Civil War Arkansas

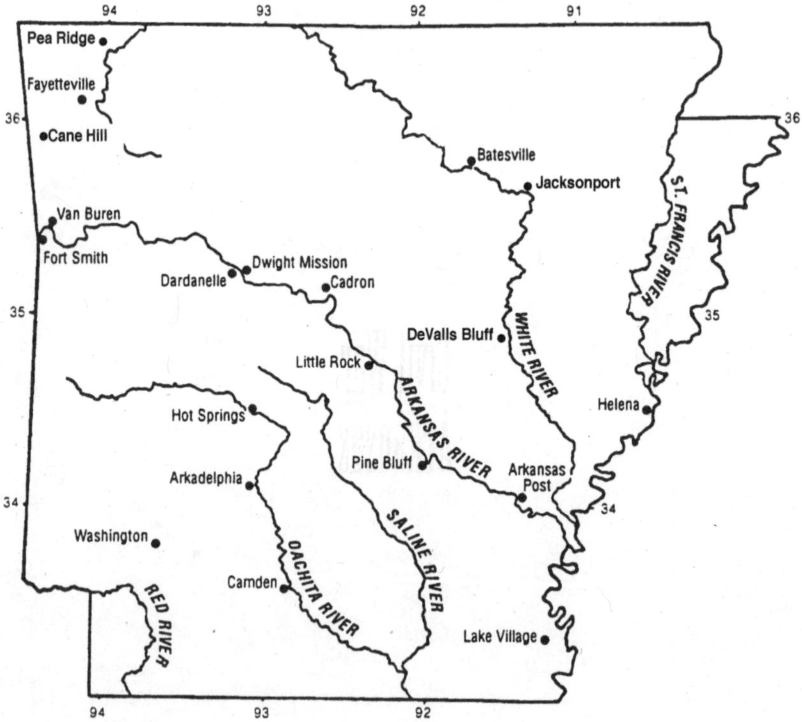

The Civil War in the West

Series Editors: Anne J. Bailey and Daniel E. Sutherland

Civil War Arkansas

Beyond Battles and Leaders

EDITED BY
ANNE J. BAILEY AND DANIEL E. SUTHERLAND

The University of Arkansas Press
Fayetteville 2000

Manufactured in the United States of America

ISBN: 978-1-55728-564-5 (cloth)
ISBN: 978-1-55728-565-2 (paper)
eISBN: 978-1-61075-099-8

25 24 23 22 21 7 6 5 4

This project is supported in part by a grant from the Arkansas Humanities Council and the National Endowment for the Humanities.

Designer: Ronie Sparkman

⊗ The paper used in this publication meets the minimum requirements of the American National Standard for Permanence of Paper for Printed Library Materials Z39.48-1984.

LIBRARY OF CONGRESS CATALOGING-IN-PUBLICATION DATA

Civil War Arkansas : beyond battles and leaders
edited by Anne J. Bailey and Daniel E. Sutherland.
p.cm. – (The Civil War in the West)
Includes bibliographical references (p.) and index.
ISBN 1-55728-564-0 (cloth : alk. paper) – ISBN 1-55728-565-9 (paper : alk. paper)
1. Arkansas–History–Civil War, 1861–1865. 2. Arkansas–History–Civil War, 1861–1865–Social aspects. 3. United States–History–Civil War, 1861–1865–Social aspects. I. Bailey, Anne J. II. Sutherland, Daniel E. III. Series.
E496 .C58 2000
973.7'09767–dc21
99-048841

Acknowledgments

The authors wish to thank the publishers of the following journals for permission to revise their original essays for the present volume:

The *Arkansas Historical Quarterly* for Anne J. Bailey, "Henry McCulloch's Texans and the Defense of Arkansas in 1862," 46 (spring 1987): 46–59; Michael A. Hughes, "Wartime Gristmill Destruction in Northwest Arkansas and Military-Farm Colonies," 46 (summer 1987): 167–86; William L. Shea, "A Semi-Savage State: The Image of Arkansas in the Civil War," 48 (winter 1989): 309–28; James J. Johnston, "Bullets for Johnny Reb: Confederate Nitre and Mining in Arkansas," 49 (summer 1990): 124–67; Carl H. Moneyhon, "Disloyalty and Class Consciousness in Southwestern Arkansas, 1862–65," 52 (autumn 1993): 223–43; Daniel E. Sutherland, "Guerrillas: The Real War in Arkansas," 52 (autumn 1993): 257–85; Kenneth C. Barnes, "The Williams Clan: Mountain Farmers and Union Fighters in North Central Arkansas," 52 (autumn 1993): 286–317; and Carl H. Moneyhon, "From Slave to Free Labor: The Federal Plantation Experiment in Arkansas," 53 (summer 1994): 137–60.

Kansas History for Kim Allen Scott, "The Preacher, the Lawyer, and the Spoils of War," 13 (winter 1990–91): 206–17.

The *Military History of the West* for Jayme Lynne Stone, "Brother against Brother: The Winter Skirmishes along the Arkansas River, 1864–1865," 25 (spring 1995): 23–49.

Civil War History for Gregory J. W. Urwin, "'We Cannot Treat Negroes . . . as Prisoners of War': Racial Atrocities and Reprisals in Civil War Arkansas," 42 (September 1996): 193–210.

Contents

Contributors

Anne J. Bailey is an associate professor of history at Georgia College and State University. She is the author of four books, including *Between the Enemy* and *Texas: Parsons's Texas Cavalry in the Civil War* (1989) and the forthcoming *Chessboard of War: Sherman and Hood in the Autumn Campaigns of 1864.*

Kenneth C. Barnes is an associate professor of history at the University of Central Arkansas. He is the author of *Who Killed John Clayton? Political Violence and the Emergence of the New South, 1861–1893* (1998).

Michael A. Hughes is an adjunct professor at East Central University, Ada, Oklahoma, and the managing editor of the *Journal of the Indian Wars.* He has written numerous articles about the Civil War in the West and the Trans-Mississippi.

James J. Johnston is a retired foreign service officer. A native Arkansan, he currently lives in Fayetteville and is the author of several articles on Arkansas history and folklore.

Carl H. Moneyhon is a professor of history at the University of Arkansas at Little Rock. He is the author of six books, including *The Impact of the Civil War and Reconstruction on Arkansas: Persistence in the Midst of Ruin* (1994) and, with Bobby L. Roberts, *Portraits of Conflict: A Photographic History of Texas in the Civil War* (1998).

Kim Allen Scott is the Special Collections librarian at Montana State University. He is the author of numerous articles about the Civil War in the Trans-Mississippi.

William L. Shea is a professor of history at the University of Arkansas at Monticello. He is the author of three books, including, with Earl J. Hess, *Pea Ridge: Civil War Campaign in the West* (1992).

Jayme Millsap Stone is an instructor of history and coordinator of undergraduate studies at the University of Central Arkansas. The essay reprinted here is her first contribution to Civil War history.

Daniel E. Sutherland is a professor of history at the University of Arkansas, Fayetteville. He is the author or editor of ten books, including *Seasons of War: The Ordeal of a Confederate Community, 1861–1865* (1995) and *Fredericksburg and Chancellorsville: The Dare Mark Campaign* (1998).

Gregory J. W. Urwin is an associate professor of history at Temple University. He is the author or editor of eight books, including *Custer Victorious: The Civil War Battles of General George Armstrong Custer* (1990) and *Facing Fearful Odds: The Seige of Wake Island* (1997).

Series Editors' Preface

The Civil War in the West has a single goal: To promote historical writing about the war in the western states and territories. It focuses most particularly on the Trans-Mississippi theater, which consisted of Missouri, Arkansas, Texas, most of Louisiana (west of the Mississippi River), Indian Territory (modern day Oklahoma), and Arizona Territory (two-fifths of modern day Arizona and New Mexico), but it also encompasses adjacent states, such as Kansas, Tennessee, and Mississippi, that directly influenced the Trans-Mississippi war. It is a wide swath, to be sure, but one too often ignored by historians and, consequently, too little understood and appreciated.

Topically, the series embraces all aspects of the wartime story. Military history in its many guises, from the strategies of generals to the daily lives of common soldiers, forms an important part of that story, but so, too, do the numerous and complex political, economic, social, and diplomatic dimensions of the war. The series also provides a variety of perspectives on these topics. Most importantly, it offers the best in modern scholarship, with thoughtful, challenging monographs. Secondly, it presents new editions of important books that have gone out of print. And thirdly, it premieres expertly edited correspondence, diaries, reminiscences, and other writings by witnesses to the war.

It is a formidable undertaking, but we believe that The Civil War in the West, by focusing on some of the least familiar dimensions of the conflict, significantly broadens understanding of that dramatic story.

Anne J. Bailey
Daniel E. Sutherland

Introduction

The History and Historians of Arkansas's Civil War

The essays in this volume represent the best recent work about the Civil War in Arkansas. All have appeared in scholarly journals during the past decade, although most of them have been updated and revised for publication here. Many other essays could have been included, but the present collection satisfies two useful purposes. First, each selection explores a military or social dimension of the war that has been largely ignored or which is unique to the war in Arkansas. Second, by pushing the traditional boundaries of military and social history, they reflect the current trend in Civil War history generally. In neither scope nor interpretation do they offer a definitive view of Arkansas's war. For instance, none of the essays touches on the causes of the war, and only occasionally do they delve into wartime political and economic issues. Yet, taken together, they provide thought-provoking insights and suggest exciting new directions for future scholarship.

Still, perspective is everything in history, so before leaping into the 1990s, it may be worthwhile to start at the beginning, which would be a hundred years ago. In 1899, John M. Harrell published the first significant work on the Civil War in Arkansas, entitled simply *Arkansas.* It appeared as part of the landmark *Confederate Military History,* edited by Clement A. Evans. Like most contributors to this multivolume set, which included a book-length military/political narrative of the war for each Confederate state, Harrell was a veteran of the war and active in the United Confederate Veterans. Born in North Carolina, he had emigrated to Arkansas in 1849, at age twenty-one, to practice law. He rose to the grade of colonel during the war and saw action in Virginia, Mississippi, and Arkansas. Harrell's pro-Southern account was very much in keeping with the partisan views that influenced most nineteenth-century "histories" of the conflict. Yet, for all that, Harrell's interpretation was surprisingly balanced in tone. It was certainly more than a personal reminiscence, and while we have no evidence to show what sources he used in his research, he more than likely consulted *Century Magazine*'s "Battles and Leaders" series of the 1880s and the government's recently published *War of the Rebellion.*[1]

Harrell stood unchallenged until the 1920s, when Thomas S. Staples and David Y. Thomas produced the first scholarly accounts of the conflict. Staples, a professor at Hendrix College and former student of William A. Dunning at Columbia University, expressed more interest in Reconstruction than the war. Yet the fact that Arkansas had early on been occupied by the Union army, thus allowing Abraham Lincoln to experiment with Reconstruction policies in the state, made the prelude to that postwar political struggle an important part of the state's wartime experience. Staples devoted nearly a fifth of his 1923 book, *Reconstruction in Arkansas,* to the war years. Reflecting the beliefs of his mentor and the so-called "Dunning school" of historiography, he characterized the state's Unionist government as inept and interpreted the postwar era as a dark period in the South's history. Scalawags, Northern carpetbaggers, and Southern blacks conspired, he said, to strip former Rebels of their rights and to establish corrupt state governments that mirrored the Gilded Age cesspool of Washington, D.C.[2]

Three years later, Thomas, formerly a professor at Hendrix but by then situated at the University of Arkansas, filled in the rest of the picture with his tremendously influential *Arkansas in War and Reconstruction, 1861–1874.* Interestingly, Thomas had been reluctant to write the book. The son of a Confederate veteran, the Kentucky-born Thomas was, nonetheless, "very much adverse to war." His pacifism alone nearly led him to reject the project, and he became downright apprehensive upon learning that the Arkansas division of the United Daughters of the Confederacy (UDC) would "assist" with his research. The UDC, armed with a twenty-five hundred dollar grant from the state legislature, had solicited Thomas to write the book, and the organization was determined that his work should vindicate the Lost Cause. Relations between the scholar and his patrons became strained at times, as Thomas resisted UDC efforts to influence his interpretation of events. Yet, in the end, his views were not all that different from the Daughters. The professor may have abhorred war, but he maintained a Confederate perspective.[3]

Thomas acknowledged divisions among Arkansans over the wisdom of secession, but he also stressed their unity of purpose once the issue had been decided. He recognized slavery as an important reason for the sectional divide, but he insisted that states rights loomed larger as a cause of secession. In all instances, he portrayed Yankees as the villains. He lavished attention on traditional military history, but he also introduced aspects of the war that had been largely ignored. He emphasized important political and economic dimensions. He appreciated the key role played by guerrilla warfare, and he devoted entire chapters to women on the home front and to Arkansans who fought in the Union army. Thomas, like Staples, had been a student of Dunning at Columbia, so he willingly embraced his friend Staples' interpretation of Reconstruction in the state. In any case, Thomas devoted fewer than 50 of 435 pages to postwar Reconstruction, and he mentioned wartime Reconstruction barely at all.[4]

Thomas's book would influence historians for decades to come, and his achievement is all the more remarkable when one considers the paltry sources available to him. There existed virtually no body of scholarly books or articles against which he could test his conclusions. He drew heavily on Harrell, *War of the Rebellion,* "Battles and Leaders," wartime newspapers, and published debates. He acknowledged having picked up "bits of information . . . here and there from sources too numerous to mention," but these must have been mostly reminiscences. Still, Thomas was not unduly concerned about careful documentation, and he even admitted, "As the book was not written primarily for mature scholars, I have not thought it worthwhile to clutter up the pages with footnotes."[5]

Because Thomas seemed to have said it all, historical writing about the war in Arkansas came to a virtual halt. Indeed, few people seemed to be interested in any part of the state's history. There was certainly no interest outside the state, and the efforts of historically minded Arkansans to preserve their heritage had consistently sputtered over the years. The Antiquarian and Historical Society of the State of Arkansas had been organized in 1837—a year after the state entered the Union—but it folded in 1842. A fitful attempt to create a similar organization some years after the war went nowhere, and not until 1903 did faculty and students at the University of Arkansas found the Arkansas Historical Society. Before the year was out, this essentially local Fayetteville group had reorganized itself as the statewide Arkansas Historical Association (AHA). Thomas, then teaching at Hendrix, was one of four original vice presidents.[6]

Two years later, the state legislature created the Arkansas History Commission (AHC) for the purpose of collecting and preserving historical source materials. The AHC also assumed responsibility for publishing collections of historical essays—though very few were related to the war—gathered by the AHA. Unfortunately, this left the AHA with no real function, and the organization folded in 1911. Professor Thomas and others tried to resurrect the AHA in 1930 without success, but another effort in 1941 paid off. The new, improved AHA committed itself not only to gathering and preserving historical materials, but also to stimulating interest in writing the state's history. Toward that end, the organization founded the *Arkansas Historical Quarterly (AHQ)* in 1942, with Thomas as editor.[7]

The *AHQ* would provide a major and natural outlet to promote the writing of Civil War history, although interest was slow to develop. In 1952, Fred Harvey Harrington, a charter member of the new AHA and a professor at the University of Arkansas before moving to the University of Wisconsin, insisted that Arkansas was "virtually an unplowed field for the historian." He admitted that the state's historians confronted several obstacles. Manuscripts, newspapers, and other original source materials were widely scattered. Few books had been written about Arkansas, which made it difficult to acquire "background material in a hurry." And not to be ignored was the fact that few publishers were interested in Arkansas topics.[8]

Harrington himself had already pointed the way out of this historical wilderness by publishing, in 1945, one of the first genuinely scholarly articles about the Civil War in Arkansas. "Arkansas Defends the Mississippi" described the role of Arkansas troops at Port Hudson during the Vicksburg campaign. The piece was typical of both amateur and academic efforts during the 1940s, as authors tended to focus either on military operations—especially battles like Prairie Grove and Jenkins' Ferry—or on military leaders, like Patrick R. Cleburne. Still, there were notable exceptions to this rule. Clara B. Eno, a prominent club woman, charter member of the AHA, and UDC loyalist, published an essay about Arkansas Confederate women in 1944. More scholarly was the first doctoral dissertation to emphasize the social consquences of the war in Arkansas, written by Maude Carmichael at Radcliffe College. Carmichael studied the transition from slave to free labor; and in 1942, while teaching at Arkansas State Teachers College in Conway, she published an article based on her research. Toward the end of the decade, Edward A. Dale, a professor at the University of Oklahoma published "Arkansas and the Cherokees," a portion of which addressed the war years.[9]

Perhaps the most remarkable work of the 1940s came from Elsie Mae Lewis. A native of Little Rock, Lewis labored under the double weight of being both female and black in an academic world that was usually cold toward both. Still, after earning an undergraduate degree at Fisk University and a masters at Southern California, Lewis completed her doctorate at the University of Chicago under Avery O. Craven in 1947. Lewis, who would spent a distinguished teaching career at Tennessee A & I, Howard University, and Hunter College, was more concerned with antebellum politics and secession than the war years; but at a time when any scholarly work on the state's history was welcomed, Lewis contributed mightily. She never published her dissertation, which dealt, in any case, more with antebellum political and economic conditions than with the crisis of 1860–61, but she did publish an article that drew on her research.[10]

Increasingly varied and sophisticated work on wartime Arkansas appeared during the 1950s, a decade in which some important political, social, and cultural studies neatly balanced more traditional military topics. Jack B. Scroggs and Ralph Wooster pushed the limits of research by Elsie Lewis and David Thomas by writing more detailed accounts of the secession crisis in Arkansas. Wooster's work later formed part of his trailblazing 1962 book, *The Secession Conventions of the South.* Lewis herself, still working on the fringes of the war, wrote a perceptive article about Robert Ward Johnson, who had led the Conway-Sevier-Johnson political clique—better known as the "family"—on the eve of the war. Robert F. Smith explored the role of the state's Confederate press in shaping public opinion. His master's thesis at the University of Arkansas, which served as the basis for much of his published work, has yet to be fully superseded. William Frank Zornow and Ted R. Worley also investigated life on the home front. Zornow addressed the use of state aid to assist indigent Confederate soldiers and their families, while Worley looked at Unionist activities, particularly the Arkansas Peace Society. Worley, who taught history in the state's public schools and at Arkansas State Teachers College, served as secretary of the AHC, and acted as editor of the *AHQ* (1953–59), was a pioneer in the modern era of Arkansas history.[11]

Other scholars explored important economic aspects of wartime Arkansas. Richard W. Griffin examined the slow evolution of industry—especially cotton factories—that began in the 1820s in the state but was snuffed out when the Union army captured Little Rock in September 1863. Mary Elizabeth Massey, a native of Morrilton who had studied as an undergraduate with Thomas Staples at Hendrix before moving on to take her doctorate at the University of North Carolina under Fletcher Green, published a pioneering article in the *AHQ,* "The Effect of Shortages on the Confederate Homefront," in 1950. Although the article did not deal directly with Arkansas, the research was drawn from her dissertation, which did include material on her native state and which would be published in 1952 as *Ersatz in the Confederacy: Shortages and Substitutes on the Southern Homefront*, an enduring classic. Massey would become the leading authority of her generation on the Confederate home front, serve as president of the Southern Historical Association in 1972–73, and reign, along with her contemporary C. Vann Woodward, who was born at Vanndale in 1908, as one of the most distinguished historians produced by the state.[12]

Military history written during the decade offered a surprising degree of variety, highlighted by several important biographies. In 1954, Daniel O'Flaherty published what still stands as the best biography of the Trans-Mississippi's most daring Confederate cavalry leader, Joseph O. Shelby. Three years later, Joseph H. Parks completed the only full biography of Edmund Kirby Smith. Robert J. Hartje wrote a revealing 1958 article about the clash between Sterling Price and Ben McCulloch over strategy in the Trans-Mississippi, an article that contributed nine years later to his biography of Earl Van Dorn. In 1959, Ralph Rea, an enthusiastic local historian of Boone County, finished writing the first modern biography of Price, a general who had an enormous influence on the war in Arkansas. Equally important, his book was published in Little Rock, indicating a new commitment of Arkansans to their history. A good biography of Albert Pike appeared two years later. Other historians offered briefer sketches of less important players. Hal Bridges, a professor at the University of Arkansas who would become best known for his 1961 biography of Daniel Harvey Hill, wrote a sketch of Confederate general William Y. Slack, who was killed at the battle of Pea Ridge. Common soldiers also received some attention, most notably from Harry N. Scheiber, who investigated the connection between the frequency with which Confederate troops in the Trans-Mississippi were paid and the state of their morale.[13]

Battles and campaigns also received deft treatment in the 1950s. In 1958 Ira Don Richards wrote the first master's thesis at the University of Arkansas to deal with a Civil War campaign—the 1864 Camden expedition. The following year, while a doctoral student at Tulane University, he published the first scholarly analysis of the battle of Poison Spring, a battle in which over one hundred black Union soldiers had been killed by Confederates. Richards suggested that surviving evidence tended to support long-standing charges of a "massacre," but he avoided making any definitive statement about the controversial episode. James H. Atkinson, a retired teacher from

Little Rock Junior College and former chairman of the AHC, published a comprehensive narrative of the Camden expedition and a detailed account of an action at Prairie D'Ane. Jack Scroggs and Donald E. Reynolds teamed up to remind scholars about the important role Arkansas played in the Vicksburg campaign. Their article focused on weaknesses in the Confederate command structure in the West, most particularly the ineptness of Theophilus H. Holmes, theater commander of the Trans-Mississippi.[14]

Two book-length studies also touched on combat actions in Arkansas. Jay Monaghan's fast-paced *Civil War on the Western Border* dealt primarily with Kansas and Missouri, but it also included chapters on the key Arkansas battles of Pea Ridge and Prairie Grove. More significant was Ludwell H. Johnson's *Red River Campaign.* Written originally as a Johns Hopkins University dissertation under the direction of C. Vann Woodward, Johnson's work brillantly demonstrated the complex political, economic, and ideological dimensions of that important Trans-Mississippi campaign. Although most of the action took place in Louisiana, and Johnson largely confined his discussion of Arkansas to a single chapter, the book contributed significantly to an understanding of Arkansas's Civil War.[15]

Yet, in some ways, the decade's pivotal contribution to military history was an article about the battle of Pea Ridge written by Walter Lee Brown. Historians had long characterized that March 1862 contest as the most important military engagement ever fought in Arkansas, and the majority agreed that the Confederate defeat ended Rebel hopes of hanging on to Missouri. But Brown, who had joined the faculty at the University of Arkansas after completing his doctoral dissertation on Albert Pike at the University of Texas in 1954, went further. He labeled Pea Ridge "one of the truly decisive battles of the Civil War." To underscore his point, and in an effort to have the western theaters recognized as being equal in importance to Virginia and the East, Brown called Pea Ridge the "Gettysburg of the West." Not only did it cost the Confederates control of Missouri, he said, but it also ended Rebel plans for "turning back the Federal advance into Tennessee" and marked the "beginning of the end for the Confederate hope of retaining control of the Mississippi." Ultimately, insisted Brown, Pea Ridge meant "the loss of the war in the West."[16]

This set the stage for an explosion of historical writing in the 1960s. The entire country, as it turned out, entered into one of its periodic fits of Civil War mania during the decade, which kicked off with the centennial celebration of the war. Perhaps no other part of the country benefited as much from the celebration as Arkansas. Certainly the Trans-Mississippi as a whole, which had received about the same minimal degree of attention from historians as it had from the Confederate government, got a boost. In 1956, James J. Hudson, who taught Civil War history at the University of Arkansas, had chided the author of a book entitled *Decisive Battles of the Civil War* for not saying more about the war in the West. The author had paid but little attention to Pea Ridge, complained Hudson in a review of the book, while Prairie Grove and other important military actions were not mentioned at all. Hudson insisted that the war in the Trans-Mississippi deserved "more thorough coverage."[17]

But in the 1960s, even Arkansas became fashionable. The state received important exposure when the Pea Ridge battlefield became a national military park in 1961. Articles about several Arkansas battles appeared in the high-profile *Civil War Times Illustrated.* And Walter Brown, who began his thirty-year reign as editor of the *AHQ* in 1960, included thirty-four Civil War–related articles in that journal during the decade. Military topics tended to dominate, and leading the renaissance was a research historian at the Vicksburg National Military Park, Edwin C. Bearss. This future chief historian of the National Park Service had first been drawn to the unplowed fields of Arkansas historiography in the late 1950s, when he published articles on the battles of Pea Ridge and Arkansas Post. He continued to write about Pea Ridge in the 1960s—the most detailed tactical studies of the battle written to that time—but he also turned his attention to battles at Helena and Pine Bluff, the 1862 White River expedition, and the Camden expedition. Most notable was his work on the campaigns in western Arkansas, especially around Fort Smith.[18]

In 1965, John L. Ferguson, the state historian and executive secretary of the AHC, published a book, under the auspices of the Arkansas legislature and the Arkansas Civil War Centennial Commission, designed to help junior and senior high school teachers tell their students about the war. The book was a treasure trove of documents, maps, illustrations, selected writings, and a calendar of the war. For Ferguson, the collection represented "the substance and the spirit of the War Between the States as it was fought in Arkansas." The previously published material included Scroggs's article on the secession crisis, an excerpt from David Y. Thomas, and an old article by Henry B. McKenzie entitled "Confederate Manufactures in Southwest Arkansas," which first appeared in the 1908 volume of the AHA *Publications.*[19]

Leo E. Huff became the other notable name associated with the 1960s. Huff completed his master's thesis on Civil War Arkansas under Walter Brown in 1964. A World War II veteran, Huff was interested in military history, but only marginally so in battles and campaigns. His work focused more on the tangential yet fascinating topics of personality conflicts in the Confederate high command, railroads and logistics, and the state's Military Board, which played a crucial role in the early defense of Confederate Arkansas. However, most important was his work on the state's guerrilla war. His was the first scholarly effort to untangle the complex yet enormously important role of guerrillas, bushwhackers, and irregular warfare. David Y. Thomas had touched on those issues in the 1920s, and a few other writers had told the stories of individual guerrilla leaders. Richard S. Brownlee had even published a landmark book about the guerrilla war in Missouri, but Huff was the first historian to document conditions in Arkansas.[20]

Other writers concentrated on traditional battles and campaigns. Ira Richards continued to refine his work on the Camden expedition. Stephen B. Oates, who completed his doctorate at the University of Texas in 1968, wrote two insightful articles about the second most notable battle on Arkansas soil, Prairie Grove (December 1862), and a little known engagement at Cane Hill (November 1862). The latter piece would form part of Oates's first book, *Confederate Cavalry in the West.* Alwyn Barr, a fellow doctoral student with Oates at Texas, published an article on Confederate artillery in Arkansas. The best overview of military operations came from Albert Castel in his detailed account of the wartime career of Sterling Price, published near the end of the decade. Castel, a professor at Western Michigan University, incorporated much recent research on actions at Helena, Jenkins' Ferry, Little Rock, and Pea Ridge, although in the last instance, he disagreed with Walter Brown about the significance of the battle.[21]

Several new trends in Civil War history emerged in the 1960s, as well. Most striking was the outpouring of unit histories that accompanied the centennial celebration. Unit histories had flowered in the last third of the nineteenth century, as veterans became authors—or, more often, compilers—to commemorate the heroics of their regiments, brigades, divisions, and corps. But the histories of the 1960s, while often written by enthusiastic amateurs and not always as scholarly as they might have been, tried to provide more historical perspective than earlier efforts. Additionally, Burton J. Williams, a professor at the University of Kansas, explored a topic that seemed a natural departure from the new interest in guerrillas, and which would become even more popular in the 1980s and 1990s. Recognizing that Southern civilians were too often left out of traditional accounts of the war, Williams looked at the impact on noncombatants of depredations by Union soldiers in Arkansas. His case study was small, involving just ten citizens in the vicinity of Batesville, but it was an important reminder about the cost of war.[22]

Another important trend toward the microcosmic view could be seen in several attempts to tell the wartime stories of individual towns and counties. This was an outgrowth of a new interest in local history, an interest that had accompanied efforts in the 1940s to preserve the state's heritage. Several counties had established their own historical journals by the 1970s, and the war was a favorite subject in their pages. Graduate students selected thesis topics that focused on particular communities, and even established scholars probed the impact of the war at the local level. Among the best efforts were articles by Ted Worley and Nola A. James on Van Buren County and Independence County, respectively. While some of these community studies, like the unit histories, were written by enthusiastic amateurs, that did not necessarily mean they lacked value. As Walter Brown wrote in his review of one such study of Jackson County, "[The author's] Confederate heritage and partisanship occasionally overcome objectivity, but in the main she has written a book based on thorough research and careful documentation."[23]

By 1970, the broad outline of Arkansas's Civil War history had been set. Earlier writers would continue to flesh out traditional themes over the next twenty years, and many new voices contributed to ongoing debates while also raising provocative questions and introducing intriguing perspectives. Among the old guard, Ed Bearss explained in greater detail the role of Fort Smith as the state's westernmost Federal outpost. Leo Huff examined the use of martial law to suppress Unionist dissenters. Donald Reynolds went beyond his earlier work with Jack Scroggs to look at Union strategy in Arkansas during the Vicksburg campaign. And Walter Brown continued to challenge earlier understandings about Pea Ridge by examining wartime charges that Albert Pike had authorized Confederate Cherokees to scalp Union soldiers in the battle.[24]

Meantime, new authors contributed to an ever more sophisticated understanding the war. The most important young scholar to appear in the 1970s was Michael B. Dougan, who earned his doctorate under the legendary Bell I. Wiley at Emory University. Dougan had published an article about the wartime role of the Little Rock press—both Rebel and Unionist—in 1969, while still in graduate school; but over the next few years he would explore the broader topics of life on the Confederate home front and antebellum and wartime political machinations. In 1976 he published *Confederate Arkansas,* the first comprehensive survey of the state's wartime experience since David Y. Thomas. Dougan, by then a professor at Arkansas State University, largely ignored military events, but he provided an excellent overview of wartime society and politics and a much needed reexamination of the secession crisis.[25]

While not concentrating exclusively on Arkansas, Robert L. Kerby provided a good narrative overview of both the home front and military operations during the second half of the war in *Kirby Smith's Confederacy,* published in 1972. His biographical approach proved popular, as military biography showed itself to be alive and well in the 1970s. Similarly, Robert E. Shalhope produced a new biography of Sterling Price that dug deeper into the nonmilitary aspects of Price's life than had Castel's book. Howell and Elizabeth Purdue wrote a useful biography of Arkansas's greatest Civil War hero, Pat Cleburne. There was no shortage, however, of traditional battle and campaign studies. In the late 1970s William R. Geise wrote an impressive series of articles, for *Military History of Texas and the Southwest,* that traced Confederate strategy and operations from January 1862 through February 1863. Geise blamed Thomas C. Hindman and Theophilus Holmes for most of the Confederacy's military setbacks in Arkansas, although he acknowledged the difficulties of communication west of the Mississippi. He also bemoaned the Richmond government's lack of interest in Arkansas.[26]

But the newest trend in military history, one that would continue through the 1990s, concentrated on the bottom end of military operations, namely, small, previously unexplored military actions and the role of the common soldier. For example, David O. Demuth, an Arkansas businessman and board member of the AHC, published articles about a skirmish at Hurricane Creek and the burning of Hopefield. The former piece explained why Union military policy was crumbling in Arkansas by the fall of 1864; the latter article revealed the sometimes brutal methods used by Federal commanders to suppress Rebel guerrillas. William L. Shea, an important new voice in the decade who completed his doctoral work at Rice University, wrote in the early 1980s about military actions at Ditch Bayou, along the Cache River, and at Camden.[27]

Of course, Bell Wiley had long since shown what wonderful things could be learned by studying the lives of Johnny Reb and Billy Yank, but the 1970s and 1980s solidified the "New Military History," and the common soldier quickly became its centerpiece. Tommy R. Thompson, a professor at the University of Nebraska, Omaha, exemplified this approach with an article about an unknown Arkansas infantryman. LeRoy H. Fischer, of Oklahoma State University, undertook the delicate task of separating fact from fiction in a major retelling of the saga of Arkansas folk hero David O. Dodd, the young lad who was hanged as a spy by the Union army in 1864. Earl J. Hess addressed two important questions posed by the New Military History: Why did Civil War soldiers fight, and how did they interact with noncombatants? Using the Federal occupation of Helena as a test case, Hess maintained that increasingly callous treatment of civilians in the summer of 1862 coincided with an evolving determination among some Northern soldiers to wage a war that would abolish slavery and reconstruct Southern society as well preserve the Union.[28]

Unit histories continued to be a popular form of military history, but by 1980 they had become more sophisticated—often involving some sort of statistical analysis—than those of the 1960s. James Willis took an unusual approach by employing a single regiment—the Ninth Arkansas Infantry—as a "unifying strand" to tell the story of Arkansas Condederates who served in the Western Theater. Writers also went beyond Arkansas military units to examine the composition and activities of other Union and Confederate units that served in the state. Kim Allen Scott, an archivist by training, explored the small-scale, personal side of the war. His analyses of the battles of Fayetteville and Cane Hill are models of their kind, and his examination of the Eleventh Kansas Infantry used a company newspaper from that regiment to take a unique look at a group of common soldiers. Similarly, Anne J. Bailey detailed small but important military actions at Whitney's Lane, Cotton Plant, L'Anguille River, and Pine Bluff through an examination of an important Confederate unit serving in Arkansas, William H. Parsons's Texas cavalry brigade. Several historians, including Bailey, examined the North's elite Mississippi Marine Brigade, which engaged in counterguerrilla operations in Arkansas. Numerous Arkansas regiments—both Confederate and Federal—have received attention since the mid-1980s; and Charles G. Williams has assessed the role of a band of overlooked contributors to the defense of Confederate Arkansas: the home guard.[29]

An important nonmilitary historian to shape the historiography of the

1980s and 1990s was James W. Woods. While still a graduate student at Tulane University, Woods wrote an insightful examination of Arkansans in the Confederate Congress; but his dissertation, published in 1987, provided a finely nuanced and detailed reevaluation of Arkansas politics between 1859 and 1861. Woods attributed the timing and circumstances surrounding secession in Arkansas to a mixture of local and regional interests, an interpretation that still reigns as orthodoxy. Fitting neatly into neither the Upper nor Lower South, said Woods, Arkansas, along with Texas, formed the "frontier" of the Old South. Few of its citizens depended on slavery, yet the state's economic future seemed to be firmly tied to the South's peculiar institution. "Tasting a new prosperity from both cotton and slavery," concluded Woods, "this small state was unwilling to part with its new economic success, even for the sake of the Union."[30]

Looking more specifically to the war years, historians addressed a variety of nonmilitary issues in the 1980s and 1990s. The popularity of community studies grew, as witnessed by excellent work on Pulaski, Jackson, Phillips, and Chicot Counties and the towns of Hot Springs and Fort Smith. Gary W. Pecquet, a professor of economics at Southwest Texas State University, took a long overdue look at the financial condition of state government during the war, while Diane Neal and Thomas W. Kremm explored the little-known story of the state's "farm colonies," an experiment akin to the "strategic hamlets" of Vietnam. The colonies made it easier for the Union army to protect Unionists from Rebel raiders while allowing loyal farmers to produce crops for themselves and their protectors.[31]

Militarily, a new wave of researchers reaffirmed the importance of Pea Ridge in the state's history. Michael A. Hughes contributed a lengthy article to a 1988 issue of *Blue and Gray Magazine* devoted to the battle, and Alvin M. Josephy, Jr., included a chapter on Pea Ridge in his survey of the war west of the Mississippi River. Stephen D. Engle dissected the role of controversial Union general Franz Sigel in the fighting at Elk Horn Tavern. David Bosse took an unorthodox approach to the action by examining how it was reported in the press. Most important, however, was a major reinterpretation of the battle and campaign by William Shea and Earl Hess. Published in 1992, their sweeping narrative combined a detailed analysis of both strategy and tactics—even down to the movements of companies and batteries—with informed discussions of logistics, medical care, and issues posed by the new military history of the 1970s.[32]

An important new interpreter of the broader war was Carl H.

Moneyhon. A professor at the University of Arkansas at Little Rock, Moneyhon teamed with Bobby Roberts, who had written about the wartime career of Arkansas politician and soldier Thomas C. Hindman, to produce a unique survey. *Portraits of Conflict: A Photographic History of Arkansas in the Civil War,* published in 1987, offered far more than the title suggested. A lucid narrative, drawing on the most recent scholarship, accompanied its striking, and sometimes rare, photographs. In addition, dozens of portraits of common soldiers and civilians formed the heart of the book's photographic record. Moneyhon and Roberts had given a face to the new military history, and the effect was dramatic.[33]

Moneyhon took the next logical step in 1994, when he updated both David Thomas and Michael Dougan with a new synthesis of the war and Reconstruction. He did not match Thomas in the detail given to military actions, but he surpassed him in his exhaustive examination of the social, political, and economic trends that defined the era. Clearly, too, Moneyhon presented a very different interpretation of Reconstruction than that of the old Dunningite. Himself a contributor to the recent literature on the impact of the war on communities, Moneyhon was particularly attuned to that aspect of the story; and his larger framework drew inspiration from Eric Foner's neo-revisionist view of Reconstruction.[34]

Moneyhon's synthesis highlighted most of the important themes in the historiography of the 1990s. Unionism and disloyalty in the Confederacy were two such issues, first addressed by Thomas and now revisited. Diane Neal and others expanded Ted Worley's earlier probing of Unionist peace societies. Several historians, building on the work of Leo Huff, tried to make sense of the complex subject of guerrilla warfare. Another innovative piece of research, which drew inspiration from the work of Elizabeth Massey, was John F. Bradbury's revealing look at the relationship between the Union army and Rebel refugees. Similarly, Clea L. Bunch published a useful article in 1997 on the reaction of Arkansas women to Federal occupation.[35]

Perhaps the most elusive and least examined topic has been the role of African Americans in the war. Scholars have studied antebellum slavery and the lives of postwar Southern blacks exhaustively, but the crucial years in between—the war years—are more difficult to document and comprehend. This is true of the entire South, not just Arkansas, and although Arkansas had fewer slaves than most other Confederate states, historians cannot be excused from their responsibility to pay more attention to this crucial subject. The only comprehensive study of antebellum Arkansas slavery, by

Orville W. Taylor, was published in 1958. It is a good, still useful book, but scholars have published an enormous amount of work on slavery generally since it appeared.[36]

Most of the work on African Americans since 1958 has been done within the framework of Reconstruction. Happily, because the U.S. government experimented with reconstruction programs in Arkansas during the war, historians have paid some attention to race between 1862 and 1865. Randy Finley's excellent study of the Freedmen's Bureau in Arkansas barely touches on the war years, but he does document the earliest contacts between the bureau and its charges, especially on the subject of health care. Other scholars have evaluated efforts to educate the freedmen; and Bobby L. Lovett, a professor at Tennessee State University, has measured the broad impact of both war and Reconstruction on the state's black population. Working from the other end of the chronological scale, Paul D. Lack has taken a unique look at urban slavery—in Little Rock—between 1830 and 1862. Also unique is A. F. Kaufman's sketch of the Fifty-fourth U.S. Colored Infantry, one of five black regiments raised in Arkansas during the war.[37]

The other racial minority to play a role in wartime Arkansas was the Native American. Arkansas bordered Indian Territory (present-day Oklahoma), and Confederate commanders in the state frequently drew on friendly Indians to supplement their forces. Pea Ridge is the most notable instance where they engaged in combat; and several writers, including Walter Brown, Roy Clifford, and Shea and Hess, have specifically addressed their role in that battle. Several classic works on Indians in the Civil War date from the first few decades of this century, those by Annie Heloise Abel and Wiley Britton being the most notable ones; but interest in the subject has slowly grown since the 1960s. Ed Bearss and others have noted the important military role played by Indians in the campaigns around Fort Smith, and several authors have described Native American actions at Poison Spring. Stand Watie, the principal Cherokee military leader—and the last Confederate general to surrender his forces—has received several military biographies, as have John Ross and John Drew.[38]

Returning to the subject of Reconstruction policy, the Federal experiments in Arkansas—the first coming in 1862 at Helena—form an important part of the wartime story. In the 1950s and 1960s bits and pieces were added to the Staples/Thomas version of events. William B. Hesseltine and Larry Gara, for example, examined the postwar roles of Arkansas's Confederate leadership, and Ruth Caroline Cowen published a useful overview of the role of the Union army in shaping early Reconstruction policy. Martha A. Ellenburg addressed the entire Reconstruction period in Arkansas in her 1967 doctoral dissertation at the University of Missouri. However, not until 1976 did George H. Thompson gather these threads to produce a modern appraisal of Reconstruction in the state. Thompson, in turn, provided a useful departure for Moneyhon, as did several other writers working on specific aspects of wartime Reconstruction during the 1980s and 1990s.[39]

Finally, and always at the heart of the Civil War, the military history of the struggle continued to thrive in the 1990s. The most significant contribution of the decade, published in the same year as Moneyhon's survey—1994—and filling in many of the military details left out of that narrative, was *Rugged and Sublime: The Civil War in Arkansas.* This collaborative effort by Moneyhon, Shea, Daniel E. Sutherland, Thomas A. DeBlack, and Kenneth Story remains the best account of the battles and campaigns in Arkansas; but it is indicative of equally fine work on individual battles, such as Poison Spring, Jenkins' Ferry, Prairie Grove, Cane Hill, Cotton Plant, Whitney Lane, and Arkansas Post. Broader military operations, including Confederate national policy toward Arkansas and the Trans-Mississippi, Union strategy before the surrender of Little Rock, and the final Confederate offensive of the war also received deft treatment. Combining military and social history, Gregory J. W. Urwin explored the role of religion among Union soldiers, and Anne Bailey examined the issue of alleged Confederate atrocities against black soldiers at Poison Spring.[40]

Military biography also remained a popular means of understanding the war. Patrick Cleburne, Arkansas's most enduring Confederate hero, continued to attract attention, most notably in an excellent book by Craig L. Symonds. Historians seemed to be particularly interested in Cleburne's unsuccessful quest to have blacks inducted into the Confederate army. Thomas Hindman, who also proposed arming slaves, finally received full biographical treatment; and Walter Brown, after decades of research and writing, converted his doctoral dissertation on Albert Pike into a monumental biography. Thomas Cutrer published the first full-length biography of Ben McCulloch, the Texan entrusted with the defense of Arkansas early in the war who died at Pea Ridge. The wartime roles of other, less central figures, such as Confederate general Daniel C. Govan, also received reappraisal.[41]

The essays selected for this volume reflect the past decade of research and writing, which, as shown, has been characterized by a refreshing diversity. The essay by Anne J. Bailey analyzes Confederate strategy in 1862. She credits Henry McCulloch and some twenty-five hundred Texans (about half of the total Confederate force in Arkansas) with delaying Union occupation of the state for over a year. Her skillful summary of the military situation at that critical point in the war also evaluates the strengths and weaknesses of the Confederate command system.

Turning to the impact of social and economic factors on military events, Michael A. Hughes explains the role of gristmills and "farm colonies" in the Union occupation of Arkansas. Gristmills often served as rendezvous points and recruiting depots for Confederate guerrillas in the northern part of the state. By 1864 the Federals believed that the destruction of those mills might temper the cyclone of irregular warfare that enveloped them. At about the same time, Union authorities experimented with farm colonies as yet another means of undermining the guerrilla threat. Both Federal initiatives proved successful in thwarting guerrillas by destroying part of the economic base that supported them.

James J. Johnston is more interested in mines than mills, but his detailed explanation of the Confederacy's niter industry offers a penetrating look at this neglected yet vital dimension of the Rebel war effort. The Richmond government depended on Arkansas to help provide its armies with lead and gunpowder, but this mission required more than the state's abundant raw materials. It also took labor, security, and transportation, none of which the Confederate government could provide in sufficient measure.

William L. Shea is interested in the reaction of Union soldiers to the "semi-savage" land of Arkansas. He maintains that an important source for the modern image of Arkansas as an impoverished backwater can be found in the reaction of these soldiers during the spring and summer of 1862. In the aftermath of the battle of Pea Ridge, as the Union army penetrated deeper into the state, the attention of the nation was focused as never before on Arkansas. Northern newspapers told their readers all they could about that exotic part of the world, which meant that they also printed hundreds of letters written by soldiers to the folks back home. Their unflattering descriptions of the state and its people left a seemingly indelible public impression.

Kim Allen Scott portrays the struggle for survival on the home front, and in very personal terms. Too often, Scott says, historians relate even the most emotionally wrenching episodes of war in a detached, analytical fashion, without conveying any of the passsion or suffering of the moment. In telling the story of the robbery of the Harvey Henderson Edmiston family by Kansas soldiers, Scott provides a striking example not only of the plight of Arkansas civilians, but also of the difficulties faced by Union soldiers in deciding how to treat noncombatants in the Trans-Mississippi.

Carl H. Moneyhon has contributed two essays to the collection. The first one explores the connections between social class and Confederate disloyalty in southwestern Arkansas. Interest in Southern Unionism has increased in recent years, along with suggestions that flagging support for Southern independence on the home front contributed significantly to Confederate defeat. Moneyhon argues that one of the most important factors in determining support or opposition to the Rebel cause was social class, as poorer folk came to believe that the war, with its attendant suffering and deprivation, was being fought in the interest of their planter neighbors.

Moneyhon's second essay examines the transition from slave to free labor, an issue first raised by Maude Carmichael in the 1940s. As the Union army strengthened it grip on the Mississippi River valley, it used slaves to operate delta cotton plantations for the profit of the U.S. government. The experiment was also intended to teach blacks the rights and responsibilities of free labor and to provide them with a degree of economic independence. Moneyhon explains why the experiment largely failed.

Daniel E. Sutherland revisits the issue of guerrilla warfare, the first scholar to do so since Leo Huff's pioneering article of 1965. Sutherland goes beyond Huff's focus on guerrilla leaders and military operations in northern Arkansas to evaluate the extent to which guerrilla warfare shaped the strategic and tactical pattern of the war in Arkansas. Specifically, he addresses three issues: the reasons men became guerrillas, their roles in Confederate service, and the effectiveness of Confederate guerrilla operations.

Kenneth C. Barnes adds to the literature on both the irregular war and the nature of Unionism by looking at a band of Unionist guerrillas, the Williams clan of north central Arkansas. The Williamses resisted involvement in the war, but the men of this extended family were finally forced to join the fighting. Though small slave holders, they had supported the Union from the beginning, and so formed a partisan company to defend their neighborhood against secessionst neighbors. Barnes also demonstrates how these wartime divisions inspired postwar political violence well into the twentieth century.

Jayme M. Stone, focusing on one of the final campaigns of the war, reminds us that set-piece battles like Pea Ridge and Prairie Grove were relatively rare in Arkansas. Skirmishes and bushwhacking characterized the crucial Arkansas River campaign of 1864–65, a campaign to determine who would control northern Arkansas. Both sides drew on Arkansans to do the fighting, an errie feature that legitimized the generic characterization of the struggle as a brothers' war. Stone's work also points to an aspect of the war that has been seriously neglected: naval and logistical operations on Arkansas rivers.

Gregory J. W. Urwin's award-winning essay addresses the controversial issue of Confederate atrocities against black Union soldiers at the battles of Poison Spring and Marks' Mill. Other scholars, including Anne Bailey, have explored this ground, but Urwin's is the most thorough treatment to date. He concludes that the murder of African Americans during and after the fighting was not senseless racial violence but part of an "ongoing program" of racial intimidation by Confederate authorities.

And what of the future? This introduction has suggested some of the gaps in our knowledge and the direction in which many historians are headed. We need to know more about the guerrilla war that dominated military operations in the state. We need to know more about Unionists and Unionism, especially why people supported one side or the other. Studies of civilian morale, whether Unionist or Confederate, are needed; and the roles of the churches, women, African Americans, Native Americans, and foreign immigrants demand far more attention than they have received. Historians need to continue to think small, too. More military unit studies and more community studies are essential means of testing larger themes. Carl Moneyhon, writing in the introduction to his survey of the war and Reconstruction, insisted that community studies were the only means of understanding the impact of the war on Arkansans. It is also time to apply one of the latest historical trends to the study of Arkansas's war, the role of memory. Fred A. Bailey has taken a step in that direction by suggesting how postwar political agendas shaped early histories of the war; but deeper, even richer, possibilities remain.[42] Such challenges as these should keep the historians of Arkansas's Civil War busy for years.

Chapter 1

Henry McCulloch's Texans and the Defense of Arkansas in 1862

Anne J. Bailey

Checking the Federal advance toward Little Rock in 1862 seemed "small indeed by comparison with the more imposing and dramatic events of the far east," noted Colonel William Henry Parsons of the Twelfth Texas Cavalry Regiment, "but momentous in results" to the security of the Trans-Mississippi Department. Not only was the possession of Arkansas at stake, continued Parsons, "but for immediate results to the fate and fortunes of Texas, few successful movements can be recorded of graver and more decisive" significance than those first campaigns which arrested the Federal drive south. Perhaps Parsons magnified the importance of the threat, but he was correct in expressing the concern Texans felt for neighboring Arkansas. Although estimates vary, at least sixty thousand Texans enrolled in the Confederate army; approximately one-half of this number served in Arkansas in 1862. Their timely arrival prevented the fall of Little Rock and deterred any Federal occupation of the state. One man stood out in this crisis: Henry McCulloch, an obscure brigadier general from Texas. Even today Henry McCulloch receives little recognition, instead his name is often confused with his older brother, Ben, who rendered distinguished service as the commander of the army defending Arkansas early in the war.[1]

By 1862, as the situation in the state rapidly deteriorated, Ben McCulloch had become a focus for controversy. Commissioned a brigadier general in May 1861, the elder McCulloch had assumed command of the forces gathering around Fort Smith. Flamboyant and aggressive, Ben could also be stubborn and headstrong. He earned distinction commanding the Confederates in their victory at Wilson's Creek, Missouri, in August 1861. But instead of pursuing the initiative, McCulloch argued with Missourian Sterling Price over future strategy; neither would compromise, and they could not agree upon any concerted plan to defend Missouri and Arkansas. To alleviate this impasse, the War Department placed both men under Major General Earl Van Dorn. McCulloch and Price paid heavily for their differences; they saw their early success fade as Federal columns moved steadily through Missouri into Arkansas, where, during Van Dorn's loss at Pea Ridge in early March 1862, the Texan was killed.[2]

More important, as the Federal army under recently promoted Major General Samuel R. Curtis took possession of northwest Arkansas, General Albert Sidney Johnston, then commanding the Confederacy's Western Department, ordered Van Dorn to join him on the east side of the Mississippi River. Hampered by bad weather, poor roads, and swollen streams, Van Dorn's movement was slow. By the time he concentrated his force at Memphis in mid-April, Johnston was dead, killed in the battle at Shiloh, and his successor, General P. G. T. Beauregard, had withdrawn the army to Corinth, Mississippi. Van Dorn's men, mostly Arkansans and Missourians, pressed on toward northern Mississippi, leaving only a token force to defend Arkansas.[3]

Van Dorn's actions forced state officials to rely upon their own ingenuity. Following Pea Ridge, Curtis had marched his army along the White River into north central Arkansas, halting at Batesville. With scouting parties within miles of the state capital, Governor Henry M. Rector moved the archives to Hot Springs and let it be known that he thought the Confederacy had sold his state down the river. Brigadier General John S. Roane, a former governor in command of Arkansas's scattered troops, declared martial law, and with the permission of General Beauregard, "appropriated" five regiments of Texans en route to join Van Dorn. This, noted Colonel Parsons, whose cavalry regiment was among those detained, "so successfully impressed Curtis with the conviction that his further advance was opposed by a newly arrived army, that he precipitately fell back to the north bank of White river, and hastened couriers to [Ulysses S.] Grant" requesting supplies and reinforcements. Roane, in fact, was so enthusiastic that he told Beauregard "he was holding four companies of Parsons Texas cavalry, and 'thought with the Texas troops,'" and those he could raise in Arkansas, that he could hold the enemy in check until Beauregard "could whip the Federals at Corinth." The Little Rock *Arkansas True Democrat* agreed when it reported in May: "Our gallant Texas friends continue to arrive. . . . Gen. Curtis is likely to have a livelier time capturing Arkansas than he expected."[4]

Meanwhile, Brigadier General Paul O. Hébert, in command of the District of Texas, had already received orders from the War Department to send all of his available forces to join Van Dorn at Little Rock. Even after learning that the Confederate army was no longer in the state, Hébert continued to move his troops toward Arkansas as quickly as he could secure transportation.[5]

To provide a quick and efficient support, the Confederacy needed a liaison between Hébert at Houston and the hierarchy in Little Rock. Henry McCulloch, a seasoned Indian fighter and veteran of the Mexican War, seemed ideal for the job. The forty-five-year-old McCulloch, who had received a commission as brigadier general just a few days after Ben's death at Pea Ridge, had intended to join his brother's old command near Corinth; but after being delayed in Louisiana, however, he realized his service would be more useful in Texas, where there was a shortage of general officers. He requested, and was granted, permission to return to the Lone Star state to take charge of coordinating troop movement. McCulloch established his headquarters at Tyler in East Texas and began the task of administering order amid confusion.[6]

McCulloch's objective was to forward support to the Confederate defenders at Little Rock. His staff carefully assessed the strength of each regiment arriving in Tyler, reported its needs, and tried to send the men across the Red River better organized and equipped. By the end of June, 13,280 men were either on the march or preparing to leave McCulloch's base; combined with the 7,400 already in Arkansas, the contingent from Texas would number 20,680. With the addition of more regiments throughout the late summer and early fall, by the end of the year an official report revealed that the Army of the Trans-Mississippi contained twenty-seven regiments of Texans, two battalions, and three batteries. As usual with men scattered in the field, this report overlooked a number of independent companies, batteries, and even entire unattached regiments. Since a count found among the papers of the Confederate quartermaster showed an aggregate and effective total of 50,000 men in the department, one might estimate that over one-half were Texas soldiers. Sickness, death, and desertion, however, kept the actual number of fighting men quite reduced.[7]

As the recruits arrived in Little Rock they reported to Major General Thomas C. Hindman, newly appointed commander of the Trans-Mississippi Department. To organize a defense of Little Rock, Hindman knew he had to mold the multitude of Texans into an effective army. In an effort to combat the shortage of forage resulting from scores of horsemen arriving almost daily, Hindman ordered many dismounted as soon as they reported for duty. This measure, naturally, incited resentment and indignation; most Texans preferred service in the cavalry and detested any mention of the infantry.[8]

Hindman's unpopular actions had sweeping results. Coupled with disease of almost epidemic proportion, irregular pay, and general discontent, many Texas soldiers openly expressed scorn for service in Arkansas. Captain E. S. C. Robertson, on McCulloch's staff, observed upon his arrival, "Everything except poverty and sickness is very scarce." And, he quipped, "The people seem to esteem the Texans very highly, and charge them high prices by way of showing their regard." As a result of the distressing conditions, desertion among the disgruntled soldiers became common and troublesome. Fearful that the fledgling army might dwindle to nothing, Hindman resorted to drastic measures—the execution of deserters. This, he concluded, "had the intended effect. The spirit of desertion was crushed."[9]

The reaction to Hindman's authoritarian methods varied. Texas captain George W. Ingram of the Twelfth Texas Cavalry complained that Hindman, who, he pointed out, was from Arkansas, considered the Texans "heathens." Echoing widespread resentment, Ingram warned, "Many of the boys in the different Texas Regiments have taken a vow to kill him at the first opportunity." But, during Hindman's short seventy days as head of the department, not all Texans criticized his procedures. Roger Q. Mills, colonel of the Tenth Texas Infantry, praised him for his efficiency and promptness in organizing his command. Mills felt that under the circumstances few men could have done a better job.[10]

Boredom often breeds discontent; yet the first taste of combat sobered many of the new recruits. While Hindman worked to reinforce Little Rock, the Federal army north of the capital began to move. Because of a shortage of supplies and news of the arrival of the Texas regiments, Curtis marched his men toward the Mississippi rather than advancing on the Confederate defenders. Hindman, having nothing but inexperienced soldiers to check the movement, ordered Brigadier General Albert Rust's cavalry to harass the army's passage across the state. On July 7, the two met near the sleepy little town of Cotton Plant on the Cache River. Colonel Charles E. Hovey of the Thirty-third Illinois Infantry recalled that as "the rebels came charging at full speed" he ordered his men to fire. "Another volley," reported Hovey, "and the ground was covered with their dead. Riderless horses rushed wildly in all directions." Captain Bryan Marsh of the Seventeenth Texas Cavalry succinctly admitted that the reckless skirmishers had been "jenteely whipped." Curtis, whose army suffered only minor casualties, arrived safely at Helena a few days later.[11]

Curtis's movement eliminated one problem, but another replaced it—the difficulty of supplying an ever growing army. Major General Theophilus H. Holmes, who succeeded Hindman as commander of the Trans-Mississippi Department, complained to Richmond that the commissary, ordnance, and medical departments were almost empty when he arrived in mid-August. Many of his men had not received "a dollar for six, eight, and ten months, and [were] now becoming clarorous for their pay." Although the secretary of war, George W. Randolph, assured Holmes that supplies were forthcoming, few arms ever arrived. Normal essentials such as shoes and clothing proved equally scarce.[12]

McCulloch, from his headquarters in Tyler, worked fervently to procure provisions that Richmond could not. He sent Capt. Robertson, son of a prominent Texas impresario, on two trips to south Texas to buy supplies. On the first of these trips, Robertson secured over thirteen thousand dollars worth of arms, ammunition, and medicine that had evaded the naval blockade along the Gulf Coast, smuggled in from British Honduras. Robertson found that Confederate credit was not accepted, and he had to procure the needed items by using his own, and Gen. McCulloch's, personal credit. So desperate was Holmes for medical supplies that he sent an expressman to intercept McCulloch's staff upon their arrival in Rome, Arkansas, in an effort to hurry the precious quinine to the army doctors.[13]

Holmes proved to be a poor choice for a department that required an aggressive commander. Late in September he reorganized the army, but his changes did not please everyone. McCulloch, who arrived in Arkansas early in the month, expected Holmes to assign him a division, perhaps even a corps, with a recommendation for promotion. Indeed, most of the Texas soldiers anticipated this. Instead, the Texans soon discovered that the department commander had other plans. Holmes divided sixteen of the Texas regiments into two divisions, assigning eight to McCulloch, and the remainder to newly appointed Brigadier General Allison Nelson. But Nelson, gravely ill at Camp Holmes near Austin, Arkansas, died within days of his appointment. (Camp Holmes subsequently became known as Camp Nelson in his honor.) Nelson's division, therefore, operated under McCulloch. In addition, Holmes ordered Parsons's cavalry to join McCulloch as scouts. Instead of forcefully utilizing McCulloch's command, Holmes's subsequent actions demonstrated that he was dilatory and vacillating.[14]

Holmes hoped to defend all of Arkansas—from the Indian Territory to the Mississippi River. He ordered Hindman, who had assumed command of the First Army Corps operating in northwest Arkansas, to take a position near the Boston Mountains south of Fayetteville in order to keep a watchful eye on Federal movements from Missouri. Holmes also sent a brigade of Texans and one of Arkansans to the uncompleted fortification at Arkansas Post on the Arkansas River, and kept the remainder, including McCulloch's division, in reserve near Little Rock.

The nearest danger was the large Federal army gathering at Helena. Holmes ordered McCulloch's division to DeValls Bluff on the White River where he believed a show of force was necessary to discourage any enemy advance. Constant rain, however, made any encounter with the enemy not only impractical, but virtually impossible. Because of the mud, African Americans impressed to open and maintain roads made little headway. Even the horsemen had trouble moving through the quagmire; only a few scattered cavalrymen ever saw an enemy soldier.[15]

The miserable weather, intensified by inactivity and illness, frustrated the soldiers. When the anticipated advance from Helena failed to materialize, Holmes ordered the troops back to camp near Little Rock. Joseph P. Blessington, of the Sixteenth Texas Infantry, recalled that although it was early October "[i]t rained, sleeted, and froze." Zachariah H. Crow of the Seventeenth Texas Cavalry, now dismounted, remembered a "march of 11 days through the mud and water up to [their] nes [knees]." Capt. Robertson wrote to his wife late in the month that even the "oldest inhabitant [did] not recollect to have seen winter set in so early, or snow falling to the depth of two inches on green cotton leaves and potato vines."[16]

Illness hit almost everyone. The hospitals, which soldiers complained were little better than hog pens, overflowed. Capt. Marsh told his wife that he never allowed his men near a hospital as long as they had money enough to pay for board at a private house. "It is really distressing," observed Capt. Robertson, "to hear the poor fellows coughing when out on dress parade, or drilling." By November, the men buried five to seven comrades a day. Supplying cavalry mounts proved another vexing problem. The land west of the White River, where McCulloch had camped, was devoid of forage as the drought of the preceding spring had destroyed most of the crops. The Confederate commissary procured corn from the bottomlands of the lower Arkansas River and shipped it by water to Little Rock, but the river had become too low to navigate, even for shallow-draft boats. Holmes continued the unpopular, but necessary, practice of dismounting cavalrymen as the forage gave out; and the remaining mounted men had to camp east of the White and Cache Rivers, where grass was abundant.[17]

Adding to the strife, the War Department had ordered seven regiments sent to the army in Virginia. Holmes, who had been promoted to lieutenant general in October, complained that he was in no position to offer aid, as he had no troops to spare and even fewer qualified commanders. McCulloch, in fact, was the only Texan ranking higher than a colonel. Holmes pointed out to Samuel Cooper, the adjutant and inspector general in Richmond, that the withdrawal of the requested regiments would be "most painfully felt." And, he observed, "All the brigades are now commanded by colonels, most of whom are not qualified to command a regiment." He felt he could not possibly comply with the order.[18]

The Richmond government continued to petition for more men. In November, Holmes received another order from Cooper, this time requesting him to send ten thousand reinforcements to Lieutenant General John C. Pemberton at Vicksburg. Distressed, Holmes procrastinated. The Federal forces at Helena had just attempted the capture of Arkansas Post, southeast of the state capital. Fortunately for the Confederates at the yet uncompleted Fort Hindman, the enemy gunboats drew too much water, and a mix-up in communications had compelled their withdrawal.[19]

Thoroughly alarmed, Holmes began to prepare a defense. He ordered one of the brigades with McCulloch to reinforce Arkansas Post, where Brigadier General Thomas J. Churchill had assumed command. With McCulloch's remaining three brigades under Colonels Overton Young, Horace Randal, and George Flournoy, Holmes sought to defend the fertile Arkansas valley, an area of rich farmland vital to the subsistence of the armies in Arkansas and northern Louisiana.

Rather than accede to Richmond's demand for more men, Holmes stalled. Writing to Cooper, he pleaded for the safety of Arkansas. To abandon the valley would open it to almost certain occupation; and for any troops to reach Vicksburg would take at least thirty days even under the best conditions. The Mississippi was over three hundred miles away and, Holmes argued, his troops, not accustomed to marching long distances, could never arrive in time to be of any use. This, coupled with the fact that the river had risen and forage was scarce, made a successful attempt to relieve Pemberton almost impossible.[20]

This disregard of orders caused some concern in Richmond. A few days later a terse message arrived from Cooper: "The President reiterates his orders that you send without delay sufficient forces from your command to General Pemberton." Holmes replied immediately that McCulloch's was the only division available, and to remove it would leave the country around Helena undefended. "Solemnly, under the circumstances," answered Holmes, "I regard the movement ordered as equivalent to abandoning Arkansas."[21]

Reluctant, Holmes hesitated. But he could not continue to ignore a direct order from President Davis. He instructed McCulloch to march his division toward Vicksburg, but three miles southeast of Little Rock Holmes ordered the Texans to halt. Instead, he directed McCulloch to proceed for Van Buren, where Hindman requested reinforcements. Federal troops were advancing on the Confederates; and Hindman's corps, reduced by sickness and casualties, amounted to only ten thousand effectives against what he estimated as twenty thousand Federals. McCulloch's division had scarcely started toward Van Buren before Holmes countermanded the order. One tired infantryman complained, "[W]e can never tell where we are going until after we get there." Another indignantly grumbled, "[I]f we came to Arkansas with the expectation of riding on railroads we would find ourselves mistaken."[22]

While the Confederate hierarchy at Little Rock held council, the Texans spent Christmas trying to anticipate what lay ahead. The men in McCulloch's division knew that Major General John G. Walker, a native of Missouri and old acquaintance of Holmes, had arrived from the East; few surmised the reason for Walker's presence. The day after Christmas, Holmes surprised all by placing the Texas division under Walker. McCulloch, on being relieved, was assigned to command one of the brigades. The troops received no explanation for McCulloch's apparent demotion; many seemed baffled at the turn of events. McCulloch made no public comment, even to his own staff. But again the Texan had been overlooked for promotion.[23]

Walker scarcely had time to reach his new command, and the men barely time to react, before Holmes ordered the division to march—this time toward Pine Bluff. They had traveled thirty-seven miles in three days when the department commander again countermanded the order; the troops returned to Little Rock over the same road. On New Year's Day the soldiers covered seven miles without any apparent destination. A frustrated J. P. Blessington complained, "It was generally believed amongst the troops that General Holmes was advised by the Medical Board to give Walker's Division enough of exercise."[24]

Meanwhile, the situation along the Mississippi River continued to deteriorate. On January 2 Pemberton reported that his men, from their position on the Vicksburg bluffs, had repulsed enemy gunboats. Exactly a week later, Churchill, at Arkansas Post, learned that a Federal fleet had entered the Arkansas River. Instructed to resist until help arrived, Churchill appealed to Holmes for support. The Texans greeted rumors of an imminent campaign with marked excitement. E. P. Petty of the Seventeenth Texas Infantry recalled, "The news of a prospect of a fight was received by the regiment with cheers . . . all are making active preparations to give the Yankees a warm reception on Arkansas soil."[25]

Churchill needed reinforcements, and quickly. But on January 11, after covering about twenty-five miles, the soldiers camped—still nearly thirty miles from Arkansas Post. On the following morning the troops advanced only five miles before learning that Arkansas Post had surrendered. One cavalryman bitterly observed, "The infantry censure Gen. Holmes for not getting Walker's Division at the Post before Churchill was compelled to surrender."[26]

Chaos followed the fall of Arkansas Post. Many of the Texans captured with Churchill were friends and relatives of the men in Walker's division. But the Texans had little time to vent their anger; the loss of Arkansas Post seemed only a prelude to the invasion of Little Rock. Nothing stood between the capital and an estimated fifty thousand Federals except a few scattered Confederate brigades. Holmes arrived at Walker's camp on the banks of the Arkansas River to take personal command; and Hindman, whose army had retreated following the battle at Prairie Grove on December 7, soon joined them.

The combined forces anxiously waited for the anticipated offensive. In their camp on the river, known to the soldiers as "Camp Freeze Out," the men built fortifications of mud, snow, and ice. "There we lay for six or seven days without tents and with but little food," recalled John Simmons, "amid snow eight inches deep, with but one blanket apiece, shivering around our campfires." Instead of an advance, the Federal gunboats retreated into the Mississippi. Unknown to the Confederates, Ulysses S. Grant, perturbed at having part of his command diverted up the Arkansas River, had ordered the fleet to withdraw.[27]

Holmes, freed from the threatened invasion, ordered the army to retreat. The weather was miserable, recalled a jaded Confederate, "and such marching poor soldiers never did before—incessant rain and mud almost insurmountable." Footsore and weary, the men trudged past deserted farms and empty plantations to arrive near Pine Bluff, where the tired Confederates settled down for a much needed rest. And, noted Captain Thomas Smith of the Eleventh Texas Infantry, although the boys arrived "in a worn out muddy condition," he found them "more lively than could reasonably have been expected under the circumstances." He believed the Texans had suffered "almost beyond endurance."[28]

But their year in Arkansas was about to end. In March 1863, Lieutenant General Edmund Kirby Smith replaced Holmes and transferred the headquarters of the Trans-Mississippi Department to Louisiana. As Grant increased his pressure upon Vicksburg, defending the Mississippi became imperative, and the new commander ordered most of the Texans to Louisiana.

How important had the Texans been in the defense of Arkansas? Certainly in 1862, when it appeared that the state, abandoned and defenseless, would fall to the Federal army, their arrival was decisive. At this crucial point Henry McCulloch took charge of the situation in Texas and hurried thousands of men to the defense of Little Rock. But McCulloch's administrative skills, excellent though they were, never won him acclaim, and he failed to prove himself on the battlefield. In July 1863 he returned to Texas, where he remained for the rest of the war, serving as commander for the defense of the western frontier.[29]

Nevertheless, Henry McCulloch and the Texas soldiers helped determine the fate of Arkansas in 1862. The response to Arkansas's plight had been quick and effective. Little Rock was no longer there for the taking; any effort to occupy the capital would have resulted in significant casualties—both Federal and Confederate. Whether or not the Army of the Trans-Mississippi could have actually turned back a Federal offensive is not important; the significance is that the Union commanders were not sure they could overrun the Texas recruits—along with the growing number of Arkansas and Missouri troops—without heavy loss. Although Holmes, slow and timid, never utilized his army effectively, any movement toward Little Rock had to wait until the Mississippi River was securely in Union hands, the army from Texas dispersed throughout the entire Trans-Mississippi Department, and the threat of invasion elsewhere made Arkansas second in importance. Thus, in September 1863, Brigadier General Frederick Steele's Federal army occupied Little Rock. The Confederates, by this time mainly Arkansas and Missouri troops, withdrew to Rockport and Arkadelphia. Although much of Arkansas, as well as Louisiana and the Indian Territory, would fall, the thin buffer zone surrounding Texas, and protected by the Army of the Trans-Mississippi, would remain until the war's end.

Chapter 2

Wartime Gristmill Destruction in Northwest Arkansas and Military Farm Colonies

MICHAEL A. HUGHES

To students of Arkansas marches and battles, the northwest counties are a uniquely interesting area. Although fewer than 13 percent of the state's 771 military actions took place in the northwest, these affairs included the engagements in the intense campaigns climaxed at Pea Ridge and Prairie Grove.[1] The fighting in northwest Arkansas was the most costly in the state. Within a thirty-five-mile radius of the town of Fayetteville, almost 30 percent of all Union casualties in Arkansas occurred, a full one-tenth of all Union casualties west of the Mississippi River.[2] A new face of war was displayed in famous Civil War tragedies like the burnings of Jackson, Atlanta, and Columbia and in the scythe-like marches of William T. Sherman across Georgia and Philip Sheridan down the Shenandoah Valley. But long before these Confederate disasters, and little known today, northwest Arkansas had already experienced total war, war without rules.

There is a fascination to the strategies, the glory, even the carnage of battle. So we may overlook certain other important aspects of the Civil War. The complicated logistics which were necessary to feed armies in the field draw little attention, nor do the individual tragedies of civilians whose goods and livelihoods were sacrificed to feed those armies. This essay focuses on the way in which campaigns in northwest Arkansas destroyed some antebellum industries, as several Ozark villages became some of the earliest victims of modern warfare. Perhaps studying the fate of several regional mills will shed some light on how armies were sustained during the war and on the consequences of military considerations taking precedence over civilian needs.

It is easy today to underestimate the critical role milling played in Arkansas's embryonic manufacturing economy. To us today, the old mill is viewed as a picturesque complement to a rural landscape, as was depicted when a facsimile Arkansas gristmill appeared in the opening scenes of *Gone with the Wind.* However, in pre–Civil War Arkansas mills symbolized industry as well as agriculture. Beyond processing flour and meal, the rural mill was the factory of its day.

The mills of northwest Arkansas, in particular, did more than just grind the corn, wheat, and rye for homes, farms, and distilleries. Area mills both sawed timber and ran planes and lathes which converted the wood into furniture and farm implements. Benton and Washington County mills carded wool, ginned cotton, and wove cloth for clothing across two states and the Indian Territory. A look at Washington County in particular demonstrates how advantageous the presence of good mills could be. In 1860 Washington County was self-sufficient in several industries. It ranked first among Arkansas counties in wool production, so was naturally almost first in the processing of wool. But even in areas where the county lacked raw materials, the mills gave it an economic advantage. For example, only five counties in the state produced fewer bales of cotton than did Washington County, but the presence of adequate mills enabled the county to rank second in the production of cotton goods.[3]

In February 1862 war came to northwest Arkansas in the form of an invasion by Union general Samuel R. Curtis. The culmination of this campaign would be the battle of Pea Ridge on March 7 and 8, 1862. But it is very possible that northwest Arkansas's milling industries were already suffering from the effects of war through a loss of laborers.

Northwest Arkansas mills were credited with employing at least eighty-eight workers in the 1860 industrial census of Arkansas.[4] But the number of mill workers was obviously larger. Since the census failed to examine several active mills, for reasons unknown, it missed counting a number of employees. Also, owner-operators and apprentices were not counted among the eighty-eight workers. And not all of the mills' workers may have been freemen, so that many non-white laborers may not have been counted. The possibility of slave mill hands is suggested, first, by the fact that the number of employees counted at enumerated textile and sawmills seems inadequate for their operation. Second, the 10 percent slave population counted in Washington County in 1860 seems too high for a county which raised few staple, labor-intensive crops. This suggests that some slaves may have labored in industry.[5] These observations, and records of the postwar occupations of some freedmen, including mechanics, suggests that part of the mill workers may have been slaves.

If they were, then the rapid exodus of slaveholders fleeing in the advance of Curtis's Union army permanently removed other mill hands. When one considers the white workers who had already joined the army, it seems clear that the war damaged the milling industries before a shot was fired in Arkansas.

Weeks before Curtis entered Arkansas, his campaign had several times, been diverted by the necessity of having to seize intact local mills. Curtis found two reasons necessitating such seizures, necessities which plagued commanders on both sides of the conflict throughout the war. First, campaign supply lines could not always provide adequate milled flour. A member of the Thirty-sixth Illinois Regiment described such a situation during Curtis's advance: "The long, slender line of communication with Rolla (Missouri), liable at any time to be broken, necessitated heavy details for its protection. . . . Supplies being nearly exhausted, subsisting off the country became a matter of necessity. . . . Foraging expeditions rapidly gathered the grain stored in the granaries; mills were set to grinding it."[6]

A second reason for capturing mills intact was that it was wiser to requisition large quantities of grain from a single miller's granary than it was to pillage it from a multitude of private homes. On March 1, Curtis noted, "[T]he burning of . . . valuable mills in Arkansas by the enemy has induced some resentments on the part of my troops[;] peaceable citizens not being at home to sell [supplies] to my quartermasters, I am compelled to take them without purchase, making settlement difficult and doubtful, occasioning irregularities which I have labored to counteract."[7]

As to paying millers for supplies to the army, only "Union men" were to be guaranteed compensation, and then in the form of quartermaster's receipts.[8] The quartermaster with the onerous task of making forced requisitions during the Pea Ridge campaign, taking "the bull by the horns" as one dispatch put it, was then a captain.[9] Within four months, however, Quartermaster Philip Sheridan would win his general's star. While Sheridan's memoirs are generally read for information on the fighting which brought him to fame, he chose to devote three pages to his victories in milling operations during the Pea Ridge campaign.[10]

Whether or not Napoleon actually coined the famous phrase "an army marches on its stomach," General Curtis felt the axiom to be true. He took no chances in preparing to feed his men. In anticipation of the 1812–1813 Russian campaign, Napoleon had ordered construction of five hundred portable grinding mills. Imitating this French innovation, the United States had stockpiled two hundred similar portable mills at western frontier posts.[11] To guard against the prospect that all local mills would be destroyed, Curtis had his men carry fifty of these hand mills. His would be the first, if not the only, Civil War campaign so encumbered. But from southern Missouri into northwestern Arkansas, Curtis's army was fortunate, for community mills were found to be largely intact or repairable.

However, Confederate general Ben McCulloch had not intended to leave any facilities intact for the benefit of the invaders. Only the haste of the Confederate retreat from Missouri and northwest Arkansas had saved the mills thus far. Three months earlier McCulloch, then regional commander, had written, "[A]s for Arkansas, every man who is a patriot and sound southern man will be the first to put the torch to his own grain or mill rather than have them left to aid the enemy."[12]

As they proceeded into Arkansas via Benton County, all went well for the Federals. But the situation further south, in Washington County, proved another matter. McCulloch aggressively sent out patrols on some unfinished business. On February 22, 1862, two days before taking Fayetteville, Curtis's Federals found themselves surrounded by a circle of fire. William Baxter, a Fayetteville resident, described what happened in the town that day: "Bands of cavalry, by order of General M'Culloch, dashed into town and began firing the buildings which had been used for military purposes . . . the steam mill, which had been furnishing the rebel army ten thousand pounds of flour per day, was consumed."[13] Baxter's neighbor, young Marian Tebbetts, had a personal interest in the destruction: "The big flour mill . . . was owned by Father and Stirman and Dixon, and was the only steam mill in that part of the country. Father begged of the officers that they remove machinery sufficient to insure it against use as a mill, but no heed was given his request and the great and useful building burned."[14]

The tenor of the times may also be gauged by the threat directed to Colonel Grenville Dodge's Union outpost at War Eagle, or Blackburn's Mill. On its way north to attack the Federal supply line back in Missouri, the Sixth Texas Cavalry Regiment stopped at the mill on February 27. There they made a request. If Dodge did not abandon the mill by noon the Texans swore they would "hang every d——d Yankee there."[15]

Between March 1 and March 3, Confederate raiders burned the Bean textile mill and the Pearson/Kidd mills at Cane Hill, west of Fayetteville. South of Fayetteville, another mill, possibly Graham's or Stelle's (alt. Steele's), was also burned.[16] In one week, Southern torches cost Washington

County the source of over seventy-one thousand dollars in annual milling production.[17] Benton County's War Eagle Mill (abandoned by Dodge's men for tactical reasons rather than because of Texan threats) met its end as well, on March 2.[18]

A chronicler of the Third Louisiana Infantry Regiment later justified McCulloch's arson, saying that "as a military necessity no one could question its wisdom and justice. . . . It was no time, in the face of a powerful and pursuing foe, to query into the motives and policy of a course . . . prompted by dire necessity, the salvation of the army, and the ultimate good of the country."[19] But others suspected such a policy might backfire on the Confederacy. Missouri State Guard general Sterling Price termed such arson "an infliction as grievous as any . . . by the enemy," while his Union opponent, Curtis, wrote, "Nothing could be more injurious to the country than this burning of mills, and the people are indignant."[20]

McCulloch's insistence on mill burning was as atypical of the early phases of the war in northwest Arkansas as it was in other areas of the country. Most commanders still conducted what Winston Churchill called "the last war of gentlemen." Just the previous January, Sterling Price, Confederate commander in Missouri, had sent an inquiry to his Union counterpart, Henry Halleck. Did Halleck not agree, Price asked, that the destruction of transportation facilities was "the legal right of a belligerent power?" But of the burning of mills Price stated, "[I]t does not seem to me that the necessities of either party requires . . . such vandalism."[21] In response, Halleck agreed that there seemed little justification for the destruction of mills.

It was fortunate for the Federals that the Confederate parties which wreaked such destruction in Washington County had acted too late to disable most of the mills of Benton County. Curtis's army already held the Confederate's former campsite at Cross Hollows, where Blake's/Black's Mill hardly gained a respite between Confederate army and Union army milling. When Curtis found the Washington County mills destroyed, he sent detachments to work Osage Mill and William Mill, in southern and central Benton County.[22] It was from these mills that several Union units, combining outpost and scouting duty with flouring operations, raced to take part in the first day of the battle at Pea Ridge on March 6 and 7.

After the Confederate defeat at Pea Ridge, northwest Arkansas became a no-man's-land from May to August 1862. Then, from August 1862 to January 1863, both sides cautiously sent expeditions into the area, in part to again utilize the mills. Confederate cavalry chieftain Brigadier General James S. Rains worked the few surviving mills near Fayetteville, and Colonel John T. Coffee's Confederate irregulars made use of the mill at Cross Hollows.[23]

Although Union efforts to trap Coffee's troops failed, the Federals seemed content with their own logistical activities; if they could not at the time maneuver the Confederates onto the battlefield, they could at least confront them in what was called "the mill business."[24] Brigadier General James G. Blunt, just across the state line in the Indian Territory, reported, "I am thrashing out and grinding wheat; a game we can play at as well as the rebels."[25]

Since mid-year of 1862, field command of Confederate troops west of the Mississippi River had been under Major General Thomas Carmichael Hindman. Ever aggressive, Hindman made plans in October 1862 to seize Fayetteville from the east and reestablish Confederate control in northwest Arkansas. His maneuvers failed at the little-known engagement of McGuire's Store at Oxford Bend, east of Fayetteville. This October 28 defeat, incidentally, deprived Hindman of the use of two working mills on the White River.[26]

When Hindman next approached Fayetteville, it was from the west. The resulting battle of Prairie Grove on December 7, 1862, once more cost Hindman control of two mills, Dutch Mills and Rhea's Mill. In a boon to historians, the wartime traumas of the owners of these two mills are well documented. The sympathies of mill proprietor William H. Rhea are evidenced by his flexible price scale. Flour was charged to Confederates at two and a half cents a pound; flour was charged to Federals at twice that.[27] Rhea saw plenty of both sides—his mill changed hands at least seven times during the Prairie Grove campaign. While we do not know how Rhea responded to the occupation of his mill by the Confederates, surviving records give his impressions of Union visits. According to Rhea, the average cost of an occupation by Union troops was $1,270.42 in goods, services, and damages. Rhea eventual billed the United States for everything from 13,100 pounds of flour to two turkeys. An early environmentalist, perhaps, the miller also attempted to charge $500 for the pollution resulting from decomposing horses.[28]

Records from the mill village of Hermannsburg, or Dutch Mills, seven miles southwest of Cane Hill, indicate that Confederates could be equally unwelcome guests. At the hamlet the German, or "Deutch," family of the

Hermanns operated what was popularly known as "Dutch Mills." On November 15, 1862, Nani Hermann recorded, "[T]his morning . . . some men were wanting the keys to our mill. . . . The bulk of the [Confederate] army had hardly gone by . . . when four men came. . . . [They] searched the house from roof to cellar, not overlooking the granary and smokehouse, and took everything they wanted." Dutch Mills changed hands four times during the Prairie Grove campaign, with increasingly destructive effect. Eventually the depredations of war forced the Hermanns to abandon the village.[29]

Another especially bad season for northwest Arkansas mill owners and other residents began about December 1863 with an unprecedented wave of Confederate guerilla activity. At this time, several mills along the Missouri line were burned. Some portions of southwest Missouri became depopulated for want of grain or the facilities to grind it into flour or meal.[30] Northwest Arkansas was little better off that winter. An elderly Washington County man residing northwest of Fayetteville on Clear Creek, which before the war had powered three mills, could by February 1864 no longer find a working mill in his vicinity. After an eighteen-mile journey to use the closest intact mill, he recorded that his fears that his grain would be seized by a Confederate bushwhacker were perhaps equalled by his fears that his meal would be seized by a Union scout.[31]

Bushwhackers were a chronic problem for the Union garrison at Fayetteville after the Federals occupied the region for good in the fall of 1863. But suddenly, in the summer of 1864, Fayetteville post commander Colonel Marcus LaRue Harrison thought he saw the solution to the guerrilla problem. "The disabling of mills," guessed Harrison, "causes more writhing among bushwhackers than any other mode of attack."[32] Perhaps Harrison believed that village mills, which were traditional places for socializing, were gathering or recruiting places for guerrillas. For whatever reason, Harrison ordered a raid on mills owned by Confederate sympathizers. During twelve August days, Walters' Mill in Benton County and Brown's Mill and Dutch Mills in Washington County were disabled.[33] This time the cost to northwest Arkansas was forty-five thousand dollars in annual productivity.[34] The destruction of Brown's Mill may have been especially satisfying to Harrison; its owner, William "Buck" Brown, was the wiliest and most effective Confederate partisan captain in northwest Arkansas. But, ironically, one of Colonel Harrison's assignments was to guard and protect mills. Exactly why Harrison undertook the raid, and whether or not he had authority to do so, remains a mystery. With the exception of Harrison's one foray, there seems to be no evidence of any other Federal destruction of northwest Arkansas mills. With the August 1864 raid over, the burning of area mills came to a close.

The 1860 industrial census of Arkansas indicates that there were thirty-five mills in the six northwestern counties of the state; almost half of these mills were in Washington County.[35] Correspondingly, Washington County was the Arkansas county most injured by the war; about half of the county's fifteen to eighteen antebellum mills were destroyed or disabled before peace came. Few mill owners, even those identified with the Union cause, were ever reimbursed for services, supplies, or losses. Miller Tandy Kidd of Cane Hill would wait fifteen years before receiving a settlement of only fifteen cents on the dollar for forage requisitions.[36]

Wartime mill destruction apparently cost Washington County its pre-war Arkansas lead in several industries. The lead in textile production, in particular, went to those counties less affected by the conflict. Only one of Washington County's smaller carding mills reappears in the industrial census of 1870.[37] And some individual communities of Washington County, like the small town of Elm Springs, declined to a fraction of their importance before they lost their mill.

Having been one of the first areas in this hemisphere to experience modern economic warfare, northwest Arkansas's agricultural and subsistence economy were already badly damaged by 1863. In the latter months of the war, a social and agricultural experiment radical for its time would be attempted for the survivors. In September and October 1864, Confederate general Sterling Price attempted a last gamble to save the West for the Confederacy with a daring expedition into Missouri. Price was defeated and driven back through southern Missouri and northern Arkansas. Price's offensive had stimulated a wave of Confederate guerrilla warfare. His defeat was followed by even more desperate and lawless fighting in the Ozarks. Even before Price's campaign developed, an observer had noted that "the country [of] . . . the Boston Mountains [was] in a very desolate, unsettled state, full of bushwhackers, thieves, and rebel sympathizers . . . committing every depredation devisable by the human mind."[38] Now, as hopes of Confederate salvation waned, the irregular warfare took an especially vicious turn, for the wives and children of Union sympathizers were singled out for revenge.

Ironically, the Union families of northwest Arkansas were bedeviled by regular Union forces as well. A group identifying itself as a "committee of the loyal citizens of Crawford County" protested that it was "impossible to keep a horse, an ox, a piece of meat, or a bushel of meal, unless so far hidden as to defy their search."[39] The Federal commander at Fort Smith was forced to admit the truth of the accusation: "Many loyal people have been shamefully treated. . . . The country is filled with irregular receipts for forage, horses, cattle, and other property which cannot be settled, but in most instances everything has been taken and no receipt given, the people turned out to starve."[40] Between the depredations of Confederate guerrillas and Union foragers, some north Arkansans did not survive the winter of 1864–65. Reports verified that several women and children between Fayetteville and the Missouri line died of starvation during the war's final winter.[41]

Tens of thousands of civilians had already abandoned northern Arkansas before that last season. In March 1864 it was reported that the border counties of southwestern Missouri were virtually depopulated.[42] Two months later officials noted that the adjoining Arkansas counties were being vacated as well.[43] By the summer of 1864, even the military population had shrunk, for neither army could find sufficient grain or forage in northwest Arkansas to continue operations there.[44] By February 1865 the counties south of the White and Buffalo Rivers were deserted as well.[45]

Many families fled to Kansas, others to Missouri; the post at Springfield, Missouri, reported on "an unending stream . . . pouring in from Arkansas."[46] Refugees remaining in Arkansas made their way to the principal Union garrison towns. The post at Little Rock sent two thousand refugees northward during the last three months of the war, without attempting to estimate those who had already gone on or still remained.[47] Fort Smith had an estimated refugee population of one thousand in May 1864, and two thousand ten months later.[48] And about one thousand persons tried to remain in northwest Arkansas as dependents of the post at Fayetteville.[49]

In many cases, refugees were family members who had fled to the encampment of a husband and father. The destitution of soldier families, aggravated by prolonged pay delays, led to absences, desertions, and thefts among Union troops recruited in Arkansas. But despite the cost in discipline and morale, no coherent departmental policy for refugee relief was formulated until April 10, 1865, ten days after Lee's surrender.[50] Until that time, each post commander was left to make his own decisions about aiding refugees. Lieutenant Colonel Irving W. Fuller at the post of Lewisburg (near Morrilton) reported as early as April 1864, "I found . . . very many destitute families in this locality, the majority of them unable to provide for themselves. These I have assisted as far as possible."[51] But, unlike Fuller, many commanders did not provide refugee assistance until the war was almost over.

The degree of assistance offered by commanders varied greatly. Department head Major General Joseph J. Reynolds at Little Rock fed up to seven hundred destitute women and children, mostly the dependents or widows and orphans of Union soldiers.[52] Colonel M. LaRue Harrison at Fayetteville performed a similar service, even going so far as to lend cash advances.[53] On the other hand, Brigadier General Cyrus Bussey at Fort Smith called the Little Rock policy "indulgence" and charged that officers like Harrison actually offended northwest Arkansans by offering them government assistance.[54]

A far more controversial relief effort was the establishment of the so-called post colonies or colony farms. In mid-May 1864 Colonel Harrison mentioned in a letter on militia formation that he was using a home guard company to protect farming west of Pea Ridge in Benton County.[55] Pleased with the results, and perhaps encouraged by a subsequent departmental order regularizing such companies, Harrison decided to create what became the first guarded farm colonies. By the end of 1864 he reported, "[P]ost colonies have been formed all over the country with little forts to protect agriculture, and they are garrisoned by home guards. Next year will be one of great abundance and large crops will be raised if protection is given."[56]

The novelty of Harrison's concept was that he was no longer thinking in terms of militia companies which happened to guard farmers. Instead he now thought in terms of agricultural settlements made up of armed farmers, perhaps not unlike Israeli kibbutzim. Major General Reynolds expressed a similar idea sent an order to Bussey at Fort Smith in February 1865. Bussey was instructed to raise companies "whose occupation is farming not soldiering" and to "sell corn, oats, and broken-down horses to those attempting to farm."[57] Such orders, it must be noted, were not intended to create a social or agricultural experiment, but to provide a means of reducing the drain on army resources.

The only set of detailed instructions on forming such colonies was produced by Harrison at Fayetteville. According to the instructions, colonies were to be produced when fifty men capable of bearing arms asked to form a home guard company and to settle their families together. They were to sign an article of loyalty to the Federal and Unionist state governments and to enroll inhabitants within a ten-mile radius of the colony. Farming was to be done on a large, defensible tract of abandoned land; Harrison stated, "[T]hey also agree to parcel out the land by vote, giving to each one all he wants to cultivate." But, Harrison insisted, they were "to have nothing in common, except defense and obedience to law."[58] So these were "collective farms" only in being on a common site and enjoying collective security.

In several cases, some effort was made to create real, though temporary, communities at the colonies. Union Valley colony, northwest of Prairie Grove in Washington County, possessed a blacksmith and wagon shop, a place for regular religious services, and perhaps the first free public school in the county.[59] Fish Farm colony, five miles downriver from Pine Bluff in Jefferson County, also operated a school.[60] Among the "freedmen's home farms," that at Pine Bluff was at least one place where education and community building were attempted among former slaves.[61]

Most of the evidence about the crops raised at such farms comes from the western Arkansas colonies, the most numerous. One clue about crops is a petition to the president from Crawford County citizens wishing to form a colony. While Lincoln received thousands of petitions requesting pardons and political appointments, this request from Van Buren was surely the only one for one thousand bushels of corn and oats, seventy-five bushels of Hungarian grass seed, and one hundred bushels of Irish potatoes and button onions.[62] Harrison's correspondence regarding northwest Arkansas refers to corn at six settlements and to a projected one-thousand-ton hay crop at Union Valley. There were eight hundred acres of wheat planted at his Pea Ridge colony, but wheat was possibly restricted to Benton County farms as most flour mills elsewhere had been destroyed.[63] None of the crops mentioned were innovative, since grains and potatoes had been staples in western Arkansas before the war.

Finding a legal basis for appropriating the large amounts of land needed could have been a sticky problem. Any one of three justifications for appropriation could have been cited: the Second Confiscation Act of July 1862, the precedent set by Grant in a general order issued in Tennessee in 1863, or an August 1864 letter from the War Department to Arkansas on emergency contingencies.[64] However, taking such a course of action would have involved lengthy correspondence with Washington and finding some quasilegal application of the precedents. Instead, officers in Arkansas simply cited the "destitute condition . . . of refugee families" and temporarily borrowed the land on the grounds of necessity.[65] Legally, all colonists were squatters, and in one ironic instance just after the war a Union regimental commander was hired as counsel by a plantation owner to evict the farmers of a colony.[65]

The number and location of colonies in Arkansas is difficult to determine. The Johnson Plantation colony was in Pulaski County below Bayou Fourche.[67] Fish Farm colony, below Pine Bluff, has been previously referred to.[68] Four colonies around Fort Smith and Van Buren, under the jurisdiction of Cyrus Bussey, were never referred to by name or precise location.[69]

The most extensive colonies were those under Harrison in northwest Arkansas. In all, Harrison planned for seventeen colonies, two in Benton County, four in Madison County, and eleven in Washington County.[70] Harrison estimated these would enroll twelve hundred men, not counting family members, and would cultivate of fifteen thousand acres.[71]

At least four "freedmen's home farms" were established in Arkansas, each in a loosely defined administrative district.[72] In contrast to the refugee colonies, the land for these farms was leased, and the goal of the farms was to be self-supporting through crop sales, whereas the refugee colonies sought self-sufficiency only in terms of feeding themselves. Also, the freedmen's farms were not prepared for self-defense but were dependent on nearby Federal garrisons. The Little Rock freedmen's farm was evidently a failure, while the DeValls Bluff operation was largely self-supporting.[73] Home Farm, within the eastern portion of present-day Pine Bluff, was perhaps the most successful effort socially.[74] A farm three and a half miles below Helena was financially lucrative initially but began to crumble after several devastating raids.[75]

Among refugee colony founders, Harrison had a very positive and optimistic view of the worth of such colonies. To him they not only relieved the refugee problem but could contribute to the war effort in other ways. For example, the men of at least two northwest Arkansas colonies actively took the field against Confederate guerrillas, thus serving as extensions of Harrison's First Arkansas Cavalry Regiment (USA) at Fayetteville.[76] And Harrison also believed that the colonies served as the bait in a carrot-and-stick plan to induce Confederates to surrender. The enemy could either be hunted down by Harrison's patrols or succumb to the bounty of the colonies in an otherwise desolate land.[77] Harrison may even have seen the colonies as a means of winning over the hearts and minds of the enemy. In the one set of records surviving from a colony, the indigent roll shows that four wives and mothers of Confederate soldiers were cared for at Federal expense.[78]

Harrison's enthusiasm for the colonies was evidently shared by Union provisional governor Isaac Murphy, for he encouraged Harrison to establish additional colonies in Carroll, Marion, Newton, and Searcy Counties as well. Harrison replied in March 1865 that he did not have enough soldiers to supervise additional counties.[79] But in May, after the Confederate surrender, he sought to have refugees in Missouri encouraged to return to Arkansas to form colonies.[80]

In contrast to Harrison, Cyrus Bussey treated his colonies at Fort Smith and Van Buren as nuisances. In fact, Bussey does not seem to have ever authorized the four colonies in his jurisdiction. Apparently the refugees themselves seized upon several abandoned plantations at about the time Bussey was ordered to assist them.[81]

It was the understanding of the Department of Arkansas that Bussey was to send to Little Rock those refugees unable to care for themselves, while permitting those attempting to farm to remain in the Fort Smith–Van Buren area.[82] Bussey, however, tried several stratagems to remove every refugee he could from his command. After complaining to Little Rock that he would need rations for at least one thousand additional persons to support the refugees until crops came up, he was promptly assured that the additional need would be met. In response to the assurance, Bussey then claimed that the previous week's estimate was in error and that there were really five thousand refugees, all "on the verge of starvation."[83] When an unfortunate Captain Warren Harper arrived from Little Rock to settle one hundred refugees on the Burrows plantation, Bussey proclaimed that they could not stay, for Mr. Burrows, "a very bitter rebel," would be upset.[84]

Perhaps not surprisingly, the formation of colonies became a point of contention between Bussey and the enthusiastic Harrison, his subordinate. Not content to bemoan having to form colonies himself, Bussey also attempted to discourage Harrison: "I fear your colonies at Bentonville and elsewhere outside of Fayetteville cannot be maintained. Rebel organizations will be formed strong enough to destroy them."[85] Yet he would argue subsequently that the absence of Confederate strength in northwest Arkansas made the colonies unnecessary.[86]

On March 31, 1865, Bussey changed tactics in his objections to Harrison's colonies. He wrote to Harrison, "[I]t is reported to me that you have issued orders compelling all the people in Northwest Arkansas to join the colonies or they would not be permitted to raise any crops, and that there are many old men and widows with small boys who cannot join these colonies and will be left to starve. . . . It is also reported that an officer of your command said in a public speech in Fayetteville . . . that he would burn the house and kill any man who would not join a colony."[87] While Harrison claimed, "I have never known anything more enthusiastically taken hold of by our people than is our colony system," Bussey wrote, "[T]hese colonies are not formed by the people, but by Colonel Harrison, who has virtually driven the people from their homes to form these colonies."[88]

Bussey offered a number of contradictory explanations for why Harrison was creating what Bussey called a "military despotism."[89] In the course of a single letter he implied that Harrison was involved in a scheme to steal and sell government rations, that he was trying to profit by selling from a private store, and that Harrison was irresponsibly giving out free rations liberally.[90] He charged that Harrison was quickly becoming the most despised man in northwest Arkansas but that Harrison was setting out to do so in order to win sufficient popularity to be elected to Congress.[91]

Was Harrison in fact coercing civilians into the agricultural colonies? Harrison did make several remarks that are suspicious, such as "[R]ebels are coming daily, and those that do not dare to come in are becoming bushwhackers," and "[N]one but the bushwhackers have so far objected [to enrollment in the colonies]."[92] Harrison did definitely see the colonies as instruments in antiguerrilla warfare, and in his carrot-and-stick approach to the Confederates the stick may have been use to prod some civilians along.

But Bussey's charges are so colored by exaggeration that it is difficult to tell to what extent they are true. Bussey swore that he had received several delegations of citizens, many of them aged, and had received hundreds of protests. But Bussey failed to submit a single affidavit or letter of protest from these irate citizens. And Bussey's claim that he had "the testimony of nearly all the officers of the First Arkansas" protesting Harrison's policies completely unsupportable.[93]

Perhaps Bussey's attacks are partially explained by the fact that while he was constantly skirmishing with Little Rock over refugee relief, Harrison's colony efforts were being praised and encouraged by the governor. Then too, his actions protected Bussey's bureaucratic backside. If Harrison's colonies succeeded, then Bussey was on record as having approved the plans; if the colonies failed, then Bussey was on record as having condemned the plans. Or, what may have been at issue were Bussey's feelings about the whole issue of Federal intervention on behalf of the refugees. As noted earlier,

Bussey's comments on free rations suggest his contempt for Federal assistance. As for selling the rations, however, he not only did not object but endorsed the idea.[94] So perhaps Bussey and Harrison confronted one another in an early and abortive skirmish of the great confrontation between the concepts of laissez-faire and the general welfare state. They certainly played out in a small way quarrels still not resolved over the proper limits of government assistance and the proper foundations of collective action.

The records of the Union Valley colony, the sole such records to survive, hint at the atmosphere of fear and alarm which attracted Arkansans to the collective security of the colonies. For example, Special Order No. 6 prohibited the wearing of hickory-dyed clothing, "the collers [*sic*] commonly known as Butternut . . . on account of its resemblance to the uniform of the rebel army . . . and to the garb of the guerrillas who infest the country."[95] On April 13, 1865, a dispatch had to be sent to the colony when its members became alarmed at hearing gunshots at Fayetteville. But the worst was over, and the need for the colonies was declining. The message read, "[T]he firing you heard is in honor of Genl. Lee's Surrender. . . . We fire today 200 guns in honor of this long hoped for event, the termination of this Rebellion. . . . We may be troubled for some time by guerrillas, but the time is not far distant when we can return to our homes with safety, and beat our swords into plow shares, and our spears into pruning hooks."[96]

Chapter 3

Bullets for Johnny Reb: Confederate Nitre and Mining Bureau in Arkansas

JAMES J. JOHNSTON

At the beginning of the Civil War Richmond viewed the Arkansas niter deposits as a valuable war resource, and, beginning in the summer of 1862, it expended manpower and funds to develop these resources. Yet, twelve months later, the Confederate Nitre and Mining Bureau relocated its mining and processing operation to Texas and northern Louisiana. What caused the Arkansas project to fail, if it did fail, and should Richmond have anticipated the problems and concentrated its efforts in Texas from the beginning?

After secession and the creation of a central government, one of the Confederates' first concerns was supplying arms and ammunition to their fledgling army and navy. Buyers for the Confederate government went north to purchase war materiel; secessionists captured United States arsenals in the Southern states, and agents went abroad to buy and ship weapons, ammunition, and other supplies to the Confederacy. The Confederate Congress created the Ordnance Bureau under Colonel Josiah Gorgas, late of the United States Ordnance Board, to coordinate all these efforts and to begin the domestic production of war materiel. The central Southern government looked to Arkansas to supply materiel for the Confederate defense, just as it looked to Arkansas for troops and the supplies to arm those troops. Gunpowder and lead to make cartridges for Confederate arms figured prominently among these supplies, and Arkansas was conspicuous as a producer of lead and of a significant gunpowder ingredient, saltpeter. Reliable gunpowder consisted of two parts saltpeter, one part charcoal, and a bit less sulphur. Arkansas had the saltpeter and could produce charcoal and sulphur. Given these raw materials, all that was needed to produce gunpowder, the Ordnance Bureau chief learned, was labor, security from hostile interruption, and transportation.

A great deal has been written about the contribution of Arkansas troops to the Confederate war effort both east and west of the Mississippi River, but relatively little has been said about the efforts of the Confederate central government in Arkansas, or the Arkansans themselves, to provide war materiel for those Arkansas troops. The Arkansas Ozarks shared with the mountains of Tennessee and Virginia deposits of saltpeter which the Confederate Ordnance Bureau looked toward as sources for that vital gunpowder ingredient. Unfortunately, the Ozarks also shared with Tennessee and Virginia less desirable aspects for large-scale, dependable niter mining: the mountaineers were independent anti-secessionists and the border areas were subject to destructive raids and occupation by nearby Union troops. Arkansas had the raw materials, but did it have the labor, security, and transportation to produce gunpowder? Virtually from the beginning of Arkansas's white settlement the land had been touted for its rich natural resources. Somehow no one had ever exploited them on a large scale, but this did not mean that these resources were not there. Could the Confederacy now exploit them to produce munitions?

Saltpeter, niter or potassium nitrate (KNO_3), for more than a millennium had been used in meat preservation, ceramics, and gunpowder production. The availability of saltpeter in America, especially for gunpowder, facilitated westward movement and played an important role during the Revolutionary War and the War of 1812. Effective British blockades forced the Americans to rely on domestic niter reserves in cave sediments; this caused saltpeter production from cave sediment nitrates to become one of early America's first and most important chemical industries. Although there were many uses for saltpeter, the primary use by the Confederacy was for gunpowder, composed, according to the Confederate *Ordnance Manual*, of "saltpetre, charcoal and sulphur." The *Ordnance Manual* describes saltpeter as "a transparent, white, crystallized salt, inodorous, anhydrous, of a cooling, pungent, and slightly bitter taste." The manual goes on to say that "[i]t occurs as a saline crust in caverns in some parts of the globe." It occurs in limestone caves in the Arkansas Ozarks.[1]

There were two stages to niter production: initial processing or leaching at the mine site and further refining either at the mine or at a refinery located elsewhere. Major George W. Rains, an Ordnance Bureau officer who in 1861 promoted small niter-processing entrepreneurs, wrote that leaching the crude saltpeter from the cave's earth was a simple process. It involved breaking the lumps of earth, placing them in barrels and pouring water into the earth-filled barrels to dissolve the saltpeter. The liquor (water with dissolved saltpeter) drained from the first barrel was run through two more earth-filled barrels before strong wood-ash lye was added and mixed thoroughly. The clear liquor became muddy and was allowed to settle until it again became clear, then it was boiled until a drop taken on the end of a stick became solid when dropped on cold metal. The liquor was then strained through a cloth into a tub and allowed to set until it became cold and crystalized. The crystals were crude saltpeter, which could then be sold to Confederate refineries. Rains stated that three men working six days using twelve barrels for leaching the cave earth could produce not less than one hundred pounds of saltpeter.[2]

West of the Mississippi River the procedure for processing the saltpeter may not have followed this procedure. William L. Marrs was detailed to work in a saltpeter mine on Cane Creek in Carroll County and at Cecil Cave, on the Buffalo River, in Newton County. He recalled that none of the Arkansas efforts were very successful, but he also served with the Nitre and Mining Bureau in Texas at New Braunfels and at Rió Frio where the cooperation was much better. He described the manufacturing in Texas as follows:

> A cave was found that contained bat guano; then logs were cut eight feet long, were split open, and troughs were made of them. Logs were built into a pen about four feet high with a log floor, boards were split out, and the cracks in the floor and sides stopped with them to retain the dirt. Large log heaps were burned into ashes, and those pens were filled with a mixture of the bat guano from the cave and the ashes from the log heaps in the proportion of two portions of dirt, or guano, and one of ashes; then water was poured into the pens to leach the dirt and ashes, like old-fashioned lye for soap-making. Then large vats or kettles were used. This lye, or ooze, was boiled until it became of a muddy thickness, when it was dipped off and placed in wooden vats to settle. When settled, it was dipped off carefully and put back into vats and boiled until it became "muddy" again; then it was dipped out into vats to cool. When it began to cool, the saltpeter formed and was ready to take out. Then it was placed in a small hopper like an old-fashioned ash hopper and two or three buckets of water poured on it to wash out the lye. The hopper was open at the bottom, so the water could run out. The saltpeter was sacked and stored. We hauled this saltpeter to San Antonio, and it was sent from there to the

> powder mill near Galveston. To manufacture powder it takes half a pound of saltpeter, one-fourth pound of sulphur, and one-fourth pound of charcoal to make one pound of powder. Put all in a mortar and beat it up together and pour in water until it is thick dough, then grain and glaze, and you have Confederate powder.
>
> Mr. Marrs says the powder was manufactured "to perforate blue uniforms."[3]

This description is similar to a description for the Ozarks as well, except that Ozark niter came not only from bat guano, but principally from saltpeter, the result of nitric acid action on limestone.

George Foster worked at the Bean's Cave Confederate niter works, and he recalled that the saltpeter cave was full of red clay that was strongly impregnated with saltpeter. The clay was mined and dumped into a battery of very large hoppers, similar to ash hoppers that housewives used to obtain lye for soap. A small stream of water slowly passed through each hopper, picking up the saltpeter in solution as it passed through the clay. Then this saltpeter solution went into the huge caldrons and was boiled or evaporated. The saltpeter accumulated as a solid in the bottom of the caldrons after all water had boiled off. It was then refined and ready for use.[4]

Major Rains also described the steps required to refine crude saltpeter on a small scale. Two hundred twenty-five pounds of crude saltpeter crystals are dissolved in sixteen gallons of boiling water and allowed to boil for about two and a half hours. The scum is taken from the surface and placed aside; the liquor is strained and poured in a long cooling trough where it is constantly agitated with wooden rakes. During the cooling, fine, needle-shaped crystals of niter form in the liquor. After washing, the niter is nearly pure and can be made into gunpowder. Rains commented that niter produced in government-operated mines did not need to be further refined. Presumably the refining process was also carried out at the mine (refer to Marrs's description above).[5]

The Confederate *Ordnance Manual* describes saltpeter refining as follows: "Wash the crude saltpetre in a large shallow pan with about 40 per cent. of cold water, stirring it well with rakes. At the end of 12 hours, withdraw the water, which takes away with it a portion of the chlorides. To free the saltpetre from earthy matters and the chloride of sodium, dissolve it by means of heat, in the least possible amount of water, in a large copper kettle."[6]

Charcoal could be easily produced by stacking wood into heaps partially covered with earth to limit the air and setting it afire. The Augusta, Georgia, powder mill relied chiefly upon cottonwood *(populus heterophylla)* from the banks of the Savannah River. The Confederates obtained sulphur by processing iron pyrites (FeS_2) with nitric acid to release the sulphur.[7]

Early north Arkansas settlers knew about saltpeter deposits and worked them prior to the Civil War to make gunpowder. The county assistant marshals who compiled the 1850 census praised the economic and environmental aspects of their counties in the mortality schedules. They reported that Madison and Searcy Counties had niter and that Madison County had lead. From 1857 to 1860 State Geologist Dale David Owen conducted a geological survey of Arkansas and found significant niter deposits in Independence, Marion, and Newton Counties, and lead in Carroll, Marion, Newton, Pulaski, and Sevier Counties. Owen wrote that Marion County's Bean's Cave, named for an early niter miner who killed his partner, was ideally located on a bluff over the White River to facilitate niter shipment. He also reported that a firm from Elgin, Jackson County, had recently bought the Bean and nearby caves to begin niter production. These saltpeter caves and lead mines in Arkansas would soon play a part in the upcoming Civil War.[8]

Just two years after Owen's *Geological Reconnaissance of the Northern Counties of Arkansas* was published, the Confederate States were looking for resources to arm themselves. Before secession the Southern states had not produced war materiels, and there were few skilled workmen and no commercial amounts of munitions were stored in the South. The only operating commercial lead mines were on the northern limits of the Confederacy in Virginia, and they were subject to interdiction by Federal forces. In its first months, the new Confederacy considered importation from Europe, augmented by domestic production, as the method to meet its supply needs. The Confederacy did not wait for the Federal blockade to reduce their imports before turning to domestic production; domestic production had been Confederate policy from the beginning. However, domestic production never reached the levels hoped for, and the Confederacy imported more munitions than it produced from its own mines and factories.

In the early days of secession the Confederacy purchased war materiels from the North, but this could only be a stopgap, and not a long-range supply policy. Nevertheless, both the Confederate government and state legislatures placed munition orders with Northern manufacturers and were having them filled. In February 1861, Jefferson Davis sent Captain (later Admiral) Raphael Semmes to New York to buy munitions, arms, and gunpowder. He was successful, and for a few weeks Semmes's supplies came south. On April 16, 1861, four days after the Confederates fired on Fort Sumter, Abraham Lincoln forbade trade with the seceded states. Lincoln's decision stopped Semmes's efforts and the importation of war materiel from the North.[9]

Davis, in early April, also sent Major (later Lieutenant Colonel) Caleb Huse to London to begin purchasing war supplies for the South. Huse had to make contracts to manufacture the materiel because there were not enough munitions in stock to supply his needs. By December 1861, thousands of modern rifled muskets and other supplies were arriving safely through the Federal blockade, declared by President Lincoln the preceding April 19, after Fort Sumter. Huse remained in Europe until the end of the war, buying military munitions on credit and dispatching them to Bermuda to be transshipped to the Confederacy.[10]

On the Confederate domestic scene, the government was fortunate to acquire a man with ordnance experience and organizational talents, Colonel Josiah Gorgas. He resigned his commission with the United States Army, where he was serving on the Ordnance Board, and, on April 8, 1861, accepted President Davis's offer to be chief of ordnance for the Confederate States of America. Gorgas made immediate preparations to manufacture powder and saltpeter and to develop lead and copper sources. The Confederate government had no powder mills except two crude ones located in Norfolk, Virginia, and Augusta, Georgia. An adequate supply of sulphur had been found in New Orleans, where it had been imported to be used in sugar refining, and plans were underway to produce sulphur from iron pyrites in Georgia. Charcoal was readily available throughout the South from trees such as the cottonwood. A niter bed had already been started in Richmond and others followed, but the Ordnance Bureau never obtained any niter from these beds, except for tests; however, some niter was obtained from earth under old houses.[11]

At the same time that the Confederate central government was exploring all avenues to arm itself, Arkansas was undergoing a similar experience, but with an added element: Arkansas had not yet decided to secede. In 1860 and early 1861 Arkansas was caught up in the secession movement and its people were torn between secession and remaining with the Union. The mountain counties in the north were predominantly anti-secessionist, and the state had not yet made a decision by April 12, 1861, the day the Confederacy fired on Fort Sumter. While Arkansas was still in the Union, secessionists from the cotton producing counties on February 8, 1861, asked for and received the surrender of the Little Rock Federal arsenal, with its arms and munitions. February 12 they seized the United States stores in Pine Bluff; April 18, the stores at Napoleon, Arkansas; and April 23 Fort Smith surrendered to the secessionists. The state legislature sent Thomas James Churchill and Christopher C. Danley to the North as purchasing commissioners with one hundred thousand dollars in appropriated funds to buy arms and munitions for the state. They spent thirty-six thousand dollars with the firm of Williams and Hatfield in Cincinnati for powder and bought twenty-eight boxes of guns and pistols, from Baltimore, which were to be shipped with the powder to Little Rock. However, the Cincinnati Home Guard and the chief of police stopped the shipment in mid-April as it was bound for the Southern Confederacy. Even before Arkansas had voted to secede, Northern citizens were applying Lincoln's trade embargo. However, secession was not long in coming. In Arkansas, the event that moved the waverers and mildly pro-Union voices to secession was President Lincoln's call for troops. After the Confederates had fired on Federal Fort Sumter, he asked for troops to put down the rebellion from all the states, including Arkansas. On May 6, 1861, the Arkansas secession convention voted to secede. Arkansas now had to ready itself for war.[12]

The conservative Little Rock *Arkansas State Gazette,* less than two weeks after secession, urged that steps be taken to secure a supply of arms and munitions and suggested developing various iron, coal, and saltpeter deposits in Arkansas. Stating that charcoal could be produced in Arkansas and probably sulphur as well, the *Gazette* maintained that, taking the advantages into consideration, Arkansas presented an unequaled field for gunpowder production and that Arkansas possessed materials for the manufacture of firearms sufficient to supply the whole Confederate force. With such enthusiasm, as demonstrated in the *Gazette* article, but with little practical experience, Arkansas began preparations for war. As impoverished as the eastern Confederate States were in manufacturing and in developed mineral resources, the western Confederate States were poorer. Nevertheless, they had hopes of producing the basic military supplies. In Arkansas, of the three elements for gunpowder, the Ozark caves produced saltpeter, charcoal was made from an abundance of trees, and the Southerners hoped to import sulphur from Mexico or mine iron pyrites from the Bellah mine in Sevier County and obtain the sulphur using nitric acid, as was being done in Georgia. Most of the mercury used to make fulminate of mercury for gun caps came from Mexico, a reliable import source throughout the war. The Confederates had confidence in the production of north Arkansas niter.[13]

In May 1861, just after Arkansas seceded, the Confederate War Department requested that Colonel Thomas Carmichael Hindman of Arkansas's Military Board deliver one hundred thousand pounds of saltpeter to the Confederate government at Memphis. A recent United States congressman, Hindman had received a colonel's commission and an appointment to the newly created Arkansas Military Board, which was responsible for raising and arming state troops. However, by August he still had not responded to the Confederate War Department's request. He had Arkansas organizational and supply problems on his mind. On July 20, 1861, Arkansas transferred its troops to Confederate service. Along with the troops went the use and control of their arms and war munitions.[14]

When it became evident that the Confederate government was purchasing large amounts of saltpeter and lead, entrepreneurs, principally from Tennessee, came to north Arkansas and began commercially exploiting saltpeter from Ozark caves and diggings. These areas had only been worked occasionally and crudely for home consumption. Patrick S. McNamara, an Irish immigrant, in 1861 worked for John Cubbins and Company in Memphis, Tennessee. He wrote: "I was John Cubbins' foreman Bricklayer in Memphis when the war commenced and went with him to oblige him by constructing furnaces at Searcy Co., Ark., Nitre works. It's a wild mountainous country and Cubbins induced me to remain with him until he got ready to leave for Memphis in April 1862. This was consequence of my popularity with the "Negroes" and the proximity of Gen'l Curtis's army." William Henry Harrison Trice from Johnson County, Tennessee, on the Virginia border, brought more than thirty slaves with him and employed nearly one hundred men to exploit the lead mines and Thompson niter cave on Cave Creek, Newton County. Texan William Bennett set up niter works at the niter cave near Whitely's Mill on Cecil's Fork of the Buffalo River (near Boxley), and Greenhaw and Company operated Bean's Cave, Marion County. Out-of-state entrepreneurs Edward Ivy and Brinkley Newell and Company also had operations and employed slaves in Newton County.[15]

In mid-1861, Robert C. Brinkley of Memphis and William E. Jones of Davidson County, Tennessee, and Commerce, Mississippi, bought three saltpeter caves in the mountains west of Batesville, Arkansas, and had a contract with the Confederate government for five hundred thousand pounds of saltpeter. On August 22, 1861, the steamboat *New Moon* delivered to Memphis thirty large kettles and a steam engine to be used at their saltpeter cave. This was probably the East Lafferty Creek Saltpeter Cave, identified by Owens in 1857 as belonging to Colonel John Miller.[16]

From Memphis, Confederate major general Leonidas Polk assumed the task of defending the Mississippi River, and in July, immediately after assuming his post, sent two chemists from New Orleans to examine the saltpeter caves on Arkansas's White River. They reported that the supply of saltpeter was virtually inexhaustible, but that the private entrepreneurs could not work the mines efficiently. The government was paying twenty-five cents a pound for saltpeter which it could produce itself for ten cents a pound. On August 7, 1861, Polk recommended to Davis that these caves be taken over by the Confederacy at once and worked by the Confederate government.[17]

Later in 1861 some niter caves in the South were being worked by the Confederate government, but private entrepreneurs were still encouraged to begin production. In 1861, Major George W. Rains, in charge of the Gunpowder Department, C.S.A., late of the U.S. Army and former assistant professor of chemistry at the U.S. Military Academy, wrote *Notes on Making Saltpetre,* in which he "earnestly appealed to his countrymen who may live near any cave, to put themselves . . . to some inconvenience in order to aid in the invaluable production." His *Notes* are simple instructions on processing saltpeter, and he lists "Articles Wanted to Make Saltpetre on a Small Scale": "One ordinary iron pot, for boiling; three or four tubs, pails, or barrels cut off; two or three small troughs; some coarse bags or a wheelbarrow to bring the earth from the cave, and four strong barrels with one head in each—empty vinegar, whiskey or pork barrels are very good—are about all the articles required for a small saltpetre manufactory. To these, however, must be added some ash barrels to make potash lye, as it is better that this should be made at the same time and place, the ashes from the fire under the pot for boiling assisting in the production."[18]

In conjunction with Rains's *Notes,* Josiah Gorgas issued a notice that the Confederate Ordnance Department would pay thirty-five cents per pound for all saltpeter delivered before February 1, 1862, to any of six collecting points throughout the South including Sandford C. Faulkner, Military Store Keeper, Little Rock, Arkansas, the only collection point west of the Mississippi River.[19]

In Arkansas after secession many supplies and provisions quickly became scarce. In May gunpowder was difficult to find on the market and prices were climbing. By December 1861, Colonel Solon Borland, commander of state troops in eastern Arkansas, felt compelled to issue orders from his command at Pocahontas forbidding speculators from purchasing and shippers from transporting foodstuffs or firearms from his district. The *Gazette* editorialized that, from the beginning of the war, the country had been infested with speculators who traveled throughout the country falsely representing themselves as Confederate agents, buying arms, ammunition, and provisions and reselling them at considerable profit. Providing for a newly created military from limited to nonexistent resources under such chaotic conditions was a monumental task.[20]

The Confederate Ordnance Bureau had established a presence west of the Mississippi and was developing arsenals at New Orleans and Baton Rouge, Louisiana; San Antonio, Texas; and Little Rock. By the close of 1861 the department had supplied the arsenals with some machinery and they were producing munitions and equipment. In December 1861, the Little Rock *Gazette* reported that Colonel Sandford C. Faulkner, the arsenal's storekeeper, had shown the *Gazette* reporter the improvements he had made in the last few weeks. He had installed a steam engine to drive lathes and machinery to make and repair guns. The reporter stated that the arsenal employees were boring rifle barrels, attaching gun stocks, and making several thousand cartridges daily, and that Colonel Faulkner was soon leaving to purchase additional machinery. The Dedman foundry at Camden produced cannon which fought at Wilson's Creek. There were two foundries in Little Rock (Robert Brodie and Drake and Byrd), one of which produced grapeshot. At Hopefield, opposite Memphis, the Memphis and Little Rock Railway shops were repairing arms. The Arkansas penitentiary was turning out gun carriages, caissons, wagons, boots, shoes, clothing, and other military supplies.[21]

At the very beginning of the war, New Orleans became a center for war materiel manufacturing. The Cook Brothers, funded by local capital, began making rifled muskets in New Orleans. The Confederate government used five hundred tons of scarce sulphur, stored there before the war for sugar refining, to upgrade the production of a local powder mill; and the Ordnance Bureau installed a stamping mill near New Orleans to produce gunpowder. North Arkansas caves provided saltpeter for the New Orleans gunpowder mill. Saltpeter from Bean's Cave in Marion County and lead from a nearby lead smelter were sent via the White and Mississippi Rivers to New Orleans. In order to avoid Federal scouting parties, the products were moved down the White River at night in small boats, running the dangerous waters of the upper river in the dark. The Confederates also worked the Boxley caves on upper Buffalo River in Newton County early in the war, taking the saltpeter via wagon to Clarksville on the Arkansas River, then shipping it downriver to New Orleans by boat. Similarly, the saltpeter cave on the James S. Thompson farm on Cave Creek in eastern Newton County produced saltpeter for the New Orleans mill, despite an early accident. Early in its operation a large boiler exploded and almost wrecked the plant. Slaves, imported into the mountains, worked with local men in mining the saltpeter in these Ozark caves. Rich lead mines near Boxley and on Cave Creek in Newton County were being rudely worked, and the Bellah mines in Sevier County were yielding lead and iron pyrites for sulphur. However, Admiral David G. Farragut's capture of New Orleans on April 25, 1862, closed this outlet for Ozark saltpeter and lead.[22]

Entrepreneurs had to furnish their niter mines with equipment before they could become operational on a large scale. The equipment was bulky, heavy, and costly. The machinery for Thompson's Cave Creek mine came from New Orleans via the Mississippi and Arkansas Rivers to Norristown, three miles south of Russellville, then was freighted sixty-five miles across the Boston Mountains to the factory site by wagon. Several large kettles of various sizes used in the Confederate niter works in Newton, Searcy, and Marion Counties are now located in private hands or museums in the area. Some are broken, reflecting the wrecking efforts of Union soldiers. Although damaged, many were still in use for hog scalding, water troughs, or feed storage as recently as 1960. Freighting these large and heavy objects by wagon over the mountain roads that one Federal officer called "rasperous" must have been immensely difficult, and the Federals believed that "with the almost impossibility of replacing the machinery, steam engines, kettles, etc., the destruction of the works was a severe blow to the rebel government."[23]

During Arkansas's first year in the war, the niter miners learned that security was to be a major problem. Operating niter works in northern Arkansas proved to be hazardous, especially after the Confederate defeat at Pea Ridge, March 7–8, 1862, gave Union forces in southwest Missouri easy access to the area. On March 23, 1862, Major General Henry Wagner Halleck, commanding the Federal Department of the Mississippi, informed Brigadier General Samuel Ryan Curtis, whose Army of the Southwest was then headquartered at Cross Timbers, Arkansas, near present-day Rogers, that the Confederate government "ha[d] about 100 negroes engaged in a saltpeter works in Marion County, a little east of Worth." As they were guarded only by a single company, Halleck thought a "detachment of cavalry from Springfield could destroy these works and free the negroes, as being employed in enemy's service." This Confederate niter works was apparently at Bean's Cave on the left bank of White River just east of present-day Fairview, Marion County.[24]

Acting on Curtis's instructions, Colonel Lafayette McCrillis in April 1862 led his Third Illinois Cavalry Regiment from West Plains, Missouri, into the area. He learned that the establishment was three miles above Talbot's Ferry on the south bank of White River and eight miles below the mouth of Little North Fork River. A party of eight men crossed over in canoes from opposite the works and, finding it lightly guarded, destroyed the operation.[25]

Further evidence that Federal forces were causing havoc with Arkansas's niter mining operations is Brigadier General Curtis's May 7, 1862, report, from Batesville, Independence County, that his cavalry had destroyed "another extensive saltpeter manufactory, which [he had] discovered about 14 miles northwest of this place." This probably was Colonel John Miller's niter cave, located four miles up Lafferty Creek and worked by Jones and Brinkley, which produced quantities of saltpeter during the Civil War. Master mason Patrick S. McNamara wrote that in April 1862 his employer, Memphis entrepreneur John Cubbins, left him in charge of his niter works in Searcy County because McNamara was popular with the slaves, and Cubbins started back to Memphis because General Curtis's army was close. It was so close, camped in Batesville, that McNamara reported, "Six of the 'Contrabands' made an 'Hegira' to Batesville and we *Skedaddled* towards Memphis, on my way I met Cubbins who requested me to return, and settle his accounts." Less than a year after the outbreak of war, the North was successfully disrupting Confederate niter mining.[26]

Similar problems were being experienced by the Confederate war effort generally. The Confederacy had lost niter mines all along the upper South under the military reverses of the spring of 1862. All but one of the important caves in operation had passed into the hands of the Union forces, and of the smaller caves, the owners had generally become discouraged or indifferent. In order to supply its troops the Confederate central government was forced to improve its munitions production capability. This decision had a decided effect on Confederate niter mining and munitions production in Arkansas. Confederate chief of ordnance Gorgas determined that he needed a separate operation to take care of niter and iron production; and he was successful, on April 11, 1862, in having the Confederate Congress approve "an act for the organization of a corps of officers for the working of nitre caves and establishing of nitre beds." He was fortunate in appointing Colonel Isaac Munroe St. John to be in charge of the new Confederate Nitre and Mining Bureau. St. John had the gift of organization and Gorgas put him in charge of the production of niter from caves and the formation of niter beds. In addition to the existing niter bed in Richmond, St. John began them at various cities in the South; but there is no evidence of any west of the Mississippi, nor did they produce any niter before the end of the war. Colonel St. John divided the whole niter bearing area into districts in charge of officers directly responsible to Richmond. On May 31, 1862, shortly after the Nitre and Mining Bureau's creation, the adjutant and inspector general's office issued a general order instructing commanding officers to detail men to the niter caves located under their commands at the request of the Nitre Bureau officer in charge, and to protect them, as far as possible, from the enemy. Also all persons employed in saltpeter mining for the Nitre Bureau, whether employees of contractors or employed directly by the Confederate government, were exempt from enrollment in the armed forces. This became a particularly touchy issue as, later in the war, recruiting officers looked upon Nitre Bureau civilians as fair game, to the detriment of the entire war effort. Quartermaster officers were to furnish supplies to the officers and men of the Nitre Bureau, and nitre officers could impress free blacks, who would be paid wages and furnished subsistence, to work in the nitre caves. Nitre Bureau officers were also authorized to impress mineral mines or niter caves if they were idle or inefficiently worked.[27]

On July 31, 1862, St. John reported the results of the bureau's first four months to Secretary of War George W. Randolph. Special attention first had been given to the home production of niter, then lead and sulphur and, incidentally, to the collection of all useful mineral information. Work had commenced and a considerable amount of private capital was invested in Arkansas, Alabama, Georgia, eastern Tennessee, and western Virginia, but unfortunately in exposed locations. On May 1, the entire home production of niter from all sources within the Confederate States, as ascertained from the powder mill books, had not reached an average of five hundred pounds daily. Under those adverse circumstances the following plan to enhance operations was submitted to the department and approved: "First, to explore rapidly, but systematically, for niter caves and deposits. Second, to stimulate private enterprise by various forms of advertisement and by affording facilities for work in prompt payment and a liberal supply of tools and equipment. Third, when advisable, to start work on government account [i.e., to employ the cave operators directly, rather than contracting to buy their products, which would give niter officers direct control over the methods of production]."[28]

Concerning the situation nationwide, which certainly applied to Arkansas, St. John stated, "Exhibit sheets on file in the Bureau office already contain entries of caves and nitrous deposits sufficient in quantity and quality to meet the ordinary demands of the Confederate Army until niter beds can be made to yield. But our power to work these natural deposits is controlled by three conditions—labor, hostile interruption, and transportation." He further reported that, in some districts, much had been accomplished, but the general result made clear that the War Department could not depend upon a large and regular supply from private sources; therefore he had begun contracting directly to work the niter caves. On August 1, 1862, activity was underway at sixteen government caves, with a force of 272 white hands and 115 slaves; and there were other private works in operation selling to the Confederacy. St. John commented that good working caves should contain at least five thousand cubic feet of earth. The nitrous earth, which usually covered the cave floor or filled up its side chambers in crevices, had to be dry and should yield at least 1 percent nitrates. It was essential in order to manufacture niter from natural deposits, he cautioned, that potash, wood, and water be within easy access outside the caves. These conditions were mentioned to explain why, out of so many known and explored caves, so few could be advantageously worked. Arkansas had several caves which met these specifications, particularly the niter percentage yield. The First Iowa Cavalry reported on the Confederate niter caves on the headwaters of the Buffalo River, in Newton County, that the niter earth yielded from 3 to 6 percent saltpeter, and commented that it was easy to obtain and cheaply manufactured.[29]

The Nitre and Mining Bureau was launched and would soon be operating in Arkansas. General Josiah Gorgas recalled the special operation of the Nitre and Mining Bureau: "These officers procured details of workmen, generally from those subject to military duty in the mountain regions where disaffection existed, and carried on extended works in their several districts. In this way we brought up the nitre production, in the course of a year, to something like half our total consumption of nitre. It was a rude, wild sort of service; and the officers in charge of these districts, especially in East Tennessee, North Carolina, and North Alabama, had to show much firmness in their dealings with the turbulent people among whom, and by whose aid, they worked."[30]

When the Nitre and Mining Bureau moved into the Ozarks its officers there found that General Gorgas's comments about their ambiance were particularly true. Gorgas later stated, about the niter operation in general: "Much of the nitre region was close to the lines of the enemy, and here and there along its great extent became debatable ground. Not seldom the whole working force had to be suddenly withdrawn on the approach of the enemy, the 'plant' hurried off, to be again returned and work resumed when the enemy had retired. Much of the work, too, lay in 'Union' districts, where our cause was unpopular and where obstacles of all kinds had to be encountered and overcome. It was no holiday duty, this nitre digging, although the service was a good deal decried by such as knew nothing of its nature."[31]

The Arkansas Ozarks, where the saltpeter caves were located, had been the home of Union sentiment since the early days of secession; the region was fertile recruiting ground for Federal regiments. Nevertheless, the Nitre and Mining Bureau officers sent out from Virginia made valiant efforts to produce the war materiel needed to arm Confederate soldiers, and certainly helped the Confederate guerrillas to carry on their war to the last days of the Confederacy. In St. John's July 31, 1862, report he commented on the operations in the Trans-Mississippi, stating that the recent transfer of the Texan contracts to the Nitre and Mining Bureau made it necessary to establish a Nitre and Mining Bureau organization west of the Mississippi. A party of three Nitre Bureau officers, selected for this service and under the command of Captain Isaac Read of Missouri, started that week from Richmond under instructions to arrange a regular system of transportation in Texas for munitions and supplies from Mexico to the Confederate commands; to examine and, if miners could be obtained, to start working lead mines in Arkansas; to examine a reported valuable saline deposit near New Iberia, Louisiana; and to resume work in the very valuable saltpeter caves of north Arkansas as soon as possible. St. John went on to say that, although work had not fairly commenced on government caves until late in June 1862, the large Arkansas contribution made previous to May 1, of seventeen thousand pounds, could not again appear until the events of the war permitted, i.e., until the Confederate forces again controlled north Arkansas. Southwide the yield during August 1862 would probably be from sixteen hundred to two thousand pounds per working day. It should have been over twenty-five hundred pounds per working day, but the prevailing anxiety to save the crops, the unwillingness to send slaves far from home and a consequent scarcity of labor, and the lamentable condition of public transportation had prevented a higher production. The last two drawbacks were receiving the earnest and anxious attention of the bureau, and when overcome could raise the home niter production to three thousand pounds per day. He went on to say that if labor and machinery could be procured, lead mining in Arkansas would be started under direct contract with the Confederate government.[32]

At the same time that the new Confederate Nitre and Mining Bureau was organizing and considering operations in its new Trans-Mississippi District, a familiar person to Trans-Mississippi military put in his appearance. On May 30, 1862, Major General Thomas C. Hindman arrived back in Arkansas as commander of the Trans-Mississippi Department. After the battle of Pea Ridge, the Confederate Arkansas forces had retreated south of the Arkansas River and Federal brigadier general Curtis had marched along the White River to Batesville, ninety miles from Little Rock. Arkansas troops under Major General Earl Van Dorn were moved east of the Mississippi early in the spring of 1862 in anticipation of a big contest at Corinth, Mississippi, and took with them all war materiel and public property. Hindman found that Van Dorn, when he returned to his native Mississippi in April 1862, took nearly everything of value including Confederate supplies in Fort Smith and all the machinery for munitions manufacturing from the Little Rock arsenal. Therefore, Hindman, in June, began an intensive campaign to make his department ready for defense. He stated, "Considering the isolation of my district and the virtual impossibility of supplying it from east of the Mississippi, my purpose was to make it completely self-sustaining." This he began to do immediately and with a vengeance. On June 9, just a week after his arrival, Hindman reported to the adjutant general, General Samuel Cooper, that he had sent agents in every direction to collect arms and ammunition by purchase or impressment and that he had "engaged in repairing those on hand and in making cartridges; commenced the manufacture of saltpeter; opened lead mines;

[would] soon be mining copper, and thereby getting a sufficiency of sulphur [from iron pyrites], and hope[d] within sixty days to be making small-arms and cannon."[33]

Hindman searched for qualified support personnel and recruited or impressed them into service. He told the Confederate adjutant general in Richmond that he must have authority to commission all officers below his own rank and to appoint, promote, and dismiss at his discretion. By August he had appointed Confederate States Navy first lieutenant John W. Dunnington, late captain of C. S. ram *Pontchartrain,* to be a colonel of artillery and had made him chief of ordnance for the entire Trans-Mississippi Ordnance District. In July, Hindman appointed Frederick P. Leavenworth, formerly topographical engineer, U.S.A., as captain of ordnance and assigned him as officer in charge at the Fort Smith depot. He similarly persuaded others to serve: Major George D. Alexander to be in charge of works at Camden, Captain G. S. Polleys to be in charge of works at Arkadelphia, and even Irishman McNamara, who wrote:

> I got to Little Rock in August and Hindman learning of my experience in the Nitre business through his Acting Chief of Ordnance Capt. Polleys he ordered me to go to Marion County and take possession of the works of Greenhaw & Co. I refused to take possession of private property without compensation to the owners; but he insisted, agreeing however to allow them a fair price, for the use of the works. He wanted to make [me] Capt. of a company of Conscripts. I refused to but agreed to try and raise the men, repair and start the works and then recommend a competent person for Capt., Lieutenants etc. I soon found out that trying to make "conscripts" work without more authority was useless, so I returned to Little Rock and receiving my commission from Col. John W. Dunnington, I was now a officer which gave me almost unlimited authority to impress everything I deemed necessary for the use of the men and works under my command.[34]

Hindman developed a chemical laboratory and manufacturing center in Arkadelphia and opened lead mines, probably including the Bellah and Davis mines in Sevier County and the Kellogg mine in Pulaski County. At Arkadelphia his Ordnance Department constructed and impressed buildings, and its shops made haversacks, knapsacks, cartridge boxes, bullets, percussion caps, and good quality powder. In addition to ordnance supplies, the chemists produced medicines: calomel, castor oil, spirits of niter, and tinctures of iron. Tools, machinery, and materials were gathered piecemeal or made by hand. Molds, furnaces, and lathes were made to cast artillery pieces, and machinery was made for manufacturing percussion caps and small arms. Transferred to Camden by November, Captain Fred P. Leavenworth purchased a foundry and machine shop, added a large lathe and other tools to make shot, shells, cannon, harness, and a distilling plant. Dr. John Seay distilled coal oil, under contract, from lignite coal twelve miles above Camden on the Ouachita River. Nash's iron works near Jefferson, Texas, supplied pig iron, and the Mississippi and Red River Railway Company provided bar iron to Camden's smiths, foundry, and machine shops. Articles appeared in newspapers giving detailed instructions on how families could prepare saltpeter from earth under smokehouses and other old buildings and giving testimonial of a woman who had done so.[35]

Hindman's initiative was at first well received in Arkansas. On June 14, 1862, the Little Rock *Gazette* stated that his policy of encouraging home manufactures was necessary to the state's existence and would promote prosperity after the war: "It will make our people self-supporting in war, and independent and prosperous in peace. The policy of distributing cotton among all who will take and convert it into thread or cloth; as well as that of encouraging the tanning of all leather, and manufacturing it into shoes, will enable the country to clothe and shoe itself and the army now, and the development of these, and other like branches of industry, at the present, are but the opening of mines which will yield immense wealth in the future."[36]

Colonel Dunnington in August 1862 opened the Little Rock arsenal again. He employed an armorer shop foreman and three gunsmiths, a clerk, a carpenter, and a "laboratorian" in charge of the laboratory making cartridges, with twenty-six laborers, including nine women who earned the same pay as their male counterparts, one dollar a day. By late August the arsenal produced one pair of musket bullet molds, one pair of buckshot molds, and ten thousand ball and buckshot cartridges. In addition they repaired 750 muskets, shotguns, and rifles. In his monthly report for August, Dunnington noted, "When I assumed command at this Post all materials had been removed to Arkadelphia. There were no persons employed. No shops opened for repair of Guns or fabrication of Ammunition. Materials, tools etc. had to be procured as well as employment of laborers. Work commenced the last part of the month." For August 1862 Dunnington estimated he would need $4,000 for working a niter cave, $1,500 for labor, $2,400 for twelve mules, and $100 for a wagon. He would also need $360 to buy twelve hundred pounds of saltpeter at thirty cents a pound. For the third quarter of 1862, this was all he supposed that he would spend on the niter cave, but he estimated that he would expend $43,655 for the post at Camden, $36,250 at Arkadelphia, $30,000 at Fort Smith, and $10,000 at the Little Rock arsenal. On November 1, 1862, Major George D. Alexander became chief of ordnance and relieved Dunnington, who assumed command of Arkansas's riparian defenses; and, now a regular Confederate captain, S. C. Faulkner resumed command of the arsenal.[37]

Hindman had reestablished the laboratory and arms repair shop at the Little Rock arsenal. However, materials were so scarce that he was reduced to using public documents in the state library for cartridge paper. He employed or conscripted gunsmiths, bought or impressed tools, and repaired damaged weapons which he had brought with him or found at Little Rock or which were turned in by troops in the field. Among the guns he rehabilitated were four iron cannon condemned by the United States government and eight others which had been buried in the ground to serve as corner posts. He reported that these twelve cannon were mounted and equipped and rendered good service in the field. Such aggressive actions on Hindman's part, which did not take into account the sensitivities of local citizens, caused resentment by Arkansans who complained to President Davis, and this figured in Hindman's recall in March 1863.[38]

After the March 7–8, 1862, battle at Pea Ridge, Confederate troops had been withdrawn south of the Arkansas River and many were hurried east of the Mississippi. Federal troops were in north Arkansas at Fayetteville and Batesville, and later at Helena; and northern Arkansans were gathering to the Federal posts and enlisting under the old American flag. Yet, despite this obvious demonstration of Confederate weakness and insecurity in north Arkansas, Confederate officialdom actively reoccupied the Ozarks and reopened the saltpeter works there, instead of moving the operation to Texas, where it was to go in late 1863. With hindsight this decision to reopen the Ozark niter caves appears costly and ill advised. However, at the time, transportation was a major drawback to a Texas operation. (One of Major Read's goals when he was assigned to the Trans-Mississippi District was to improve transportation for Mexican imports.) And General Hindman brought hope of organization and success to post–Pea Ridge Arkansas. Also, Confederate prospects throughout the South looked good in late 1862.

Taking these points into consideration, it is understandable that the Confederacy believed that Ozark niter cave production was more viable than the transportation-plagued west Texas niter caves.

St. John had ordered Captain Isaac Read to be officer in charge of the Trans-Mississippi Nitre and Mining Bureau operation. On August 19, 1862, while en route to his command, Read ordered his assistant, Lieutenant R. LaMar Sprigg, to go to north Arkansas to examine the saltpeter caves and mineral deposits and to report as soon as possible to Read at Little Rock. Traveling by way of Austin, Springfield, Clinton, Burrowville (Marshall), and Yellville, Sprigg visited the site of the Marion County niter works destroyed by McCrillis's men the previous April and now being rehabilitated by McNamara. Dunnington continued to push the reopening of Bean's Cave. On October 13, Confederate agent P. S. McNamara received six hundred dollars from Chief of Ordnance Dunnington "to be expended by [him] in the name of said Jno. W. Dunnington at Nitre Cave in Marion County of this state which [was then] being worked by [him] for a/c of the Confederate States Government."[39]

Read arrived in Little Rock November 10, accepted command of the niter mining works from Dunnington as the superintendent of the Trans-Mississippi Nitre and Mining Bureau, and immediately began a four-day inspection trip to the sulphur works near Magnet Cove, Hot Spring County. The existing records do not indicate when the sulphur works was established near Magnet Cove, nor exactly where it was. It was not used before the war, or the immediate post-secession newspapers would have touted the resource. Owen mentions a considerable vein of iron pyrites on Moses Wood's farm, not far from Magnet Cove. It was probably this resource, or one very similar, which the Nitre and Mining Bureau processed with nitric acid to release the sulphur, as was done in Georgia. As an indication of its importance, Sprigg and Read visited the sulphur works within days of their arrival in Arkansas.[40]

On November 26, after returning from Magnet Cove, Read started for northern Arkansas to examine Bean's Cave. However, before he reached Marion County he learned that the Federal forces had again destroyed the saltpeter mining operation. On the same day that Read left for the north, Colonel Dudley Wickersham, Tenth Illinois Cavalry, destroyed the Bean's Cave niter works, and also those at Dubuque, farther up White River, as well as an arsenal and storehouses at Yellville. The Federals believed that the Confederates would not attempt to make Yellville into a depot again.

However, the Confederates were quickly back in operation. As Gorgas said, their practice was "to be suddenly withdrawn on the approach of the enemy, the 'plant' hurried off, to be again returned and work resumed when the enemy had retired." Two weeks later Captain Milton Burch of the Fourteenth Missouri State Militia Cavalry led a forty-man mounted expedition into Marion County, where, December 11, he learned that the Confederates had reopened a large niter works at a saltpeter cave beyond the river. He rested his men and horses until midnight, then pressed on, arriving at the cave at noon on the twelfth. The Rebels, mistaking Burch's men for a returning party of their own, were caught off guard and did not discover their error until it was too late. They surrendered without firing a shot. McNamara and at least twelve conscripts were captured. Burch destroyed the saltpeter works, reporting that it was a "gigantic works, having cost the rebel Government $30,000." In three more days, the captured commander told him "they could have had $6,000 worth of saltpeter ready for use." Ironically, this was the same works that Wickersham had reported destroyed in November, but which appeared to Burch to have been unmolested since the previous spring, when McCrillis's detachment from General Samuel R. Curtis's army had damaged it.[41]

The Confederate Nitre and Mining Bureau continued to operate niter works farther south in the Arkansas Ozarks, specifically on the bluffs along the Buffalo River and its tributaries. These mines, although perhaps not as handy for transportation as the Marion County mines, were less accessible to Federal cavalry raids and therefore operated longer. The Confederate Nitre and Mining Bureau had found that it was more reliable and efficient to work the saltpeter caves and lead mines "on government account," rather than through a civilian contractor, such as John Cubbins. Consequently, captains and lieutenants of the Nitre and Mining Bureau were posted in charge at every mining and production center. Several saltpeter caves in an area would be worked together as a production unit. August 9, 1862, Captain William S. Davis received a monetary advance as "government agent in charge of works at Nitre Cave Newton County." He had probably been placed in charge, under Hindman's niter production program, at Thompson's on Cave Creek. In January 1863, Read inspected the niter operations in the western and northern parts of the state, traveling from Little Rock to Fort Smith to Clarksville, where he traveled twenty miles to "Gileon Mountain." He returned to Fort Smith, and after visiting General Hindman's headquarters in Crawford County, he went to Bennett's Cave in Newton County and

Burrowville in Searcy County before returning to Little Rock.[42] Captain Read, the Missourian, just missed the catastrophe that occurred to McNamara in December. Only a month after a Federal raid destroyed the Bean's Cave works, Major Joseph W. Caldwell, First Iowa Cavalry, on January 10, 1863, led a detachment of his regiment from their camp at Huntsville, Arkansas, to Kingston and beyond, searching for the Confederate saltpeter works in Newton County. He found and destroyed the Bennett niter mine and processing operation on Cave Mountain above Boxley and another about four miles below on the Buffalo River. Read had been there only days before. The First Iowa captured seventeen out of twenty men employed there and destroyed fourteen buildings, two steam engines, three boilers, eleven iron kettles, half a ton of saltpeter, three Concord wagons, and two carts. Also, sometime in 1863, Union forces destroyed the Thompson Confederate niter works on Cave Creek in Newton County. Certainly they were destroyed by February 1864, when the Federal Second Arkansas Cavalry crossed into Cave Creek valley and camped about the ruins of the Confederate saltpeter works.[43]

St. John had stated that labor, hostile intervention, and transportation would determine his production of saltpeter. Hostile intervention in the form of Federal raids in April 1862 had seriously disrupted, if not closed, Bean's Cave and Lafferty Creek cave, and perhaps others not mentioned. In early 1863 Union forces were largely withdrawn from north Arkansas to support the siege of Vicksburg, giving Captain Read and his assistants the opportunity to develop the north Arkansas niter caves. At least twelve different caves were worked in north Arkansas at this time (see appendix 2 at the end of this chapter). Surviving records indicate some of the activity at this time. In February 1863, John Campbell went to Little Rock on business for the Searcy County Nitre Works. On March 18, 1863, Lieutenant Sprigg received $2,332 at Rory's Mill on Middle Fork of Sylamore Creek, Izard County, to develop niter works there. April 28, Read purchased various equipment, including a coffee mill, for the saltpeter caves in Marion County.[44]

The Federals had not shut them down. Searcy County's isolation gave their mining operations protection from Federal scouting parties until later in the war. Confederates collected saltpeter from Niter Bluff on the north bank of the Buffalo River below Tomahawk and Little Rocky Creeks. A nearby spring provided water and, until the 1940s, there was evidence of log troughs and a stone foundation. Several miles away, near the confluence of

Spring and Big Creeks, northwest of Big Flat the Confederates worked the Saltpeter Cave. One headquarters supervised about two hundred local men who worked the several small operations in Searcy County and freighted the saltpeter to Arkadelphia and other manufacturing points.[45]

Besides security from hostile interruption, another of St. John's requirements for an operable niter mine was finding personnel to work the niter mine, which was a problem throughout the Confederacy. On several occasions Gorgas, chief of ordnance, had the secretary of war emphasize that ordnance workers, particularly Nitre and Mining Bureau personnel, were necessary for the war effort and were not to be conscripted. Slaves were used throughout the Confederacy in both mining and factory operations. However, in north Arkansas this was not practicable. Slaves were used early in the war at the Searcy, Marion, and Newton County mines, but they did not last long. The slave workers in Marion County had tempted General Halleck in April 1862 to send a force to destroy the munitions works and to take the slaves as contraband, and Curtis's Federal troops in Batesville had prompted Cubbins's slaves in Searcy County to escape there. The free blacks who had long resided in Marion County—119 were reported in the 1850 census, making it the largest free black community in any Arkansas county—did not constitute a sympathetic atmosphere for Confederate use of slave labor. On at least one occasion a free black, Willoughby Hall, guided a Federal force to a Rebel saltpeter mine in Marion County and the works were destroyed. In Newton County local inhabitants recall war stories of blacks being used to work the mines on Cave Creek. The increase in the number of slaves taxed in Newton County, from 24 to 46 between 1861 and 1862, is attributable to Confederate niter and lead mining. William H. H. Trice, the Tennessee lead and niter miner on Cave Creek, was taxed in 1862 for 30 slaves. Two other newcomers, Brinkley Newell and Company and Edward Ivy, were each taxed for 3 slaves the same year. Entrepreneurs such as Trice and these two had apparently learned that leasing local slaves for niter works, as was often done in other parts of the South, was not feasible in the Arkansas Ozarks. There were simply not many slaves in 1860—24 in Newton County, 93 in Searcy County, and 261 in Marion County—and many of the slave holdings consisted of female house slaves or lone male field hands. John M. Hensley of Searcy County, who owned 12 slaves in 1860, was the largest slaveholder in his county or in neighboring Newton County.[46]

Because slaves were not a feasible manpower resource in the Ozarks the

Confederacy had to rely on local labor. The central Arkansas Ozarks were not heavily populated and many men had been recruited or conscripted for the Confederate military. In addition, this area had been a center of Unionist opposition to secession and the home ground of a secret society opposed to involvement in the Civil War. This was certainly not an ideal area to expect ardent supporters for the Confederacy. However, Gorgas and St. John found that this was true in other areas of the upper South where niter caves were located. Confederate sympathizers in the Ozarks preferred occasional service in guerrilla bands, which proliferated in the area, rather than service with regular Confederate units outside the area. Unionists had fled to Missouri for refuge, and those men who hoped to remain nonaligned hid in the hills. As early as spring 1863, scouting parties and recruiters from both sides preyed upon any male found in these north central Arkansas counties, either drafting or killing those they found. The area was certainly not a good area to recruit labor for Confederate niter mines, although niter mine duty as guards or laborers might have appealed to some in preference to regular Confederate service or hiding in the hills. McNamara found that he could not make the conscript mountaineers work without more authority. However, Mum Treat, employed at Bean's Cave, Marion County, in December 1862, and recalling his working experience, implied that the conditions were not too bad: "When the Federals attacked the works there were 23 men present who were in charge of Perry Tucker; Fate Moreland, as cook and waiter. Our camp was on the summit of the bluff, and consisted of the few log huts, two of which was filled with dried beef. The men were paid 60 cents a day in 'Chattanooga money' which was good currency at that time."[47]

Lieutenant General Theophilus Hunter Holmes (C.S.A.), commander of the Arkansas District in General Edmund Kirby Smith's new Trans-Mississippi Department, in the late spring of 1863 found at least a temporary solution to the manpower shortage in the niter mines. He had stragglers from several Confederate units rounded up and marched to the mines for labor service. This plan, building on previous practice, was partially successful. Since at least August 1862, under Hindman's push to revitalize the Trans-Mississippi, Arkansans had been reassigned or conscripted to serve as niter cave guard units attached to the various niter works. Their enforced service may have made them less dedicated to protecting the operations and may help to explain the complete surprise the Federal troops seemed to enjoy at almost every operation against niter mines. Kirby Smith praised Holmes for his wise and energetic measures to bring back absentees and to provide for the comfort of the men, which caused them to return to their colors and to fill up regiments, reduced to mere skeletons after the battle of Prairie Grove, December 7, 1862. Holmes detailed eighteen deserters from Searcy County's Company F, Thirty-second Arkansas Infantry, to the niter works in that county; and men from Company D, Twenty-seventh Arkansas Infantry, also recruited from north Arkansas, were detailed to Nitre and Mining Bureau operations.[48] James Bratton, corporal in Searcy County's Company F, and one of Holmes's soldiers detailed to the niter mines, recalled that he and his brothers, after the battle of Prairie Grove, "[r]an away and came home and worked in a saltpeter works on Buffalo and Big Creek, until in December [17], 1863, when Capt. Naypner [Archibald D. Napier, Co. I, Third Arkansas Cavalry, Union] out recruiting for the Union army, came into the cave, and [he] and John and France [James's brothers] went out with him and stayed with the Federal army until [they] were discharged.[49] Four others of Company F, assigned to the niter works in Searcy County, also went with Napier. Three more joined Captain Benjamin F. Taylor's Company M, Third Arkansas Cavalry (Union), in early 1864.[50]

Such incidents reduced the Nitre and Mining Bureau's workforce. In October 1864, Gorgas complained that while two years previously it had been difficult to get machinery, now they had a surplus and could not get workmen to run it.[51]

The holiday from Federal raids of Nitre and Mining Bureau chief Isaac Read, recently promoted to lieutenant colonel, did not last long. After the July 4, 1863, fall of Vicksburg, Federal troops returned to Arkansas and increased the security threat; and the third of St. John's dictums, transportation, became an even weightier determinant in supplying the Trans-Mississippi Department. In February 1863, when President Davis appointed Lieutenant General Edmund Kirby Smith as commander of the Trans-Mississippi Department, replacing Holmes, he cautioned Smith to make his department self-sufficient, as the central government could no longer support him across the Mississippi. Conversely Mexican imports, particularly of mercury used in the early part of the war for fulminate of mercury in percussion caps, could no longer be supplied east of the Mississippi. After the Trans-Mississippi Department became cut off from the rest of the Confederacy, Mexico became its prime supplier of all types of war materiel, some produced in Mexico, such as mercury, some bought by Huse in Europe and transshipped in Bermuda. Few railroads and the long distance between the Rio Grande and the battlefront seriously limited this traffic, even though imports from Mexico had long been significant to Confederates east of the Mississippi. In six months during 1862, niter from Mexico delivered east of the Mississippi was equal to 17 percent of Confederate home production, but imports from Europe were even more significant, exceeding home production. Even within Arkansas, where distance between source and demand had been closer, but over poor roads, Federal operations complicated the situation by interdicting shipments to the cartridge manufacturing laboratories, and eventually forced the Confederate Nitre and Mining Bureau out of Arkansas. On September 10, 1863, Federal major general Frederick Steele marched his troops into Little Rock, thus effectively closing the Arkansas River and north Arkansas to normal Confederate control. Transportation from the niter works in north Arkansas to Arkadelphia in south Arkansas became impossible. The White River was the only navigable river to traverse the niter mining region, and access to the Arkansas or Mississippi Rivers from the White had been closed since early 1862 when Federal forces regularly began operating between Batesville and Helena. Without railroads, the rough mountain roads were the only option, and they were a bad one. From the beginning of the war, throughout the Ordnance Bureau's domain, the arsenals and factories had been scattered throughout the Confederacy because poor transportation required arsenals and factories to be placed near the source of supply. It was recognized that it would have been more efficient to have fewer places of manufacture, but by dispersal the Ordnance Bureau could avail itself of local resources of labor and material.[52]

Even before Steele took Little Rock in September 1863, the Confederate command was concerned for the safety of munitions factories. In May the foundry at Camden was moved to safer quarters at Shreveport, Louisiana, and by early June, Kirby Smith's chief of ordnance was establishing this foundry there at his departmental headquarters. Kirby Smith wrote to President Davis, "Its vicinity to the iron mines, the facilities for transportation, and the inland position of Shreveport make it the most desirable selection within the department for such an establishment."[53]

As General Steele pressed closer to Little Rock and central Arkansas, more and more Confederate ordnance machinery was moved out of his path. Major General Sterling Price, commander of the Confederate District of Arkansas in the disabled Holmes's place, began moving the ordnance and public stores to Arkadelphia on July 24, as soon as he assumed command of the district. The Little Rock arsenal's last month of operation was August 1863; and Captain S. C. Faulkner, post commandant, in his report for that month noted that during the last week in the month nearly all the stores at the arsenal had been packed and sent to Arkadelphia. On August 29, Price learned that Federal forces were occupying Monroe, Louisiana, threatening his line of retreat and the stores and machinery left at Camden. Therefore, he ordered the Camden stores to Arkadelphia as well. Arkadelphia was only a stopping place en route to Texas, however. The Nitre and Mining Bureau left Little Rock in early September, stopping from two to four days at the new state capital in Washington, Arkansas. Confederate brigadier general William Steele, commander of the District of the Indian Territory, wrote, July 7, that since assuming command six months before, he had been forced to set up a shop in Fort Smith to repair small arms left behind as debris by Hindman, because he could not get arms and ordnance stores through the regular Confederate supply system. The Federal troops forced the evacuation of Fort Smith in late August, and Confederate brigadier general William L. Cabell reported that he had made preparations to protect and send off the public property at Fort Smith, probably including William Steele's repair shop. He had all the ordnance, tools, and materials loaded and sent to Waldron, Scott County.[54]

On April 30, 1863, President Davis appointed Major Thomas G. Rhett, Confederate chief of ordnance and artillery, under new Trans-Mississippi Department chief of ordnance Major General Benjamin Huger. Delayed en route, Major Rhett, by October 22, had arrived and reported that establishments for ordnance work had been in full operation at Little Rock, Arkadelphia, and Camden, and an arms repair shop at Fort Smith, but they had recently been ordered to places of safety to avoid the approach of the Federal forces. The machinery, tools, stores, and men from Little Rock arsenal were sent to Tyler, Texas; those from Arkadelphia were sent to Marshall, Texas; and the machinery, tools, stores, and men from Camden, to Shreveport, Louisiana. The Little Rock arsenal monthly reports end in August 1863 and commence in Tyler, Texas, with the September 1863 report. Rhett was constructing a powder mill at Marshall, Texas, and concentrating saltpeter, sulphur, lead, and iron there. Marshall would be the depot for supplies arriving from Mexico, including lead, niter, powder, sulphur, and percussion caps. At the end of October, Steele's Federal cavalry took Arkadelphia, only to learn from Union sympathizers that all of the machinery had been sent to Marshall, Texas.[55]

Major General Benjamin Huger had been assigned to the Trans-Mississippi Department as the new chief of ordnance in early 1863, but the fall of Vicksburg delayed his arrival at his new post until fall 1863 when he met the Confederate retreat from Arkansas. In January 1864 he reported the whereabouts of his personnel, stating that Nitre Bureau officers Major Isaac Read and Lieutenants R. LaMar Sprigg and Edmund Harrison had gone to the productive niter caves in west Texas (New Braunfels and Rio Frio) after abandoning the niter caves in northern Arkansas and the lead mines in Sevier County before the Union advance. The rich niter caves in west Texas and the powder mill in San Antonio continued to provide the Confederate forces with ammunition until the end of the war.[56]

With poor security from Federal attack, inadequate labor, and difficult transportation, the Confederates certainly were justified in pulling their ordnance works out of the Ozarks and removing them to a more secure Texas. However, it was the removal of the processing plants at Little Rock, Arkadelphia, and Camden to Texas which rang the death knell for the Nitre and Mining Bureau in north Arkansas.

Nevertheless, all the Confederate saltpeter mining activity did not go from the Ozark hills in September 1863 when the Nitre and Mining Bureau moved to Texas. The Big Creek saltpeter cave in Searcy County was operating in December 1863, when Federal captain Napier raided it. In January 1864, four months after the Nitre and Mining Bureau left Arkansas, Colonel Robert R. Livingston, commanding the Federal District of Northeastern Arkansas, headquartered at Batesville, ordered Lieutenant Colonel William Baumer, commanding the First Nebraska Cavalry, to destroy a Confederate powder mill in operation on the North Fork of Sylamore Creek, a tributary of the White River in Izard County. Later Baumer reported that he had burned and destroyed "Rohrer's" (Rory's) Mill on the middle Fork of Sylamore Creek, Izard County. On March 13, 1864, Captain Samuel E. Turner led a detachment of the Sixth Missouri State Militia Cavalry from Yellville to the Buffalo River and had brushes with several small squads of guerrillas and "destroyed some extensive saltpeter-works on Tomahawk Mountains." This was the Buffalo River Niter Bluff saltpeter works, in Searcy County, which had been operated by the Bratton brothers and other stragglers from Searcy County Confederate companies before they joined the Federal army. Captain Sol S. Keen, of the Confederate Nitre and Mining Bureau and resident of adjoining Marion County, deserted from the Confederate service and was taken prisoner in March 1864; he may have belonged to the Tomahawk niter works. Not all of the Confederate stragglers went over to the Union; some remained dedicated Confederates. The November and December 1863 muster roll for Searcy County Confederate captain James Harrison Love's Company C, Seventh Arkansas Cavalry, has the following comment: "This Company hant ben in no fite sence the Poin Bluff fite. Theas men hom' I reported Diserted is in North of the Arkansas River with Captain Love fiten the federls Ever chance tha get."[57]

The Confederate guerrillas in north Arkansas needed ammunition, and no doubt they obtained weapons and ammunition from dead and captured Union soldiers. They also maintained niter mines and made gunpowder as they had before the war started. Sometime after the battle of Prairie Grove (December 7, 1862) Confederate guerrilla Captain George T. Maddox and others established themselves in a cave near the Madison-Newton County line. He wrote, "[W]e also got another old gentleman named Hudson (who had been a powder maker in the Salt Petre cave in the Cumberland mountains of Tennessee) and he made powder for us. It wasn't very good, but answered the purpose when we were short of good powder." The quality of the homemade gunpowder was frequently a problem. In Marion County, Captain Bent Music, home on sick leave from the Confederate army, gathered a few men together to ambush a band of marauding guerrillas. When the man who was the bait led the bushwhackers into Music's trap only a few of Music's weapons would fire: "Their powder, like most everything else, was homemade, being made at the saltpeter cave on White River, about five or six miles from the battleground, and it was a damp rainy day and the powder, not being very good anyhow, got damp, so it wouldn't burn, and that fact gave them the scare and also saved the lives of some more very bad men."[58]

Of St. John's three criteria for a successful niter mining operation—labor, security from hostile interruption, and transportation—which ones, if any, caused the Nitre and Mining Bureau's withdrawal from north Arkansas? Labor problems they certainly had, with the disaffected and sometimes pro-Union mountaineers. One has only to remember the success of Federal captain Napier at the Big Creek niter cave in Searcy County, where he recruited heavily from the Confederate niter workers, to realize that the mountaineers were a real problem. Union recruiting of Confederates was certainly not unusual in counties along Arkansas's Buffalo River. Slaves were really out of their milieu in this part of Arkansas, although there were a few, and unsympathetic free blacks in Marion County served as guides to Federal scouts. North central Arkansas did not have an infrastructure to support and guard the large slave population needed to put the niter mines in full operation. In addition, Arkansas slave owners since late 1862 had been taking their property to Texas, and safety, to avoid Federal troops. So even in south Arkansas there was not an available slave workforce to lease for the mines, assuming that a slave owner would permit his capital so far from his control in such a dangerous location. A slave workforce that could be liberated was a strong temptation to Northern commanders, such as General Halleck when he suggested a raid on the Marion County Bean's Cave in March 1862 because he could free slaves engaged in war production. Also, this isolated position on the frontier was a strong temptation for slaves to escape to the Union army. Yet, Confederate guerrillas managed to operate saltpeter works for at least six to eight months after the Niter Bureau went to Texas.

St. John's second criteria was a secure environment. The March 1862 Union victory at Pea Ridge opened north Arkansas to Federal penetration. Union forces successfully raided the Confederate niter works and destroyed irreplaceable equipment and the results of weeks of work. The very commercially productive niter caves in Marion County, because of their ideal location for easy transportation, were under the watchful eye of Federal commanders and were raided again and again. Loss of equipment to Federal raids was a severe setback to the South, because real replacement costs were so high. However, Union forces did not, or could not, take full advantage of the opportunity to occupy all of the northern Arkansas counties. In 1862 only the areas around Fayetteville and Batesville were occupied; the northen tier of Arkansas counties were controlled from posts in Missouri, and the rest of north Arkansas only occasionally was raided. Destructive Union raids on Confederate niter mines, particularly in Marion County, did not keep them closed. Gorgas commented that much of the niter region became debatable land, so close to the enemy, and frequently the whole working force suddenly withdrew with the plant when the enemy approached, to return again and resume work when the Federals left. This is apparently what happened in Marion County. Niter works in the interior of north Arkansas remained inviolate until early 1864, when the Federals expanded their sphere of control there to include permanent occupation of Arkansas's northern tier of counties. Small niter works operated by Confederate guerrilla bands existed much longer, because Federal activity in north central Arkansas was never strong enough to completely dominate those hills and hollows. Confederate guerrillas existed in small bands of five or six in the Arkansas Ozarks and used powder made from their own niter caves.

Adequate transport, the third of the niter chief's points, had been lacking in north Arkansas since Federal forces became strong enough in 1862 to interdict traffic on the White River. Without railroads and with rough roads over hilly terrain, rivers were the only adequate means of transportation for large quantities, and the White River was the only navigable river in north Arkansas. State Geologist Owen praised Bean's Cave on the bank of the White River for its outstanding location which provided easy transportation, and he commented that the Coka and Mitchell lead mines in Carroll County were only eight or ten miles from the White River at Dubuque. Federal officers complained about the rough terrain and poor roads in north central Arkansas. Mule-drawn wagons may not have needed four-lane highways, but steep hills were difficult to manage, requiring doubled harnessed teams to get them up and down the hills; and streams and rivers were difficult to cross. Animals needed the scarce forage. Nitre and Mining Bureau forage requests from 1862 to 1863 speak of no more than eighteen horses or seventeen mules at any one time, and no oxen. The niter works in Newton and Searcy Counties were from forty to seventy miles from the White and Arkansas Rivers. Those that worked the mines remembered that, after the fall of New Orleans, which was easily accessible by river transportation, the saltpeter was freighted to Arkadelphia, over 160 miles away.

Despite the anomaly of continued isolated saltpeter works operated by guerrillas, the Confederacy's Ozarks niter mining enterprise was a failed effort. It came no closer to meeting the needs of even the guerrillas than the guerrillas' activities came to solving the strategic or tactical needs of the Confederacy. The Confederacy's Ozarks niter mining effort failed because it failed to meet St. John's three criteria: labor, security, and transportation.

Arkansas saltpeter caves with nearby water and wood for charcoal had been tempting resources for Confederate development. In addition, the Marion County niter caves and lead mines were blessed with easy access to the White River, a transportation thoroughfare, and Arkansas niter and lead were close to the front—production was close to consumption in the Trans-Mississippi. Furthermore, in August 1862, General Curtis was blockaded in Helena, so Confederate efforts were unmolested. Hindman had arrived in Arkansas and was bringing order out of chaos. Throughout the South the prospects were upbeat, and the Confederacy was hopeful. The summer of 1862 was the high tide of Southern hopes; and the newly formed Nitre and Mining Bureau could no more see the fall of Vicksburg, the loss at Gettysburg, and the debacle at Helena than they could predict the arrival in twelve months of Federal general Frederick Steele in Little Rock and their own withdrawal to Texas. In the summer of 1862, operating saltpeter works in the Ozarks and munitions factories and laboratories in Little Rock and south Arkansas seemed viable, and anticipating the need to move to Texas at that date required the same prescience as forecasting the ultimate fall of the Confederacy.

Appendix 1

A comparison of the equipment that we know about reveals the following:

Equipment	Marion County	Newton County
	Bean's Cave[a]	Boxley[b]
Buildings	5	14
Steam engines	1	2
Kettles	26	7[c]
Boilers	6	3
Safes	?	1
Wagons	1[d]	3
Carts	?	2
Mules	12[d]	?
Tools	Carpenter	?
Blacksmith	?	
Total value	$30,000	?

Note: For bits of information that we know about other operations, the Searcy County Niter Cave on Buffalo River had six large iron kettles, the largest being seventy-two inches in diameter and thirty-nine inches deep. The First Iowa Cavalry reported that they destroyed four iron kettles at the niter cave four miles downstream from the Boxley cave. There is also tradition of a boiler exploding at Thompson's niter cave on Cave Creek, Newton County.

? This information is not available.

a U. S. War Department, War of the Rebellion: A Compilation of the Official Records of the Union and Confederate Armies (128 vols., Washington, D. C.: GPO, 1880–1901), ser. 1, vol. 22, pt. 1, 159–61.

b U. S. War Department, War of the Rebellion, ser. 1, vol. 22, pt. 1, 213.

c 800 lbs. weight

d Based on Col. John W. Dunnington's purchase record in Nitre and Mining Bureau, Compiled Confederate Military Service Records, RG 109, National Archives.

Appendix 2

The following are niter caves or lead mines which were actively worked during the Civil War or which were mentioned in contemporary literature as potential sources for the Confederacy.

Baxter County (then part of Marion County)

*Barnett's Bluff, west of Monkey Run, Mr. Davis, operator.[a]

Carroll County

*Cane Creek niter works. William F. Marrs worked at this site under a Lieutenant Kincaid.[b] Coka and Mitchell diggings (lead), T 20 N, R 19 W, now Lead Hill, Boone County. The distance from these mines to navigation on White River, at Dubuque, was from eight to ten miles.[1]

Cleburne County (then part of Van Buren County)

Niter Cave located southeast of Shiloh.[c]

Independence County

*Lafferty Creek Cave, located four miles up creek from mouth, Colonel John Miller's "saltpetre cave," worked by Robert C. Brinkley and William E. Jones of Tennessee.[d]

Hot Spring County

*Sulphur Works near Magnet Cove, probably located on or near Moses Wood's farm where Owen reported a considerable vein of iron pyrites.[e & f]

Izard County

*Rory's Mill, niter works, Middle Fork of Sylamore Creek.[f & g]
Niter diggings high up on Jackson's Creek.[g]
Niter diggings near Rocky Bayou, three miles down Jackson's Creek.[g]

Lawrence County

E. W. Haughton's diggings (lead), on Stennett's Creek, Sec 10, T 17 N, R 2 W.[h]

Madison County

*Near Madison's northeast county line.[i]

Marion County

*Bean's Cave, Sec 28, T 20 N, R 15 W, on the White River, operated first by Greenhaw and Co., then by Captain P. S. McNamara on behalf of the Confederate government.[j]

*Dubuque.[k]

Lead mines on the waters of Sugarloaf, Hightower, and Jennings Creeks.

Wood's mine, Sec. 13, T 19 N, R 17 W.

New York Company's diggings, on Sugarloaf Creek, T 20 N, R 17 W.

Molton's diggings, on Jennings Creek, one and one-half miles above forks.

Seawell's diggings, 4 miles below Molton's, T 19 N, R 17 W.

Armstead Hudson's diggings, Sec. 19, T 20 N, R 17 W.

McCarthy's diggings, T 20 N, R 18 W.

Jemmy's Creek diggings, near the forks.[l]

Montgomery County

Mentioned as possible location in 1861 *Arkansas State Gazette* article.[m]

Newton County

*James S. Thompson Cave, Cave Creek, Sec. 27, T 15 N, R 19 W. It was first operated by W. H. H. Trice, using slaves and local men, then by Captain William S. Davis for the Confederate government.[n & o]

*Lead mine near Thompson's Cave.[o]

*Bennett's Cave (Boxley), and two niter caves nearby, Bat Cave, or Saltpeter Cave, on Cave Mountain above Boxley, and a second niter cave about four miles down Buffalo River. Lead mine located nearby, T 16 N, R 22 W, on Villines Creek. T. B. Fowler worked in this cave, 1861–1862.[p]

*Cecil Cave (or Cove) Niter Cave(s). William F. Marrs worked at this site under a Lieutenant Kincaid. This could be the Boxley Cave on Cecil's Fork of Buffalo River or it could refer to Cecil's Cove, T 17 N, R 21 W.[b]

Pulaski County

*Kellogg's lead mine. Owen writes, "The most important mineral locality which has come under my observation, in Pulaski county, north of the Arkansas river, is situated on Kellogg's creek, and known as the 'Kellogg lead mines.' The principal mines are in township 3 north, range 11 west, and about ten miles north of Little Rock. . . . From long disuse, the shafts from which the ore was raised, have become filled with water rubbish, earth and rocks, washed in or detached from the mouth of the pits, so that there is no opportunity, now, of inspecting the condition of the ore in place." Major Isaac Read, January 3, 1863, requested clothing for Negroes working in lead mines in Pulaski County. January 16, 1863, he had requisitioned tents and wagon sheets in order to move the force working Kellogg mines to Sevier County.[q]

Searcy County

*Niter Bluff, located on north bank of Buffalo River below Tomahawk and Little Rocky Creeks, Sec. 24, T 16 N, R 16 W.[r]

*Saltpeter Cave, located in a bluff near the confluence of Spring and Big Creeks, northwest of Big Flat in the Ozark National Forest.[r]

A Captain Richardson was in charge of the Searcy County niter works after John Cubbins and Co. departed in April 1862.[s]

Sevier County

*Richard W. Bellah mine, Sec. 27, T 7 S, R 32 W, produced iron pyrites as well as lead. Several forage vouchers paid at Paraclifta indicate that it was the administrative seat for the Sevier County Nitre and Mining operation.[t]

Davis Mine, Sec. 10, T 7 S, R 30 W, was opened in 1843 for lead ore and was operated intermittently until 1916.[u]

Washington County

Orion Rieffs Cavern. Reiff's properties were located in Sec. 18, T 15 N, R 29 W, and Sec. 31, T 16 N, R 30 W. Tested by Owen, who commented that it did not have a large percentage of saltpeter.[v]

* Evidence that location was actively worked during Civil War.

a Mary Ann Messick, History of Baxter County (Little Rock, Ark.: International Graphics, 1973), 217–28. This area was in Marion County during the Civil War.

b "Gunpowder for the Confederate Army," Confederate Veteran 14 (1906): 119.

c George Haddock, Report of a Geological Reconnaissance of a Part of the State of Arkansas, Made during the Years 1871–'72 (Little Rock, 1873).

d U. S. War Department, War of the Rebellion: A Compilation of the Official Records of the Union and Confederate Armies (128 vols., Washington, D. C.: GPO, 1880–1901), ser 1, vol. 13, 371 (hereafter cited as OR); Haddock, Report, 57; David Dale Owen, First Report of a Geological Reconnaissance of the Northern Counties of Arkansas, made during the years 1857 and 1858 (Little Rock, 1858); "Saltpeter in Arkansas," Des Arc Weekly Citizen, October 16, 1861, 2:2; Mrs. Elmer Kirk, "The Saltpeter Mine of 1862," The Independence County Chronicle, April 1962.

e David Dale Owen, Second Report of a Geological Reconnaissance of the Southern Counties of Arkansas, made during the years 1859 and 1860 (Philadelphia, 1860), 106; Lieutenant R. LaMar Sprigg, travel voucher from August 19 to November 25, 1862, in Confederate Nitre and Mining Bureau, Compiled Service Records, RG 109, National Archives (hereafter cited as CSA N & M Bureau, NA).

f Lieutenant R. LaMar Sprigg, CSA N&M Bureau, NA; OR, ser. 1, vol. 34, pt. 1, 65–66.

g Haddock, Report, 46.

h Owen, First Report, 63, 209.

i George T. Maddox, Hard Trials and Tribulations of an Old Confederate Soldier (Van Buren, Ark., 1897), 16–17.

j Captain Patrick S. McNamara and Major Isaac Read, CSA N&M Bureau, NA; Owen, First Report, 53–55, 224–26.

k OR, ser. 1, vol. 22, pt. 1, 794.

l Owen, First Report, 46–53, 55–58.

m "Army and Munitions of War," Little Rock Arkansas State Gazette, May 18, 1861.

n OR, ser. 1, vol. 34, pt. 1, 93; Owen, First Report, 84–86; Haddock, Report, 322–35; Owen, Second Report, 229–30. Owen's chemist stated that this was quite a strong niter-earth, and ought to be profitable, if properly managed. Raymond B. Stroud, Robert H. Arndt, Frank B. Fulkerson, and W. G. Diamond, Mineral Resources and Industries of Arkansas, Bureau of Mines Bulletin 645 (Washington, D. C.: GPO 1969), 307.

o "Memoirs—James Town Greenhaw 1869–1958," Newton County Homestead (April 1960), 47–48; Little Rock Arsenal Monthly Reports, Civil War: Miscellaneous Records, RG 109, National Archives.

p OR, ser. 1, vol. 22, pt. 1, 213; Major Issac Read, CSA N & M Bureau, NA; Stroud et al., Mineral Resources, 307.

q Major Issac Read, vouchers dated November 29 and December 3, 1862, and January 16 and 24, 1863, CSA N & M Bureau, NA.

r "Helped Make Powder in Civil War," Marshall (Arkansas) Republican, newspaper clipping ca 1915.

s Nitre and Mining Bureau voucher in John Campbell file, Union Provost Marshals' File of Papers Relating to Individual Civilians, RG 109, National Archives; Captain Patrick S. McNamara, CSA, N & M Bureau, NA.

t "Manufacturers in Arkansas," True Democrat, January 2, 1862, c. 2, p. 2;

Owen, Second Report, 110–11; Major Isaac Read, CSA N & M Bureau, NA; Stroud et al., Mineral Resources, 373.

u Stroud et al., Mineral Resources, 373.

v Owen, First Report, 115–16; Owen, Second Report, 256.

Chapter 4

A Semi-Savage State: The Image of Arkansas in the Civil War

William L. Shea

For a century and a half Arkansas has been portrayed as a backwater populated by impoverished and uncultured hillbillies. Historians seeking the sources of this unbecoming image have noted the cumulative impact of the observations of antebellum travelers, the gyrations of Arkansas political and religious figures, and the stereotypes perpetuated in literature, films, television programs, and comic strips. There is, however, one important source of this image which has not been examined: the public and private observations made by thousands of Northern soldiers and civilians who came marching through Arkansas during the Civil War.[1]

Federal incursions into Arkansas began with the Pea Ridge campaign, when the Army of the Southwest drove from Rolla, Missouri, to Helena, Arkansas. The Pea Ridge campaign is not well remembered today, but in the spring and summer of 1862 things were very different. "At that day it was a celebrated undertaking and papers throughout the country were filled with its recital," stated an Iowa veteran and historian named Addison A. Stuart.[2]

The Pea Ridge campaign and the widespread national publicity which attended it lasted six months. It was the longest and most difficult operation of the Civil War up to that time and was by far the deepest overland penetration of Confederate territory until the "March to the Sea" over two years later. Consequently, information from the victorious Army of the Southwest, and about the alien and rebellious land it traversed, was eagerly sought and disseminated in the North. Correspondents' reports appeared in major newspapers from St. Louis to New York. Hundreds of soldiers' letters were printed and reprinted in daily and weekly newspapers across a dozen states, and thousands of additional letters were passed around among family, neighbors, and friends. In the postwar decades numerous diaries, memoirs, and regimental histories dealing with the Pea Ridge campaign were published in newspapers and magazines or in book form for the further edification of Northern readers. Unfortunately for Arkansas, news from the front tended to be less than complimentary.

The officers and men of the Army of the Southwest varied considerably in terms of their political attitudes and their social, economic, and educational backgrounds, but they were Midwesterners all. Their world was a rolling prairie landscape dotted with hardwood forests and carpeted with productive farms and bustling towns and cities—the heartland of America. Their first reaction to Arkansas often was to compare the state to the only other place they knew, to see it through Midwestern eyes, to judge it by Midwestern norms. Arkansas was, wrote a Federal cavalryman, "a wonderful change of scenery to the boys from the Illinois prairies." These men in blue uniforms—mostly young, mostly away from home for the first time—were strangers in a strange land. For them, encountering an alien physical and cultural environment was a fascinating yet unsettling experience. Perhaps their state of mind is best summed up in a few poignant lines penned by that same Federal cavalryman: "We buried our first dead comrade near the Arkansas line, buried him in his uniform by the bank of a little creek among the hills and fired a military salute over his grave, and left him all alone in the woods. Had we buried him on some prairie knoll it wouldn't have seemed so lonely to us."[3]

The Army of the Southwest began its six-hundred-mile odyssey into the heart of Dixie by advancing from southern Missouri across the Ozark Plateau into northern Arkansas. The Federal soldiers—overwhelmingly flatlanders—quite naturally were struck by the unfamiliar physical environment. Initially they responded much like tourists in any day and age encountering something novel. One man noted that the scenery "extorted frequent expressions of admiration from many." An Iowa officer informed his wife that "the scenery has been beautifully grand," while an Illinois soldier reported "the most beautiful scenery I ever beheld in my life." Sentiments of this sort were expressed by a great many others in nearly identical terms. The army's young assistant quartermaster, who obviously had not been to Europe, told his father how "our marches over the mountains winding around in the ridges remind me of the pictures of Napoleon's army in the Alps."[4]

Sparkling mountain freshets and seemingly endless forests fascinated the Midwesterners. An Indiana soldier informed his hometown newspaper of "the clear cool streams and springs of water that run through nearly every valley," and a Kansas cavalry officer told his brother that Arkansas "is one remarkable countrey for fine streams of pure running water." At the outset of the campaign a cavalryman atop a bluff peered southward and observed with wonder that "Arkansas is almost an unbroken forest." Six months later a weary infantryman from Wisconsin confirmed that initial observation. He told his sister that "*all* this state where we have been is *thickly* wooded."[5]

The invaders from the rich prairies of the Midwest also were intrigued with the rocky composition of the Ozark Plateau. "I frequently amused myself pushing loose large rocks to see and hear them fall in the abyss below," wrote an energetic Kansan. Most Federal soldiers, however, were content merely to observe the rocks, not wrestle with them. An officer with a fine eye for detail noticed that near Pea Ridge "the hills seem formed of rocks, splintered and riven fine, just as we see them prepared for macadamized roads." A second officer observed that along the Arkansas-Missouri state line the ground for vast distances was "covered deeply with flinty fragments of rocks, ranging in size from a hickory nut to a hen's egg." A soldier with a somewhat broader perspective wrote home that "the ground is covered with stones from the size of a pea up to cliffs of two hundred feet in height of solid rock." He added that "the green pines and cedars look very pretty on the barren stony hills."[6]

An Illinois regimental surgeon provided a plausible explanation for the widespread interest in lithology. The Ozark Plateau, he wrote, is "composed of millions of little rocks thrown together in one huge pile. Its surface is literally nothing else but fractional pieces of stone—and these the soldier must have for his bed." A footsore and perhaps backsore Illinois officer assuredly spoke for vast numbers of his comrades when he summed up the strange terrain as being "oh so rough and rugged and rocky."[7]

Within a few weeks the excitement of the trek had faded considerably. The desperate battle at Pea Ridge in March 1862, the onset of torrential spring rains, and the difficulty of operating in what was essentially a frontier region all began to take a toll on the morale and attitude of the Federals. What had been novel or interesting gradually came to be seen as alien and undesirable. A soldier ominously observed that "to one used to the broad prairies and cultivated fields of the north, this is a most forbidding region." Descriptions of the landscape assumed a more negative character. "I doubt if few of the habitable portions of the globe presents a more dreary and uninviting wilderness," concluded an Illinois man. "We are in a perfect wilderness," wrote another, "where not any thing is to be seen but trees stumps hills and rivulets."[8]

Words almost failed an Indiana infantryman who wrote that the Army of the Southwest was lost in "one of the most rantankerous, half-manufactured sections of the country you ever saw." A former professor of rhetoric at the Illinois Normal School called upon his collegiate vocabulary in describing the region as "barren, desolate, uninhabitable, and repulsive" and "as devoid of any attractive features which should characterize a civilized country, as perdition itself could well be." Another Illinoisan said as much with fewer syllables: "Of all the country that I have ever seen, for sterility and rockiness this 'takes the rag off the bush' as the saying is." Briefer yet was a Wisconsin soldier's fervent declaration that "another such a God-forsaken country was never seen by mortal man."[9]

What shortly before had been considered a mountainous wonderland now was described as a "gloomy and forbidding region of chert hills and pine forests," "a country of the most weird and uninviting character," "an uninhabited, cheerless, and arid region," and "the most desolate country I ever saw," crisscrossed by the "awfulest roads man ever traveled." A formerly fascinated soldier now concluded that Arkansas was "barren of everything that would make it attractive to an Illinoisan."[10]

After Pea Ridge the Army of the Southwest turned eastward towards the distant Mississippi River. As the Federal troops struggled across the center of the Ozark Plateau, they were shocked at the people and the way of life they encountered. "You have no idea how miserably poor the inhabitants of this section of the country are," wrote an Illinois officer to his mother. "They have barely enough to keep body and soul together which I suppose they make by hunting and I do not think they are fit for anything else," commented another Illinois soldier. A staff officer recorded for posterity that northern Arkansas "was very thinly settled by a wild semi-civilized race of backwoodsmen" whose houses and farms were of the most primitive character. An Iowa artilleryman agreed, describing the inhabitants as "backwoodsmen, half hunter and half farmer, with seeming little industry at anything, living in rude cabins located in the narrow valleys along the creeks, cultivating a few acres of ground to corn, potatoes and pumpkins." A Kansas cavalryman, no stranger to frontier conditions, noted in his diary that "every thing has the appearance of being made just for present use and not to last." An Iowan observed that "not one house in ten has any window. Their school houses and churches (and they are very scarce) have a log sawed out to admit light." The scarcity of churches in Arkansas was noted by many Federal soldiers. Apparently the state was still several decades away from becoming the buckle on the Bible Belt.[11]

Few Federals had anything complimentary to say about the Arkansans they met in the countryside. Quite a number of soldiers remarked that the natives—later generations would derisively call them hillbillies—matched their ramshackle buildings. One man observed that "there is a general appearance of slovenliness, as if they had all come to the conclusion that there was no use trying to be decent." Another concluded that "the majority of them have scarcely enterprise enough to make themselves useful in life." The list of derogatory comments was practically endless. Arkansas was a "semi-savage State," declared a soldier's letter that found its way to the popular *New York Tribune.* "The people are ignorant," wrote an Illinois infantryman. "This is the case wherever we have traveled, and aside from the towns, the natives can neither read nor write; schoolhouses are almost or quite unknown. Many families are met with, none of whom ever saw the flag of their country till we brought it here." An Iowan also described Arkansans as "ignorant and lazy," adding that the state was "decidedly a land of corndodgers and poor fiddlers."[12]

Some of the Federal soldiers could not contain their scorn. One disgusted Midwesterner declared that "the indolent, go-easy, do-nothing squatters" he encountered in northern Arkansas would "make the fairest, sunniest land in the world look dark and gloomy." Another opined that "the few who live here and there look as if they were banished from civilized society for their evil deeds." A Kansas soldier informed a friend back home that in Arkansas "most of the *Natives* did not seem to know whether there was any other country or not. We told them a few things about America which quite astonished them. They in return quite satisfied us. If I had time I would tell you some things that would beat the 'Arkansas Traveler.'" An Iowa soldier informed his beloved that "here the people are ignorant in the extreme. . . . having no schools of any consequence and 'book larnin' but little sought after." He described the inhabitants as "idle and shiftless, being too indolent to make a decent living on a farm of two hundred acres and ten negroes to help them." He closed in a condescending tone: "I wish you were here to go with me to the country and see some of my acquaintances (of a recent date). I know you would be amused at the expressions they sometimes make."[13]

An even more disparaging—if slightly ungrammatical—observation came from an Indiana cavalryman in a letter to his fiancee: "You have often read and heard tell of the curious ways that the people have in this state, but the stories was never bad enough to be true." In a similar vein a Wisconsin soldier wrote that "I have often heard and read of the ignorance of the Southern people, but I have never been so fully convinced of the fact, until I have had an opportunity of conversing with them." Decidedly harsher in tone was this remark by a Cincinnati newspaper correspondent traveling with the Army of the Southwest: "The semi-barbarous condition of Arkansas has become proverbial in this country; and yet no one who has not traveled in the State can have any just idea of the ignorance and immorality that prevail there. If a foreigner were set down in this Patagonia of places, and told that it was one of the component parts of the Great Republic, famous for its schoolhouses, railways and newspapers, he would not believe a story so apparently self-contradictory." It appears safe to conclude that Arkansas's reputation was well established before the Yankees came.[14]

Another newspaper correspondent, this one from St. Louis, probably summed up the prevailing feelings of the officers and men of the Army of the Southwest when he reported that:

> We are marching through a region where the sound of the church bell is never heard, where a large portion of the country is a wilderness, and the inhabitants of the small and narrow valleys are far separated from each other and, following a rude and primitive method of agriculture, they give but little attention to religion or education. The farm houses are nearly all built of logs, and half of them, at least, are of the poorest description, with chimneys built on the outside, of sticks and mud, a yard with a rude fence, and all manner of animals occupying the enclosed space, but not a tree or shrub or spot of green grass for the eye to rest upon. Occasionally a better specimen of homestead is seen, with forest trees filling the yard, but such houses, and orchards, and lawns as you find in the New England, Middle and Western States, are nowhere to be found here, although many of the inhabitants have lived here over twenty years.

All in all concluded a Federal officer, Arkansas was a "miserable poor country" with a population "whose only heritage was wretched poverty."[15]

The female of the species naturally was of particular interest to the young Midwesterners and their comments about "Ozark Beauties," while not always complimentary, were usually more good-natured. The day the Army of the Southwest entered northern Arkansas two young women stopped to chat with the troops of a passing Illinois regiment. The soldiers enjoyed the brief diversion but one wag observed that it looked as though the women combed their hair "by crawling through the brush-fence after the pigs." Combs and brushes seem to have been in short supply everywhere in the hills. After buying chickens from a "dirty-faced barefooted" female of about sixteen years, a Federal engineer remarked, "Oh what a country for tangle-haired girls and tumble-down log houses."[16]

On a more positive note, an Illinois officer chanced upon a "quite pretty girl" near the Pea Ridge battlefield, a discovery which prompted him to exclaim, "O what a miracle." A Missouri soldier met a "quite handsome secesh Gall" in the same neighborhood a day later and recorded the memorable event in his diary. (Is it possible they encountered the same attractive female?) An Iowa soldier on patrol dutifully reported sighting "some feminine rebels, who were good looking but very illiterate." At least as common, however, were references to sallow, emaciated, "harpy-like females" who smoked, drank, cursed, expectorated, and engaged in any number of disgusting habits. None of the hundreds of letters and diaries reviewed for this essay contain any hint of romantic attachment or sexual attraction between the Yankee invaders and the rustic belles of the Ozark Plateau. Even by Victorian standards such an absence is unusual.[17]

Small-town Arkansas females were rarities (there being so few small towns along the army's route), but when encountered they caused something of a sensation. Typical were remarks made by Federals who briefly occupied Pocahontas. The soldiers commandeered the local printing press and cranked out one or two editions of a paper they called the *Division Register.* In a front page article the military journalists reported the discovery of "something we have not seen since leaving St. Louis—handsome young ladies." They went on to say that "if those who decamped are as good-looking as our samples, the country must be a paradise for young men. And after seeing the snuff-dipping, tobacco-chewing specimens along our march, they are truly refreshing." Apparently there was a yawning gap between urban and rural life in mid-nineteenth-century Arkansas, even when "urban" usually meant miniature metropolises of only a few hundred souls.[18]

Despite the occasional sighting of well-dressed (and presumably well-coiffed) females, the Federals were impatient with their isolation in an unfamiliar and difficult environment inhabited for the most part by an impoverished and uneducated people. They began to view "the wilderness wilds of the 'Arkansaw Nation'" as a place distinctly distant and different from the land they had left behind. "We greatly dislike the idea of stopping out here in this wilderness to remain in ignorance, by never seeing a newspaper or getting any authentic news," wrote an Illinois soldier. "It would be a great consolation to us all to hear once more from the United States, as we are getting anxious to know how things are progressing in a civilized nation." A second Illinoisan wrote to his wife that "I had begun to think that we are getting so far from 'America' as the boys say, that I had almost begun to give up all hopes of hearing from the outer world again very soon." Another complained to his spouse, "I don't want to be anywhere where I can't buy things for money!" After weeks of travel across the Ozark Plateau a disoriented Federal soldier headed a letter, "Way down here some place I don't know where." An unhappy young soldier informed his parents in distant Iowa that "it would please me very much to be taken out of this awfull country." Near the end of the campaign an Iowa officer confided to a wounded comrade convalescing in St. Louis, "I am glad our little army is going to 'America' and I am sure I don't blame you for not wanting to come back to Arkansas." After three months of marching across what he termed "the wilds of Arkansas," an Illinois officer announced to his hometown newspaper that "I am perfectly willing that this shall remain forever an *enemy's* country." Such sentiments seem to have been shared by a great many of his fellow soldiers.[19]

The Army of the Southwest eventually emerged from the highlands and reached Batesville. Located on rolling hills above the White River, the little Independence County community was a sight for sore eyes. Batesville was "the most beautiful town I have seen in the West," enthused an Illinois soldier. "Its streets and residences are beautifully laid out and ornamented. I was much surprised to find so pretty a town." A staff officer concluded that "Batesville is one of the prettiest places I have ever seen. It is a perfect grove." An Ohio artilleryman described the town as "the prettiest villa I have seen either in Missouri or Arkansas. The citizens seem to exhibit a good deal of taste in cultivating flowers and laying off their yards to suit the tastes of the fanciful." Not to be outdone, an Illinois cavalryman informed the readers of his home town newspaper that "a more lovely place cannot be found anywhere." Equally enthusiastic comments can be found in dozens of surviving letters and diaries. (The town seems to have made a better impression than the townspeople. After lavishly praising Batesville in a letter to his wife, an Iowa officer noted, "Were this country settled by intelligent and northern people I would move to Batesville at the close of the war *sure.*" Another Iowan remarked to his fiancee that while Batesville was indeed an attractive little town, it would only become "a place of considerable importance if a few enterprising *Yankees* would settle here.")[20]

Batesville appealed to the Federal soldiers for two reasons. It was, of course, the first real town most of them had seen in quite some time. A weary infantryman observed that "to men who for months had been wallowing in camps or wandering over the fag-ends of creation, it seemed a paradise." Another foot soldier noted in his diary that he and his comrades spent most of a day wandering about the streets and "stareing at the houses not having seen civilization for nearly eight months." Probably more important, and certainly more often mentioned, was the fact that Batesville seemed so familiar, so much like what they expected a town to be. An Iowa officer observed significantly that the place "had much the appearance of a northern town." A young and homesick Illinois soldier wrote to his parents that Batesville "seemes like my good old home Trumanburg." Another Illinois soldier, who was born and raised in New Hampshire, informed his wife that the appearance of the town "would lean one to believe that he was walking the streets of a New England village but for the ebony hue and shining ivory of the infernal Darkie which is everywhere visible." A cavalryman writing to the editor of his local newspaper gave Batesville his ultimate accolade. "It is," he said, "the handsomest town I have seen since I left Illinois."[21]

The nearby settlement of Jacksonport was described in quite different terms. "The soldiers consider it the meanest secesh place we have found yet," reported an Illinois officer. An Iowa officer called it "an awful mean and rowdy place." Another Iowan called it as "an ill-looking village of strong rebel proclivities," adding that it was almost deserted except for some "spiteful and malignant rebel women." The men in the ranks agreed with their superiors, referring to Jacksonport as a "very miserable town" and generally denigrating the place. "Part of it is ashes and the rest ought to be," was a typical comment. The Federals were struck by the intensely pro-Confederate attitude of the local population. An Ohio soldier informed his sister that the townspeople were secessionists "and they are not afraid to say so either." Women made faces at the invaders, and one disgusted Midwesterner observed that "even the little boys call us 'yankees.'"[22]

After spending several weeks in the Batesville-Jacksonport area, the Army of the Southwest pushed on to Helena across the alluvial flatlands of the Delta in the middle of an Arkansas summer. "The weather was intensely hot," wrote a rather romantically inclined Illinois cavalry officer, "and the road lay through the malaria-breeding swamps and fen-lands where the trailing masses of Spanish moss on the great trees wave like mourning bands over the reeking lands." Another cavalryman, a bit more straightforward, informed his wife that "the sun shines hot enough to suit the wishes of a man with the ague," adding that the troops now had a notion of "how it is in haydes." Other soldiers were even more direct. One told how "the country literally steamed with heat," and another described the lower White River valley as a "wooded wilderness of fever nests and mosquito pests." The Federals did not think the white inhabitants of the Delta were much of an improvement over the denizens of the Ozarks. An Illinois officer termed it an "indolent, heathen country," and one of the few Ohio soldiers in the army even went so far as to say after the war that "the country between Batesville and Helena was the most backward in civilization and cultivation of any we saw in the South."[23]

While tramping through what one officer, anticipating H. L. Mencken by half a century, called "the miasmatic swamps of Arkansas," the Federals encountered some of the state's less endearing fauna. An Illinois soldier informed the readers of his home townpaper that "these swamps abound in snakes, lizards, tarantulas, and all varieties of creeping and crawling things, calculated to affect one with feelings of horror and disgust. It was no unfrequent thing to see some of the boys up in the middle of their sleeping hours hunting, with a lighted candle, for snakes, lizards or *what-nots* under their blankets." Ticks especially fascinated and repelled the Midwesterners. "The wood ticks of Arkansas were a burden to us," recalled a cavalryman. "As one of the natives expressed it, there were 'oodles of them,' meaning a great many. I remember that once I sat down on a friendly looking log . . . and when I got up there were platoons of them on the march up my legs from my boots to my waist. At night before trying to sleep we usually sought the aid of a friendly comrade who would help to pick them off where we could not get at them ourselves. They attacked our horses as well as ourselves." Another soldier described how "the wood ticks crept over us by the thousands, biting like savages."[24]

Other insects did not go unnoticed. An Iowan wrote of seeing "more lightning bugs than could keep out of each other's way," and enduring nights when "the bugs and mosquitos kept up a noise like bees swarming." Indeed, hardly a Federal account is without references to camping among reptiles or battling mosquitoes and ants "of the largest caliber known to natural history." Northern readers might easily have concluded that eastern Arkansas was only a step removed from the Amazon basin.[25]

As the Army of the Southwest marched along the White River through Augusta and Clarendon, the Midwesterners came face to face with slaves and slavery on a large scale for the first time. "It was a country of large plantations with armies of strange looking negroes who streamed into our camps and attached themselves to our columns," recalled an Illinois officer. "They were the most wretched lot of human beings that we boys had ever seen. We were short of supplies ourselves, but we had to share what we had with these strange camp followers. We set them to work when there was work they could do." An Iowa staff officer informed the folks back home that "[t]he only correct information we could possibly obtain was from the negroes, who invariably told us where the bacon was buried or concealed in the brush as well as of the whereabouts of the corn whiskey, etc." An Illinois soldier wrote much the same thing to his local newspaper: "Negroes have thronged the road side as we passed, and thousands would have followed us if they had been encouraged to do so. With a few exceptions, they are the only friends we have here, and they are all willing to fight or render us any other service we may ask of them."[26]

Even though it was only the summer of 1862—six months before the issuance of the Emancipation Proclamation—black Arkansans appeared to know what the arrival of Federal soldiers meant to them. An Illinois man informed his wife that "the slaves seem to understand the matter very clearly and are on the alert to make escape by any opportunity." He added that even before leaving Jacksonport twelve runaway slaves had attached themselves to his regiment. A Wisconsin soldier reported that by the time the Army of the Southwest reached Helena everyone had gotten used to huge numbers of refugee slaves "wandering around the camp as thick as blackberries."[27]

Like a magnet, the Army of the Southwest attracted those seeking a new life free of bondage. Major General Samuel R. Curtis, the Federal commander, did not encourage blacks to accompany his column, but he did not discourage them either, and he made it clear to them that they now were free to do as they wished. Many decided to follow their liberators. "Some two thousand slaves—men women and children—have come to our camps desiring freedom," wrote a Kansas regimental surgeon. Other estimates of the number of refugee slaves accompanying the army range up to four or five thousand. "On our march the negroes had fairly swarmed around us," recalled a cavalryman in blue, "coming from every mansion, log cabin, and habitable place in the whole region. Some of the women had taken the finery belonging to their mistresses, and putting it on, strutted alongside of the column with great bundles on their heads. Little children walked briskly, while old men and young plodded on as [if] their lives depended upon reaching some place in front; exactly what place they neither knew nor cared. So excited a body of humanity seldom was seen before;

here was the realization of the hopes of liberty which they had kept alive for years." So much for the cherished Southern myth of slave loyalty and docility, at least in eastern Arkansas.[28]

Few of these conservative Midwesterners were abolitionists. In fact, an Iowa soldier probably was correct in saying that initially the Army of the Southwest "was permeated with a strong proslavery element." Arkansas slaves often were described as being "little better than savages" and a "miserable degraded set." Nevertheless, the grim reality of the Peculiar Institution had a radicalizing effect on many Northern soldiers. One declared that "I am not yet quite an Abolitionist but am fast becoming one." Another confided to his wife, "*We know up north nothing of slavery.*" An Illinois officer elaborated on the underside of slavery in a letter home: "Now I have witnessed the unnaturalness of slavery with my own eyes and with disgust. [There is] not a single slaveholder, or at least very few, who don't sell their own children. All the house servants are mulattoes, who often bear a striking likeness to the children of the household." Whether atop the Ozark Plateau or along the White River, the Federal soldiers found reasons to depict white Arkansans as degenerate, brutal, and immoral.[29]

As the Army of the Southwest approached Helena, the weary soldiers were impressed by the older and better established farms in Phillips County. "The country for the last dozen miles is beautiful," wrote a St. Louis newspaper correspondent, "grand plantations of cotton and corn on the right and elegant residences on our left. An air of wealth prevails." A Wisconsin soldier told his sister of houses "which surpass any I *ever* seen in point of extravagance and wealth and I *have* seen some costly mansions in Wisconsin and Illinois." Helena itself, the terminus of their epic march across Arkansas, impressed the Federals considerably less. It was variously described as "one of the hardest and hottest secesh holes in the South," "the resort of gamblers and rogues of all grades and capacities," "a sickly detestable village," and a "dirty nasty town" which "should be sunk." Nevertheless, the Federals were happy to be there. St. Louis journalist William Fayel concluded his account of the epic campaign across Arkansas with these heartfelt words: "Mighty glad to get out of the wilderness." Hardly a man in the Army of the Southwest would have disagreed.[30]

Despite their own difficulties, the Federal troops were aware of the devastation the Pea Ridge campaign inflicted upon the state. "Desolation, horrid to contemplate, marks every section of the country through which the army has passed," wrote one distressed Midwesterner. "Houses are deserted and fast going to ruin; fences are pulled down and burned up; orchards are ruined by hitching horses and mules to the trees; fields are left uncultivated and an air of sickening desolation is everywhere visible." An Iowan noted, "Such scenes cannot be described, but will last with me while time lasts. Fields all burned out, houses, barns, cotton-gins, and fences burned, and the smoke mingling with the dust darkens the heavens. . . . Slaves trying to follow. No white men to be found. Women crying but makes little impression on us." And from a third Federal pen: "I am roaming over the wilds of Arkansas, and desolating the country as we pass. We make a clean thing of almost everything as we pass along, in the way of forage, both for man and beast." One depressed Federal soldier summed it all up in two stark sentences: "Both armies are engaged in destroying; what the enemy leaves, our men destroy. The enemy destroys Union property, and the Union troops destroy secesh property—and there being only the two kinds of property, it is *all* destroyed." As sketched by many in the Army of the Southwest, the Arkansas wilderness was fast becoming a wasteland.[31]

This essay includes only a fraction of the surviving descriptions of Arkansas that appeared in Northern publications or were circulated in unpublished form among family and friends. It does not and cannot include the innumerable oral accounts from the thousands of Federal soldiers who returned home to tell tales of their travels in deepest Arkansas, tales which probably grew a bit more colorful with each retelling. Were these accounts accurate, or were they hopelessly prejudiced by wartime passions? It is, of course, impossible to be certain in each instance, but it appears that most reports from Arkansas in the first half of 1862 were not distorted to any serious degree by the emotional fervor of the times. The officers and men of the Army of the Southwest generally expressed themselves in matter-of-fact terms. Like soldiers in every war, they often resorted to sarcasm, exaggeration, and heavy-handed humor to make a point or enliven a narrative, but their comments and observations reveal little discernible antagonism toward Southerners in general or Arkansans in particular.[32]

Probably more important than wartime animosity in coloring the impressions of the invaders was the combination of their own backgrounds, the antebellum reputation of Arkansas, and simple geography. The Army of the Southwest was composed of Midwestern men and, for the most part, northern and eastern Arkansas were alien and unappealing places by Midwestern standards. Under these circumstances it was natural for the Federals to notice the differences between what they had known at home and what they experienced on the march. In a strongly complementary fashion the unhappy antebellum popular image of Arkansas predisposed the invaders to notice those features which reflected and reinforced widely accepted stereotypes of backwardness. Finally, the Army of the Southwest traversed some of the most sparsely settled and least developed areas in Arkansas, indeed, in the entire Confederacy. Even today, a substantial part of the Federal route is heavily wooded and lightly settled. When these psychological, cultural, and geographic factors are considered, it is not surprising that the Midwesterners were unimpressed with Arkansas.

Even taking these factors into account, there can be little doubt that most of the observations made by the Federal soldiers depicted people and places as they really were. It is an inescapable fact that large sections of Arkansas remained in a primitive condition a quarter of a century after the state's premature admission to the Union, and would remain so for decades more. Descriptions of Arkansas by Confederate soldiers from other parts of Dixie often were couched in terms quite similar to those used by Northerners. A fair example comes from the pen of a Texas cavalry officer helping to ward off the Army of the Southwest. The Texan informed his wife,

> We have been in such a wild, mountainous and unsettled country, that we have heard from nobody and seen nothing but wild and rugged mountains, steep and precipitous cliffs of rock—almost impassable and unfathomable mountain gorges. The counties of Yell, Scott and Franklin in this state, taken all together, are the most rugged and worthless country I ever saw. . . . We divide the country into three parts, to wit: Arkansas, Arkan*saw* and Rackensack, and we are all of the opinion that we are now, and for several days have been, in Rackensack. Whatever induces one to live in such a country, and almost literally starve and perish here, I confess is a mystery to me. The people, men, women and children, go bareheaded, barefooted and almost destitute of clothing. How they live through the winter frost and snows which must be severe up here, I cannot see. The houses are built of poles and are open and half of them [are] without covering. And yet for fine timber the country is unsurpassed. The people are absolutely too lazy to turn around.

Such comments make it rather difficult to distinguish between allies and enemies, but easier to conclude that both were describing Arkansas much as it really was.[33]

In the final analysis, however, questions of bias and accuracy are irrelevant. Long before the outbreak of the Civil War Arkansas had a widespread reputation as a wilderness populated by crude backwoodsmen. The descriptions of the state produced by the soldiers of the Army of the Southwest reinforced this negative image and gave it widespread circulation among hundreds of thousands of Americans who had never been exposed to the dubious musical merits of the "Arkansas Traveler."

News from Arkansas soon disappeared from the front pages of Northern publications as attention shifted to other fronts, but the damage had been done. The Pea Ridge campaign was more than a military and economic disaster for Arkansas; it also was an important step in the development of a popular image which plagues the state to this day.

Chapter 5

The Preacher, the Lawyer, and the Spoils of War

Kim Allen Scott

The day the Yankees came to his farm, Harvey Henderson Edmiston probably watched the approaching caravan of wagons and blue-clad soldiers with a hint of quiet self-confidence. The forty-five-year-old Washington County, Arkansas, farmer had a secret weapon in his pocket on this cold December day in 1862: a note signed by Brigadier General James G. Blunt himself, guaranteeing the safety of Edmiston's property from government confiscation.[1] Harvey managed to wangle his safeguard from the Federal commander sometime during the previous two weeks when the contending armies of North and South swept past his property on their way to the bloodletting at Cane Hill and Prairie Grove, Arkansas. He considered himself fortunate in convincing Blunt of his loyalty, especially since he had sold a pair of mules at a handsome profit to the Rebels just two months previous at Evansville.[2] The four hundred Confederate dollars gained from the sale were safely stashed, and with his oldest son, Tom, away in the southern part of the state, Harvey only had his youngest children at home, presenting an acceptable picture of domestic tranquility to any inquiring Northern soldiers.

Captain William A. Martin, Company G, Seventh Missouri Cavalry, and commander of the forage detail, reined up in front of Edmiston's house with a group of teamsters and "contraband" laborers. He informed Edmiston that his men needed supplies for the hungry soldiers of the Army of the Frontier and demanded to know what foodstuffs the farmer had in his home. Edmiston fished out his safeguard and presented it to the Yankee officer, explaining that with five children in his household, all under the age of ten, he really had no food to spare.[3]

"I don't care for your paper!" snapped Martin callously, "I have my orders and we'll take your property anyway!" He brushed past the bewildered farmer and entered the house, quickly surveying a large stash of fine red apples stored in the loft while his teamsters helped themselves to half a hog in the smokehouse. Edmiston watched helplessly as the marauders loaded up the pork and Captain Martin directed a second wagon load of soldiers to enter the house to get the apples.

This next group of soldiers terrified Edmiston even more than had Captain Martin. They were Kansans, and as they leapt from the wagon in front of his house, Edmiston saw that they were armed with the largest guns he had ever seen. Staring beyond their huge, brass-barreled muskets, he studied the faces of the six soldiers, memorizing their features as they pushed through his doorway. They may have laughed roughly as they loaded up the eight bushels of fruit, bragging about the reception their comrades in Company B would give them when they returned with the prize. Edmiston probably even heard the name of their regiment as they drove off to rejoin the caravan heading toward Cane Hill: the uniformed robbers were from the Eleventh Kansas Infantry.[4]

The impact of the Civil War on Arkansas residents like Harvey Edmiston has been the subject of several published articles. Historians usually tell the story of civilian suffering during the conflict by presenting a broad overview of many different events, separated by time and distance, in order to best utilize the scant records available for consultation. While they may be valuable contributions to our understanding of the past, these generalized historical inquiries usually fail to give the reader a sense of what passions motivated civilian and military participants in Arkansas during the terrible Civil War years. Explaining away the depredations committed by the Union and Confederate armies simply as wanton acts of warfare is to reduce historical figures to stereotyped cardboard cutouts. By focusing the historical microscope on the events surrounding one particularly well documented occurrence, the robbery of the Edmiston farm on December 12, 1862, this study may help the reader gain a better sense of the 1860s zeitgeist in northwest Arkansas. Nineteenth-century people, just like their twentieth-century counterparts, were a complex mixture of petty jealousies, hatreds, and prejudices. Occasionally they acted on their impulses with predictable results, as Harvey Edmiston found out the day the Yankees came to his farm.

Before we can fully understand the incident which occurred at the Edmiston farm in 1862, the careers of two pivotal characters in the story, Colonel Thomas Ewing, Jr., of the Eleventh Kansas Infantry, and Colonel William F. Cloud, of the Second Kansas Cavalry, must be discussed. As the results of this investigation will demonstrate, the friction between these two men probably had as much to do with the pilfering of Edmiston's apples as the six privates who actually lugged the fruit away.

Privilege and ambition: these two themes appear to dominate the life of Thomas Ewing, Jr. Born in 1829 and the son of a United States senator from Ohio, Ewing enjoyed a comfortable childhood befitting of his family's status and influence. That influence was shown clearly when young Thomas worked at several appointed government jobs in Washington, D.C., even before his 1854 graduation from Brown University.[5] After receiving his law degree from the University of Cincinnati in 1855, Ewing traveled to Kansas Territory where he established a law partnership with his brother Hugh and brother-in-law, William Tecumseh Sherman. His talents as a barrister remained largely untapped, however, because Ewing, in the words of one researcher "found town lot speculation and the making of loans to settlers far too exciting to allow much time for the mundane practice of law."[6]

Thomas Ewing's political portrait is somewhat difficult to draw. In regard to slavery, he politely could be referred to as a "moderate" whose pragmatic alliance with Kansas abolitionists did not interfere with opportunities to make money. For example, when it appeared that the free-state movement had gained the upper hand in Kansas after 1857, Ewing not only accepted a politically expedient figurehead position on the board of the Leavenworth, Pawnee, and Western Railroad Company (which had been organized by pro-slavery advocates), but also lobbied Congress for land grant assistance with Andrew Jackson Isacks, a Louisiana-born advocate of Southern rights.[7]

By the summer of 1862 any aspiring Kansas politician could see that an acceptable service record would not hurt his chances to continue in public service; and Ewing, who had been appointed chief justice of the Kansas Supreme Court in 1861, prepared to accept a commission as colonel of a new regiment of infantry being organized for the Union cause. He stumped the state for recruits to fill the ranks of the Eleventh Kansas Infantry and met with enthusiastic response everywhere he spoke. It is possible that political ambition also could account for some of the motives spurring the men who flocked to Ewing's banner. He wrote to his father in late August describing the calibre of volunteers attracted during his recruiting tour: "The people are greatly aroused, and men of the highest character and intelligence are going in as privates. In Jackson County every lawyer (5) volunteered—three ministers, three merchants, and every county officer save one. There will be a great deal of competition for the company and field officers, there being so many qualified for the places."[8] In Topeka, newspaperman Edmund G. Ross managed to convince the personnel in his printing office to join him in Ewing's regiment, while another editor, Preston B. Plumb of Emporia, also jumped on the military bandwagon. Thomas Moonlight, a Leavenworth County attorney who held a captain's rank in the adjutant general's department, resigned his commission when Ewing offered him the lieutenant colonelcy of the Eleventh.[9] All three of these men had been outspoken abolitionists, and their election to the various officer's positions during the regimental balloting that September may have suggested to Colonel Ewing what the rank and file of Kansas voters expected of their leaders.

When the Eleventh received the call to the front on October 4, 1862, it was armed hastily with oversized antique Prussian muskets, the only weapons the quartermaster at Fort Leavenworth had to spare. Shouldering the .72-calibre smoothbores, the regiment marched south to join Brigadier General James G. Blunt's division of the Army of the Frontier and help smash the rebellion. Their long and uneventful journey ended temporarily at Pea Ridge, Arkansas, on October 25, when the Eleventh reported for duty at General Blunt's headquarters. Blunt, a former physician who had been so active in the Kansas abolitionist movement that he worked with the likes of John Brown, placed the Eleventh in the third brigade of his division under the immediate command of Colonel William Frederick Cloud of the Second Kansas Cavalry. Ewing was at odds with his new commander almost immediately.

The personality of William F. Cloud is harder to assess than Thomas Ewing's because, unlike the lawyer turned soldier, Cloud's personal papers do not appear to have survived. Like Ewing, Cloud was an Ohio native who traveled west to seek his fortune, but there the similarity between the two ends. Cloud's parents were simple farmers, and he early showed a disposition for two widely divergent vocations: soldiering and preaching. When the war with Mexico broke out, Cloud joined the Second Ohio Infantry as First Sergeant of Company K and stayed with the army all the way from St. Louis to Mexico City. After the war he lived for a time in Michigan, and then emmigrated to Kansas in the year of 1858. There he became active as a preacher in the Methodist Church and ran a haberdashery business at Emporia until his services as a soldier were again required in 1861. He accepted a commission as major of the Second Kansas Infantry in early May and saw combat during Brigadier General Nathaniel Lyon's southwest Missouri campaign the following summer. Cloud's regiment was used up badly at Wilson's Creek, losing nearly a third of its number, and later became reorganized as a cavalry force under his command as colonel.[10]

Regardless of his military talents, Colonel Cloud appeared every inch a soldier with his intellegent eyes, drooping mustache, and shoulder-length hair. He quickly established a reputation as a no-nonsense disciplinarian with a genuine concern for the welfare of his troops. During a September 1861 expedition in Jefferson County, Missouri, Cloud overruled his commanding officer and ordered a withdrawal of his men when overwhelming enemy forces threatened the Union soldiers with annihilation.[11] Troopers of the Second discovered their leader would not tolerate the molestation of civilians when he approved a drumhead courtmartial conviction on July 10, 1862. Private John Bell of Company I was found guilty of raping a woman near Iola, Kansas, and was hanged.[12] Cloud also demonstrated his compassion and tact later that month when he was sent to escort Chief John Ross of the Cherokee Nation to the Union lines, along with the tribe's archives, from Tahlequah in the Indian Territory. Even though he had just returned from fighting hostile Indians farther west on the plains, Cloud treated his charges "with the distinguished consideration due them."[13] In the words of one admiring officer who served under him, Colonel Cloud was "[a] man easily approachable, stood little on his dignity as a commanding officer, mingled freely with all classes, chatted pleasantly with all who came to him, and made them feel that all were equally interested in the Union cause, which championed the rights of the plain people, and he easily won their respect and confidence."[14] With such attributes as those listed above, it is easy to see how the diverse backgrounds of William F. Cloud and Thomas Ewing, Jr., could have led to a stormy military relationship.

Colonel Cloud may have first run afoul of his ambitious subordinate during the battle of Fort Wayne, in Indian Territory on October 19, 1862. General Blunt received word that a large force of Confederates were gathering in the Indian Territory just west of Maysville, Arkansas, and determined to drive them out. Colonel Ewing eagerly sought to lead his regiment against the enemy for the first time and became enraged when Cloud galloped past the slow-moving infantrymen with the Second Kansas Cavalry, routing the enemy before the Eleventh could even arrive on the field. In a letter to his wife written a few weeks afterwards, Ewing expressed his contempt for his commanding officer, predicting, "He and I will have a collision certain. . . . If he had any brains I could stand him better, but he has none. He is not fit to command more than a company."[15]

Following the fight at Fort Wayne, the Army of the Frontier settled into a lengthy bivouac at Lindsey's Prairie, a wide expanse of grassland on the state line about twenty-five miles southwest of Bentonville. Here Cloud and Ewing continued to irritate each other while performing the boring duties of foraging and drill. Even their animals appeared to sense the animosity between the two. At a grand review of the division held in mid-November, Colonel Ewing had the Eleventh at attention in its proper place among the other regiments while Colonel Cloud cantered up on his horse to inspect the troops. Cloud extended his compliments to the commander of the Eleventh and Ewing ordered his regiment to present arms. Cloud's horse, probably excited by the unexpected glare of one thousand brass-barreled muskets held forth in the bright November sunshine, suddenly kneeled down in front of Ewing, causing the infantrymen to titter nervously in the ranks while the cavalryman struggled to retain his seat.[16] If there was ever any chance the two soldiers might resolve their differences, it may have evaporated after the farcical debacle of this review.

The difference of opinion between the former lawyer and the former preacher over the treatment of civilian property proved to be their most hotly contested issue. During the fall of 1862, the Army of the Frontier operated in northwestern Arkansas under the direction of Special Order 87, which regulated the confiscation of Rebel property. Congress had passed the Second Confiscation Act on July 12, 1862, allowing the Union army to use captured Rebel property at its own discretion, but each particular unit interpreted the law in varying degrees of severity by means of special orders. The exact particulars of Special Order 87, the guidelines that General Blunt's army used to implement the Confiscation Act, may never be known since a whole copy does not appear to have survived.[17] However, one can safely assume Colonel Cloud particularly concerned himself with paragraph 8 since he quoted it angrily in an exchange with Colonel Ewing that December. According to Cloud, paragraph 8 stated that the "order to take property from disloyal persons must be issued from the brigade or division headquarters," and he insisted that the proviso be observed. Ewing, and many men in his command, may have been convinced that almost all Arkansans could be classified as "disloyal" and resented headquarter's restraint on their plundering. Unlike Cloud, Ewing had been a resident of Kansas since the turbulent days of the mid-1850s and sympathized with the passions his men felt against Southerners. Even soldiers from other Northern states who had never personally suffered depredations at the hands of pro-slavery "border ruffians" could feel the same callous attitude of Kansans concerning Arkansas civilians. As one Iowa boy stationed at Helena bluntly put it, "If my hand touches any rebbel's [*sic*] valuables I expect they will stick to my fingers."[18]

As long as General Blunt ordered the raiding, no conflict between Cloud and Ewing over confiscation could ferment. During the interim between the battle of Fort Wayne on October 22 and the battle of Cane Hill on November 28, Ewing's men participated in numerous foraging expeditions which involved the confiscation of civilian goods. William Brown, a miller who lived near Elm Springs, Arkansas, became one of the earliest Arkansas settlers to experience the Kansas brand of warfare on November 4 when a contingent of the Eleventh Infantry under Major Plumb arrived to confiscate livestock, grain, and vegetables from the "rank secech."[19] Other settlers were raided during the expedition and a tannery burned at Cincinnati, all with the blessing of the commanding officer of the Army of the Frontier.

Circumstantial evidence suggests that Blunt may have repented his army's vigorous pursuit of property as the weeks dragged on. Aside from the two known safeguards he issued to Arkansas civilians in December 1862,[20] Blunt also authorized the publication of a statement by troops under his command; it denounced the pillage by some, calling the acts "disgraceful to the perpetrators and calculated to bring discredit upon the whole army and upon the cause for which the army is fighting."[21] Colonel Ewing probably grew impatient with any softening on the issue of confiscation at headquarters and sided with subordinates who opposed Blunt's demonstrations of leniency. "I am afraid I will have trouble here with Blunt as well as Cloud," wrote Ewing to his wife on December 2, "but cannot well explain the cause, all of which, however, are traceable to political jealousies."[22] Regardless of whatever political jealousies Ewing may have been referring to, his subsequent correspondence shows that bickering over confiscation played a major part in the former lawyer's estrangement from his commanding officers.

Squabbles over civilian property rights were temporarily forgotten on November 28, 1862, during the battle of Cane Hill, Arkansas; but the test of wills between Ewing and Cloud continued in another fashion. General Blunt's spies informed him on the twenty-seventh that a large force of enemy cavalry occupied the southwestern Washington County town of Cane Hill, and he immediately organized an expedition against the Confederates. More than five thousand men, including the Eleventh Infantry and the Second Cavalry, marched until midnight to reach a point about fifteen miles from Cane Hill. At 5:00 on the morning of the twenty-eighth, Blunt's army resumed the march by following a rather difficult and little-used country lane which led directly south to the town. Colonel Ewing's men struggled along gamely with their heavy muskets, while Colonel Cloud's horsemen rode in file behind them, probably urging them on at an uncomfortable pace. When advance elements of Blunt's command made contact with the enemy at 10:00 A.M., the Eleventh Kansas was still several miles behind struggling over a steep hill. Blunt urgently requested reenforcements, and once more Ewing watched the horsemen of the Second gallop past his doughboys to engage the enemy. Vowing not to be left behind again, Ewing ordered his men to march alternately at quick and double-quick steps, a grueling pace even without the encumbrance of their heavy packs and weapons.[23]

The Confederate force at Cane Hill had no intention of holding back the superior numbers hurled against them and made a running fight. Brigadier General John Sappington Marmaduke, commander of the Rebel army, only made stands long enough to delay his pursuers before withdrawing farther south toward the safety of the Boston Mountains. The constant running, deployment of flanking skirmishers, and reforming to continue the chase proved particularly hard on the Yankee infantrymen. Ewing described the situation to his wife: "My regiment was nearly run to death, going incessantly from 5 A.M. to 9 P.M., and travelling full 35 miles with their blankets on their backs—and yet Cloud complained of them for not outracing the cavalry which kept the road during the fight while we struggled through the bush for ten miles—the puppy!"[24]

When the Yankees went into camp at the Confederates' old position at Cane Hill, it appeared as if the Army of the Frontier would undergo another lengthy, boring bivouac with little to do other than forage and drill. Colonel Cloud now decided to express his own views on army discipline by issuing General Order 15 on December 4, 1862. The former preacher declared that his brigade would observe a regular system of drill and daily inspections during their stay in the enemy's country, and ordered Colonel Ewing to "adopt such police regulations as [would] secure at all times the men in [his] entire command in camp (except those on detail)."[25] Ewing disobeyed the last proviso almost immediately by allowing several members of Company E to commandeer an abandoned printing office in the village for production of a regimental newspaper, but he at least insisted that his men follow closely the regulations found in paragraph 3 of Cloud's order. This command required that, in order to conserve ammunition, no one was to fire a weapon without authorization and demanded an arrest penalty for discharging a gun for any reason other than combat. The men of the Eleventh did follow paragraph 3 to the letter, if not the spirit, as became evident after the battle of Prairie Grove.

The Rebel army under the command of Major General Thomas C. Hindman met the combined forces of the First, Second, and Third Divisions of the Army of the Frontier at Prairie Grove, Arkansas, on December 7, 1862. After a vicious one-day fight, during which the Eleventh Kansas performed gallantly on the battlefield's western section, the regiment again retired to camp at Cane Hill and resumed their foraging expeditions to supplement the hardtack, salt pork, and coffee provided by the quartermasters.

On December 12, 1862, Lieutenant William V. Phillips, Company C, Eleventh Kansas Infantry, rode out from the main camp at Cane Hill to inspect a guard post manned by soldiers belonging to Company I. The darkened sky threatened rain that afternoon, and when Phillips arrived at the outpost he discovered the men half famished after twenty-four hours of watching for the enemy near an Ozark farmstead. The soldiers had been sent on guard without a meat ration, and when they tired of gnawing on the tasteless hardtack wafers stuffed in their haversacks, they killed one of the hogs they saw milling around the farmer's house. Remembering the strict orders against discharging their firearms, the obedient soldiers bayonetted the pig before confiscating it. Several chickens also were killed. By the time Phillips reached them, the guard detail had butchered the hog, neatly dressed the carcass, and obviously wanted to return to camp in order to roast their booty. Phillips dismissed the men and watched the soldiers file slowly back down the road. Private Keithley and five of his comrades also carried sacks of apples, probably liberated from the same farm with the pork and poultry, as they disappeared in the gathering gloom of twilight.[26]

Unfortunately for the privates of Company I, Colonel William F. Cloud picked that very evening to inspect his outposts and met the plunderers along the road. Purple with rage at the ragtag caravan of thieves, Cloud demanded their names and unit, and then threatened each one with flogging for their pilfering.[27] Cloud was still seething with anger at his headquarters the next morning when a local farmer who asked to see the commanding officer was shown to his tent. The long-haired cavalryman listened patiently as Harvey Henderson Edmiston told his story about the stolen apples and then Cloud inspected the farmer's crumpled safeguard signed by General Blunt. This report provoked Colonel Cloud. The situation Edmiston described, that of losing half a hog and several bushels of apples by Kansas soldiers, appeared to be exactly the same as what Colonel Cloud had seen along the roadway the previous evening. Cloud sat down at his camp desk and scribbled out two documents, both addressed to Colonel Thomas Ewing, Jr.

The first document Cloud penned detailed the crimes as far as he understood them and demanded the arrest of First Lieutenant Josiah McAfee, Company I, for dismissing the guard and allowing his men to plunder civilians. Cloud finished with a curt order for Ewing to search his entire regiment for large red apples, and arrest all soldiers found in possession of the same, and a warning that "these things *must* cease!"[28]

Colonel Cloud then turned his attention to Edmiston. Calling an orderly to his tent, the cavalryman ordered an escort for the farmer and handed him a second note: "Col. Ewing; The bearer is the man who had his safeguard violated yesterday. You will assist him in identifying the guilty parties, and if any are convicted, report the same for punishment."[29] Edmiston took his leave from Colonel Cloud's headquarters and headed for the camp of the Eleventh Kansas, while the cavalryman occupied himself with other matters, likely satisfied that the unlawful members of Ewing's infantry would be brought to justice. But if the former preacher felt that justice had been served by issuing the two orders, he failed to reckon with the skillful manuverings of the former lawyer under his command.

When Colonel Ewing received the first note from Colonel Cloud, he went to work on the first loophole he found. Lieutenant Phillips of Company C, not Lieutenant McAfee, had relieved the guard yesterday, and Ewing called Phillips to his tent for an explanation. The young subaltern, probably with Ewing coaching him, prepared a carefully worded statement correctly identifying himself as the officer who dismissed the guard, but disavowing any responsibility for the bayonetted hog and stolen apples. Phillips's defense for relieving the guard was based entirely on the weather: he maintained that it was raining when he made the decision to dismiss the outpost.[30]

The next piece of business required considerable tact on the part of Colonel Ewing. Harvey Edmiston arrived in the camp and the regiment formed into line while the colonel escorted the farmer past the men.

Edmiston singled out privates Robert Owings, James Wells, A. J. McCleary, Joseph Stanley, Duelly Bronson, and James Terril, all of Company B, as the men who entered his house the day before. There was little use in denying their guilt, but Colonel Cloud's specific charge against the soldiers was for violating Edmiston's safeguard rather than stealing the apples. Ewing carefully interviewed Edmiston to establish the exact sequence of events. The farmer had to agree that the privates standing before him were indeed the ones who took his apples, but the nasty officer who waved aside his safeguard was not among them. Ewing then wrote out a statement for the accused enlisted men, admitting that they took the fruit but only after being ordered to by Captain William Martin. Turning to Edmiston, Ewing read the statement and requested the farmer to endorse it. Edmiston wrote the following on the bottom of the document: "So far as the transactions referred to and partially set forth in the statement tends to implicate the men whose names are signed above, the statement is correct."[31]

Apparently satisfied, Edmiston returned to his farm while Ewing prepared an addendum to his statement: "You will perceive by the enclosed that the charge of forcing the safeguard does not lie against my men," he smugly informed the preacher, "and that the case is one out of my jurisdiction and directly under yours."[32]

When Colonel Cloud received the two reports from the Eleventh Kansas Infantry the next day, he had to admit the lawyer had outfoxed him: "Your skill in clearing your foragers is commended, especially in view of the fact that a wagon master's order is permitted to render null and void the orders of division and brigade commanders. . . . When I charge men with straggling and marauding, I propose to sustain the same, especially with an eye witness. If Lieutenant Phillips was in charge of the guard, you will for the present release Lieutenant McAfee and return him to duty."[33]

But Ewing was not finished. Angered to distraction over Cloud's incessant meddling with his command, the former lawyer decided to act before army headquarters made permanent by promotion any of the current brigade command positions occupied by Colonel Cloud, Colonel William Weer, and General Frederick Soloman. On the night of December 14, 1862, Ewing dipped his pen in acid to write a confidential letter to Brigadier General James H. Lane, the fiercely abolitionist Kansas political leader, in regards to the relative merits of the Army of the Frontier's brigade commanders: "As to Cloud, he is as high, as Colonel, as his capacity warrants. A general should have capacity beyond a drill and a dash. . . . But there are other things to be considered. Weer and Cloud both cling to the West Point policy of treating treason as respectful and the property of traitors as sacred. Under cover of a clamor against mean and detestable outrages rarely occurring and universally condemned, they would prohibit all use of secession property."[34]

Just how "rarely" these outrages occurred is a matter of conjecture. What the few extant manuscript sources from Washington County residents suggest is that plundering by Union troops in the fall of 1862 was the norm, rather than the exception. Amanda Braly, a widow living just south of the Cane Hill area, wrote to her son in the Confederate army on November 15 and reported that one of the family hogs was killed by soldiers and that her corn supply was uncertain because "the soldiers ha[d] been feeding of it."[35] Not even obvious Union sympathizers were spared. On the night of December 12, Yankee soldiers visited the house of Lina Hermann at Dutch Mills, just a few miles away from the Edmiston place. Just as Harvey Edmiston had done that same afternoon, the German housewife presented a safeguard signed by General Blunt, but the soldiers took what they wanted anyway.[36] Rumors of the Yankee pillaging in Washington County spread far beyond Arkansas's borders. Albert O. McCollum, a soldier in the First Arkansas Cavalry stationed in Mississippi, became unsettled when he heard rumors from home in February 1863. "Since the Cane Hill fight I have heard the Federals took all your horses and Old Sam and the wagons," he wrote to his parents near Fayetteville.[37]

In his letter to General Lane, Colonel Ewing sidestepped the issue of the frequency with which his men plundered civilians by resorting to political rhetoric. He emphasized his point for the "privileges and just indulgences of our noble soldiery" by asserting that "the Democratic, not the Republican policy, prevails in the Army of Republican Kansas," and appealed that the promotion to the third brigade commander be granted to Colonel William Phillips, then in command of one of the Union army's Indian regiments.[38]

Ewing did not stop pestering his commanding officer after sending his letter to General Lane. He ordered his men to seize any good mules they came across on December 20 and was again reprimanded by Colonel Cloud for violating Special Order 87.[39] As if to purposely antagonize his superior, Ewing the next day sent directly to Cloud a routine request for chickens and vegetables from Dr. J. D. Adams, superintendent of one of the emergency hospitals at Cane Hill. Cloud returned the request with an exasperated reply for his subordinate to check the division regulations.[40]

Ironically, Ewing's feud with Cloud jeopardized the one thing he cared the most about: his military record. The commander of the Eleventh exhibited extraordinary bravery on the field at Prairie Grove, but he worried that Colonel Cloud would prevent his rightful citation in the official reports. During the confusion of the battle, Ewing acted temporarily under the orders of Colonel William Weer of the Second Brigade, and although Weer praised highly in his report all the soldiers who followed his orders during the fight, he also added, "Due credit will doubtless be given them in reports from their proper commanders."[41] Ewing sent a copy of Weer's indirect commendation to his wife on December 18, complaining, "I suppose Cloud would slander the whole regiment if he could without flagrant and notorious falsehood. As it is, he will probably not allude to it. He is the pettiest creature out of petticoats."[42]

But Cloud did allude to the Eleventh Kansas in his report of the battle, and in a manner which should have shamed his suspicious subordinate: "Colonel Ewing of the Eleventh, and the captains and lieutenants . . . are all worthy of their brave commands. These officers went into the thickest of the fight and staid [*sic*] there until by order or necessity the whole line fell back to more effective positions."[43] In all fairness to Colonel Ewing's suspicions, it should be stated that Cloud wrote his report on December 18, three days after Weer had submitted his own. It is possible that the former preacher felt compelled to mention the Eleventh favorably after reviewing the text of Weer's report.

The feuding between the preacher and the lawyer came to an end with the closing of the year 1862. Ewing indicated in a letter home to his wife that his officers planned to petition for placement in another brigade, and by December 31 a general reorganization of the Army of the Frontier's First Division accomplished just that.[44] Colonel William Weer replaced General Blunt as division commander, and the Eleventh Kansas was placed in the First Brigade under Colonel William R. Judson. Colonel Cloud accepted the command of the Second Brigade, consisting of his own regiment, the Second Kansas Cavalry, and the Tenth and Thirteenth Kansas Infantry. The Third Brigade, incorporating all three Indian regiments, fell to Colonel William A. Phillips.[46]

Colonel Cloud finished out his Civil War service in Arkansas and the Indian Territory, gaining many battlefield distinctions but no further promotions. He holds the somewhat unique distinction of being the only Civil War cavalry commander ever to have captured four enemy steamboats, during a brilliantly executed raid on Van Buren, Arkansas, at the end of December 1862. He also took part in a daring rescue of a surrounded Union army garrison at Fort Gibson, Indian Territory, in July 1863, breaking through the enemy lines with a numerically inferior force and fighting his way back out again.[46]

Following the war, William Cloud made his home in Carthage, Missouri, where he served as a collector of internal revenue for the U.S. government. Toward the end of his long life, Cloud wrote a history of Mexico, which, if not a sterling testament of racial tolerance, at least demonstrated his continuing interest and sympathy for people and cultures different from his own. He died in Kansas City in 1905.[47]

Thomas Ewing, Jr., achieved even higher goals than avoiding further service under Cloud's command. On March 13, 1863, Ewing was promoted to the rank of brigadier general and eventually given command of the District of the Border in western Missouri. Time and military honor had not mellowed his philosophy for dealing with Southern sympathizers, however. Following a vicious raid against Lawrence, Kansas, in August 1863 by William Quantrill's guerrillas, General Ewing issued the notorious "Order Number 11." This manifesto forcibly depopulated four border counties of Missouri which had been used as a base by the guerrillas and made no distinction between those who were loyal to the Union cause and those who sympathized with the Rebels.[48]

Thomas Ewing never lived down Order Number 11. The incident became permanently associated with him after artist George Caleb Bingham produced the dramatic painting *Orders Number 11* in 1879. The painting, which depicted a Missouri farm family being forced to vacate their property by dispassionate Yankee soldiers, quickly became an American classic and visually reinforced the image of Thomas Ewing, Jr., as a ruthless conqueror.[49] After the war Ewing eventually returned to Ohio, where he unsuccessfully attempted to claim his father's old position in the Senate and the governorship of the state. He never got any further than two brief terms in the House of Representatives after Buckeye voters became acquainted with his war record. Ewing died in 1896 after being run over by a New York City streetcar.[50]

Harvey Henderson Edmiston survived the war with his family and farm intact. In fact, the Edmiston farm is still in the hands of his descendants, making it one of the oldest continuously owned family farms in Washington County.[51] The thievery of Edmiston's apples had two results pertinent to our inquiry, however. Thomas Alexander Edmiston, Harvey's eldest son, enlisted with the Thirty-fourth Arkansas Infantry on November 22, 1863, at Camden, Arkansas.[52] He no doubt joined Company B of this Southern regiment because it consisted almost entirely of his neighbors from Washington County, but the timing of his decision to enter the Confederate service could possibly be a result of the treatment his family received from Kansas soldiers the previous fall.

Edmiston probably experienced further loss of his property as the war dragged on, and he kept a tally of his damages. On June 17, 1871, he filed a claim with the federal government for $527 in compensation. Although the farmer had adequate documentation to present his demand to Fayetteville claims agent George W. M. Reed, there is no record that the government ever repaid him for the losses he endured during the 1862 animosity between the preacher and the lawyer from Kansas.[53]

Chapter 6

Disloyalty and Class Consciousness in Southwestern Arkansas, 1862–1865

CARL H. MONEYHON

In the spring of 1863 violence broke out within Confederate Arkansas. Soldiers deserted from military camps, avowed Unionist organizations appeared, and armed clashes took place between men who stated their hostility toward Confederate authorities and loyalists who continued to support the Southern cause. The struggles of 1863 took place not in the mountains, areas where support for the war had always been lukewarm, but particularly in the southwestern counties that had been part of the expanding cotton-growing area of the state before the war. Ultimately the Confederate national and state governments had to use military force against their own population. This paper examines what happened in Arkansas during this period, what caused the uprising, and its impact upon the war effort.

In writing about the Southern Confederacy, historians recognize the existence of significant internal opposition to the Confederate government across the South. Personal rivalries, regional jealousies, ideological conflict, and struggles between the states and central government all contributed to this friction. Scholars have seen these problems as important factors helping to produce Southern defeat. Scholars also have been aware of another aspect of the South's domestic problems, the existence of a more difficult to explain antagonism toward the government and also the war among the common folks. This opposition appeared in almost every Southern state. Desertion, draft dodging, and outright rebellion against Confederate authority marked its existence. The outbreak that took place in Arkansas against the Confederate government in the spring of 1863 appears to have been an uprising of the latter type.[1]

Determining what caused this hostility within the Confederacy's general population has been an important concern of historians, but also a topic that has defied easy answers. The earliest explanation of what might be called popular resistance to Confederate authority saw it as an individual response to conditions and policies produced by flagging Confederate prospects. Ella Lonn, for example, saw growing suffering among civilians as undermining civilian and military morale and producing desertion and efforts at keeping out of the army. In a variation on this theme of individualism, Albert Moore found a cultural cause. When the Confederacy implemented conscription to fill the depleted ranks of its armies, it implemented a policy that necessarily produced conflict, for conscription ran counter to the hearty individualism of Southerners and failed to harmonize with the "individual instincts of southerners and with their conception of manhood."[2]

More recently, historians have seen growing antagonism between social classes as another factor promoting internal opposition to the Confederacy. Studies that have focused particularly on Southern towns have found that at least by 1863 poor whites particularly were disillusioned not only with the war but with what they considered to be the class-based policies of their government. As a result they participated in food riots, evaded the draft, and resisted the collection of taxes. The discovery of class conflict as a source of wartime political dissension emerged from urban studies; but some recent work, such as Wayne K. Durrill's *War of Another Kind*, a study of Washington County, North Carolina, has found considerable strife among planters, yeoman farmers, and the poor of the countryside as well.[3]

Although recent scholarship has identified a variety of sources of discontent, the full extent and exact nature of such insurgency remains uncharted at least in part because we know so little about what was taking place at the local level. Concerning the role of class conflict in producing the South's internal strife, it may be said that Emory M. Thomas's conclusions drawn in 1979 still hold true. While class conflict in towns is now accepted as at least one explanation for expressions of disloyalty, the amount of disloyalty inspired by class resentment in the countryside is "unknown." Thomas's observations indicate that more studies of uprisings against Confederate authority throughout the South, but especially outside of towns and regions where dissent might be expected, are necessary to gain a full understanding of what drove popular opposition to the Confederate cause after 1863.[4]

The upheaval in southwestern Arkansas happened in just such a place. On December 29, 1862, General Theophilus Holmes, commanding the

Trans-Mississippi Department, informed Confederate president Jefferson Davis of the difficulties that had developed throughout his district. He wrote, "My situation is one . . . full of perplexities not the least dangerous of which is the growing disaffection to the war among the people. With power to declare martial law I can suppress it but without this I cannot tell where it will end." Through the early months of 1863, Holmes's predictions were fulfilled, and Confederate authorities reported widespread hostility to the Confederacy, hostility that ranged from resistance to conscription to raids by armed bands against loyal Confederates. This disaffection was particularly strong among the people of southwestern Arkansas, especially in the counties lying to the west and south of the Saline River. That section witnessed the most widespread opposition to Confederate authority and saw the harshest efforts to suppress it.[5]

In 1860 conditions within the southwestern counties offered few clues to predict the emergence of such anti-Confederate sentiment. Although settled and developed primarily in the decade immediately prior to the outbreak of the Civil War, the region constituted one of the most dynamic sectors of Arkansas's cotton frontier. Plantation agriculture had taken hold particularly in the bottomlands of the Saline, Ouachita and Red River valleys. In addition, these counties each had significant slave populations. These factors make events there particularly interesting for they suggest widespread discontent even in an area that theoretically should have strongly supported the Confederacy.[6] Social patterns within the southwestern counties also offered no indication of the presence of bases for strife in the antebellum years. Religious and ethnic differences within the counties reflected patterns similar to those throughout the state. Contemporary observers generally considered their local communities to be relatively egalitarian. They were in part bound together by their belief in economic opportunity for all whites in society. Though poor, yeomen farmers and landless whites believed that they could expand their property holdings, acquire slaves, and climb the social ladder within the existing system. That does not mean, however, that they did not recognize distinctions within their society. They were aware, at least, of the existence of different classes. These seemed, however, inconsequential.[7]

In the secession crisis the white voters of the southwestern counties showed considerable unity. In the 1860 presidential election, all of the counties except Hempstead and Columbia gave majorities to the states' rights candidate, John Breckinridge. In the state secession convention, delegates from Hempstead and Ouachita Counties voted against secession on March 18, but the other southwestern counties strongly supported this action. This support for secession cut across class and other social lines. Concerning class issues in the crisis, John Brown, a diarist in Ouachita County, believed that backing for secession actually may have been strongest among the lower classes. Brown reached this conclusion from two observations. First, reflecting his Whig politics, he believed that the Democrat-secessionist leadership found it easier to dupe the lower classes. Second, he thought that the poor saw secession as a chance for change, and they supported it believing they had nothing to lose and much to gain from the disruption of the status quo. But no apparent social divisions emerged in 1860 or early 1861.[8]

Further evidence of solidarity among whites in the southwest could be seen in the general support for war that they exhibited in the wake of the firing on Fort Sumter and Lincoln's call on the state for troops to suppress the rest of the South. Young men from all classes flocked to the Confederate colors in large numbers. At Camden thirteen companies totaling thirteen hundred men organized by September 1861. This number constituted about three-fourths of the adult white male population of 1860. Other counties experienced similar responses. In Union County, according to a later estimate, over fifteen hundred men joined the Confederate army. The latter figure is particularly impressive considering that the census of 1860 showed only thirteen hundred men in the county between the ages of twenty and fifty. John Brown captured the zeal that swept Camden when he wrote on May 30, 1861, "[T]he excitement intense. The whole country is arising—and our people are perfectly wild."[9]

In the winter of 1862, however, Confederate authorities noted signs of discontent among Arkansas soldiers and civilians throughout the state. Arkansas units stationed at home suffered high rates of desertion. The civilian population appeared generally demoralized and hostile to General Thomas Hindman, military commander in the state, who had imposed draconian measures on the population to muster the resources necessary to resist a Federal invasion in the summer of 1862. Opposition to Hindman grew so widespread and strong that President Jefferson Davis appointed Major General Theophilus Holmes to replace him. When Holmes arrived he discovered that disillusionment with the Confederate cause ran deep. Although Hindman clearly was an issue in creating the problem, Holmes offered a broader assessment of causes in a letter written to President Davis on December 29, 1862. He described the situation as desperate. Holmes attributed the disaffection to four major causes: A drought that summer had produced food shortages throughout the community. Uncontrolled inflation had seriously undermined the position of the poor, many of whom barely managed to survive. The troops had been badly maintained and most had not been paid. Finally, there was almost universal opposition to the exemption provisions of the Confederacy's conscription law. Of particular concern was the exemption of one white man on each planation for each twenty or more slaves.[10]

Holmes did little to allay concerns, however, and unrest intensified in the first months of 1863. Southwestern Arkansas particularly witnessed increasing displays of opposition to the Confederacy. A full accounting of what happened is difficult because wartime public records for these counties are limited. Only one newspaper published in the period remains in existence. In addition, few letters, diaries, or even memoirs have surfaced belonging to people from this area who were there during the war. Nonetheless, enough information exists to provide some sense of the extent and nature of the protests. The sources indicated a widespread resistance to Confederate authority.

Among the first signs of trouble was the report of a mutiny of those who had been ordered to report for duty. At the conscript camp at Magnolia in Columbia County, conscripts made a public demonstration of their intention to resist the conscription law. Ordered to report, many of those who arrived at the camp decided not to submit to the law. On January 6, 1863, led by a Parson Butler, some forty or fifty persons "young & old" formed a line on the parade ground to show their intention to resist conscription and then walked out of camp.[11]

By February, some men had formed secret organizations that proclaimed openly a desire for an end of the war and a return to the Union. Judge Brown heard that many in the Camden area had joined groups pledged to resist military authority, especially conscription. At least one of them, a band in Ouachita County, had reportedly armed itself to resist any military force that authorities might send to enforce the law. In Calhoun County a "union league" led by William J. Wyatt formed, and its members swore an oath to support each other against conscription and the Confederacy. A Union scout found the same type of opposition in Clark County, where Unionists had organized and had armed and equipped themselves with Confederate supplies. The scout believed they would cooperate with any Federal movement into the area. General Holmes received reports indicating that these secret societies were numerous.[12]

Although it is difficult to measure the number of men who became part of this opposition, it is clear that public officials thought it was significant enough to pose a threat. Judge Brown heard that several of the bands organized around Camden consisted of between twenty and forty men. Residents of Pike and Clark Counties informed officials that Captain Greer's company of dissidents in Pike County had as many as three hundred men in it. A band active near Arkadelphia claimed to have at least eighty-three men. Confederate authorities never offered their own assessment of the numbers involved, but they agreed that the numbers were large. Federal estimates suggest that the numbers may have been even larger. After Lieutenant Colonel Henry C. Caldwell of the Third Iowa Cavalry led a Federal expedition into Clark and Pike Counties in 1864, he reported that there were hundreds of "loyal" men, hiding in the mountains bordering the southwestern counties, who claimed to have fled from their homes to avoid being hanged by Confederate authorities.[13]

The appearance of such groups caused both authorities and local civilians to wonder what had taken place to produce such a crisis and to speculate on what had generated such disloyalty. Some of those reporting on what was taking place believed that deserters from the Confederate army formed the core of the disloyal groups gathering locally. One observer contended that bad food, exposure, hard duty, and news of the destitution of their families made them natural recruits to dissident groups. Thus they slipped away from the army, sometimes in whole squads. In Pike County a Captain Greer, alleged to have been a captain of a company that had been raised in Jefferson County and who had failed to pass his examinations, led one such band. When he deserted he took many of his men with him, and they established themselves at "Greasy Cove," a mountain pass at the head of the Little Missouri River. From there they raided the nearby neighborhoods and challenged Confederate authorities to dislodge them. It was clear, however, that the Greer band included more than deserters. The *Washington Telegraph* described it as consisting of "deserters, disaffected persons, and turbulent characters."[14]

While individual reasons clearly played a role in the growing resistance to Confederate authority and conscription was a major issue, from the beginning the opposition clearly was more broadly based. Central to its existence was the breakdown of social order and a growing antagonism among the region's lower classes against the elites. Judge Brown was one of the contemporary observers who believed that authorities deluded themselves when they assessed what was happening as a simple phenomenon. In addition to the deserters who left the army because of their disaffection, Brown believed that many more who resisted conscription were family men who were unwilling to leave their families. And, of course, sincere Unionists who had always opposed the war found an avenue for their political beliefs in joining such groups. That the issue of conscription had unified individuals motivated by varying reasons and had led to widespread unrest amazed Brown. He observed the existence of a "spirit of disloyalty beyond what was expected."[15]

In addition to a reaction against what might be called specific complaints, Brown recognized that disaffection was rooted primarily in the section's lower class. The specific issue that produced disaffection, military service, raised questions among poorer Arkansans concerning broader issues such as the purpose of the war and whether their leaders reflected their interests. Some contemporaries found that poorer members of society believed that the rich were using them and that conscription was the final proof of that abuse. The exemption of slaveholders seemed patently unfair. These observers concluded that certain members of the lower class, as a result, took leadership roles in the growing anti-Confederate movement. In noting the "collisions" that took place in surrounding counties that February, Judge Brown recorded that the majority of resisters were poor men who were reluctant to leave home because they feared for their families. Sam M. Scott, the editor of the *Arkansas Traveller,* who visited the area in April, concluded that opposition to the Confederacy was clearly rooted among the poor.[16]

An examination of the backgrounds of those individuals known to have opposed Confederate authority lends support to the analysis of Judge Brown and Sam Scott. All of those identified as dissidents in Ouachita and Calhoun Counties came from the yeoman class. Although Southern born and bred and the backbone of society, they now opposed the course of the Confederate government. Benjamin F. Nutt, who joined the Union League of Calhoun County, provides a representative example of the type. Thirty-three years old in 1860, this Alabama-born farmer from Locus Bayou Township had $300 in real property and $350 in personal property. Married and the father of five children in 1860, he joined others in the county in 1863 in opposing Confederate authorities. Although the precise details of his actions remain unknown, at some time Confederate authorities identified Nutt as a leader of the resistance and he was arrested and hanged.[17]

Ultimately, the growing dissatisfaction of the yeomanry transcended individual resistance and produced ideas among the dissidents, ideas that identified the basic issue in their conflict with Confederate authorities as one of class. While the extent to which this class-based critique of the government circulated among the lower classes cannot be determined precisely, it is clear that Confederate authorities perceived the existence of the class argument and were concerned with its effect. In their frantic efforts to counter class-oriented discourse with their own propaganda, Confederate civilian and military leaders provided important indirect evidence of its existence. The area's principal newspaper, the *Washington Telegraph,* took elaborate measures to assure citizens that neither the conscription law nor the war itself reflected the interests of the slaveholding elite alone. Indeed, John Eakin of the *Telegraph* became the foremost spokesman for the Confederate effort at beating down class hostilities.

Eakin began with an editorial published on December 17, 1862. In it he defended the conscription law from those who charged that the exemption provisions were nothing more than a way to allow the rich to escape duty while using up poor men in the army. He justified exemption as necessary for the protection of local communities. Eakin wrote, "Some one *must* be with the slaves: that is certain. The poor creatures are liable to be led astray and ruined. They need control, discipline, kindly advice. They must be cared for and clothed. They must be kept at work, and, by the products of their industry, support our armies." According to Eakin, the law was not intended to benefit the rich but was solely for the good of the community. He went on, "[I]f these views seem reasonable to the conscript, it may quiet his murmurs, and cause him to look with less discontent upon the more fortunate owner of slaves, who is called to remain at home. It may satisfy him, also, that our rulers have not drawn a line between him and his neighbors. That they may not have pandered to the wealthy, and oppressed the poor."[18]

In a second editorial that appeared on the same day Eakin provided evidence that the protest against conscription had raised questions about the entire character of the war. Someone was asking why the war was being fought. In an editorial entitled "For What Are We Fighting?" the newspaperman defended the war as a struggle to protect the idealized society believed to have been in existence during the antebellum years. All Southerners, and the poor especially, had a stake in Confederate victory. "It is a miserable fallacy," he wrote, "to say that the poor man has no interest in this war." The Southerner's country's survival was at stake, and Eakin believed it was a country that offered whites more advantages than any other in the world. Eakin concluded, "If we fail, the poor man goes to hopeless poverty, and he and his posterity, with here and there a lucky exception, become hewers of wood and drawers of water for capitalists whom he can never hope to rival."[19]

As Confederate authorities organized to suppress the armed bands gathering in southwest Arkansas, Eakin wrote on February 4, 1863, that the people suffered from a false idea that the war was for the protection of slave property. The idea flourished and he complained that it would not die, despite the fact that the slave states of the South offered white men the best country in the world in which to exist and be free of a class system with social rankings. He concluded, "Throughout the South the poorest man of decent morals is the peer of the proudest. . . . Such is the social system for which we contend."[20]

Not all leaders, however, minimized the concerns of the poor or tried to convince them of their common interests with the rich. From an unexpected quarter, Rufus K. Garland, brother of Confederate congressman Augustus H. Garland, defended the revolt of the poor and demanded publicly that officials become sensitive to the concerns of that class. In a letter to the *Washington Telegraph,* Garland contended that Southerners were accustomed to a classless society and that was what made the conscription law so unacceptable. "It will be seen," he wrote, "that any legislation which *may be construed* into an effort to make distinctions of this kind [class distinctions], will meet with opposition from them [poor men] sooner than in another other country on the globe." Garland believed that dissatisfaction was based firmly in the awareness of the lower classes of these distinctions and the desire to protect themselves from abuse.[21]

The Confederate authorities found themselves with a broad-based and widespread revolt on their hands, but they refused to recognize the legitimacy of the popular complaints or to make accomodations with the dissidents. They refused to listen to Garland's warning. Instead, they moved aggressively to suppress with force the individual and organized opposition. Clearly, Confederate authorities believed that what was taking place in southwest Arkansas was very serious. As early as December 1862, General Holmes mentioned to President Davis that he needed permission to declare martial law in order to control conditions that promoted dissent. He finally asked for that permission in January 1863. In a letter to Senator Robert W. Johnson on February 16, he indicated that the situation was out of hand and described disaffection as so rampant and strong that he was not sure he could "put down" the disaffected "without an outbreak." Holmes represented opposition to conscription as "universal" in a letter to Major General John G. Walker two days later and described it as dangerous, especially when "sustained and strengthened" by deserters and jayhawkers. Davis finally suspended the writ of habeas corpus on January 29, and Holmes acted on February 9 to impose martial law.[22]

Holmes, having secured the suspension of the writ of habeas corpus, acted immediately to suppress what he termed local "disaffection." The general authorized the enrollment of partisan ranger companies for use in rounding up deserters, enforcing conscription, and suppressing dissent. A company of citizens from Pike, Polk, Hempstead, and Sevier Counties organized under his authority to suppress "lawless associations" in the mountains of Pike, Polk, and Montgomery Counties. They proclaimed their willingness to go anywhere at a "minute's warning" to relieve loyal citizens from such groups. Holmes apparently also detached regular Confederate army units for service in the task.[23]

The units sent into the area and the local militia units moved quickly. The commander in the field was Major James T. Elliott. Elliott was a prominent resident of Camden who had been president of the Mississippi, Ouachita, and Red River Railroad before the war. In July 1862, he received a commission as a major in the Confederate army and was named provost marshal for the Second District of Arkansas. Subsequently, he was appointed enrolling officer and commandant of conscripts for the southwestern quarter of the state. Elliott took the field that spring to lead local militia and detached companies of Arkansas and Texas cavalry against the dissidents.[24]

No records remain of the extent and nature of Elliott's operations in the southwest, but Holmes informed relatives in March that he had sent "three or four active and sharp expeditions" into the area and noted that the "principle [*sic*] leaders" of the uprising had been killed or captured. Judge John Brown had no details to provide, but recorded in his diary at the end of February that "collisions" had taken place between organizations opposed to conscription and the authorities.[25]

Several specific clashes provide some evidence of the actions carried out by Elliott's troops. Henry Merrell, one of the owners of a cotton mill in Pike County, reported that one local group of partisans had been organized under Captain Morgan to attack the Greer camp on the Little Missouri in Pike County after they had attacked a Mr. Henderson, who was carrying salt from Sevier County to Hot Spring County. In an attack probably in late January, the Confederate company "stormed their entrenchments and broke them up." In the battle some were killed outright, but their leaders, Greer and a man named Clark, were hanged. Others apparently were taken prisoner and sent to Little Rock, but there is no record as to what happened to them.[26]

In Calhoun County an episode took place referred to cryptically in the press only as the Calhoun County Rebellion. It perhaps was associated with the organization of the "union league" in that area. At least three members of this league were hanged as a result of the government's action in the county—Dick Gammell, Cabet Sillimore, and Benjamin Nutt. In April, Henry G. Orr of the Twelfth Texas Cavalry informed his sister that his unit was guarding "one 'Jay Hawker,' as they [were] styled—men who organized to resist conscription—he [was] from Calhoun County." Three weeks later he noted, "[T]he jayhawker we had here several weeks ago was taken home (to Calhoun County) and hung there." This may have been the alleged captain of the group, William J. Wyatt, who was arrested by military authorities and held for a time as a jayhawker. Another individual, Simon D. Simmons, was indicted for being a member of a secret society, although the court record provided no evidence of crime or of the individual's involvement in the local movement.[27]

On February 15, a Confederate force attacked another group that had been operating on the Ouachita River in the vicinity of Arkadelphia in what locals referred to as the battle of McGrew's Mill. Captain Henry B. Stuart, circuit judge for Clark County, led the company and attacked a band led by a Captain Brown. The Confederates declared victory, claiming to have killed eleven and wounded large numbers more and to have captured twenty prisoners. Brown's men left the area, although they reported that they had rebuffed the Confederate force, losing only two killed and four wounded to the Confederate loss of sixteen killed and twelve wounded. Brown's group, claiming to be pro-Union, then escaped to northwest Arkansas where some of the men reputedly joined the First Arkansas Infantry (Union) at Fayetteville.[28]

Individuals recorded continuing clashes between the military and civilian groups in the weeks that followed. Citizens of Calhoun, Dallas, and Ouachita Counties met on March 12, 1863, to organize independent citizens' companies to defend themselves against lawless clans of "jayhawkers, and others avoiding the conscription law and now laying out in the swamps and secret places in the country." The citizens committee pledged revenge against all members of such clans and cooperation with cavalry acting in the area under Major Elliott. Judge Brown noted in his diary that troops in the Camden area had clashed with bands of armed "civilians" and that many of those civilians had been shot, hung, or had left the country to join the enemy.[29]

In addition to military action, Confederate military courts prosecuted dissidents vigorously, even after violent clashes came to an end. The extent of the actions of the military courts is unknown because of the nature of the record, but Unionists contended that the violence against them was widespread and at least some men were tried and executed by the courts. In 1865 one of the military judges for the state, George C. Watkins, was arrested and charged with treason for presiding over trials in which "hundreds" of conscripts were tried and shot, and no records of the proceedings kept. Unfortunately, at least as far as understanding more fully the operations of the Confederate courts, Watkins never came to trial and no evidence of his activities was presented.[30]

At least some indication of the work of the courts may be found in the appeals made to civilian courts after martial law was suspended in February 1863. Some of those arrested by military authorities appealed for release to the civil courts. These appeals led to a serious clash between military and civilian authorities. Applying for writs of habeas corpus on the grounds that the military had interfered with civil justice, they asked to be placed in the hands of the civilian courts. Incomplete district court records for the period make it impossible to determine how all of these appeals came out, but Confederate authorities tried to prevent the releases of men they had arrested. In one instance in April 1863, Circuit Judge Lafayette B. Green issued a writ for William J. Wyatt which local military authorities refused to honor. Green and others protested to the governor and commanding general about this refusal by the military to obey civilian authorities. Military authorities, in turn, actively protested any action that would release Wyatt from their custody. Conscript commander Benjamin F. Danley wrote to Harris Flanagin on April 4 and requested that the governor "prevent the interference of the civil authorities" in the punishment of Wyatt, who

Danley called a notorious jayhawker. Wyatt's fate is not known with certainty, but as has been shown, there is every reason to believe that the military continued to hold him and probably executed him in the end.[31]

On the surface the efforts at suppressing the opposition appeared successful. Confederate leaders reassured each other that they had acted quickly enough to get the situation under control. As early as February 25, the Little Rock *True Democrat* reported that it was "gratified to learn that the dissatisfaction at the exemption clause of the conscript act . . . ha[d] subsided." Calling opponents "jayhawkers," the editor observed that they were "beginning to see the error of their ways" and concluded that "their numbers [were] too small and the material too unprincipled to hang together long." Holmes officially proclaimed the upheaval in the southwest at an end when he informed the president in March that he did not believe he would have to resort to further use of force in suppressing disaffection. In a letter in April, he concluded that his actions had "relieved [him] from apprehension": "They are now put down everywhere and quiet is restored." These conclusions, however, were premature, and violent resistance to Confederate authorities continued through the rest of the war years.[32]

General Holmes may have been optimistic about the impact that his actions against the active dissenters had on general disenchantment with the Confederate cause, but reports from the southwest indicated that while he may have dispersed some of the armed groups, the resistance did not die that spring. Sam Scott informed Flanagin in April that he found opposition untamed. In a letter to the governor, Scott reported that in Clark County "the spirit of discontent, in regard to the conscript law, [was] far from being allayed—rather increased." Further, Scott found that the idea that the upper classes were against the poor persisted. He found that "the old cry of poor men being obliged to fight for the rich may be heard on all sides."[33]

The refusal of the class-based criticism of the Confederate government to die was apparent in the continued effort by Eakin and the *Washington Telegraph* to counter the idea. In September 1863, Eakin once again called for class unity in the face of the growing military crisis. He wrote, "You have been accustomed to see your fellows around you rising by industry in the social scale step by step to the highest rounds of the ladder. You have congratulated yourself that you live in a country where this was possible to all. . . . Know, then, that they will never be possible in a Union forced upon us by the calamities of war."[34]

It is also clear that General Holmes had failed to suppress the operations of dissident bands in the mountains to the north of the southwestern counties. Judge Brown reported that Jayhawkers existed in force in these areas. Other information indicates that many of these bands carried out a continuing war against those who tried to suppress them. The reduction of the war into one of personal vendetta that characterized the northern counties emerged in the southwest. In Pike County, Captain Morgan, commander of partisans that had destroyed the Greer band, was ambushed and killed later in the war. In addition, Captain Flowers, another "regulator," was also assassinated by ambushers in Hot Spring County.[35]

State agents sent throughout the southwestern counties that autumn found, if anything, that the anti-Confederate sentiment had expanded, that it remained widespread, and that the military had failed to suppress it. Benjamin Danley wrote to Flanagin from Washington, Arkansas, in September, "[A] great many deserters and refractory conscripts in the country . . . are running at large and will continue to do so until an armed force can be produced to arrest them." Captain Barton J. Brown informed the governor from Columbia County on October 6 that there was "undoubtedly a Union sentiment prevailing among a large class of citizens here & nothing but assistance [would] insure prompt action."[36]

In fact, the Confederacy never regained the hearts of many of the people of southwestern Arkansas during the war. Soldiers returning from the front increasingly expressed dissatisfaction with their leaders and with events. Authorities were forced to turn to more draconian measures to procure soldiers or to secure cooperation from civilians. A Union officer, Lieutenant Colonel Henry Caldwell, returned from an expedition into southwestern Arkansas in 1864 and reported that Union sympathizers there had told him of continuing persecution of Unionists and others who opposed the war by Confederate authorities. He wrote, "Every conceivable means has been used to force [them] into the rebel service; they have been hung by scores; they have been hunted down with blood hounds by the slaveholding rebels of Red river Valley; they have been robbed of their property, chained and imprisoned."[37] By the war's end General Joseph O. Shelby received orders for his forces to impress for service every man they encountered between the ages of sixteen and fifty, and his men were instructed to ensure their compliance by using "all the force in [their] power, and when necessary [they] shot them down." Any solidarity among white Arkansans in support of the Confederacy had clearly given way.[38]

The dissent which began in the spring of 1863 in southwestern Arkansas had significant implications for the state through the rest of the war and into the postwar period. Mobilization of white Arkansans against the Confederacy forced the Confederacy to respond with force. Jayhawkers, Unionists, or deserters prowled on the edges of Confederate Arkansas and consumed military resources, energy, and time. Their existence and the need for troops to suppress them did not disrupt the war effort significantly, but their presence did undermine civilian morale to some degree. Of course, the presence of Confederate troops who despoiled civilians was an equally oppressive burden felt by civilians and makes it difficult to measure the extent to which the dissenters alone undermined civilian morale.[39]

The problems in southwest Arkansas contributed more directly to Confederate defeat in other ways. Many men left the area as the friction grew and some clearly joined the Union army. Dissidents from Clark County joined Colonel M. La Rue Harrison at Fayetteville in the autumn of 1863. Approximately three hundred men joined a Union expedition in November 1863 at Caddo Gap so that they could enlist in a regiment being organized by a Colonel Arnold. Arnold was from the area and led a party of scouts that had accompanied the expedition.[40]

In addition, events helped produce a collapse of local communities. If the white population of southwestern Arkansas had been united before the war began, clearly the internal war that broke out after 1863 tore the fabric of their society. For a significant number of poor people, the war destroyed, at least for the moment, any belief that they shared a common destiny with their wealthier neighbors or that the antebellum and wartime leadership reflected their interests. Reports of social conflict indicated that soldiers and rural folks were particularly hostile toward town folks. Hostility was felt between those who left and those who remained.[41]

As has been seen, however, this fragmentation of society increasingly took on class tones; and the conflict contributed to a growing sense of class consciousness or class division within the state. The immediate cause for dissent may have been dissatisfaction with Confederate military service and conscription, but from the beginning those who fought for the Confederacy came to see themselves as poor men who were having to fight a war to benefit rich men. Their own opportunities were being squandered in a conflict that had no goal other than the protection of slavery. Their fight was not only with conscription but also with the ruling class.

The extent and role of internal strife in Arkansas during the war also had implications for the postwar history of Arkansas and the South as well.

For example, it helps explain why opponents of the Democratic party during Reconstruction relied heavily on class appeals when seeking political support. They thought that they could secure broad backing from among the state's poorer whites, men who had been the object of military suppression. When a correspondent of the Little Rock *Republican* linked the Democratic party with the "gentlemen" who had brought starvation, death, and devastation to the "wool hat and cooperas breeches" men, gentlemen who had caused poor farmers and mechanics to be conscripted while they were "at home wallowing in their riches," he was appealing to the interests of a very real constituency.[42]

At the same time that the disarray of society, a disarray that had grown during the war years, makes sense of Republican political strategy, it also raises questions about the course of Reconstruction. No matter what had taken place during the war, the old leadership regained power by 1874, only eight years after the end of the war. That political end ultimately required the old elites to either suppress dissent among whites or regain their trust and support. Any understanding of that result must ultimately come to grips with how the Democratic leadership accomplished that end. In Arkansas and probably the rest of the South, history must take into account how the question of social conflict among whites, conflict that had been generated by the war, was resolved.

In the end, the conflict within southwestern Arkansas did not decide the outcome of the Civil War, although it added to the complicated picture producing that result. What did happen, however, was the collapse of the harmonious white society that had existed before the war. In the end, it left an Arkansas not only where individuals nurtured personal grievances but also where a potential conflict between poor and rich whites always lurked in the background. Thus, the struggle in the southwest helped to shape future Arkansas history.

Chapter 7

Guerrillas: The Real War in Arkansas

Daniel E. Sutherland

In May 1862, the colonel of the Ninth Illinois Cavalry reported that the body of one of his men, Private Philander W. Pringle, had been found lying in a swamp near Jacksonport. He was the third man found shot and the second to have died since the regiment's arrival. These shootings mark in a very real sense the beginning of guerrilla warfare in Arkansas, for Private Pringle had been murdered by a partisan. "A most bitter and malignant spirit" prevailed throughout Jackson County, reported the colonel. "This morning," he expanded on May 24, "a small band was seen in the timber having arms in their hands. These people will conceal their weapons and appear as good Union men," he complained. The colonel needed advice. "I wish to know what course to pursue with regard to the guerrillas in this county," he concluded to General Frederick Steele, "and hope you will issue a proclamation telling the people hereabouts what they may expect in case they continue to commit murders as heretofore." Henceforth, Federal military commanders in Arkansas would have to take guerrillas into account.[1]

This is how the Civil War was fought in Arkansas: ambushes, midnight raids, often with civilians treated as combatants and neighbors turned predators. Not a war within a war, as some historians have suggested, not even a second war, but *the* war. Traditional set-piece battles did unfold at places like Pea Ridge and Prairie Grove, but most of the fighting, most of the terror and suffering in wartime Arkansas, came from irregular warfare, and it devastated the land and people. Virtually every part of the South, especially remote or rugged regions like the Appalachians, suffered the ravages of guerrilla fighting, but Arkansas and Missouri may have witnessed the most sustained combat of this kind.

A large literature exists for guerrilla warfare, but only recently did very much of it explore the War between the States.[2] Virgil C. Jones and Richard S. Brownlee published the first historical studies of Civil War guerrillas during the mid-1950s. Jones concentrated on the eastern theater while Brownlee described the Trans-Mississippi. Both authors focused on the exploits of romantic or notorious guerrilla leaders, such as John S. Mosby, William C. Quantrill, and William T. "Bloody Bill" Anderson. They largely neglected the social and economic impact of guerrilla warfare on Southern communities, and they seemed uninterested in the lives of the guerrilla rank and file.[3] The situation improved but little in the 1970s, although Albert Castel produced a slender survey of the guerrilla war across the South, and Don R. Bowen grappled with the issue of why men turned to guerrilla war in Missouri.[4] But not until the 1980s did historians finally consider the broader implications and consequences of the guerrilla war. Since then, a series of excellent books and articles by Phillip S. Paludan, Michael Fellman, Thomas Goodrich, Benjamin Franklin Cooling, Noel C. Fisher, and others have begun to untangle the extremely complex world of Civil War guerrillas.[5]

The first serious consideration given to the guerrilla war in Arkansas came in 1965 with an article by Leo E. Huff. Yet Huff largely followed the Jones-Brownlee prescription of concentrating on partisan leaders. He noted the social chaos and physical destruction produced by guerrilla warfare, but he backed away from any systematic analysis. Some important work on the irrregular war in Arkansas has been done since then, yet most of it remains buried in masters theses and doctoral dissertations, many of which focus on larger wartime issues.[6]

This belated appreciation of the guerrilla war generally and Arkansas guerrillas in particular is not difficult to explain. Guerrillas have been as hard for historians to pin down as they were for Federal and Confederate regulars. Surviving official records, such as *War of the Rebellion,* frequently mention partisans, but usually in the most obscure manner. Private records of the war, principally correspondence and diaries, reveal little about guerrilla operations. For a long time, the story of Arkansas's irregular war remained an oral tradition. Not until the late nineteenth century did surviving guerrillas write or dictate their stories, and piecing together the entire story from these colorful fragments, even against the backdrop of private and official records, is a formidable job. Thus guerrillas have remained shadow warriors, "ghosts," as both Jones and Brownlee suggested.[7]

Useful and intriguing as these early attempts to understand Arkansas's guerrilla war have been, a topic with such rich potential for exploring the nature of the war warrants more comprehensive treatment. This can be done only by moving beyond traditional tales of heroism and knavery, beyond the exploits of acknowledged bandits and bushwhackers, to consider how partisan fighters helped to shape the strategic and tactical patterns of the war. Our understanding of the topic being so limited, it seems logical to start small and focus on three specific subjects: the reasons men became guerrillas, their roles in Confederate service, and the effectiveness of Confederate guerrilla operations.

If ever necessity bore a child, it fought as a guerrilla for the Confederacy's Trans-Mississippi armies. Guerrillas became important adjuncts to the Rebel army in Missouri by the autumn of 1861. Indeed, Missourians, owing to their participation in the Bleeding Kansas border war, had been honing their skills as guerrillas for several years by that time. The first skirmishes in Arkansas came in February 1862, and as Federal columns penetrated as far south as Fayetteville and Batesville, Arkansans became guerrillas in self-defense. The Confederate government had not committed nearly enough troops to Arkansas, and Federal soldiers easily overpowered or simply bypassed local defense forces. Sensing their impotence against well-armed and numerically superior forces, Arkansas defenders struck the enemy's flanks and rear. A member of a Texas "spy company" (detached scouts) stationed at Little Rock reported that a half dozen of his friends took to the bush in early May to harass the advancing Federals. "I don't suppose it is expected for our little company to fight them much," he reasoned, "but to watch them close and occasionally get one or two." Such would be the pattern of guerrilla operations for companies like his for the remainder of the war.[8]

As overwhelmed communities across the Upper South found themselves in similar straits by April 1862, the Confederate government authorized, through the Partisan Ranger Act, the use of irregular units. General Earl Van Dorn, in mid-May 1862, became the first Confederate commander to recruit guerrillas in Arkansas. He had little choice, for in the chaotic aftermath of his army's retreat from Pea Ridge, in March, hundreds of men had deserted to fight in isolated bands, most of them in northwest Arkansas. General Thomas C. Hindman, commanding the Confederacy's Trans-Mississippi District, gave his official blessing to the formal organization of guerrilla bands, or "independent companies," in June. He also continued to use already existing bands, both those that had arrived from Texas and Missouri and the ones recognized by Van Dorn. The new companies, formed into groups of ten or more men, were to arm themselves and receive pay and allowances only for subsistence and forage. Companies would elect their own officers and, in theory, be "governed in all respects by the same regulations as other troops."[9]

And just here appeared the strongest attraction of partisan warfare. Frequently detached from what might be called the *paper army,* with all its regulations, guerrillas thrived on independent action. The Partisan Ranger Act and Hindman's directive legitimized the sort of freewheeling operations favored by many Arkansas Confederates. George T. Maddox of Madison County left regular Confederate service after the battle of Prairie Grove. "That kind of warfare did not suit me," explained Maddox. "I wanted to get out where I could have it more lively; where I could fight if I wanted to, or run if I so desired; I wanted to be my own general." Maddox and men like him were fighters, not soldiers, and they acknowledged no formalities of war or restrictions on how, when, or where they might strike the enemy. Joseph M. Bailey of Carroll County served as a Confederate volunteer for two years before joining an "independent company" in northern Arkansas. "Most of these men," he concluded of his fellow partisans, "preferred the free but more hazardous life of independent soldier and scout, to the more irksome duties of the regularly organized forces of the Confederate Army." Yet another partisan found the style of warfare exhilarating. "It is very exciting to be in the enemy's country not knowing what moment we will be attacked," he cavalierly informed his worried wife. "When we camp, we hunt for a swamp and then move before day."[10]

Men who had been serving in Confederate units outside Arkansas or distant from their homes often deserted the paper army, not just to do as they pleased but to fight *where* it most mattered, near their homes. Men subject to conscription, if sympathetic to the Confederate cause, often did the same. Even citizens not subject to conscription—middle-aged men and boys—sometimes took up arms as "bushwhackers" to defend their homes. When Federal troops and jayhawkers launched raids in the vicinity of Petit Jean, "daily and nightly . . . stealing and often publicly taking all the good Horses, Saddles, Bridles, Guns & ammunition, Provisions, etc.," local folk acted. "We are driven to the necessity a few of us," complained a man seeking help from Confederate authorities, "of laying in the bushes in order to guard their passes to our neighbourhoods every night, with only a force of 20 or 25 men and boys."[11]

One partisan officer took exception to the image of guerrillas as deserters and outlaws who contributed nothing to the Confederate cause. "Theas men hom' I reported Diserted is in North of the Arkansas River with Captain Love," he asserted, "fiten the federls Ever chance tha get." Captain Love was Captain James Harrison Love, a farmer from Searcy County in peacetime, but organizer and leader of an independent company that fought in and around Love's home on the Buffalo River through most of the war. Only when Confederate authorities expressly ordered Love's men elsewhere (just three times during the war and never for more than three months at a time) did they stray from Searcy County. In this respect, it is not insignificant that General Hindman, when recruiting partisan bands in June 1862, specified that all companies would "serve in that part of the district to which they belong." Even General Samuel A. Curtis, commanding the Federal Trans-Mississippi Department, recognized this favored mode of organization when he referred to the partisans opposing him around Batesville as "county guerrillas."[12]

General Theophilus H. Holmes, so often denigrated as "Granny Holmes," understood what motivated the guerrilla. Holmes, a West Point graduate and veteran of the Seminole and Mexican wars, disliked partisan warfare. He intended to wage war "upon honorable principles and upon the rules of warfare among civilized nations." On the other hand, Holmes knew that, should the Federals ever occupy Arkansas, and should Confederate fortunes east of the Mississippi take a similarly dismal turn, Southerners would "rise as individuals and each man take upon himself the task of expelling the invaders." Holmes informed a Northern officer, "We hate you with a cordial hatred. You may conquer us and parcel out our lands among your soldiers, but you must remember that one incident of history, to wit, that of all the Russians who settled in Poland not one died a natural death."[13]

Revenge and personal vendetta also counted for much. The origins of this impulse varied. Some people sought revenge against neighbors who had persecuted them for supporting the "wrong" side. Others used the war as an excuse to right old wrongs and settle family feuds. Revenge also explains why partisans, as well as men in the regular forces, sometimes crossed the line between soldier and brigand. Once violence had been done to one's family, neighbors, or home, retaliation frequently followed. This became especially true along the Arkansas-Missouri border, where the families of Confederates and persecuted Unionists, many of them reduced to flight across the border, lived cheek by jowl. "Thus situated," recalled Joseph Bailey, "we were subject to numerous raiding parties from Missouri on the North, and the mountain country [often Unionist territory] to the South. Most of the raids were made more for plunder, than to wage war on armed men." The war became a "struggle for supremacy and revenge," he insisted.[14]

Additional testimony stresses the strength of this motivation. General

Dandridge McRae, who freely utilized detachments of partisans, believed, "The large majority of these who joined the guerilla bands had deadly wrongs to avenge and this gave to all their combats that sanguinary [*sic*] which yet remains a part of the guerilla's legacy." Guerrillas, he added, practiced "individual vengeance acting through a community of bitter memories." Men like George Maddox often "went to the bush" to retaliate against Kansas Jayhawkers, Confederate and Federal deserters, and "natural thieves" who had harassed, robbed, or murdered civilians. "They [guerrillas] would have staid in the regular army if it had not been that their friends had been so cruelly treated as they had," he elaborated.[15]

The use of guerrillas also suited military and physical conditions in Arkansas. The terrain clearly favored guerrilla actions. Mountains and deep rivers cloaked the northern half of the state; swamps blanketed the delta and much of the southern part. Baron Carl von Clausewitz would have nodded approvingly. No Arkansas partisan had read the untranslated Clausewitz, but his masterpiece, *On War*, stressed the "benefit of terrain" for defensive guerrilla operations. Federal armies soon learned the wisdom of Clausewitz. One general, perplexed by his subordinates' inability to control the guerrilla menace in northwest Arkansas, advised a colonel, "Posts and highways are not the places to find bushwhackers. The by-ways and mountain paths your men know so well are the real tracks to glory and honor. Night marches, sudden attacks, ambuscades, and untiring pursuit are the only cure for bushwhackers and guerrillaism." Even an untutored partisan ranger could appreciate the Confederate advantage of terrain. "There has been more done here and with fewer men than any other part [of the state]," he reported from swampy White County. "So it does not require many men to harass a considerable army."[16]

Guerrilla warfare also suited the objectives of Confederate strategy in Arkansas. Hindman, in 1862, expressly charged his "independent companies" with conducting the type of operations pursued by guerrillas in Missouri, that is, "destroying wagon trains and transports, tearing up railways, breaking the telegraph lines, capturing towns, and thus compelling the enemy to keep there a large force that might have been employed elsewhere."[17] From 1862 until the end of the war, guerrillas, often described in Federal reports as "wandering Confederates and marauders," "thieves," "railraiders," "pirates," and "demons," reveled in such actions, as well as in stealing horses and mules, firing on riverboats, capturing Federal stragglers and foragers, and confiscating Federal supplies. They even stole cotton from Federally leased plantations, cotton that could be sold at large profits by 1864. In one particularly successful operation between Little Rock and Benton, guerrillas employed the services of several staunchly Confederate women to drive wagons loaded with purloined cotton.[18]

Perhaps the most annoying element of guerrilla strategy—and certainly the most costly in economic terms—was the disruption of river traffic and the confiscation of river cargo. "From here to Memphis, guerrillas line the shore," reported a frantic Federal from Helena early in 1863, "and are as familiar with trade as if they had sent for their goods." The guerrillas held the boats, lifted the cargoes, and then served as "commissaries to the interior." The United States government seemed to be "feeding them [the Confederates] with one hand and fighting them with the other." Colonel Archibald S. Dobbin, deemed "a notorious brigand" by some Federals, annoyed in every conceivable way Federal boats along the White River between St. Charles and Clarendon. A. C. McCoy's band seized and burned Federal boats near Helena. What was worse, Rebel merchants frequently sold these confiscated goods, even to the Federal army. "The people on the route are all rebels," complained one general of traffic along the White River, "implicated in purchasing the property and horses and mules stolen from the leased plantations." The general recommended in May 1863 an "abrogation of all trade stores on the Arkansas and White Rivers, and to allow no trade on the Mississippi" until peace was restored.[19]

Guerrilla strategy, if not official Confederate strategy, also recognized terrorization of civilians as a legitimate goal. Unfortunately, the best *method* of achieving the *goal* of terror was, likewise, terror. Confederate partisans insisted that they acted only in kind. "The guerrillas who traverse the country shoot every Union man they see mercilessly," insisted a Federal colonel from Carrollton in March 1863. "The operations of the enemy's guerrillas in Arkansas," he continued, "are far more vindictive and remorseless than anywhere else under my observation." At Batesville, toward the end of the year, another Federal colonel had to prohibit the organization of a pro-Union home guard for fear that its members would suffer retribution. The countryside was "fearfully lawless," he insisted. "When a man commits himself to the Union now, he must stay with the Federal troops for safety, and dare not go home." These remarks came several months after the capture of Little Rock and the supposed "occupation" of northern Arkansas.[20]

Down in Montgomery County, far from either Carrollton or Batesville, conditions remained similar well into 1864. Both the citizens of that county and a company of the Fourth Arkansas Cavalry (Union) sent there to protect them beseeched Little Rock for reinforcements. "Deeds of cruelty and barbarity that would shame Indians are of daily occurrence," wailed the petitioners. On one day alone, guerrillas had shot a woman and her year-old baby, she in both shoulders, the child in both arms. Next, they mowed down a doctor, and as he lay mortally wounded, the guerrillas finished him off by blowing out his brains. They shot a second man on the same day in a "brutal and cowardly manner." Generally, loyal citizens complained, "The plundering of houses, breaking and burning of cotton cards, wheels, etc., belonging to Union citizens is of common occurrence."[21]

Finally, a short-term yet dangerously potent motivation for waging guerrilla war during 1864 centered on that year's Northern election. If the Confederacy could intensify and prolong the war to the point where George B. McClellan, the Democratic "peace" candidate, could be elected president, Southern independence might be won. At the very least, a magnanimous surrender might be negotiated. Thus, guerrilla activity revived all across Arkansas in the summer of 1864, in part because partisans had been encouraged by the failed Federal Red River campaign, but more directly because of the election season. Attacks on riverboats, Federal patrols, and communication lines highlighted the resurgence. Confederate soldiers and guerrillas reported themselves in high spirits. "I learn on fair authority," insisted a Federal general to President Lincoln from DeValls Bluff, "that the explanation of this unusual feeling is that the rebel leaders have represented that by prolonging the war and successfully resisting the Federal authority a little longer they will defeat your election." Confederate civilians understood the stakes, too. "My opinion is that we are getting stronger and they weaker every day," observed a Judge Hayes from Chicot County, "and if we can hold our own the present [political] campaign will bring things to a *crisis* in the North."[22]

Recognizing the spirited determination of these guerrillas, Confederate leaders in Arkansas sought to channel their fiery brand of warfare against Federal forces. Indeed, regular Confederate troops had no option but to tap guerrilla strength. One cannot emphasize too strongly the determination made in Richmond that nearly every other area of the Confederacy held priority over the Trans-Mississippi for the distribution of troops and supplies. Jefferson Davis had not even given adequate protection to New Orleans before it fell in April 1862. Thus Confederate military commanders in Arkansas knew that if they were to have any chance of defending the state, they could do so only with the aid of guerrillas. That the inclination of individual partisans and the strength of their style of combat fit the Confederacy's strategic purposes was fortuitous.[23]

Confederate commanders early on sought to integrate guerrilla operations into their strategic plans. Van Dorn accompanied his call for partisans with specific instructions for immediate action. His irregular adjuncts were to "harass" the Federal flanks and rear, disrupt supply lines, destroy supplies, and defend all crossing points along the Arkansas River "to the last extremity." Van Dorn stressed that he relied entirely on these "isolated" bands "to act promptly and energetically in resisting and defeating the invasion of the State." Likewise, Hindman, who had been particularly impressed by the victory of partisans at Lone Jack, Missouri, in August 1862, determined to defend Arkansas with independent companies assigned as "guides, scouts, and guerrillas." He raised an irregular force of nearly five thousand men in just a few months. The turning point toward heavy reliance on guerrilla tactics and forces came as a result of Confederate defeat at Prairie Grove, in December 1862. That battle clearly showed the inability of the Rebels to match the numbers of Federal invaders. Thereafter, the Confederates emphasized guerrilla operations and raids, and even the raids depended on partisan bands for their implementation and success.[24]

These units could be formidable. The most effective guerrillas were tough hombres, armed to the teeth and prepared to shoot first and ask questions later. One can imagine these determined men swaggering through the countryside, ready to obliterate any challenge to their domain. One man, seeking permission to form a "spie company," envisioned having a "fine time going in the Yankee lines" to collect plunder and gather information about the enemy. "We will expect to be treated as Jay Hawkers," he reflected matter-of-factly, "or Gurillers when caught, and will do the same with all Yanks we catch." Colonel Thomas H. McCray, himself something of an irregular, knew precisely the sort of men to recruit for his personal escort. While issuing orders to execute all independent and renegade bushwhackers, both Northern and Southern, McCray also recruited Captain Howell Rayburn (known as Doc Rayburn or Yellow Doc) and his band of some forty guerrillas to protect him and his staff.[25]

Rowdy Texans, many of whom answered the call for help from Arkansas, struck terror in the hearts of Union soldiers. Members of Colonel William H. Parsons's Texas cavalry brigade, which often served on detached service as scouts and raiders if not genuine irregulars in Arkansas, were particularly ferocious fighters. "[The Federals] have a great deal more fear of Texas Rangers than they have of the devil," boasted a member of Parsons's "Swamp Fox" regiment. Another ranger insisted, "[The Federals] have a wholesome dread of the Texans—they dont like our mode of fighting. I believe the Texans mode of fighting is to hurt somebody no matter how that is." A member of Alfred Johnson's "spy company" delighted in telling how he and his friends routed a Yankee camp. "When the yell was raised," he chuckled, "the Fed captain told his men, 'Texas Rangers.' He broke and told them to take care of themselves." Yet another man observed, "The Yankees are as afraid as death of the Texans and curse us for everything they can think of for 'bushwhacking' them."[26]

Independent companies frequently worked in conjunction with regular Confederate troops from mid-1862 until the end of the war. Quantrill brought his guerrilla band south to act as scouts for Rebel cavalry during the winter of 1862–63. In a battle at Fayetteville, in April 1863, the colonel of the First Arkansas Cavalry (Union) identified four companies of "bushwhackers" operating with General William L. Cabell's troops. Far from being mere bushwhackers, most of the men were led by recognized partisan captains, including William "Buck" Brown and Peter Mankins. Additionally, the first battalion of Parsons's Twelfth Texas Cavalry formed part of Cabell's command. In January 1864, General John S. Sanborn, commanding the District of Southwest Missouri, faced the threat of raids into Missouri by twelve hundred to two thousand "Confederate soldiers and bushwhackers" who had rendezvoused in Newton, Searcy, Izard, and Carroll Counties.[27]

The two largest Confederate raids into Missouri—led by General Joseph O. Shelby September through November 1863 and by General Sterling Price September through October 1864—drew on guerrillas to supplement their columns.[28] Indeed, Shelby's raid depended absolutely on them. "Consolidate and organize them [independent bands] into full companies," came the word from Shelby's headquarters. "Should any refuse resort to any means you deem best to enforce the order."[29] Recognizing the independence of the partisans, the Confederate government in this and similar periods of recruitment always depended on the popularity of individual partisan leaders, themselves sometimes commissioned officers, such as Thomas R. Freeman, McCray, Dobbin, George W. Rutherford, Sidney D. Jackman, and John T. Coffee, to attract recruits in regions where they were known and trusted as protectors of Confederate property and as loyal Rebels. A glance at Confederate tables of organization shows many similar uses of unbrigaded and company-size units serving as adjuncts to Confederate units in Arkansas.[30]

Not that Confederate commanders ever had as much control over these irregulars as they would have wished. Hindman, evidently foreseeing this problem, had placed all partisans under the supervision and direction of the provost marshal's command, but that system of regulating them collapsed within a few months. Partisans resented any attempt by Confederate authorities to interfere with their preferred way of doing things. Fiercely independent bands even remained jealous of one another in some instances, particularly when thrown together in joint efforts. "The various commanders of regiments, companies, and squads have been possessed of a vexatious spirit of dissension and strife, refusing to co-operate with each other, embarrassing the cause and weakening their strength," complained Jo Shelby in the summer of 1864. He expressed dismay over the "barrier of pride and jealousy" that retarded his efforts to unite disparate bands in a common cause. Shelby, on another occasion, became incensed when Colonel Thomas R. Freeman, a sometimes partisan commander, allowed his men to roam the countryside on visits to friends, on hunting expeditions, and to engage in a little bushwhacking. Freeman must immediately order his men back to camp, insisted Shelby, and be prepared to cooperate with regular Confederate forces if he and his men wished to be "recognized as a legitimate command."[31]

Even more worrisome to authorities were those partisan bands whose enthusiasm for the cause—or whose desire for vengeance—led them to "acts of lawlessness" against Arkansas civilians. One of the earliest and most notorious of such actions came against Isaac Murphy, the state's best known Unionist. A swarm of some 150 partisans swept over Murphy's Huntsville home in December 1862. They committed "deprivations" against all Unionist families in the vicinity, but they marked Judge Murphy's family for particular abuse. The marauders carried away everything of value or utility from the Murphy home and left the women, "stripped of everything but what was on their bodies," in a "destitute condition." Refugees provided another inviting target, most often as they trudged northward to seek havens in Federally held portions of Missouri.[32]

And just here lies the thorniest—and perhaps insolvable—riddle involving Arkansas's guerrilla war. Which bands were legitimate and which the freebooters? Which raids and attacks were sanctioned by Confederate authorities and which were launched for private gain? Both Confederate generals and partisan privates appreciated the confusion, and no loyal Confederate wished to be associated with the lawless elements. Confederate authorities, ever sensitive to charges that their partisans had exceeded the bounds of decent behavior, expressed particular chagrin when roving robbers and bushwhackers were mistaken for Confederate auxiliaries. One beleaguered partisan captain, already contending with a numerically superior Federal force in Montgomery and Yell Counties, expressed outrage when civilians in his vicinity reported horses being "jayhawked" by men who claimed to be members of his command. "There has been men in the country committing crimes on my credit," he complained, "and if I find them the weather is two hot to Ride horses to headquarters with any such caracters."[33]

Other Confederate partisans resented the renegades, too. James H. Campbell, serving on "detached service" with Leslie's Battalion, McRea's Brigade, complained that northwest Arkansas was "over-run with deserters, guerrillas and thieves" in the latter part of 1863. All of these scoundrels claimed to belong to either John S. Marmaduke's or Jo Shelby's command, but they spent their time stealing horses and preying on defenseless farmers. "They became so bold and reckless," complained Campbell, "that the battalion to which I belonged was compelled to protect the country and our friends." Consequently, he added, "a very bitter feeling worked up and continued between members of our battalion and this band of desporadoes" who spent more time seeking "plunder and money than serving their country." It did not help matters that most of these brigands hailed from Missouri. Not surprisingly, Campbell's battalion soon received orders to execute any of "these guerrillas" whom they captured.[34]

What was worse, these senseless raids produced havoc in neutral or even pro-Confederate neighborhoods. "We have been tossed and tumbled about considerably by both the Feds and our own soldiers," complained a resident of Chicot County, "and then by bands of independent marauders—calling themselves 'guerillas' and having authority from almost any or every general in the Confederacy or out of it." Another man in the same neighborhood supported this opinion. "What the yankees are unable to get, our own soldiers—or other men in arms—seem to think legitimately belongs to them as spoils of war," he muttered. "The citizen is regarded as lawful prey, nothwithstanding he is the main stay of the army."[35]

For concerned Confederates, it was simply a matter of good public relations. When the "jayhawking captains" of Shelby and Marmaduke raided into Missouri, they went as a "mob" and adopted the "pirates' law of property," admonished one Confederate colonel. "No respect is shown to age, sex, or condition," he complained to President Jefferson Davis. In contrast, he continued, the Federal commander in Arkansas, General Frederick Steele, had earned a reputation for "forbearance, justice and urbanity." Indeed, Steele's sympathetic treatment of known Rebels and slaveholders had even made him suspect in the eyes of Unionists. Partisan leaders thus received orders to control their rambunctious men. "The citizens must and shall be protected in the possession of their property," particularly their livestock, insisted Jo Shelby. "They have thus far shown every disposition to assist us, but if this detestable system of 'jayhawking' is not broken up they will soon come to prefer the Federals to us."[36]

Confederate authorities had to rely on the popularity and forceful personalities of partisan leaders to discourage banditry, just as they relied on those same men to recruit and form partisan bands. Alf Johnson's sway over his men won the respect and allegiance of people in the vicinity of Brownsville. "It is because we have a noble leader," explained one of his admiring men. "He can now get this whole people to follow him." This same man reported on another occasion, "There is not a family east of White River but is willing to do anything for any of our company." Thus in the spring of 1864, while summoning partisans to rendezvous for impending operations, Confederate authorities asked guerrilla chieftains to arrest all "jayhawkers," whether Federal or Confederate, who had committed "outrages upon the citizens." People guilty of such crimes were to be executed and unorganized bands "broken up." Moreover, partisans must give vouchers to all citizens from whom they requisitioned goods and equipment.[37]

Ultimately, the value of Confederate partisans depended on their military effectiveness, and judged by that standard, the Confederacy possessed an extremely useful weapon. The Federals themselves betrayed the guerrilla impact on their operations in four distinct ways: Through warnings to Confederate partisans, through retaliation, through the organization of antiguerrilla forces, and by adopting strategies to combat guerrilla activity.[38]

By September 1862, Federal and Confederate commanders in Arkansas engaged in a heated correspondence over which of their men were in fact guerrillas, the relationship of irregular and semi-regular troops to regular forces, and the proper treatment of captured partisans. Thomas Hindman protested the news that a "notorious rebel leader of guerrilla bands" in Missouri named Poindexter was to be executed as a spy. Are "these men termed 'guerrillas'. . . to be put to death . . . or treated as prisoners of war?"

he asked Federal general James Totten. How did the acts of Poindexter differ from those of a Federal soldier named Chrysop who had murdered an unarmed Confederate hospital steward in Carroll County, Arkansas? Totten replied that Poindexter had been apprehended behind Federal lines in civilian garb and was, therefore, a spy. As for guerrillas generally, continued the Yankee, they were but "robbers, horse-thieves, and assassins innocent of any honorable impulses." He would not comment on the Chrysop case, but Totten insisted that captured guerrillas would not be treated as prisoners of war.[39]

General William T. Sherman replied to a similar letter from Hindman, who had accused the Union army of ignoring established "usages of civilized warfare." Hindman's protest extracted a smile from Sherman. Call them what you will, guerrillas or partisan rangers, said Uncle Billy, no one who served without a uniform could expect to be treated as a soldier. Sherman also delivered a warning. If the Confederate army continued to use "ununiformed bands," the United States would be forced to field its own guerrillas. And "at that game," promised Sherman, "your guerrillas would meet their equals, and the world would be shocked by the acts of atrocity resulting from such warfare."[40]

In October, Theophilus Holmes continued the debate with Samuel Curtis. The focus again fell on treatment of ununiformed men. Were they soldiers or spies? Holmes maintained that given the unholy "war of extermination" being visited upon the South, a war, accused Holmes, that had extended to the arming of slaves in eastern Arkansas, the Confederacy must use all possible means to resist Northern aggression. Besides, insisted Holmes, it was unreasonable to expect that the South would allow the North to dictate how the war would be fought. "We cannot be expected to allow our enemies to decide for us," reasoned Holmes, "whether we shall fight them in masses or individually, in uniforms, without uniforms, openly or from ambush."[41]

In April 1863, faced with an expanding guerrilla war in the Trans-Mississippi and an escalation of the eastern war, Federal general in chief Henry W. Halleck issued guidelines to curb the unrestrained war predicted by Sherman. War Department General Order No. 100, issued to the Department of the Missouri as General Order No. 30, defined four types of "guerrilla" service. Of the four types, only the "partisan," who operated on detached service as "part and parcel of the army," was deemed worthy of the name soldier. All other "guerrillas" were declared outlaws, to be punished, if apprehended, by death. They included "insurgents," "brigands," and the "guerrilla proper." The last named group, insisted Halleck, made "petty war chiefly by raids, extortion, destruction, and massacre," and "almost always" degenerated into "simple robbers and brigands."[42]

That would seem to have resolved the issue. Unfortunately, these guidelines appeared halfway through the war, and even at that, they represented only the North's view of the matter. Confederates continued to insist that even "partisans" clad in blue uniforms, if they acted under government commission, must be recognized as legitimate members of Confederate service. They also rejected the Northern definition of proper guerrilla actions, which confined legitimate operations to the disruption of the "enemy's lines of connection and communication."

The first Federal warning to Confederate guerrillas in the field, as opposed to protests against their use through official channels, followed swiftly on the heels of efforts by Van Dorn and Hindman to recruit partisan bands. After having his White River gunboats and transports fired upon from the woods opposite St. Charles, Colonel Graham N. Fitch, commanding the Forty-sixth Indiana Volunteers, warned the inhabitants of Monroe County, "This mode of warfare is that of savages." If the attacks continued, insisted the colonel, all local people would be held responsible, their property subject to seizure or destruction. When Hindman remonstrated that he had commissioned these so-called guerrillas as independent companies, Fitch, refusing to back down, replied, "You must be aware that your captains of tens will soon become little else than highway banditti, more terrible to citizens of your own State than to soldiers and sailors of the United States."[43]

Retaliation against local noncombatants and refusal to allow guerrillas their rights as prisoners of war became the most widely used means of restricting partisan operations. When Admiral David Dixon Porter chose the latter as a means of protecting his river vessels, General Holmes retaliated by insisting that for every Confederate denied his rights as a prisoner he would respond in kind. Frederick Steele, facing six companies of rampaging guerrillas between Clarendon and Helena, tried a variation of Fitch's threat. He cleverly applied for civilian assistance in checking the menace by warning them that Rebel guerrillas would devastate the countryside if allowed to operate unimpeded, and that it therefore behooved civilians, whatever their sympathies in the war, to help curtail irregular operations. By the summer of 1862, the United States government had embraced retaliation against civilians as a legitimate means of controlling guerrillas, although, in fact, commanders in the Trans-Mississippi had been doing so independently since early in the war. The most notorious example of officially sanctioned vengeance came when General Thomas Ewing issued his General Order No. 11 in retaliation for William Quantrill's sacking of Lawrence, Kansas.[44]

Threats continued to spew forth from Federal headquarters, and at a rate that betrayed the effectiveness of the guerrilla campaign. In November 1863, the Federals issued a warning to bushwhackers engaged in cutting telegraph lines in the vicinity of Fort Smith: captured bushwhackers would be hanged from every pole along lines where wires had been cut. Early in 1864, the Federal commander in northeast Arkansas promised kind treatment to all bushwhackers and guerrillas who voluntarily surrendered and swore loyalty to the United States. He likewise promised to take "extreme measures" against all guerrillas who continued in the field and against all civilians who harbored them. "My desire is to restore peace and prosperity to this portion of Arkansas," he informed partisan leader Thomas Freeman, "but if I am compelled to resort to the sword to enforce it, rest assured that sufficient energy will be exerted to speedily overrun the country."[45]

When verbal and written threats proved insufficient, Federal authorities retaliated swiftly and rarely tempered justice with mercy. The rules were easy to understand, and as early as August 1862, Federal troops had learned them. "Guerillar Bands . . . is prowling through this country almost all times and every place," swore a Union soldier from northwest Arkansas. "*But that game is almost played out for there* are strict orders against taking any more prisoners that is found in arms or as bushwhackers, but to leave them on the ground we found them on." Colonel Robert R. Livingston, commanding Federal troops in northeast Arkansas more than a year later, proclaimed, "My business here is to put down rebellion and exterminate guerrillas." Later that same year, in May 1864, Livingston instructed his men to "follow the usual rules" in tracking down partisans. They were to kill "all [Confederates] who wear our uniform and all positive jayhawkers or guerrillas." Confederates soon learned the rules, too, and proceeded to play the same game. "The Federals did not practice taking prisoners in this country," reported Joe Scott. "Every man or nearly so that fell into their hands was almost sure to be killed unless he [the captor] was a first-class Federal."[46]

Frustrated Federals, unable to strike solidly or potently at their elusive prey, sometimes settled for easier targets, such as the families of known guerrillas or of Confederate sympathizers generally. This was the strategy Ewing had employed in Missouri. In Arkansas, after "lawless men" had ambushed a forage train at Osage Fork on King's River in April 1863, Colonel William Weer directed the lieutenant commanding the expedition to "destroy every house and farm, etc., owned by secessionists, together with their property that cannot be made available to the army." Weer reasoned that the bushwhackers had been "encouraged and entertained by the inhabitants in that vicinity," and, therefore, the entire neighborhood must pay the price of rebellion.[47]

By 1863, the Federals had unleashed their counterguerrilla campaign. In March of that year, Colonel Weer, commanding troops at Carrollton, complained, "The operations of the enemy's guerrillas in Arkansas are far more vindictive and remorseless than anywhere else under my observation." In early April, Weer, shocked by the "boldness" of Confederate partisans who would "hang around" his camp, informed General John M. Schofield, "I am enveloped in a cloud of guerrillas." In order to resist them, Weer requested permission to raise "an independent organization of citizens" to help hold the country. These men, he stressed, would have to serve locally, lest their families fall prey to "murderous bushwhackers." Frederick Steele faced a similar threat. "It is my opinion that several regiments of good troops could be raised in Arkansas within a short time, for the purpose of putting down guerrillas and operating against the rebel army," asserted Steele in September 1863. The following month, he received permission to recruit "companies of loyal citizens" to defend their own neighborhoods and "subsist upon the enemies of the Government."[48]

Most of the men in Federal antiguerrilla units and Unionist partisan bands were recruited from Arkansas, Texas, and Missouri—the same sources that filled Confederate partisan ranks—with additional volunteers coming from Kansas. Whatever their origins, these men delighted in harassing Confederate sympathizers. The most effective of the volunteer regiments was the First Arkansas Cavalry (U.S.), but its methodical and disciplined challenge to the Rebels was too tame for Unionist guerrillas. Captain Martin D. Hart, a "renegade Texan," loosely coordinated several Federal guerrilla bands that threatened Rebel communications and committed "numerous outrages" against citizens between Fort Smith and Dardanelle. "Farmers are wanting to go to work," complained a man from Ozark of Hart's activities, "but there will be but little done in regard to farming unless those thieving jayhawking villains are hunted down and hanged." Hart and his men were eventually captured and Hart hanged by Confederate (Texas) partisans, the only Confederate forces capable of dealing with them.[49]

Tangible irony clings to Confederate assessments of the difficulties attendant to cornering Federal guerrillas. "The topography of the country where these parties operate is of such a character as to render pursuit useless," reasoned General William Steele, "unless the men are well mounted and the pursuit is kept up without relaxation." More than that, Arkansas Unionists knew the ground as well as their Rebel foes. An Iowa soldier observed of some Confederate deserters who had volunteered to act as Union scouts, "[T]hey are acquainted with the country and Know who are loyal and who are not. They have brought in a good many Guerrillas and bushwhackers."[50]

Confederates, like the Yankees, sometimes found it hard to distinguish between Union regulars and irregulars, but there could be no mistaking the destructive swath left by Unionist guerrillas on the march. A Confederate partisan captain, tracing the path of a Union raid from southwest Missouri through northwest Arkansas, discovered that the Federals had "murdered every Southern man that could be found" at Carrollton. On the Osage River in Carroll County, they had burned fifteen homes and accompanying outhouses. These "Hessians," as the captain called them, had "hoisted the black flag" and shown no mercy. Their "guide and principal leader" in Arkansas was a former Baptist preacher in Carroll County named Thomas Crysop (the Chrysop of whom Hindman had complained a year earlier?). Other bands, led by such men as William J. Heffington, Jacob E. Yoes, and Thomas Wilhite, preyed on both sides as freebooters.[51]

Yet the Federals, like the Confederates, sometimes found it hard to control their irregulars, or even many of their regular troops. Consequently, Federal commanders periodically issued strong warnings to their men about the need to respect and preserve private property, including Rebel property. Still, some officers admitted defeat. Even if able to curb violence against civilians, they found it nearly impossible to eradicate other forms of exploitation. "Many loyal people have been shamefully treated," reported the Federal commander at Fort Smith. "The country is filled with irregular receipts for forage, horses, cattle, and other property which cannot be settled, but in most instances everything has been taken and no receipts given, the people turned out to starve."[52]

The guerrilla impact on Federal operations may be seen most clearly in its effect on military strategy. The very fact that the United States organized its own partisan bands, despite the repugnance most military leaders had for irregular fighting, suggests a dramatic influence. It also suggests a tremendous amount of frustration on the part of Federal officers seeking to curtail partisan activities. "This trying guerrilla war-fare," concluded one officer charged with fighting Confederate river raiders, "[is] phoenix-like in its character, subdued, yet day after day rising up out of the ashes of its defeat again to menace us." An officer in an Iowa regiment, harassed by guerrillas near Pea Ridge in late 1862, expressed amazement at how swiftly and silently the enemy could strike. Following one encounter, he mused, "I could not help thinking all the time that it was strange that an enemy could be within 5 miles of us, & come up and attack us, & none of our 20,000 men know any thing of it or of their presence in the vicinity."[53]

The mere threat of guerrilla attacks spooked Samuel Curtis. Early in the war, while commanding Federal forces in Missouri, Curtis vacillated and delayed for months before invading Arkansas, even when specifically ordered to do so by Henry Halleck. Curtis feared that guerrillas in Missouri would seize the state if he withdrew sizable numbers of troops. By the end of the year, having committed his men south of the Missouri border, Curtis suddenly reversed his thinking. He entertained exaggerated fears of an invasion of Missouri from Arkansas, an invasion that could have succeeded only if spearheaded by considerable numbers of partisans. Meanwhile, Hindman gave partisan bands under John Coffee, Jeremiah V. Cockrell, Upton Hays, Dewitt C. Hunter, Sidney Jackman, and Henry Tracy "free rein" in the northwestern part of the state. Their raids and harassing actions forced John Scofield to devote a substantial number of his troops to protecting southwest Missouri.[54]

Thereafter, the threat posed by guerrillas to Unionists, Federal garrisons, supply lines, and communications often dictated Federal troop movements. Following the 1862 raid on Huntsville, a Federal colonel asked that "a strong cavalry force" be stationed there to protect citizens and the fragile communication line to Springfield, Missouri. Another Federal officer, in 1864, recommended that a post be established near Marshall Prairie to protect Unionists and agricultural stores in Carroll, Marion, and Searcy Counties from guerrillas. Throughout the last half of the war, Federal troops rushed hither and yon to block anticipated or ongoing guerrilla threat.[55] Entire commands sometimes had to be deployed with the guerrilla menace in mind. "The dispositions you have made," John Schofield informed Frederick Steele in November 1863, "with the addition of some cavalry along the White River, to prevent the organization of guerrillas, will, I believe, be the best we can do until operations elsewhere will allow you to advance."[56]

In northwest Arkansas, always one of the hottest regions of guerrilla activity, Colonel Marcus La Rue Harrison, the Federal commander at Fayetteville who led the First Arkansas Cavalry (U.S.), undertook an extraordinary action in the summer of 1864. Believing that gristmills in Benton and Washington Counties served as rendezvous points as well as sources of supplies for local partisans, Harrison ordered the destruction of three mills, one of them owned by partisan captain Buck Brown. "The disabling of mills," proclaimed Harrison, "causes more writhing among bushwhackers than any other mode of attack." The statement expressed the colonel's frustration at being unable to crush the elusive partisans. The extraordinary feature of his actions, however, was that Harrison had been expressly charged with protecting and maintaining the mills.[57]

The situation facing the Federal army in Arkansas bore an eerie resemblance to that facing the United States Army in Vietnam, for it seemed to men like Schofield and Steele that while they controlled the towns, most of the countryside belonged to Rebel guerrillas. "I think our company can soon drive them [Federals] inside the corporation or at least their pickets can't stay out," boasted a partisan operating near St. Charles. "They don't move a peg without our seeing them." Expanding the Vietnam analogy, Federal authorities toward the end of the war organized military farm colonies similar to strategic hamlets (or Israeli kibbutzim) in several parts of northern Arkansas. Under the colony program, armed Unionist families settled on confiscated lands near Federal garrisons to farm and live as safely as wartime conditions would permit. On occasion, colonists actively took the field against Rebel partisans, and at least one Federal colonel regarded the colonies as active and effective weapons in waging antiguerrilla warfare.[58]

By July 1864, General Napoleon B. Buford, commanding the District of Eastern Arkansas, felt compelled to raise the issue of Federal strategy in Arkansas. "Why do we continue to occupy the interior of Arkansas?" he asked in a private letter to several other generals, including Ethan Allen Hitchcock, Lincoln's former general in chief. Buford never referred to "guerrillas" per se, but his objections to defending Arkansas's rugged interior all pointed to the severe losses in men, animals, and equipment suffered by the Federals in their efforts to battle guerrillas on their own ground. Buford advocated securing the towns on the fringes of the state, particularly along the Mississippi River, or on island fortresses in interior rivers. The entire issue of whether or not to abandon Fort Smith in late 1864 and early 1865 revolved around the guerrilla threat. Ultimately, the argument for maintaining the fort was decided by a sense of guilt at leaving so many Unionists to the "mercy of guerrillas." Assessing the situation throughout the state, General Christopher C. Andrews informed Lincoln from Little Rock, "[T]he country seems to have degenerated into bushwhackers. It is hardly safe to go out of our lines a mile. I believe Union people are suffering more to-day in Arkansas than ever before since the war commenced."[59]

Clearly, the subject of Confederate guerrilla activity is complex. Having come to grips with the motivation of Confederate partisans, their role in the defense of Arkansas, and their effectiveness in disrupting Federal invasion plans, how much do we really know? Not much, or at least not as much as we might know. The complex organization of guerrilla bands must be explored; and a social profile of these partisan fighters, based on census reports, tax and court records, and similar sources of evidence, would make for a fascinating study. A systematic analysis of the impact of guerrilla warfare on the civilian population is in order, a study, incidentally, that could easily branch off into badly needed research on the refugee problem in Arkansas. More work on the river pirates, particularly their impact on the wartime economy of Arkansas, is needed, and on, and on. The history of the Civil War in the Trans-Mississippi remains largely untold. If, as suggested here, the guerrilla war is the key to understanding the Trans-Mississippi war, then the beginning of wisdom begins in the mountains and swamps of Arkansas.

Henry McCulloch and his Texans saved Arkansas by delaying Union occupations for over a year.
Photo © Milo Mims.

Rhea's Mill was typical of the rendezvous points favored by Confederate guerrillas and targeted by M. LaRue Harrison. *Courtesy Special Collections, University of Arkansas, Fayetteville.*

Union soldiers complained about the "semi-savage state" of Arkansas even as their foraging parties stripped communities bare. *From* Frank Leslie's Illustrated Newspaper. *Photo by gary Shepard.*

This saltpeter cave in the Ozark National Forest, Searcy County, was a valuable military asset to the Confederacy.
Courtesy James J. Johnston.

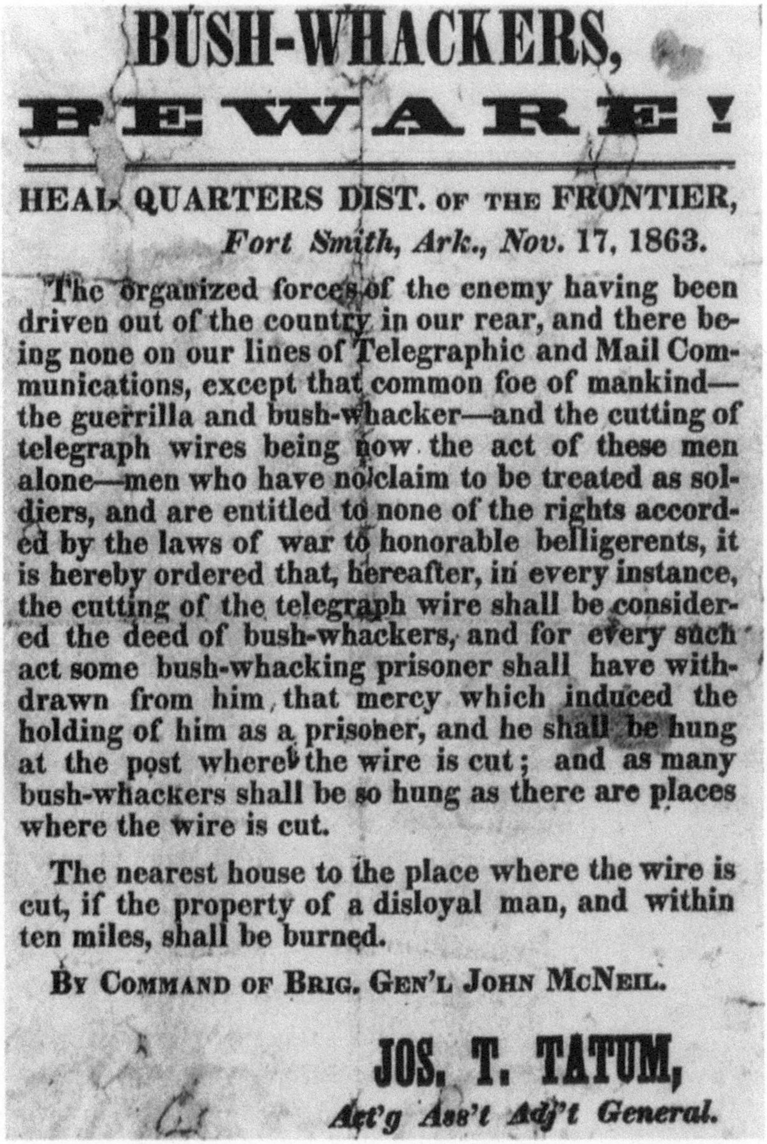

BUSH-WHACKERS,

BEWARE!

HEAD QUARTERS DIST. OF THE FRONTIER,

Fort Smith, Ark., Nov. 17, 1863.

The organized forces of the enemy having been driven out of the country in our rear, and there being none on our lines of Telegraphic and Mail Communications, except that common foe of mankind—the guerrilla and bush-whacker—and the cutting of telegraph wires being now the act of these men alone—men who have no claim to be treated as soldiers, and are entitled to none of the rights accorded by the laws of war to honorable belligerents, it is hereby ordered that, hereafter, in every instance, the cutting of the telegraph wire shall be considered the deed of bush-whackers, and for every such act some bush-whacking prisoner shall have withdrawn from him that mercy which induced the holding of him as a prisoner, and he shall be hung at the post where the wire is cut; and as many bush-whackers shall be so hung as there are places where the wire is cut.

The nearest house to the place where the wire is cut, if the property of a disloyal man, and within ten miles, shall be burned.

BY COMMAND OF BRIG. GEN'L JOHN MCNEIL.

JOS. T. TATUM,

Act'g Ass't Adj't General.

Federal commanders struck back ferociously at the guerrilla menace, as seen by this warning posted at Fort Smith in 1863.
Courtesy the Littlejohn Collection. Photo by gary Shepard.

The plight of these refugees from Fayetteville may well have turned them into Unionists and against the Confederate government. *From* Harper's Weekly. *Photo by gary Shepard.*

Confederate guerrillas reward themselves with the easy pickings of a sutler's train. *From* Harper's Weekly. *Photo by gary Shepard.*

Captain Thomas Jefferson Williams, leader of a tough band of Unionist guerrillas. *Courtesy of Polly Church.*

"Contrabands" at work in 1864 near Helena, possibly on one of the Federal army's leased plantations. *Courtesy Nebraska State Historical Society, Lincoln.*

The gunboat U. S. S. *Cricket*, seen here patrolling the White River, made a tempting target for Confederate snipers and guerrillas. *Courtesy Special Collections, University of Arkansas, Fayetteville.*

The execution of these captured black teamsters is almost sanitary compared to the atrocities committed at Poison Spring and Mark's Mill.
From Harper's Weekly.
Photo by gary Shepard.

Little Rock, Arkansas became the seat of Union occupation after September 1863.
From Harper's Weekly. *Photo by gary Shepard.*

Chapter 8

The Williams Clan: Mountain Farmers and Union Fighters in North Central Arkansas

KENNETH C. BARNES

The War between the States brought a true localized civil war to the hill country of north central Arkansas. Neighbors turned against neighbors as sentiments divided sharply between Union and Confederate loyalties. This study will examine the impact of the Civil War on one extended family of hill farmers, the Williams clan of Conway County. They supported the Union, but what they wanted most was security for their home and families. This they failed to achieve. The war took away adult male members of the household, brought physical deprivation, and caused the women and children to flee their homes as refugees. The collapse of civilian authority and military discipline in the area brought guerrilla war from 1863 to 1865. The nasty blood feud between the Unionist Williams family and their Rebel neighbors surrounded them with a web of violence they could have never before imagined. After the war a bitter acrimony between Democrat and Republican families led to a cycle of political violence in Conway County which lasted well into the twentieth century.

The Williams family epitomize a type about whom we know little from the historiography of Civil War Arkansas. During the war expatriate Arkansans such as Albert Webb Bishop and James Demby tried to publicize the plight of Arkansas Unionists to a Northern audience.[1] However, contrary to the old adage, the losers, not the victors, wrote the history of the war in Arkansas for almost the century that followed. Most of the men of substance and education in Arkansas supported the Confederacy. After the war, these dashing and often articulate Rebel leaders wrote the history of the war in Arkansas from the Confederate point of view.[2] The more objective historical scholarship of the last thirty years has indeed taken seriously the Union dissent within the state. With more than eight thousand white Arkansans volunteering for service with the Union army, only Tennessee surpassed Arkansas among Confederate states in numbers of native troops in blue. However, discussions of Unionism in Arkansas have focused on the debates of articulate lawyers like David Walker and Jesse Turner, who debated the issues in newspapers and in the secession conventions in 1861.[3] Much less is known about the experiences of the ordinary Arkansans who became foot soldiers for the Union army. Mostly illiterate subsistence farmers from the Ozarks, they did not leave memoirs and letters to tell their own story. Richard Current, the author of a recent book on white Southern Unionists, calls these men the unknown soldiers of the Civil War.[4]

The men of the Williams clan, headed by Thomas Jefferson ("Jeff") Williams, were in many ways very typical of those in northwestern Arkansas who supported the Union.[5] Williams and his family came to Arkansas from the hill country of Franklin County, Tennessee, in 1844. Jeff Williams and his two brothers, John and Leroy, had first seen Arkansas in the spring of 1838 when as members of the Tennessee militia, they "escorted" a party of Cherokees west through Arkansas to Indian Territory. For the Williams brothers, there must have been irony and some anguish to this task. Their mother, Rebecca, was the daughter of a full-blooded Cherokee.[6] They must have liked what they saw in the near wilderness of Arkansas, for six years later, shortly after the death of their father, the entire clan of five Williams brothers, three sisters, and their families packed their belongings and moved to the state.

Clearing land in the hills of northern Conway and southern Van Buren Counties, they were among the first white settlers in the area. Jeff Williams built a log house on 160 acres in Conway County near the present community of Center Ridge. He became relatively prosperous in the years preceding the Civil War. One of the few farmers in the area who could read and write, he also preached for a small congregation of the Disciples of Christ. In 1860 Jeff Williams was one of only two slave owners in the township, with a female slave, aged twenty.[7]

Even though a slave owner, Jeff Williams apparently remained devoted to the Union during the sectional politics preceding the Civil War. He named two sons, born in the 1850s, Henry Clay and Daniel Webster, for the Whig senators from Kentucky and Massachusetts who symbolized anti-sectionalist loyalty to the Union after the Compromise of 1850. Jeff Williams's political views were reflected in a public meeting held to discuss the secession crisis soon after Lincoln's election, in December 1860 at the county courthouse in Springfield. He served with four other men as a committee to draft resolutions expressive of the sense of the meeting. The committee deplored that "a sectional party" had elected Lincoln. But because this election was constitutional, Williams's committee regarded it as insufficient grounds for secession. They recommended that their state senator and representative vote for no man for U.S. Senate who believed Lincoln's election a sufficient cause for secession. The committee condemned both Northern and Southern fanatics and their inflammatory speeches calculated to inflame the public mind. At this public meeting the citizens of Conway County resolved their support for the Union and their rights under the Constitution. One of these rights, the report concluded, was the right to own slaves.[8]

Several other counties in northern and central Arkansas held meetings and sent anti-secessionist resolutions to Little Rock. In Van Buren County, where two other Williams brothers lived, a public meeting drafted a statement opposing secession, upholding Union, but maintaining the constitutional right to "property." Just to the west in Pope County, a mass meeting at the courthouse in Dover became so rowdy that the voice vote on secession resulted in a shouting match. Eventually the crowd of over five hundred voted by removing themselves to separate corners of the courthouse lawn for a headcount. After voting down the secession position by a margin of four to one, the majority "marched three times around the public square, under the old Stars and Stripes, during which time thirty-three guns were fired for the Union."[9]

Apparently Jeff Williams, like most of the hill people of northern Arkansas, did not oppose slavery. These mountain farmers simply did not see slavery as a significant enough cause for secession from the Union. At the secession convention in March 1861, Unionists acted upon these sentiments and defeated the ordinance for secession. However, the convention agreed that Arkansas should secede if Lincoln waged war against the six Southern states that had already left the Union. After the firing began at Fort Sumter, a second convention in May took Arkansas out of the Union and into the Confederate States of America.

In the Williams's neighborhood troops began organizing immediately for the Rebel army despite the anti-secessionist position declared six months earlier. In May one unit formed at Lewisburg, on the Arkansas River near the present town of Morrilton. The largest settlement in the county, Lewisburg was a commercial outpost where planters from the bottomlands alongside the river sold their cotton. In June and July, the Tenth Arkansas Cavalry formed at Springfield, the county seat, with nine companies drawn from Conway and neighboring counties.[10]

But clearly from its very beginning the war divided the loyalties of the hill folk of northern Arkansas. The earliest known organized resistance to secession came when Unionists in Conway, Van Buren, and several other counties of northern Arkansas formed underground "Peace Societies" in the fall of 1861. According to surviving oaths and constitutions, the purpose of the secret societies was to protect members, their families, and property from their "enemies." Whether these enemies were Confederate authorities, soldiers, or merely unsympathetic neighbors is unclear. Local authorities in several north Arkansas counties apprehended members of the society, tried some for treason, but impressed most of them in units of the Confederate army.[11]

No Unionists were taken into custody in Conway County, but it is reasonable to suspect Jeff Williams's involvement with the Peace Society. Edmund Stobaugh, one of the ringleaders arrested just a few miles away in neighboring Van Buren County, like Jeff Williams, was a Disciples of Christ preacher. The Williams and Stobaugh families saw each other often before the war at church gatherings. After his arrest and impressment into the Confederate army, Stobaugh served as a chaplain until his death in Corinth, Mississippi, in 1862. Ananias Stobaugh, also arrested in Van Buren County and impressed, was luckier. He deserted and escaped back to Arkansas, and by June 1862 Ananias Stobaugh, with two other Stobaugh kin, had joined Jeff Williams's band of Union resistance.[12]

Carl Degler, the eminent southern historian, has said that the severest test of Unionist sympathies for Southerners was their willingness to serve in the invading Federal army. In his study of Southern Unionists, Richard Current suggests that a combination of patriotism, courage, and opportunity motivated Southern loyalists to enlist in the Union army.[13] Jeff Williams and his family seem to have had all three. Besides their Unionist convictions, the disruption of their lives in spring 1862 encouraged the Williams men and several of their neighbors to join the Union army. After the Union victory at the battle of Pea Ridge in early March, Arkansas Confederate troops were sent to Corinth in northern Mississippi to halt Grant's advance south through western Tennessee. Some of the Arkansas troops arrived just in time for the costly defeat by Grant's troops at Shiloh. A great blow to the Confederacy, the effect on Arkansas was no less dramatic. With the shift of Arkansas troops to Corinth, the state stood defenseless in the face of an advancing Union army.

In the meantime, a Federal force with upwards of twelve thousand men under General Samuel R. Curtis moved south from Missouri into Arkansas. On May 4 Curtis's troops halted near Batesville. The presence of a large Union army in north central Arkansas had an electrifying effect. In fact, instead of making the region safe, the arrival of the Union army may have disrupted life even more. The Union army did not conquer and occupy; it merely passed through. However, Governor Henry Rector fled Little Rock, courts suspended their functions, and civil authorities virtually stopped exercising their powers. Many Arkansans refused to accept Confederate money; consequently it so depreciated that it became practically worthless. Extortion and price gouging in necessities of life "menaced the poor with actual starvation."[14]

Adding to the chaos in May 1862 was the threat of conscription of sons and husbands into the Confederate army. The Confederate Conscription Act of April 16, 1862, made military service compulsory for men aged eighteen to thirty-five. Governor Rector, alarmed at the Union advance, in early May began raising a state militia for the defense of Arkansas. He even threatened secession from the Confederacy if Rebel leaders abandoned the Trans-Mississippi West. By the end of May, agents were scouring the countryside raising two forces: a Confederate army unit and an Arkansas militia. Union reports from northern Arkansas in May described the as "in a state of terror" from the impressments into service.[15]

In Jeff Williams's home territory the pressure to enlist was intense. That spring a local planter, Anderson Gordon, raised a new Confederate company in northern Conway County, a company which eventually became part of William Cabell's brigade under General Sterling Price. In June General Curtis noted large numbers of Rebel troops moving near Clinton, just north of the Williams family farms, and captured a Rebel colonel who had been raising troops in the area. Albert Webb Bishop described how Rebels held township meetings in northern Arkansas to raise troops. When someone failed to participate, Webb said, "personal notice was given." Any tardiness to enroll brought surveillance, abuse, and insult from one's neighbors. Jeff Williams, at age fifty-one, was not a likely candidate for the Rebel army. But he had three sons and three sons-in-law of conscription age. His son Leroy, aged nineteen, at one point went to a Confederate camp at Grand Glaize on the White River and enlisted, he said, just to keep the Rebels from killing his father. But the next day he slipped away and came back home to Conway County.[16]

By early June Jeff Williams and about forty others from Van Buren County and northern Conway County had banded together and made their way through Rebel territory to join General Curtis in Batesville. Another group from Conway County arrived a few days later. Jeff Williams's band included his four sons, three sons-in-law, two brothers, four nephews, and a brother-in-law. Leroy said, "All of us were pretty well kin folks. . . . We ran away from Conway Co., to prevent being conscripted by the rebel army." The official report of Arkansas Union troops, presented to U.S. Congress after the war, said the men from Conway County "were compelled to flee to the army, be killed, or go into rebel service." Just one day after they arrived in Batesville these volunteers were in Federal uniforms, drawing equipment and rations.[17]

Word about the Williams's opposition to the Confederacy spread quickly in Conway County. On August 5, a young Rebel soldier sent to guard a grain depot at Cadron (about twenty miles south of the Williams's farm) wrote home to his mother in Pine Bluff, "Some time ago there was a whole company formed here who immediately on their organisation [*sic*] joined Curtis' army of invasion. All these things seem to indicate a very strong union feeling in our midst which I have no doubt has been fostered by the Conscription Law."[18]

The group from Conway County were not the only Arkansans who fled to the Union army. One of Curtis's colonels reported that men fleeing impressments were "flocking in from all quarters." About forty men had similarly banded together in Independence County to resist conscription and had traveled to Batesville. Authorized to muster volunteers for six or twelve months of service, Curtis recruited three additional companies of six-month men in Independence and Izard Counties in June while Jeff Williams's men remained in the Union camp in Batesville.[19]

Evidently these Arkansas volunteers expected that their service in Curtis's army would be part of an effort to hold their home territory for the Union. In other words, they wished to become the home guard companies envisioned by the Peace Societies the year before. One native Arkansan, Captain James W. Demby of the Second Arkansas Cavalry, served with Jeff Williams's company that fall and described the men as refugees who had come to Batesville for safety. They became soldiers, he said, so that they could "assist in chastising those who forced them to seek that refuge." According to Captain Demby, General Curtis gave them a cold shoulder upon arrival. More troops could have been raised, but Curtis did not seem to want them. Demby said that many of the Arkansas volunteers who came into Curtis's camp and offered their services eventually returned home disgusted. Their fate became then the choice between conscription into the Rebel armies or hiding out in the woods and swamps for the months to come.

No evidence suggests that the Williams men and their neighbors had joined the Union army intending to fight away from their homes. Like other Union supporters in northern Arkansas, they must have been dismayed when Curtis's army moved out of the area as speedily as it came. According to Demby, Curtis had promised the Arkansas volunteers that they would remain in the Batesville area, and they felt surprised and deceived when the march from Batesville began. The soldiers recruited in Independence County remained at their homes, not in Curtis's camp in Batesville. Late in June when General Curtis unexpectedly began his march south. Men were summoned from home so suddenly that some had no chance even to say goodby to families or take a change of clothing.[20]

After camping almost two months in Batesville, Curtis was running out of supplies. Jeff Williams and the other raw Arkansas recruits marched with Curtis's army in late June southeast along the White River. After a week of marching, the force engaged Rebels at the Cache River near Cotton Plant. Union reports estimated Confederate losses at 200 (123 actual bodies were found). Union losses numbered only 7 killed and 57 wounded. Jeff Williams's company experienced no casualties in the three-hour battle. Instead of turning west from Cotton Plant and moving toward Little Rock, the rather timid General Curtis moved southeast to Helena, which had already been occupied by Federal troops after the fall of Memphis in June. Through the hot plains and malarial swamps of east Arkansas, the march from Cotton Plant to Helena covered only thirteen miles per day. The heat and wretched conditions took a heavy toll in sickness even before the troops arrived in Helena. Union soldiers from the Midwest wrote home about the experience, describing the area as "'a wooded wilderness of fever nests and mosquito pests.'"[21]

Once in Helena the morale and health of Williams's men began to deteriorate. The four companies of Arkansas recruits were mustered into service as the First Arkansas Infantry Battalion. The men from Conway County formed the nucleus of Company B. They elected Jeff Williams as captain, George Galloway as first lieutenant, and Nathan Williams, Jeff's oldest son, as second lieutenant. These four companies of Arkansas volunteers then elected, almost unanimously, an Arkansas man as their battalion leader. Instead Curtis made Lieutenant Colonel John C. Bundy their commander, as Demby described him, "A young fop of a lieutenant from the North" who received his post because he was Curtis's pet. Demby said Bundy's conduct and manners only increased the Arkansas men's distaste for the Union army.[22]

Curtis's army was virtually penned up in Helena for months to come. In this post that Union soldiers described as "a dirty nasty town," a "sickly, detestable village," and "the resort of gamblers and rogues of all grades and capacities," Williams's company did some drilling but otherwise sat inactive. Morale dipped low as the men of Williams's company also were consumed with worry about the security of their families left behind. According to one member of the battalion, First Lieutenant Calvin Bliss, the men received little news from their loved ones and feared that they were suffering under the hands of lawless brigands and Rebel neighbors bent on retribution. Camped in Helena, they could do nothing to protect their families, nor could they provide sustenance which became increasingly scarce as two rival armies passed through the state.[23]

It became more apparent that these mountain men had not enlisted to be ordinary Federal foot soldiers. Most of the men had brought horses with them, fearing their Rebel neighbors would steal them if they were left behind. According to Captain Demby, who served in Helena with Jeff Williams's men, Curtis had promised the Arkansas volunteers that they could keep their horses and become a mounted infantry unit. However, Union authorities in Helena did not allow them to forage in the countryside nor draw forage from the quartermaster. As a result, most of their horses either died of starvation or were stolen. The men either sold the remainder for a trifle or gave them away. The paymaster for the Union camp in Helena, a Major Mitchell, even refused to pay the First Battalion on the grounds that General Curtis had no authority to raise such a unit. After Curtis transferred to St. Louis by September, Military Governor John Phelps intervened to get payment for the men.[24]

Besides problems with morale, the hot months of late summer in Helena brought rampant disease to the crowded camp of soldiers and thousands of black refugees who had swarmed in from plantations in eastern Arkansas. Federal officers continually complained to their superiors about the health problems in camp. For good reason it became a well-known saying among Union men that they had rather "go to Hell than Helena." Dozens of the Arkansas volunteers died there from dysentery, pneumonia, typhoid fever, measles, and other camp diseases. Leroy Williams said nearly all of his company "were dead or nearly dead at Helena from diarrhoea." When two of his sons, Morton and John, did not improve from the care of the regimental surgeon, Captain Williams apparently had the money to place them in a boarding house in town and hire a private physician, Dr. Jack, to care for them. Jeff Williams became so sick with chronic diarrhea in August that the camp surgeon judged him unfit for duty and requested a twenty-day leave of absence. He must be removed from Helena, the doctor said, to save his life. On September 24 an order of General Frederick Steele discharged Jeff Williams from service on account of his continued ill health. However, he stayed with the company until they were mustered out in December. The sickest men in the company were sent by boat upriver to the army hospital in St. Louis. By October 20 there were not enough healthy men to perform camp duties, and army command ordered the entire First Arkansas Battalion removed from Helena to Missouri. They traveled by boat up the Mississippi River and arrived at Benton Barracks, the large Union base in St. Louis, on October 28, where they remained until they were mustered out of service on December 31, 1862.[25]

Illness traveled with the company upriver, however, and the deaths only continued in St. Louis. Captain Demby, who also was transferred from Helena to St. Louis, grandiloquently described the plight of the First Arkansas Infantry Battalion: "Arkansas volunteers' tale of woe and mortality in Helena is truly appalling, unprecedented among any other troops within our knowledge. Physically and mentally dejected, under bitter disappointment and blighted hopes, new diseases were contracted and old ones aggravated, producing incurable complications, ending either in immediate dissolution, or a lingering and painful semi-existence. Their hospital accommodations and medical attention were better adapted to produce, rather than remove disease. Many of them were really murdered."[26]

After six months of inglorious service in the Federal army, about 150 of 382 members of the First Arkansas Infantry Battalion had died of disease. None died in battle. Of the 75 men in Jeff Williams's Company B, 34 died, 5 were discharged early because of ill health, and 13 went to a hospital but recovered. Two-thirds of Captain Williams's company either died or went to a hospital. Jeff Williams's brother John died in Helena of "nervous disease" while another brother, Riley, died of pneumonia in St. Louis. He also lost a nephew and a brother-in-law to disease. Both he and his eldest son, Nathan, were discharged early because of ill health.[27]

These Union men from Conway and Van Buren Counties had fled to the Union army in Batesville for self-protection and with hopes of establishing security for their property and families. Instead, their six months of service in the Union army brought them death and lingering illness. In the words of James Demby, they were dejected moreover because "they were unable, during the whole term of service to render any assistance to their families or friends, whom they had left helpless in the hands of their enemies."[28]

Stranded in St. Louis, Jeff Williams and the remnant of his company dared not to return to their homes in Rebel territory. Instead they made their way toward Springfield, Missouri, where a large Union force under General James G. Blunt had headquarters. There they joined a considerable throng of Unionist refugees from Arkansas pouring into southwestern Missouri in early 1863. Somehow the Williams men communicated with their family back home. Captain Williams's wife, Margaret, and their younger children, perhaps with others in the clan, made the dangerous journey through the Ozarks to Missouri. For the next eight to ten months, they stayed in Douglas County, Missouri, just southeast of Springfield.[29]

The Williams men worked as scouts with a Missouri cavalry regiment. Whenever a scouting party went south to the Arkansas line, Leroy Williams said, he volunteered to go along. In his account written thirty-five years later, Confederate colonel John Harrell described how Union scouts, Missouri and Arkansas Federals, swept down from Missouri in 1863 and ruthlessly raided Rebel families in northern Arkansas. Although Harrell's account is hardly objective, these Federal bands were apparently quite lawless. Leroy Williams described how he captured a horse in a skirmish with Confederates while traveling south from Springfield with a cavalry unit. When he arrived in Fayetteville, the First Arkansas Cavalry took his horse, Leroy said, but the soldiers stole him another one.[30]

While Williams's group scouted in Missouri, Union troops began an offensive aimed toward central Arkansas. The Federal force at Helena repelled a Rebel attack on the same day that Vicksburg fell, July 4, 1863. With new confidence General Frederick Steele moved toward Little Rock in August as General Blunt's men moved south from Missouri toward Fort Smith. By early September the Arkansas River valley lay for the first time in Union hands.

As the Federal armies moved into central Arkansas, Jeff Williams's family and most of his company returned to Conway County. A few stayed in Missouri. George T. Bird joined the First Arkansas Cavalry stationed in the Springfield area. Joseph Vaughn signed up with the Eleventh Missouri Cavalry, which operated in Indian Territory until the end of the war. One survivor of Company B, Wilson Shewmake, married a Missouri girl in Rolla, then moved to Illinois until the war ended. Those who returned to Arkansas fell in with army units traveling south to Fayetteville and Van Buren. From there they followed another unit east along the Arkansas River back to Lewisburg in Conway County. From Lewisburg they walked twenty miles north to their homes, having been gone over a year. The survivors of Company B were not the only Arkansas men returning to the state. General Blunt wrote from Fort Smith in September that Union men who had been driven to the mountains to save their lives were coming in to enlist by scores. One Conway County resident later recalled that after the Federal army took Little Rock, "draft dodgers" who had fled to Missouri returned to the area; many of these, he said, "were plain outlaws."[31]

On September 15, five days after he took Little Rock, General Steele issued special orders authorizing the Union men of Conway County to form themselves into a company for the purpose of protecting themselves, their families, and their homes against Rebel violence and depredations. By these orders Jeff Williams organized an independent company of which he became captain and commander. A U.S. mustering officer swore the men into service at the Union camp near Lewisburg. Captain Williams's son Nathan was first lieutenant. One year before, the commanding officer of the First Arkansas Infantry Battalion, John Bundy, had discharged Nathan Williams early, saying that he was "physically and mentally incapacitated for the duties of an officer and ought never to have been commissioned." Nathan Williams would take over command of the independent company at his father's death in 1865. The company included Williams's other sons, Leroy, John, and Henry, several sons-in-law, and some other survivors of Company B. Still suffering from chronic camp ailments and hardly able to fight, they feared they would be killed by Rebel bushwhackers if they lived at home. With General Steele's orders, the men finally had authorization to form the home guard company envisioned earlier by the Peace Societies. As one of the members said, "The only way we could stay near home was by being in that company."[32]

With the Federal push into central Arkansas and the Arkansas River valley, the Rebel command retreated south of the Arkansas River. The Confederate state government moved to Washington, in southwestern

Arkansas. Meanwhile, the Union army established posts at Little Rock, Pine Bluff, DeValls Bluff, Brownsville, Lewisburg, Dardanelle, and Fort Smith. Many Rebel soldiers north of the Arkansas River deserted rather than retreat to the south with the Confederate army. By September 1863 the Rebel army in north central Arkansas had broken up into small bands of guerrillas and marauders operating in the vicinity of their homes. With this situation and the return to northern Arkansas of Union sympathizers who had hidden out in Missouri, a more vicious stage of guerrilla war set in which would last until the Confederate surrender in 1865.

Captain Williams's ragtag independent company tried to protect their families and property against the deserters and guerrillas that ravaged north central Arkansas in 1863 and 1864. Most likely, they exacted retribution as well against their Rebel neighbors. Union and Confederate authorities agreed that inhabitants of the area were terrorized, although each side placed the blame on the other. In his memoirs written in 1918 Herbert Jones described how outlaws roamed the countryside of Conway County and pillaged at will. He blamed the Federal garrison in Little Rock for taking little interest in the welfare of people in the hinterland. Actually General Steele repeatedly had requested additional troops to occupy central Arkansas and protect loyal citizens, but Federal authorities turned him down. Steele's orders from Washington instructed him to concentrate his troops against the main forces of the enemy, not to use them to protect the country from guerrillas and robbers.[33]

By 1864 law and order had collapsed in Conway County outside the Union post in Lewisburg. John Harrell recounted how the fear of raiders and guerrillas (mostly Federals, according to Harrell) drove citizens in northern Arkansas from their homes. Many, he said, took their bedclothes to the hollows and thickets and slept outdoors in the coldest weather for fear of being murdered in their beds. When Colonel Robert R. Livingston reoccupied Batesville for the Federal army in December 1863, he found the area "so fearfully lawless, and murders so common" that he refused to organize home guard companies of loyal citizens. He felt certain that if he formed such groups, Confederate guerrillas would murder many of them and take their arms. Concerning the Batesville area, he said, "When a man commits himself to the Union now, he must stay with the Federal troops for safety, and dare not go home."[34]

These conditions brought the Williams band into close association again with the Union army. Recruited from central Arkansas, the Third

Arkansas Cavalry was mustered into duty at Little Rock in February 1864. Led by Colonel Abraham Ryan, the unit was sent up the Arkansas River to Lewisburg to hold territory "infested by numerous guerrilla bands who were robbing and murdering Union families." Finding it too dangerous to live in their own homes, Jeff Williams's independent company spent their time in the bush or at the Federal garrison at Lewisburg. The Williams company obeyed the orders of Colonel Ryan and drew rations, ammunition, and clothing. On occasion, Williams's men traveled and fought with the Third Arkansas. They did not have to answer to roll call and received no pay. The primary role for Jeff Williams and his men was to scout their home territory and provide intelligence for Colonel Ryan. As Williams's son put it, "We stayed around home most of the time and scouted about after bushwhackers."[35]

The nemesis for the Williams company in north central Arkansas was a band of Confederate guerrillas led by Colonel Allen R. Witt. In the summer of 1861 Witt had organized men from Conway and Van Buren Counties into a Rebel company called the Quitman Rifles, which became part of the Tenth Arkansas Regiment. Sent to Mississippi in time to fight at Shiloh in 1862, the regiment retreated to Louisiana and elected Witt as commander. Witt and the entire Tenth Arkansas were captured at the Federal assault of Port Hudson in the summer of 1863. Union authorities paroled the enlisted men, and they returned to Arkansas. Witt and ninety-four other Rebel officers were placed aboard the U.S. gunboat *Maple Leaf* bound for the Federal prison at Fort Delaware, New Jersey. While at sea the prisoners, with Witt as one of the leaders, overpowered the Federal guard and took the ship. They landed behind Rebel lines and escaped. Witt made his way back to his home territory in Arkansas and reorganized his men just as Jeff Williams and other Arkansas Federals were returning to the state from Missouri.[36]

From their home base in Quitman, about twenty miles east of Jeff Williams's farm, Witt's guerrillas, like Williams's Raiders, lived in the bush and operated semi-independently. Cut off from the Confederate military and political leaders south of the Arkansas River, Witt's troops apparently received no pay and lived off the countryside.[37] Colonel Ryan considered Witt's men to be bushwhackers, while in a letter of 1865 Witt referred to Williams's independent company as a group of jayhawkers and marauders. W. W. Garner, a Rebel soldier in south Arkansas, wrote to his wife in Quitman, Witt's hometown, late in 1863. She had been visted by a group of Federals who refrained from taking her horses, apparently because she told them she was the wife of a Mason. Jeff Williams was a blue lodge Mason. Garner hoped his wife would not get visited again, but if she was, he said, "I would far perfer [*sic*] the regular Feds to the low-flung militia, for I don't think that ever an honorable man went into such an arrangement as they do. I look on them as cowards, jayhawkers, and thieves generally." Although both Witt's men and Williams's Raiders were authorized units, they operated in a no-man's-land which lacked both civil law and military discipline.[38]

Throughout the last eighteen months of the war, Witt's men scoured the countryside of north central Arkansas, harassing Union expeditions and scouting operations. In return, detachments from the Third Arkansas at Lewisburg chased Witt's men back to Quitman where they evaporated into the landscape. On one occasion, Jeff Williams's son Leroy accompanied a detachment of the Third Arkansas, under Captain Archibald Napier, which killed seven of Witt's men and captured seven more. Leroy Williams boasted that he had saved Captain Napier's life and had wounded and taken the prize catch, a Rebel Captain Livingston. Witt, however, eluded the Union grasp.[39]

With the Federal and then Confederate offensives in Arkansas during the spring and summer of 1864, both Williams's and Witt's bands worked closely with their respective commands. In March Federal troops advanced to challenge the Confederate force massed in southwest Arkansas. Some of Witt's men made their way through Union lines to join in the battles in April of Poison Spring, Jenkins' Ferry, and Marks' Mill. Some of the Williams's company apparently accompanied Colonel Ryan's force from Lewisburg in the campaign. Leroy Williams claimed he was with the Third Arkansas when he killed a Rebel officer in Cleveland County, the location of the battle of Marks' Mill.[40]

In mid-May, the dashing Confederate general Joseph Shelby crossed the Arkansas River at Dardanelle with twenty-five hundred men, sending the Federal garrisons there and in Lewisburg into shock. Colonel Ryan evacuated the Lewisburg post and floated his arms and munitions downriver toward Little Rock. Shelby's troops entered Lewisburg but found the place malignant with smallpox. Ryan had cleverly placed the supplies left behind in houses where disease was raging, and the Rebels left them untouched. Jeff Williams and the independent company accompanied the five hundred troops under Ryan's command as they fell back to Cadron Creek.[41]

Instead of moving toward Little Rock as expected, Shelby took the Dover-Batesville Road and marched northeast. Ryan was ordered to move north to engage and harrass Shelby. Instead he sent Williams's company with a small force north toward Clinton to intercept Shelby. But with his main force Ryan marched from Cadron northeast toward Searcy and then indecisively backtracked west to Quitman and Springfield. There Ryan's men joined with two additional Federal units which had marched north from Little Rock and Pine Bluff. While these thousands of Federal troops marched somewhat aimlessly in Conway and Van Buren Counties, Shelby's men marched around them to the north, passing through Clinton on May 23. The two large armies never met. By the end of the month Ryan reoccupied Lewisburg as Shelby reached the White River above Batesville and camped. Ryan received the blame for letting Shelby slip through.[42]

As Shelby's men marched on the road between Dover and Clinton, they camped just a few miles from Jeff Williams's farm in north Conway County. Williams's younger brother, William Day Williams, had stayed home with his family while his kin served in the First Infantry Battalion and then the independent company. Nonetheless he fell victim to Rebel violence. A short way down the road from Shelby's camp, William Day had gone out to work in his cornfield with his son, Frank, and John McGinty, a Union soldier home on furlough and still in uniform. Around lunchtime they took a break from their labor, and the two boys took off their clothing for a dip in Point Remove Creek, which ran alongside of the Dover-Clinton Road. While swimming they saw the Rebel army coming down the road. Jumping out of the creek, they put on their clothing, grabbed their guns, and started running away, shooting as they went. The Confederates gave chase and captured the Williams men. They shot John McGinty, left him for dead, and marched William and Frank off to Batesville. Separated when they arrived, young Frank Williams never saw his father again. He was told his father was killed and his body thrown in the White River. The Rebels then released Frank with a message to return to his uncle Jeff: "Quit killing men, or we're going to come get him."[43]

Jeff Williams and his men sought safety during the summer of 1864 inside the Union camp in Lewisburg as north central Arkansas remained an extremely dangerous place for native Federals. Even families of Union men flocked to the garrison for protection. In July 1864 orders were issued for all soldiers' wives and children in the Lewisburg post to be moved to a secure camp on the south side of the Arkansas River. From their headquarters near Batesville, Shelby's force swept the countryside in north central Arkansas clean of forage, food, and men. Finding deserters and lawless men roaming the area, Shelby raised several thousand troops over the summer.[44] On September 7, Confederate generals Price and Fagan crossed the Arkansas at Dardanelle with three brigades, more than eight thousand men, to reinforce Shelby and begin a planned attack on Missouri. Again Union commanders expected Price to turn toward Little Rock. Ryan once more began the evacuation of Lewisburg. Leroy Williams volunteered for a mission to travel downriver to meet and destroy a Federal boat laden with supplies, to keep it from falling into Rebel hands. Leroy met the steamer at the Fourche la Fave River and assisted in burning it. Ryan paid him forty dollars for his service, the only cash money Leroy said he ever received from the Third Cavalry.[45]

With the evacuation of Lewisburg, Captain Williams's company presumably fell back with Ryan's men to Palarm Creek near Little Rock. Meanwhile Fagan and Price traveled north through Conway County and joined up with Shelby's men near Batesville. Except for a detachment of the Third Arkansas which engaged Fagan's troops at the Point Remove Creek in northern Conway County, the large Confederate force made its way through central Arkansas without opposition. By mid-September the combined forces of the three Rebel generals marched north to Missouri. North central Arkansas became a safer place for Arkansas Unionists during fall 1864 as Colonel Witt's guerrillas and other irregulars went with the Rebel army to the Missouri campaign.[46]

With the demoralizing defeat at Westport, near Kansas City, the Missouri raid failed miserably, and the Arkansas Rebels late in 1864 returned south to once more terrorize native Unionists. By the beginning of 1865, Colonel Witt's men decided to silence Jeff Williams, the Union scout and spy. The threat had been communicated the summer before through young Frank Williams. Sometime that same summer, Rebels made another threatening gesture to the Williams family. According to oral history, Jeff Williams's son Leroy had come home to visit his mother. As he slept that night he was alerted to the Rebel approach when his horse began pawing and neighing. Leroy vaulted out of bed, wrapped a cloak over his shoulders and jumped on his horse. As his horse cleared the paling fence surrounding the yard, shots rang out. Leroy escaped unharmed although his cloak was shot through with several bullet holes.[47]

On the night of February 12, 1865, Rebels made good on their threats. Colonel Witt, with sixty to a hundred of his men, surrounded Jeff Williams's log house near Center Ridge, shortly after he and his sons had come home to visit their family. Foreseeing his fate, Williams turned to his wife, Margaret, and said, "My time has come." As he opened the front door, guns in hand, a volley of buckshot struck him from twenty-five yards away. He was killed standing in his own doorway. Margaret picked up his guns and placed them in the fireplace, apparently to keep the Rebels from taking them. Two or three younger children were asleep in the back room when the gunshots awakened them. They rolled out of bed and under them for cover. Family stories suggest that the Rebels beat the Williams women before they left. Leroy's wife, Sarah Jane, was pregnant, and in one account, almost lost her child after the Rebel guerrillas punched her in the belly with their gunstocks.[48]

Enraged and vengeful, Leroy Williams pursued Witt's men on horseback as they moved west toward Dover. He chased one unlucky Rebel to the edge of a bluff on the mountain just south of the Williams farm. There the man shimmied down a chinquapin tree and eluded Leroy, who could not follow on horseback. Peering over the edge of the bluff, Leroy saw below the form of a man looking down at the palms of his hands. He tracked the man later to the house of a woman who had taken him in and and dressed his wounded hands. Leroy had the woman cut off the bandages to see the wounds, then shot the Rebel dead on the spot.[49]

Leroy caught up with Witt's band on the evening of his father's death and killed three men as they watered their horses at the Point Remove Creek. He came on the men again later after they camped at Sucker Creek, near the community of Cleveland. Riding through the camp, he shot four more. Williams descendants still speak of Leroy's ability to ride with a gun in each hand, holding the reins of his horse with his teeth.[50] The next day Leroy and the Williams men joined with a party of seventy men from the Third Arkansas Cavalry sent by Colonel Ryan to pursue Witt. Over the next three days they chased the Rebels to Clinton and then to Quitman where Witt's men dispersed. Although Witt again eluded the Federal's grasp, they brought five of his men back to Lewisburg as prisoners.[51]

Both Williams descendants and the descendants of the Rebels they were chasing tell the story of how the Williams men tracked their father's killers to Clinton. The Williams men followed one of the Rebels into a store in town. As the clerk behind the counter, a Pate man, went for his gun, Leroy Williams shot him in the hip. Meanwhile the man Leroy had pursued slipped out the back door. Descendants of Clinton Rebels who tell this story add that after the Williams men shot the Pate man, they poured out the blood from his boots and wore them away. Family tradition holds that Leroy Williams alone killed as many as sixteen members of the Rebel posse who had shot his father.[52]

Ryan sent word to Union headquarters in Little Rock about the killing of Jeff Williams, "the noted scout." James Demby, who had known Williams at Helena, eulogized him as a true patriot and esteemed friend in the Union magazine he published in Little Rock, the *Home Aegis.* The death of Jeff Williams, however, did not mean the end of his independent company. On February 22 special orders came from Little Rock promoting First Lieutenant Nathan Williams to captain of Williams's Independent Company of Scouts and Spies.[53]

After Lee surrendered at Appomattox, Colonel Witt and other guerrillas in Arkansas still held out. Witt wrote to the Union commanders in Little Rock in May and June requesting that they disarm the independent companies such as that headed by Leroy and Nathan Williams, "[W]ho say what they do is under the direction of the U.S. authorities." Surely Federal authorities in Little Rock must not be aware, Witt said, "of the many murderous crimes and outrageous depredations" they had committed. Witt claimed he had brought this to Colonel Ryan's attention earlier in the winter, but Ryan took no action. Fearing retribution, Witt refused to surrender until the independent squads were disarmed. He asked further that Federal authorities restore order by using soldiers from other states to occupy Arkansas, "not to send men of this State, who have personal grudges."[54]

Witt had good reason to fear. The Williams men were hell-bent on revenge. Even Henry Clay Williams, who had just turned fourteen the week before his father was shot, had then joined the independent company to avenge his father's death. According to one account, in 1865 the Williams company rode on horseback to the house of George Harden, a Van Buren County Rebel, whose wife tried in vain to pursuade him to hide. He responded that he was tired of hiding and would try talking to the men. After speaking with them at his front gate, they rode off. But one of the Williams men turned his horse and shot Hardin dead. Mary Holmes, an old-timer in Conway County who in her youth knew Jeff Williams's sons well, recalled the story of how Leroy tortured one unlucky Rebel during the war. With an auger he bored a hole in a tree, she said, and carved a wooden peg about the same size. Forcing his captive to stretch his hands high over his head and stick his thumb in the hole, Leroy then drove in the peg onto the man's thumb. Leroy apparently deserved his nickname, "Wild

Dick." When Leroy Williams applied for a military pension in his old age, the examiner described him as a "pretty tough customer in his day and sort of a daredevil, hardened by the killing of his father." Leroy's grandson, Lonnie Maxwell, recalled hearing him reminisce about his Civil War experiences with another member of the company not long before his death in 1924. When asked how many men he had killed, Leroy responded, "Too many, but I like [lack] three more."[55]

In Conway County the bitter feelings between Confederates and Union supporters in the hilly northern part of the county lasted for years after the Civil War. When the radical Republican Powell Clayton became governor of Arkansas in 1868, he immediately organized state militia companies drawn largely from the old Unionist areas of the state. In Conway County the Republican militia virtually waged war that fall against Democrats and Ku Klux Klansmen. The veterans of the Williams independent company volunteered for militia service and renewed their past battles against Rebel neighbors.[56] In August Clayton called for the Williams militia to march south to Lewisburg to settle a violent standoff between ex-slaves and white citizens. Before they arrived, however, Clayton traveled by steamer to Lewisburg and defused the crisis himself. He sent a courier north toward Springfield to stop the militia. The men at first refused to disband, according to one account, because they had taken orders before leaving Springfield for coffee and dry goods which they were to bring back from the looting of Lewisburg.[57]

The conflict climaxed in December when several stores and homes in Lewisburg were burned, and both blacks and Klansmen were lynched. On December 8 Governor Clayton declared martial law in Conway County and put the county under the control of four Republican militia companies, three white and one black. One of the white companies was led by a Williams man. The *Arkansas Gazette* charged that the militia had caused, not quelled, the violence in Conway County. According to the *Gazette,* the militia had lynched several Klansmen, then murdered a Democratic merchant, looted his possessions, and set fire to his shop. The commander of the militia vigorously denied the accusations. Martial law lasted only a few weeks in Conway County. By March 1869 civil authority was restored and the militia companies disbanded.[58]

When Reconstruction in Arkansas ended, these former Unionists lost political power and became an isolated minority. Ex-Confederate officers Colonel W. S. Hanna and Colonel A. R. Witt represented Conway and Van Buren Counties in the Constitutional Convention of 1874, which ended

Reconstruction in Arkansas. Southern Democrats again ran Conway County. They even moved the county seat from Springfield in the northern part of the county south to Lewisburg, a Democratic stronghold. Richard Current's study of Southern Unionists argues that this pattern prevailed throughout the South, that Unionists were socially ostracized and shut out from local power for years after the Civil War.[59]

The acrimony between Republicans and Democrats in Conway County, however, surfaced viciously again in the 1880s. With heavy black migration into the county, and an agrarian populist movement which split the white vote, Republicans won the county elections in 1884 and 1886. Conway County became the scene of the most flagrant political violence in Arkansas as Democrats fought to regain power. A resurgence of Klan activity brought lynchings and voter intimidation in black precincts. The violence culminated in the congressional election in 1888 between Democrat Clifton Breckinridge and Republican John Clayton, brother of the former Reconstruction governor and Republican party boss. At Plumerville, a black majority precinct, Democratic ruffians stole the ballot box, and later shot off the ear of the Republican Federal election supervisor. Finally in January 1889 they assassinated candidate Clayton while he was at Plumerville taking testimony about the contested election.[60]

The Union veterans and their families in the northern part of the county led the resistance to these Democratic shenanigans. In March 1890 they had chartered a post of the Grand Army of the Republic (G.A.R.) and the Sons of Veterans in Center Ridge. Ex-Rebels thereafter organized a chapter of Confederate Veterans to the south in Morrilton, the new county seat. These camps were not merely social clubs where war stories were retold; they had a political purpose. The pro-Democratic *Gazette* charged that the G.A.R. and Sons of Veterans camps in Center Ridge were actually Republican clubs, and that these Republicans in the northern part of the county were plotting violence against Democrats. The paper reported that these Republicans had threatened to burn down Morrilton if they lost the election and had ordered dozens of Winchester rifles from up north to prepare for the violence.[61]

In the congressional race that fall, Clifton Breckinridge, who had been unseated by the House of Representatives because of the electoral fraud in Conway County two years before, campaigned vigorously to regain his seat. He even scheduled a pitch to the hostile Republicans in Center Ridge. Midway through his speech at a local church, someone fired a gunshot and disrupted the meeting. While walking back to his hotel afterward,

Breckinridge's companion was knocked to the ground with a malicious blast from a slingshot. The *Gazette* charged that it was an assassination attempt against the candidate, one which could be expected in Center Ridge, "a Republican stronghold, containing many of Clayton's old militia brigands." Galloway and Frank Williams, sons of the crusty old veteran Leroy Williams, were charged with attempted assassination. On election day in the following November, the *Gazette* reported that an angry Republican mob from Center Ridge, "composed of the noted Williams gang," marched two by two into Plumerville, the site of the previous stolen election. They shot up the town with their Winchester rifles and stood guard at the polling place until the results of the election were called.[62]

Republican power in Conway County waned in the 1890s as Jim Crow laws removed the black Republican vote. White Republicans, the former Unionists in hilly northern Conway County, again became an isolated minority. The northern townships of the county, however, maintained Republican politics well into the twentieth century. In 1920 when Republican candidate Warren G. Harding won the presidential election, one long-time resident of the area remembers hearing the celebrations in Center Ridge from five miles away.[63] Until his death in 1927, Frank Stobaugh, the drummer for Williams's independent company, led a ritual parade every Memorial Day in Center Ridge. Wearing his Union uniform and beating his old drum, he headed a small procession of gray-headed Union veterans to the local cemetery. He continued the tradition even when he was the only survivor, with his grandson following behind him carrying the U.S. flag.[64]

The Williamses and their like do not figure in the standard histories of the politics and battles of Civil War Arkansas. But yet the survival of such a substantial body of oral history among Williams descendants indicates the traumatic and personally significant nature of their Civil War experiences. Doubtless, the story of the Williams clan is like that of many ordinary mountain folk of the state. For the Williams family and their neighbors of Conway County, the war meant disruption of their family life, tragic violence which took life on both sides of the conflict, and a cycle of retributive feuding which continued for generations. The transformation of Jeff Williams from a Disciples of Christ preacher into a guerrilla fighter, his cruel death, and the brutal retribution his sons exacted well reveals the moral chaos the Civil War brought to Arkansas.

Chapter 9

From Slave to Free Labor: The Federal Plantation Experiment in Arkansas

CARL H. MONEYHON

The Civil War ended slavery practically in the American South long before the Thirteenth Amendment brought it to a legal close. Wherever Union armies marched, slaves seized the opportunity to take their freedom and leave their slave owners. The new freedmen were ill-equipped, however, for their new status. Starving and ill black refugees quickly overran Federal camps in the South. Humanitarian and military concerns demanded a solution that would help these contrabands, as they were called, as well as relieve armies in the field from caring for the ex-slaves. One of the government's solutions was to place freedmen on plantations as free workers. Government-supervised plantation labor became a laboratory that tested ways of adjusting slave labor to the new circumstances of freedom. These plantations also allowed many freedmen to take the first step toward their own economic freedom.

The Federal plantation experiment took place everywhere in the South occupied by Union troops, but historians have examined most closely the effort on the Sea Islands of Georgia and South Carolina and the Natchez plantations in the Mississippi River valley. These scholars concluded that while the free labor experiment failed to secure for black people the status of landowners, it did give them ownership of their own persons. In particular the programs assured an end to physical coercion of labor, encouraged independent family, religious, and social life, and required compensation. The experience provided blacks who lived and worked in Union-occupied areas the confidence necessary to determine for themselves the meaning of freedom in the postwar world. The effort to help slaves adjust to their new circumstances was made in Arkansas as well, but little is known about the experiment there or its results. This study examines the end of slavery in Arkansas and the federal program to help the freedmen adjust to freedom.[1]

In Arkansas slavery began to collapse with General Samuel R. Curtis's invasion of the state in the spring of 1862. Thousands of slaves abandoned their masters and joined the line of march as Curtis's army moved down the White River, then settled in at Helena on the Mississippi River. As Union forces moved elsewhere in the state, masses of slaves joined the marching columns. Boston Blackwell, a slave from Jefferson County, summed up the slaves' view of the Union army when he recalled, "[I]ffen you could get to the Yankee's camp you was free right now."[2]

Helena became the first site at which large numbers of slave runaways gathered. Able-bodied men were hired to build fortifications or chop wood for the Federal fleet on the Mississippi. Many women worked as cooks or laundresses. For many, however, Helena offered nothing; and conditions among the freedmen became extremely harsh, as the freedmen were unable to support themselves. Through the spring and autumn of 1863 the Federal commanders at Helena, in order to provide some relief, attempted to send the freedmen gathered near their camp to communities in the North. One treasury agent in the Mississippi valley captured the desperation of the situation when he wrote of the freedmen, "They are the helpless, down-trodden Victims of this War—crushed between the two contending parties as a corn is ground between the upper and nether millstone."[3]

A government-organized effort at addressing problems such as those existing at Helena first took shape in the spring of 1863. Secretary of War Edwin M. Stanton sent Adjutant General Lorenzo Thomas to the area to initiate a program that would enable black refugees to "support themselves and to furnish useful service in any capacity to the Government." Thomas recruited black troops, hired laborers, and provided some relief, but he also proposed that the government use blacks as farm workers. A program implemented earlier in western Tennessee and northern Mississippi by John Eaton, Jr., an army chaplain from Ohio who had been named general superintendent of freedmen in the Department of Tennessee by General Ulysses S. Grant in December 1862, provided the basic model for Thomas's plan. The basic idea was to lease abandoned and confiscated plantations to loyal men, who would then hire freedmen. Thomas described his plan as one that would "line the banks of the Mississippi River with a loyal population and . . . give aid in securing the uninterrupted navigation of the river, at the same time . . . give employment to the freed negroes whereby they may earn wages and become self-supporting." Thomas intended that the work on the plantation would be the first step toward freedom, providing not only financial independence but understanding of the culture of free labor.[4]

In orders issued on April 18, Thomas named Chaplains Jacob G. Forman and Samuel Sawyer as supervisors of freedmen's affairs in the Helena area with instructions to lease plantations and hire freedmen to planters. The two accomplished very little that year because the program had been announced so long after the time to plant had passed. At the end of the year they had leased only two estates in the vicinity of Helena. The great majority of freedmen remained in the contraband camp created near the town. The chaplains related that health and living conditions among the freedmen in the camps continued to deteriorate.[5]

In October 1863 President Abraham Lincoln transferred responsibility for the leased plantations from the army to the Treasury Department. William P. Mellen, special agent in charge of the First Special Agency of the Treasury Department, assumed control of matters in the Mississippi River valley and issued new regulations for leases. He created three subagencies for Arkansas with offices at Helena responsible for lands from the mouth of the St. Francis River to the mouth of the Arkansas River; at Skipwith Landing, Louisiana, with control over land from the mouth of the Arkansas to Carroll Parish, Louisiana; and at Little Rock, supervising lands in Pulaski and Jefferson Counties along the Arkansas.[6]

Mellen's agents began leasing lands on January 20, 1864, and many planters signed contracts and engaged laborers under the Treasury Department's regulations. These regulations, which raised the wages of agricultural workers above those of the previous year, provoked widespread protests from prospective lessees. In response President Lincoln reversed his initial decision to place all operations under the Treasury, and on February 28, 1864, he ordered General Thomas to reassume direction of the entire program. Thomas immediately restructured the plan. He divided responsibilities between the army and the Treasury Department. The Treasury's First Special Agency, under Mellen, supervised leases. The army assumed responsibility for supervising labor contracts and caring for the freedmen. Under this reconstructed program, the plantation labor system in Arkansas moved forward.[7]

Arkansas never attracted as large a number of lessees as the Sea Islands along the Atlantic coast or Natchez. The delays in developing the system in the spring of 1864 did not help matters. Because Treasury operations within the state were divided among different offices, a full accounting of plantations that were leased by loyal tenants cannot be made; however, by the end of 1864 the superintendent of freedmen's affairs indicated that freedmen who had signed labor contracts were working on at least one hundred plantations in the state. As many as thirty-six farmed in the vicinity of Helena. Another forty planters held land in Chicot and Arkansas Counties. The Treasury agent at Little Rock never reported the number of farms leased in his district.[8]

At the beginning, most of the plantation lessees were white Northerners. To lease a plantation, the prospective renters had to swear that they were loyal to the United States government and the Constitution, that they had taken no part in the rebellion, and that they would not provide aid, comfort, or support to those in rebellion. While Arkansas did not attract a large number of Northern lessees, those who did come came from a wide variety of states. The Helena office leased land to men from Illinois, Iowa, Massachusetts, New York, and Wisconsin. Many of these men were discharged Union army officers. M. D. Landon, an antislavery reporter for the *New York Tribune,* who rented eleven hundred acres outside of Helena, was one of the more prominent lessees. Only one of the Helena leaseholders, Henry F. Hooker, was a native Arkansan.[9]

Treasury Department regulations also ensured that most of the plantation leases consisted of relatively large parcels of land. Although Mellen's instructions required that preferences be given to those wishing to lease small tracts, they also required that the lessee demonstrate the ability to stock and cultivate the land. As a result, small farmers with scant financial backing had little chance to rent land from the government. Treasury agents tended to lease most of the land in large tracts. The size of farms leased at Helena in 1864 ranged from 275 to 1,100 acres. The supervisor of freedmen's affairs in Arkansas reported that statewide the average size of farms that made labor contracts through his office was 503 acres. The government's program essentially perpetuated large-scale farm operations as had existed before the war.[10]

While Treasury agents rented land and issued permits for trade, General Thomas named Colonel John B. Eaton, Jr., as general superintendent of freedmen for the Department of Tennessee and the state of Arkansas to supervise freedmen's affairs. Ordered to exercise "general guardianship of all interests of the freed people," Eaton's office issued permits for the use of free labor and administered labor contracts. The general superintendent was to protect the rights of the freedmen and ensure that they were industrious and fulfilled their contractual obligations. In January 1864 Eaton designated Major William G. Sargent as superintendent of the District of Arkansas. The district office was located at Little Rock, with local offices at Helena, Pine Bluff, DeValls Bluff, and Fort Smith.[11]

The freedmen's officials brought the freedmen together at home farms, farms supervised by the army and worked by the freed people who could find no alternative employment, and registered them. Those males who were fit for military service usually were enlisted in the army. The aged, infirm, and orphaned received employment at the home farm itself, raising cotton and growing their own food. The rest were required to seek outside employment. The superintendent of the home farm sent those freedmen who could not find work on their own to leased plantations to work for planters who applied for laborers. By the summer of 1864, Major Sargent reported that 3,561 of over 5,000 freedmen under his supervision were at work on plantations. Of that total, 1,045 were at Helena, 200 on the White River, 958 at Little Rock, and 977 in the vicinity of Pine Bluff. Another 391 were employed on Islands No. 63 and 76 in the Mississippi River.[12]

After January 1864 the army was supposed to supervise plantation labor, but General Thomas did not establish guidelines concerning contracts until March 11, when he issued Order No. 9. As a result, many farm operators signed labor agreements based upon the Treasury Department guidelines of the previous year. As late as February 17 Treasury agents and individual planters in Arkansas remained unclear about lines of authority in the management of labor affairs. Especially unclear was whether the regulations of the Treasury Department or the army took precedence in Arkansas operations. Thomas added to the general confusion of supervising labor when he sanctioned the use of the Treasury system as well as his own.[13]

Treasury regulations classified laborers into three categories with corresponding differences in wages. Physically fit persons from twenty to forty years of age were designated as No. 1 hands who were paid $25 per month for men and $18 for females. No. 2 hands included persons from fifteen to nineteen and forty-one to fifty, with pay of $20 for men and $14 for females. No. 3 hands included workers twelve to fourteen and over fifty, to be paid at a rate of $15 for men and $10 for females per month. Hands with physical defects or other infirmities were to be separately classified by the superintendent. Treasury regulations required that lessees pay at least one-half of the monthly wage each month. The laborer had the option of receiving the wage in cash, food, clothing, or other necessities. The lessee could provide supplies, but the Treasury required that supplies be of good quality and that the provider charge no more than 15 percent above wholesale price.[14]

The army's wage guidelines and overall goals were considerably different. The army provided for a lower pay scale but required farm operators to furnish, at their own expense, several major services. The basic wage rates were similar; all males over the age of fourteen received $10 per month, and females $7 per month; children and those too feeble to provide full labor were paid one-half these rates. The army required that planters hold back one-half of the freedmen's wages until the end of the year and urged, if possible, that no monthly cash payments be made. The planter was to provide free, as a part of the laborers' compensation, healthy rations and comfortable clothing. In addition, reflecting the army's belief that the program was more than simply one to provide workers for plantations, the planter was to provide such basic services as medical care and school for children.[15]

From the beginning, the system worked in a way that failed to be much more than one that gave plantation lessees workers. Treasury and army agents complicated contractual arrangements when they allowed farm operators to negotiate agreements that did not set specific cash settlements. Some laborers signed contracts that gave them a share of the crop at the end of the season, an agreement similar to the postwar contractual relationship that historians Roger L. Ransom and Richard Sutch have called "share wages." The freedmen working for Thomas J. Jordan of Horne's Landing, Mississippi County, signed one such contract. First-class hands received a share of one-fourth of the proceeds from the crop; second-class hands, one-fifth; and third-class hands, one-sixth. Jordan's contract allowed him to write off all expenses incurred by his hands against their proceeds.[16]

The system was intended to familiarize black workers with free labor, but except for a new system of compensation, work differed little on the government-supervised plantations from the way it had been under slavery. The continued employment of large numbers of workers on individual plantations was one aspect of this continuity, particularly in the counties along the Mississippi River where large-scale operations could be better protected from Confederate raids. The Treasury Department reported in March that the number of hands on twelve leased plantations at Helena ranged from 25 to 115 each. These twelve leases accounted for over half of the total number of labor agreements signed that spring. In Chicot County three lessees each contracted to use 320 hands of all classes. The labor forces in Chicot County were large even by antebellum Arkansas standards. Lessees in the interior of the state generally did not have forces so large, although the hiring of 25 to 30 workers was common.[17]

On the larger farms and plantations, most lessees and native operators continued to use gang or squad labor directed by a boss or overseer to cultivate the crops. At Pine Bluff the operation of Patrick Benjamin employed an ex-slave by the name of Reuben as the "head man or boss-workman." Chaplain A. Severance Fisk, assistant superintendent in charge of freedmen, after a tour of plantation districts that included Helena, concluded that many lessees, inexperienced in the management of black labor and the cultivation of cotton, had hired overseers to direct their operations, and these overseers directed the labor of freedmen just as they had managed slaves.[18]

While planters hiring freed labor were prohibited from flogging or otherwise punishing their workers, military orders made it clear that workers would be required to work. The former slaves were "not relieved from the necessity of toil." The worker would be held to the "fulfillment of his engagements." Army regulations imposed significant controls on the lives of the freedmen. Thomas's Order No. 9 required that workers give "respectful, honest, [and] faithful labor" to their employers for ten hours a day in the summer and nine hours in the winter. Employers could penalize workers with a forfeiture of pay for "indolence, insolence, disobedience of orders, and crime." Workers were to remain on their plantations unless authorized to leave.[19]

As the system developed, a further complication arose because of the army's practice of allowing loyal native owners to engage free laborers under government regulations. In other areas of the South, the labor experiment carried out by the army took place almost completely on land leased by Northerners. In Arkansas, however, from the beginning many of the freedmen worked not on leased plantations but rather on plantations that remained in the hands of their original owners, who army observers believed had little real interest in helping the freedmen achieve economic freedom. If a native planter subscribed to the necessary oath and agreed to abide by government regulations, he received a permit to purchase supplies from within Federal lines, grow cotton, and sell his crop. Mellen believed at the beginning of 1864 that if given ample protection "hundreds" of native planters would agree to farm under the Treasury Department's rules. While no government documents mentioned the total number of such plantations, some Arkansans in Arkansas, Chicot, Crittenden, Jefferson, Phillips, and Pulaski Counties resumed farming under Federal guidelines.[20]

Making the system even more difficult to direct, the army also allowed freedmen to lease and work some farms. The military's concern that such farmers operate only in areas that could be protected meant that freedmen's farms existed primarily in the Helena area. By midsummer of 1864 one report indicated that at least forty freedmen rented lands directly from the government in that district and were farming them with their own means. Black lessees in the vicinity of Helena operated on a smaller scale than other tenants, with the smallest lease being twenty-five acres and none larger than seventy-five. A visitor later in the year noted that, statewide, "many" blacks had been given the opportunity to farm on their own, but the total number is impossible to reconstruct, and few details remain as to their operations.[21]

In the first year's activities in Arkansas, at least some freedmen subleased land from other lessees as well. Freedmen's officials reported that some others cultivated the plantations of their former owners, in effect leasing the land and working it for a share of the crop. In a typical contract a Helena resident allowed one of his former slaves, William Peyton, to set aside ten acres to be farmed by himself. The former slave owner provided the land and apparently credit for supplies. Peyton negotiated on his own with the Treasury Department for permission to secure bagging and rope for the cotton. In another Phillips County lease, the resident plantation owner gave her hands land to garden and permitted them to grow cotton on it for themselves. They worked the land with the planter's teams, and she superintended their efforts. In turn, she received the right to buy the cotton from them at the end of the year. Such arrangements undoubtedly provided agricultural labor in Arkansas with valuable experience in making the transition from slavery to freedom. The problem is that the documentary evidence is so scanty that it is impossible to determine the number of such contracts.[22]

Without question, the primary goal for the freedmen within the army's free labor system was to provide them with an opportunity to secure the money necessary to help themselves. As the system developed and operations began, the possibility that this primary economic goal would be secured became less certain. Many problems interfered with the actual operations of the farms in the summer of 1864. One problem that many lessees faced was that the Federal government could not provide adequate protection from Confederate raiders. Operators of government-authorized plantations reported daily fights with men who tried to steal mules and other plantation equipment. In addition, Confederate guerrillas operated near the plantations, threatening the freedmen who worked for Yankees with annihilation. As a result, the Union army built two forts manned by disabled black soldiers to protect operators of plantations in the vicinity of Helena. M. D. Landon built his own fort, Fort Landon, on the lands that he farmed. Still, such efforts were not enough.[23]

Confederate cavalry staged heavy raids on the Helena plantations on August 1 and 3, 1864. Thomas Heaton reported from Helena that between three hundred and four hundred laborers had been driven off the land and that all the mules and supplies had been taken by the Confederates. The lessees were reported to be discouraged, and some of the blacks who had leased land sold out their crops. Apparently, however, the Confederate raiders failed to destroy the cotton; according to Heaton, "[It] 'still lives' & must I think produce a pretty good yield in spite of Jeff Davis or the devil."[24]

Another problem faced by the lessees was an infestation of cotton worms in August; this did what Confederate raiders had not done. Agents reported that much of the crop planted in central Arkansas had been destroyed by the worms. From southeastern Arkansas agents indicated that the cotton worms had eliminated nearly five-sixths of the crop in the district encompassing Chicot and Arkansas Counties. Major Sargent reported that the worm had "nearly ruined the crops," although he believed that the planters had not been completely discouraged. The superintendent indicated that they had saved enough of the crop in most cases to "pay expenses" if not make a large profit.[25]

In addition to trouble encountered in producing a crop, considerable conflict developed between laborers and employers that summer. Early in 1864 many farm operators took advantage of the disagreements between Treasury and army authorities and renegotiated contracts with their workers in which they manipulated the system against worker interests. Thomas's regulations allowed the planters to cut back immediately on the cash that they were paying out to their laborers and also to control their costs by directly controlling what the workers consumed. The number who chose to renegotiate contracts using army rates rather than those of the Treasury is not known, but many appear to have done so. Among the freedmen, this appeared to be unfair and the result was disillusionment with the entire labor program. Following a tour along the Mississippi River, a tour that took him to Helena, Chaplain Fisk reported that hands complained of the reduction of wages: "They awoke one day to find that the employers' part of the contract was broken, but *their's* kept whole."[26]

As the season progressed the lessee-worker tension continued to increase. By the end of the year, planters complained that the freedmen were not working as hard as the operators thought they should nor were they completing the hours in the fields for which they had contracted. A group of planters interviewed at Helena told military officials that they received no more than six to eight hours of work per day from their hands and only about four days per week. They also criticized the freedmen for possessing poor work habits, so that even when they worked little was accomplished. All of this was intended as an argument either for cutting the pay owed to the freedmen or reducing future wages.[27]

Especially during the harvest season in the autumn, many lessees tried to force more work from their laborers. Some tried to get the government's assistance, demanding that the army assure that the freedmen fulfill their contracts. When the army refused to provide provost marshal guards to police the laborers, planters took matters into their own hands. Treasury and army regulations both denied planters the use of the "lash, paddle, and all other cruel modes of punishment" to discipline labor, but at least some lessees and managers used physical force. Chaplain Fisk reported that on some plantations "blows and kicks have not been infrequently administered." Major Sargent and others thought that the worst offenders were the resident planters for whom "the rule is unfortunately somewhat different." Chaplain Fisk, however, reported that a "certain roughness and severity of manner . . . has been used foolishly, on almost all plantations."[28]

A few lessees believed that many of the planters were responsible themselves for the lack of productivity among the freedmen. M. D. Landon informed William Mellen that the freedmen on his land worked well and that he was astonished at the "economy, saving care, happy hopeful contentment, and every day industry" of the freedmen. He credited his success to offering good pay and settling regularly with his hands. Landon recognized that the freedmen on some farms did not behave as well as his, but blamed it on employers who treated the freedmen more like slaves, paying them infrequently and providing only low wages. Convinced that planters often were responsible for poor labor, one military official contended that those who paid their workers regularly received as much as one-third more labor.[29]

When the planting season of 1864 ended and accounts were settled the disputes between planters and laborers became even more serious as parties tried to settle their various claims to the crop that had been grown. When the crop was in and sold, employers totaled up bills for goods sold to the freedmen and subtracted time lost and other penalties from potential wages. The army agents observed that few freedmen received any cash at all after the deductions were made. The freedmen did not understand what had happened, and officials were concerned that employers had gone out of their way to produce these results, cheating their workers by charging excessive rates for supplies or making false reports concerning the loss of time.[30]

In some cases the means used by employers to cheat workers were even more openly dishonest. Some employers tried to avoid paying wages by causing the workers to break their contracts. Colonel L. B. Thomas reported that some lessees drove their freedmen off the land by cutting rations, provoking quarrels, or creating guerrilla scares. When the workers left the plantation, technically they had broken their contract, thereby freeing the employer from honoring his obligations.[31]

In the end few freedmen made more than a subsistence living during that first year, although planters made enough to encourage them to try again in 1865. Many workers ended the season in debt. Military investigations of the numerous problems that had arisen between workers and employers concluded that no single cause had been responsible. Obvious dishonesty and the abuse of workers had taken place. Some laborers had without any provocation failed to honor their contracts. At the same time other factors contributed to what generally were considered the poor results of the first year of work. Chaplain Fisk recognized the complexity. While aware that fraud had taken place, he also found that many of the heavy charges against the freedmen for lost time and supplies they had received were justified. They were also inevitable given the disruption of labor by guerilla raids, bad weather, and sickness. The need of the freedmen to purchase extra supplies to relieve their destitution also was a necessary expense. In the end, however, Fisk suggested that poorer yields than expected, plus the higher anticipated cost to the laborer, had led to settlements that had given the freedmen so little.[32]

Whatever the sources of the problem, the fruits that they received in their first experience with "free labor" seriously disappointed many freedmen. Officials found widespread disillusionment among the workers. Colonel Thomas noted that with no pay at the end of the year the freedmen could see little difference between their lives as free laborers and as slaves. Freedmen in the districts responded by slowing down their work in some cases. Thomas found that the free worker "look[ed] only at results. He

[saw] that the white man ha[d] received his labor, and ha[d] paid him with food and clothing,—about the same he used to get."[33]

The system failed to give freedmen economic independence, and it proved equally disastrous in developing the attitudes about labor that had been hoped for. Among many freedmen's officials the concern with the development of these attitudes was as important as the establishment of the laborers' economic independence. From the beginning the leased plantation program envisioned not merely putting the freedmen to work but also teaching them the values essential for survival as free laborers. Industry, respect for property, and individual responsibility were to be learned by doing, not simply imposed upon the freedmen by force. At the end of 1864 they believed there had been little change. While officials noted improvements in this area, they believed that much remained to be done. In their view, the freedmen's failure to understand basic economic principles was at least partly responsible for the debts they amassed during the first year. Success required that the plantation experiment educate the freedmen to behave as free men in the broadest social sense.[34]

At the end of the 1864 season, officials who worked with the freedmen looked at the previous year and tried to explain why there had been so little success. In the end it was clear that the government's program as it had been carried out in Arkansas was partly to blame. Among their conclusions was the realization that they did not have the means to carry out effectively Thomas's broader plan. There were not enough agents to ensure that the freedmen were not cheated in their contractual relationships or to ensure that the freedmen received the educational resources intended by Thomas. Military needs decimated the numbers working with the freedmen when officers were ordered back to their regiments in the summer of 1864 and no new men were assigned to freedmen's operations. Repeated changes in staff also hindered systematic operations. Concerning the post at Helena, Major Sargent reported in the spring of 1865, "[T]his Post has been prolific in superintendents. . . . The constant change has resulted unfavorably to the blacks."[35]

In addition, some of the staff proved incapable or unwilling to perform the tasks assigned to them. When Lieutenant James H. Rains took over the Little Rock superintendency in January 1865, he found everything in disarray and condemned his predecessor for being unconcerned about the needs of the freedmen. Rains claimed that "trade, traffic and pecuniary interests, to all appearances, had occupied the time and attention of those whom [they] had supposed to be interested in the welfare of the Freed people." Also in Little Rock the supervisor of the home farm was removed when the state superintendent found that he not only kept inadequate records but lived with a woman who was not his wife.[36]

As a result of problems with the government administration of freedmen's programs, many of the broader components of the labor experiment were left in the hands of the lessees and planters who had hired black laborers. This class, overall, proved inadequate to that task and failed to carry out efforts that would have achieved the objectives of the government's policy, especially regarding the improvement of the freedmen's work habits and values. Schools were supposed to be created to that end, but few such schools ever opened on the leased plantations. Major Sargent reported that while schools had been organized in towns and on home farms, with a few exceptions they had been neglected on the plantations. In a particularly damning indictment of the system's failure to help the freedmen achieve broader social goals, Chaplain Fisk observed that little had been done for educating the freedmen and that many of the planters actually opposed the idea of providing schools. He concluded, concerning the lessees, that "no class of men, engaged in pushing their fortunes in hazardous ventures of this sort, will stop for educational or moral effort among the people."[37]

To deal with these problems, freedmen's officials urged that future efforts should emphasize placing the freedmen on smaller units of land where they would be allowed to farm independently rather than hiring them to plantation lessees. Freedmen's officials with the army generally agreed that the freedmen who worked on their own achieved the greatest economic success and learned more rapidly how to operate as free men. At Helena, Chaplain Herrick reported that on the lands belonging to Confederate general Gideon Pillow, the "Deputy place" and the "Casteel place," which had been set aside specifically for freedmen to work on their own, the freedmen had been "prosperous." The successful lessees wished for more land and other freedmen now wanted to work on their own as well. Herrick also found that the independent farmers were not only more industrious, self-denying, considerate, and calculating than farm laborers, but also possessed greater self-respect. General N. B. Buford, commander of the Garrison at Helena, went so far as to recommend that leases only be made to freedmen.[38]

When planting was renewed in 1865, despite the conclusions of the men who supervised the freedmen, little changed in the operation of the system. When the plantations were leased in the winter of 1864–1865, army agents tried to put into practice some of the lessons learned the previous year, but they found altering the system difficult. Part of the problem was that the end of the war was in sight and the future of the army's and the Treasury's role in the South was not clear. Questions existed as to what would happen to leased plantations once the war ended. As a result, the number of leases made by the Treasury Department in Arkansas declined in 1865. In the Little Rock District, the department's agent reported twelve plantations leased in Pulaski County, five in Jefferson County, and one in Prairie County. In the Helena District, officials reported approximately twenty-three plantations leased by the end of the spring. All plantations in southeastern Arkansas were abandoned. The number of leased plantations thus dropped from about one hundred to forty-three.[39]

The Treasury Department continued to lease land to the remaining lessees in large blocks rather than encouraging the freedmen to take up smaller parcels. The records of the Helena office of the Treasury showed that the average lease made that spring was nearly 580 acres, with the largest being that of W. J. Warwick, who leased some 4,000 acres of land originally owned by the heirs of John H. Craig.[40]

The reasons for the basic continuity were complex, but possibly not the least of the reasons was the resistance to changes by the lessees. They responded with hostility to attempts to break up the large leases and distribute land to the freedmen, possibly realizing that this would undermine their control over the labor market. William Sanderson, who was leasing Gideon Pillow's Swan Lake plantation in Phillips County, complained that if he was not allowed to renew his lease in 1865, he would lose thousands of dollars that he had been forced to invest in the plantation by the Treasury before he could operate it. Yankee troops had destroyed all of the improvements on the plantation when they moved into the area in 1862. Before he could raise a crop Sanderson had constructed eighteen cabins, built a gin house, repaired the barn, and repaired the engine and boiler on the gin—an investment of some eight thousand dollars.[41]

At the same time Treasury agents expanded the number of permits given to native planters to grow cotton. This opened up more plantations and workers for military supervision, but did nothing to put freedmen onto farms of their own. By the spring of 1865, many ex-Confederates considered their cause hopeless and after swearing an oath of allegiance operated their own farms under government supervision. E. T. Diamond of Helena reported that he had secretly contracted with his servants to operate his plantation in 1864, but had made no public record of it "for fear of personal violence and injury to the contrabands." To secure the supplies necessary to gather and bag his crop, he now made his contract public and expressed his intention of operating under Treasury regulations. George B. Peters, another Helena planter, agreed to employ his slaves as free laborers since Confederate soldiers had "been expelled from my region of county." Others joined Diamond and Peters, and by the end of the spring of 1865 the Treasury had registered 232 plantations at Helena as operating under government auspices and 209 of that number were run by actual owners. At Little Rock, twenty-five local planters secured permits to operate their plantations under the government's system.[42]

The expansion of permits issued to local planters ultimately played a major role in the reduction of the number of white lessees. The practice also discouraged any effort at placing freedmen on farms of their own. Still, some gains were made toward this goal. At Little Rock officials allowed freedmen to continue to lease portions of the home farm. Some outright leases of abandoned plantations to freedmen were made as well. Thomas Bass was one of these lessees and he hired fifty-seven workers. Officials also encouraged lessees and owners of land to sublease their lands. William Sanderson, who leased a farm in Phillips County, was one who operated in this manner. Sanderson gave "faithful and trusty" freedmen pieces of ground to work on their own, proposing to furnish food, clothing, animals, and tools in return for an interest in the crop. The numbers allowed to farm their own land, however, remained small in proportion to the total number of freedmen at work.[43]

After March 3, 1865, control over the labor contracts passed from the military to the newly created Bureau of Refugees, Freedmen, and Abandoned Lands. Major Sargent continued to direct the effort in Arkansas but under the authority of the Freedmen's Bureau. The 1865 plantation system differed little from that of the year before. Throughout the state over fifty-two hundred laborers signed contracts under bureau supervision. New wage rates were established for workers, increasing the pay for first-class males to twenty-five dollars per month, plus rations. Some effort was made to control spending by the freedmen by prohibiting planters from keeping account books for their laborers. The bureau's rationale was that account keeping only offered a greater opportunity for whites to swindle the freedmen. They also recognized that such arrangements generally were unsatisfactory to the freedmen.[44]

The problems of the previous year persisted, however. Major General Alexander McDowell Cook found that at Helena the freedmen working on leased plantations were "not well care[d] for by these *truly loyal men* of the north who [came] down here to get rich in a few seasons, at the expense of the colored people." By the end of the season, many of the same problems of 1864 reappeared as lessees and landowners took advantage of whatever opportunities they could find to cheat the workers of their final settlement. James H. Rains, a bureau agent at Little Rock, indicated in August that he had noticed "a disposition to oppress the Freed laborers" by the lessees. Little had changed.[45]

Again, Freedmen's Bureau officials believed that the best results were being accomplished where freedmen had been able to obtain small quantities of land and were working it themselves for wages or shares. In a report for June 1865, Henry Sweeney at Helena indicated that many more wanted to cultivate tracts from between twenty and fifty acres, but that they were unable to obtain such lands. Ultimately, the bureau agents were convinced that some sort of system of subletting land (something like the subsequent tenant system of farm labor) provided the best mechanism for educating the freedmen as well as providing them economic opportunities. In fact, within two years after the war this system of agricultural labor would dominate every portion of the Arkansas plantation region.[46]

Whatever the causes, efforts in 1864 and 1865 had done little to help blacks gain economic independence. Similar to Federal operations elsewhere in the South, the programs carried out in Arkansas provided little protection for the laborers—either from Confederate raiders or in their contractual arrangements with employers. Good intentions existed among many of the military and Treasury officials who worked with the freedmen, but these produced little in the way of real solutions to the problems that kept the freedmen from making money. The overall effort was driven in Arkansas primarily by the attempt at making the leased plantations economically productive, and the system usually worked to the advantage of the lessee, not the freedmen.

The failure extended to the broader goals of aiding the freedmen to establish communities and values that would have aided in securing full freedom. In other areas of the South the wartime labor experiment included efforts to encourage the development of independent family, religious, and social life for blacks. In Arkansas the profit motive ruled the experiment. If the freedmen learned anything, they discovered that their freedom could be circumscribed all to easily. Freedmen's officials testified about the lessons the freedmen had learned in their numerous reports. One official, Lieutenant Colonel. L. B. Eaton, after a visit through Arkansas in the autumn of 1864, concluded that the freedmen usually expected to receive no full return for their labor. Eaton noted, "[The] rights of blacks . . . have been so long outraged by the whites, that they [blacks] are exceedingly distrustful." After two years of work, Henry Sweeney of the Freedmen's Bureau concluded that little had changed. Sweeney found that freedmen were suspicious and distrustful in all dealings with whites, particularly those arrangements involving written contracts. Restricted by their inability to read and write, they knew "that in all written documents (such as contracts to labor & c.) they [were] liable to be swindled by unprincipled white men." The plantation experiment provided hard lessons for the future.[47]

Chapter 10

Brother against Brother: The Winter Skirmishes along the Arkansas River, 1864–1865

JAYME MILLSAP STONE

Compared to the Civil War's eastern theater, Arkansas, at first glance, seems insignificant. Outside of a few major engagements, such as the battles of Pea Ridge, Prairie Grove, Helena, and Jenkins' Ferry, the war in Arkansas was largely a matter of skirmishing and guarding supply lines. Such tasks, according to historian Michael Fellman, were "not a poetic test of men's souls."[1] But while these routine efforts did not always provide glory, they were important and should not be neglected by historians.

In 1965 the historian Edwin C. Bearss constructed a basic outline of the state's final skirmishes along the Arkansas River, mostly from information in *The War of the Rebellion: A Compilation of the Official Records of the Union and Confederate Armies.*[2] This article, using previously untapped primary sources (letters, diaries, recollections of various soldiers, church and government records, and newspaper accounts), attempts to expand on Bearss's historical reconstruction. Bearss, for example, did not point out that many Arkansas soldiers, both Federal and Confederate, were recruited from and served in the Arkansas River valley and the adjacent counties. As a result, military operations along the Arkansas River, such as the action at Dardanelle and other nearby clashes during the winter of 1864–1865, literally pitted Arkansan against Arkansan, brother against brother.

The struggle began in earnest when, after two years as a Confederate state, Arkansas began its return to Union control following the battle of Helena on July 4, 1863. Shortly after this engagement, Union major general Frederick Steele began his march toward Little Rock. On September 10, Steele forced Confederate major general Sterling Price to abandon Little Rock and retreat south of the Arkansas River. Virtually simultaneously with Steele's occupation of Little Rock, Major General James Blunt took Fort

Smith, on the Arkansas River at the state's western boundary, for the Union. These victories gave the Federals control of the Arkansas River and the surrounding valley, thus forcing the Confederates into southern Arkansas. Adjusting quickly to the new political order, towns along the river, including Dardanelle, between Little Rock and Fort Smith, adopted resolutions in support of the United States government. While most of the principal towns along the river fell into Union hands, the countryside remained under tenuous Confederate control. This was to cause a great deal of trouble for citizens of both persuasions outside the protection of garrisoned towns, as "neighbors stole from neighbors in the melee."[3]

The explanation behind this turmoil was rooted in the state's secession struggle. Secession had not come easily for Arkansas. In February 1861 Arkansas voters, especially those from the northwestern quarter, soundly rejected the idea. Events at Fort Sumter and the subsequent decisions by Virginia and Tennessee to join the Confederacy, however, proved enough to sway both political and public opinion. By May 1861 Arkansas was on its way out of the Union, even though many complained that secession was being forced on the people. The romantic fantasy of war eventually faded as law and order broke down and neighbor began to turn against neighbor. In March 1862 the Union army won the most significant Federal victory in the Trans-Mississippi theater, the battle of Pea Ridge (Elkhorn Tavern). In the future, Arkansas adjutant general Albert W. Bishop predicted "a retributive future for those men, who, in the spring and summer of 1862, from Fort Smith to Little Rock, and from the Arkansas river to the Missouri line, hunted their old friends and neighbors like wild beasts of the forest simply because they were true Union as their fathers made it."[4]

Despite the Federal victory at Pea Ridge, Unionist sentiment of any degree was dangerous in Arkansas. One soldier likened it to being "placed between two fires—and flanked beside." Loyalty to the Union would be easier to proclaim once the Federals completely regained control of the state. Until that day, men were reluctant to risk injury to their families; instead, they maintained a "discreet silence." Only men of "uncommon nerve" dared to profess allegiance to the Union publicly while parts of the state continued under Confederate control.[5]

After the Steele-Blunt successes of September 1863, public sentiment shifted toward a renewal of Union support. Meanwhile, dozens of small bands of Rebel deserters resorted to guerrilla warfare. They had left the Confederate army to protect their families. As soldiers, they had to follow orders and quarter with their companies. As deserters, they could take refuge with relatives and exact revenge on the Federals who, they claimed, were now burning out their homes and murdering their families. Reporting to the Arkansas adjutant general, one Union officer, First Lieutenant Frank Pease, testified that the territory north of the Arkansas River was "infested by numerous guerrilla bands, who were robbing and murdering Union families in the most barbarous manner that human depravity could invent." In a recent article by historian Daniel E. Sutherland, compelling evidence shows that the war in Arkansas was irregular, destructive, and often very personal.[6]

Responding to the violence, the Union army proceeded to raise troops for the protection of the region's loyal citizens. One Union regiment raised to combat the guerrilla threat was the Third Arkansas Cavalry, mustered into service in February 1864 and quartered at Lewisburg, upriver from Little Rock.[7]

The new regiment's commander, twenty-nine-year-old Abraham H. Ryan, was a member of General Steele's staff. As commander of the District of Arkansas, Steele had Ryan transferred from the Seventeenth Illinois Infantry and elevated by three steps in grade to the colonelcy of the Third Arkansas Cavalry. A Unionist newspaper published in Little Rock, the *National Democrat,* applauded Ryan's promotion, calling him "a thorough soldier and most admirably adapted to his present command." The paper bragged that the Third Cavalry's officers were "most or all of them Arkansas men, and judiciously chosen."[8]

The "brave and patriotic" rank and file was filled with men recruited primarily from the river counties of Conway, Yell, Pope, and Pulaski. Nearly 93 percent of the men in the Third Arkansas Cavalry enlisted in the Arkansas River valley. These troops desired to "fight alone for their homes," but some came with a serious potential defect—many of the new Federal recruits came wearing Confederate gray.[9] For example, Company G of the Third Arkansas was composed, in part, of related Confederate families from the Enola and Lewisburg areas.[10] During the early months of the war, Governor Henry M. Rector had offered many Union sympathizers a choice of entering either the Confederate army or prison. By early 1864, with Federal forces now in control, some soldiers who had been pressed into Confederate service took the first opportunity to change sides. Believing them sincere in their dedication to the Union, Colonel Ryan gladly accepted the services of these former Butternuts and those offered by partisans such as Williams's Independent

Company of Scouts and Spies. Led by Captain Thomas Jefferson Williams, the scouts and spies not only provided protection for area loyalists, but conducted reconnaissance and raiding missions for the Third Arkansas Cavalry. These partisans, largely related by blood or marriage, had fled Conway County during the early months of the war to avoid Confederate conscription. Family concerns eventually led them to return home, where their attention shifted to harassing their Rebel neighbors and protecting their Federal ones.[11]

Ryan's obligations did not end with the safety of these locals. He was also expected to keep Confederate forces south of the Arkansas River and to keep the river open for navigation between Fort Smith and Little Rock, duties rarely exciting and never easy.

In 1864, Ulysses S. Grant, general in chief of the Union armies, decided to restrict operations west of the Mississippi River and concentrate his forces in the eastern and western theaters. Grant instructed Major General Edward R. S. Canby, commander of the Military Division of West Mississippi, to limit operations to those necessary to keep open the lines of communication, lines that included the Arkansas River region between Fort Smith and Little Rock.[12] The very nature of the Arkansas River made this mission especially difficult. As one Union soldier put it, the Arkansas was "one of the changeablest rivers," he ever saw, "rising one day and falling the next."[13] Its reputation was that of a glorified drainage ditch whose unpredictability would complicate Union efforts to control the countryside.[14]

The unreliable river caused transportation problems and great hardships for the Union garrison stationed at Fort Smith; it was forced at times to subsist on half or quarter rations. Sufficient corn and other crops had been planted in the river valley in 1864, but at harvest time the food rotted ungathered for lack of field labor. When the water levels were up, Federal steamers could travel from Little Rock to Fort Smith in four days. Unfortunately for the garrison, the Arkansas River for much of the winter of 1864 was too low for navigation, thus making supply unreliable. The alternative supply route was overland. Two hundred wagons traveling from Fort Scott (near the Kansas-Missouri border) were necessary to carry the payload of one Federal steamboat. Similarly wretched conditions in the Indian Territory demanded that these goods be shared with Fort Gibson, the Cherokee capital in the Indian Territory. There simply was not enough to go around.[15]

According to one report, five thousand animals died for lack of forage that winter, and Major General Joseph J. Reynolds, who succeeded Steele as commander of the District of Arkansas in November 1864, contended that the garrison at Fort Smith could not possibly provide protection for loyal citizens outside the lines, much less those in Kansas or Missouri. Thus, Reynolds considered Fort Smith a "dead weight."[16] With these problems in mind, General Canby ordered Fort Smith evacuated in mid-December 1864.

Upon hearing the news, the Unionist governor of Arkansas, Isaac Murphy, and the Arkansas General Assembly literally begged President Abraham Lincoln not to abandon the region to the "merciless ravages of the bushwhackers and robbers . . . [thus causing] the most loyal portion of Arkansas to become a scene of ruin and desolation."[17] C. P. Bertrand, the former mayor of Fort Smith, also wrote to the president, pointing out that to abandon the city could have serious political ramifications: "Do you know that this abandons one entire Congressional district and the whole of another, save two or three counties, and that two-thirds of the members and perhaps three-fourths of the Legislature, now in session here, are furnished from the district of the country thus to be abandoned and given up?"[18]

There were other considerations, too. According to General Steele, the removal of the Fort Smith garrison would endanger Fort Gibson and Union influence over the Native Americans in the Indian Territory. Steele believed that without the support these forts provided, the Indians would be "compelled to plunder the settlements of the whites or starve." The Five Civilized Tribes, occupying part of what is now the state of Oklahoma, were harshly divided during the Civil War. When the Indian Territory was under Confederate control, thousands of pro-Union Indian families had fled to refugee camps in Kansas. Instead of finding a safe haven, they found disease, starvation, and death. Union-supported Indian raids exacerbated the Native American feuding, and animosity was great on both sides. The Indian Territory returned to Union control after the December 1862 battle of Prairie Grove, but Fort Smith and Fort Gibson were still unable to distribute adequate aid despite widespread foraging. Army officials greatly feared that if the Federal presence at Fort Smith was withdrawn, loyal Indians might resort to raiding more than Confederate Indians.[19]

Likewise, the regimental commanders of the Fourth Arkansas Cavalry (U.S.) and the First Arkansas Infantry (U.S.) joined with Colonel Ryan of the Third Arkansas Cavalry in a plea to President Lincoln not to evacuate Fort Smith, claiming that those civilians, "fortunate enough . . . to get away with their lives, would . . . come to our military posts as beggars." To abandon Fort Smith would succeed only in seriously demoralizing Arkansas's Union troops. It would also give the Rebels a secure place from which to conduct fresh raids north of the Arkansas River, putting northern Arkansas and Missouri at risk.[20]

Thanks in part to this letter-writing campaign and to the efforts of Lieutenant Colonel Bishop, who traveled to Washington to "remonstrate against this most disastrous proceeding," President Lincoln pressured General Grant to countermand the orders to evacuate Fort Smith. This abrupt turnaround forced a scramble to reoccupy the town in a manner likened by historian Carolyn Pollan to an "unorganized fire drill."[21]

It was in this atmosphere of confusion that the task of sending supplies upriver by steamer to Fort Smith began in earnest. On January 9, 1865, Brigadier General John M. Thayer, commander of the District of the Frontier, headquartered at Fort Smith, sent a desperate dispatch to Little Rock, saying, "[E]vacuation or no evacuation, I beg that boats will be sent."[22] To complicate matters, Union scouts scurried into Lewisburg (upriver from Little Rock) on New Year's Day with reports estimating that 900 to 1,500 Confederates with three pieces of artillery were camped at Dardanelle, about twenty-five miles northwest of Lewisburg, and at Beatty's Mill, near Petit Jean Creek. First Lieutenant Orville Gillet, Jr., of the Third Arkansas Cavalry recorded in his concise but informative diary that "news came in of 900 Rebs being at Dardinell [*sic*]. Scout sent out to see."[23]

In conversation with Federal scouts, some of the locals claimed that the Confederates intended to raid supply boats headed toward Fort Smith. The civilians believed that the Rebels were Missourians commanded by the legendary Brigadier General Joseph O. Shelby; however, this was only a rumor.[24] The troops around Dardanelle were actually Colonel William H. Brooks's Thirty-fourth Arkansas Mounted Infantry, Colonel Robert Crittenden Newton's Fifth Arkansas Cavalry, and Colonel Erasmus "Ras" Stirman's Arkansas Cavalry Battalion.

In the fall of 1861, Brooks and Stirman had worked together in organizing several companies for Confederate service, and they continued to remain closely linked throughout the war. Although their commands originated in Washington County, approximately 43 percent of Brooks's regiments and about 30 percent of Stirman's enlistments came from Pope, Pulaski, Yell, Crawford, Sebastian, and Franklin Counties—all bordering the Arkansas River. In Stirman's correspondence with his sister, he frequently mentioned the Pope County town of Dover as a popular place to rest, visit friends, and recruit troops.[25]

Likewise, Newton, "barely more than a youth" when he entered Confederate service, recruited throughout the Arkansas River valley. The twenty-one-year-old Colonel Newton usually enlisted older men over forty, boys under eighteen, and others exempt from Confederate service; unfortunately, only a scant number of their regimental records survived the war.[26]

In an August 1864 letter to his fiancée, Captain Fontaine Richard Earle of Brooks's Thirty-fourth Infantry cherished "a hope of expelling the Feds from Arkansas river by fall." By mid-December, Major General John Bankhead Magruder, Confederate commander of the District of Arkansas, granted Earle's desire for action. He instructed Brooks, Stirman, and Newton to move into the river valley and attempt to block navigation between Fort Smith and Little Rock.[27]

General Reynolds at Little Rock and Colonel Ryan in Lewisburg were disturbed by the reports of such a large concentration of Confederate troops in the area.[28] Union reconnaissance confirmed the troops to be those of Colonels Brooks and Newton. They occupied Dardanelle, but they had failed to reach the north bank, having been repulsed by several Kansas regiments traveling downstream. Lieutenant Gillet of the Third Arkansas (U.S.) reported in his diary, "[O]ur scouts [are] skirmishing across the river at Dardinell," and "[T]he rebs up the river got cut to pieces by our men that came down from Fort Smith."[29]

Faulty Union intelligence now suggested that the Butternuts were actually more interested in commandeering cattle and evacuating pro-Confederate families than endangering Federal boats along the river. Colonel Ryan, whose paramount concern was to hold Dardanelle (important because of its location on the southern bank of the Arkansas halfway between Little Rock and Fort Smith), was anxious to take advantage of the situation. He asked General Reynolds on January 4, 1865, to send five hundred men and a section of artillery to help with an advance on the unsuspecting Confederates. Reynolds denied Ryan's request, citing a shortage of available Union cavalry.[30]

Meanwhile, new reports from scouts noted that the enemy, consisting of Newton's and Stirman's troops, had moved six miles southwest to a place called Bogg's Mill. Brooks's regiment remained at Beatty's Mill. As rain mixed with snow fell during the night of January 5, the river began to rise, making it unfordable at Dardanelle. Ryan ordered Captain Davis Hamilton at the Third Cavalry's outpost in Norristown (Dardanelle's sister town across the Arkansas) to destroy all ferries and skiffs to prevent their use by enemy forces.[31] The rain and snow continued, causing muddy roads and high creeks, but despite the inclement weather, scouts continued their reconnaissance missions.[32]

On the evening of January 12, Hamilton informed Ryan that the Confederates were encamped at Bogg's Mill near Dardanelle and at Rocky Crossing on Petit Jean Creek. The next day, the Federal steamers *Admiral Hines* and *Lotus* reached Lewisburg from Little Rock. On board were 276 dismounted cavalrymen of the Seventh Army Corps under Major James D. Jenks of the First Iowa Cavalry. Ryan ordered Jenks to head upriver until he met the steamer *Alamo,* which was carrying Lieutenant Robert W. Wylie's detachment of the Third Arkansas Cavalry and 50 infantrymen of the Eleventh U.S. Colored Troops. After the boats rendezvoused, Wylie informed Jenks that it was safe for the boats to continue upriver toward Fort Smith. In compliance with their orders, Jenks and his men disembarked at Norristown and the steamers moved on.[33]

Also on Friday, January 13, the steamers *Annie Jacobs* and *Chippewa* arrived at Lewisburg loaded with sixty days worth of supplies for the desperate garrison at Fort Smith and a message from Ryan ordering Jenks to occupy Dardanelle, which the major did at 10:00 A.M. on January 14. Writing in his diary at Lewisburg, Lieutenant Gillet noted, "2 Steam Boats went up the River with 13 Pieces of Artillery to help our boys fight the Rebs at Dardinell."[34] Ryan was determined to advance on the "lively" Rebels, despite the reluctance of the Little Rock command to send reinforcements. According to his correspondence, Ryan believed that the troops on the steamers, plus a detachment of the Third Arkansas Cavalry, would be able to "clean them out" and "open [the] way for boats to Fort Smith."[35]

By noon on the fourteenth, the last of the steamers had cleared Dardanelle.[36] The boats proceeded upstream to Fort Smith without incident. As the troops began to settle in at Dardanelle, however, scouts rode into town with a report that a force of one thousand to fifteen hundred Rebels, led by Colonel Brooks, was approaching the town from the southwest by way of the Danville road. Jenks then gathered his men into three stockades that guarded the land approach to Dardanelle. Although Lieutenant Gillet's diary claimed that Jenks was provided with thirteen artillery pieces, the major's cannoneers unlimbered only two guns for the protection of the garrison.[37] The Federal force was seriously outnumbered, but the odds were evened somewhat by the fact that the Confederates possessed only one cannon.

When fighting commenced at 2:00 P.M., the sounds of battle could be heard as far away as Lewisburg. Gillet recorded, "[I] heard Canonading up the River. Supposed to be our Boys engaging the enemy at Dardinell."[38]

Supported by two field guns, the entrenched Federals prevented the Confederates from destroying the fortifications with their single gun. Lasting about four hours, the action was sharp and resulted in several Union casualties. One of the most notable men wounded was First Sergeant William Ellis of the Third Wisconsin Cavalry. Though hit three times, Sergeant Ellis refused to abandon his position. It was only after he was wounded a fourth time that he obeyed orders to report to the rear. Under Resolution of Congress, Number 43, Ellis was awarded the Congressional Medal of Honor for "gallantry in action at Dardanelle, Ark." Thus Ellis, English by birth, became the first in Arkansas to be so honored by Congress.[39]

Ryan's report stated that the Rebels left "completely whipped," and this received confirmation from W. S. Jett. Private Jett, a boy of sixteen when he enlisted in a company of Dover youths led by Confederate Colonel Stirman, noted that he saw several comrades "badly wounded, and several horses killed so we could do nothing but retreat which was done in good order."[40]

Colonel Ryan originally reported that Union casualties stood at twenty-five, but this tally was later amended to one killed, fifteen wounded, and two missing.[41] One of the missing was a Lieutenant King, perhaps Patrick B. King of the Third Arkansas Cavalry, who reportedly had been taken prisoner during the skirmish. Ryan gave high praise to the leadership of Major Jenks and his officers, but in accordance with the custom of not acknowledging the deeds of enlisted men, no mention was made of the bravery displayed by Sergeant Ellis in the official report. Ryan estimated Confederate casualties as one commissioned officer killed and about sixty to eighty enlisted men left wounded—an exaggeration. One account, however, claims that the bodies of at least fifteen dead Rebels were left behind, not to be discovered for two days.[42]

Confederate General Magruder reported that the troops of Colonel Brooks attacked a heavier Union force near Dardanelle and "drove him into his works." In contrast to this official line, the young Private Jett reflected that they had intended to charge, "but [we] were too slow about it and they [Union] took advantage of some stockades."[43] Magruder placed Confederate losses at only one killed and fifteen wounded. Jett discovered the death of his friend Mack Jordan of the Dover area. The Confederates claimed to have killed eight and wounded nineteen.[44]

Both sides claimed victory at Dardanelle. Although the Confederates accrued heavier losses, they successfully melted into the darkness, leaving the Federals in fear of a renewed attack at dawn. Major Jenks frantically sent a courier to Lewisburg with a plea for support, and Ryan responded promptly, dispatching an additional sixty troopers of the Third Arkansas Cavalry and an ambulance loaded with ammunition under Major Daniel W. Mason. More wagons followed, carrying one hundred soldiers of the Eleventh U.S. Colored Infantry.[45]

The news of the attack on Dardanelle sent the Little Rock command scurrying to send troops upriver. General Reynolds now realized that the loss of Dardanelle would prevent the supplying of Fort Smith. Consequently, he immediately issued orders for the Fortieth Iowa Infantry and a section of Ohio light artillery to move upriver with a shipment of ammunition for Sharps and Enfield rifles. Lieutenant Gillet noted back in Lewisburg, "Steamboat Devenport went to Dardinell with reenforcement for our men and took rations to our men."[46]

General Reynolds's about-face concerning Ryan's request for troops can best be explained by his correspondence with President Lincoln's chief of staff, Major General Henry W. Halleck. Concerned that he had not received any reports from Arkansas and fearing that Fort Smith was being abandoned, Halleck directly ordered General Thayer on January 10 to observe General Grant's orders and secure Fort Smith. Despite his personal belief that Fort Smith should be evacuated, Reynolds notified the chief of staff that the post would be held and that supplies were being sent upriver despite the appearance of the Rebels at Dardanelle. The river had dropped nine inches in the past twenty-four hours, thus making a crossing by the Confederates a real possibility and further threatening the Federal boats carrying supplies. This communique, sent the same day as the fight at Dardanelle, committed Reynolds to protecting the Arkansas River supply line. Prudence now required that he send Colonel Ryan the support the colonel had requested.[47]

The evening after the action at Dardanelle, scouts arrived in Lewisburg with another report that the dreaded Confederate General Shelby was near Dardanelle with a large Confederate force bent on occupying Fort Smith.[48] In light of this report and convinced that Lewisburg was secure, Ryan headed for Dardanelle, where he arrived late in the evening on the fifteenth.[49]

Colonel Ryan's prompt answer to the threat on Dardanelle and Fort Smith was encouraged by more than the need to protect the supply lines along the Arkansas River. For Ryan, it was a matter of personal honor and perhaps revenge. In May 1864 General Shelby had crossed the Arkansas River at Dardanelle with a force of twenty-five hundred men. The approach of so many Confederates had caused the Third Arkansas garrison stationed there to flee in panic, overloading a flatboat that consequently overturned, drowning a number of men. As Shelby's horsemen had moved downriver toward Lewisburg, Ryan had hastily moved his outnumbered troops farther away. Despite the swift retreat, Ryan had been able to protect the regiment's supplies and documents by hiding them in Lewisburg homes under quarantine for smallpox.[50] Nevertheless, the movement of Shelby's troops had posed a real threat to the Union hold on the Arkansas River. Colonel Ryan's instructions had been to block Shelby's movement north, but the Confederates had been able to slip around the Federals and proceed north to the White River, an action for which Ryan had personally received blame. This low point in Ryan's career was exacerbated by the declining morale of the Third Arkansas, resulting in numerous desertions.[51]

Given the trouble and embarrassment that Shelby had caused the Union forces in Dardanelle and Lewisburg just eight months earlier, it seems plausible that Ryan's decision to proceed to Dardanelle and direct the efforts firsthand was an attempt to redeem his reputation. Upon his arrival late on January l5, Ryan learned that Brooks had not renewed the anticipated attack, but had moved up the south bank of the Arkansas River in pursuit of the Federal steamboats. The *Annie Jacobs* and the *Chippewa* were able to outrun the pursuit, resulting in the Federal belief that Brooks's attention would now return to the Dardanelle garrison.

With the *Davenport*'s arrival in Dardanelle on the morning of the sixteenth, Ryan had the reinforcements needed to prepare Dardanelle for another attack. He immediately employed his troops in throwing up earthworks to fortify the approaches to Dardanelle.[52] These ramparts were constructed of materials gathered from the local churches, which were destroyed on the colonel's orders. The personal memoirs of Henry Pattillo Barry, a Yell County Confederate, recounted that the Baptist church was taken to pieces and used for army purposes when Colonel Brooks "was trying to take Dardanelle in the winter of 1864–65. Col. A. J. Bryan, of the U.S. Army (now of East Orange, N.J.) gave the order to tear it down."[53]

Along with the local Presbyterian church, the Dardanelle Baptist Church was, "by proper authority," confiscated and stripped of its weatherboarding and flooring for the "construction of breastworks and for firewood." The

Baptist congregation, pleading loyalty to the Union during the late period of the Civil War, filed suit against the United States in 1908 for damages and was awarded three thousand dollars "in full compensation for use, occupation, and destruction of said church by the Federal forces."[54]

As nightfall approached, excited scouts galloped into Dardanelle and reported that the Butternuts had been reinforced by the Second and Fourth Arkansas Confederate Cavalry Regiments. The Confederate troops were said to be surrounding Dardanelle in preparation for a dawn attack.[55] When the anticipated attack did not materialize, Colonel Ryan became convinced that it would occur two days later on the nineteenth, noting that the enemy's campfires could be observed in five directions. Intelligence suggested that the Rebels were planning to take Dardanelle in order to force the evacuation of Fort Smith.[56] Ryan's conviction that a siege was in the offing and the resulting anxiety among the Union forces were reflected in the diary entries of Lieutenant Gillet back in Lewisburg. Each day between January 15 and 20, Gillet recorded that there was, "no news from up the River . . . no news from [our] troops at Dardinell."[57]

Tensions were high as yet another bogus report of Confederate reinforcements reached Lewisburg. The Texas Brigade of Colonel William H. Parsons was thought to be camped just eight miles away. Parson's "Hell Yelpers" were renowned for their suicidal frontal assaults, and the thought of Brooks being supported by the forces of Shelby, Gordon, Morgan, and now the legendary Parsons caused Ryan to focus his attention on the defense of Dardanelle. According to Bearss, all these reports of reinforcements were instances of false intelligence, probably carefully planned and spread by the Confederates to cover their actual intentions.[58] Consequently, while the Union troops were fortifying Dardanelle and Union scouts were reporting phantom enemy troops, the Confederates were upriver, waiting for their opportunity to strike at the Federal steamboats returning to Little Rock from Fort Smith.

As Ryan prepared Dardanelle for a Confederate attack, Brooks carefully positioned his troops along the south bank of the Arkansas River upriver from Dardanelle. The Federal steamers *Admiral Hines, Chippewa, Lotus,* and *Annie Jacobs* had arrived in Fort Smith on the fifteenth with over five hundred tons of supplies for the suffering garrison. According to the pro-Union editor of the *Fort Smith New Era,* the arrival of the steamers was most gratifying to the brave troops stationed there: "They had been reduced to short rations for so long that we fear they will hardly know how to dispose of all the good things Uncle Sam sent them."[59]

After a two-day layover in Fort Smith, the convoy cast off from Van Buren on the seventeenth and headed downriver. Each steamer carried a small armed guard, officers bound for home on furlough, and numerous civilians seeking escape from the harsh conditions of northwest Arkansas. On board the *Annie Jacobs,* the largest of the four, more than five hundred haggard refugees, many without blankets, shoes, or adequate clothing, shivered in the dead of winter.[60]

Traveling with the *Chippewa* in the lead, the steamers were ambushed at 1:00 P.M., according to a *Fort Smith New Era* account, by a Rebel band under command of the notorious Brooks. Hiding in the brush along the river near a bend called Ivey's Ford and using a six-pounder gun, the Confederates hammered the *Chippewa* at close range and forced it to the south bank of the Arkansas. Official Confederate reports noted that eighty-two prisoners, plus numerous refugees, were captured. The Confederates removed all valuables from the boat, including ornate rugs, according to local folklore. After looting the boat, the Confederates moved back into cover to wait for the next victim, the *Annie Jacobs.*[61]

As the *Annie Jacobs* rounded the bend at Ivey's Ford, Colonel Thomas M. Bowen, on furlough from the Thirteenth Kansas Infantry, peered through a pair of field glasses at the *Chippewa* and noticed that it was ablaze. Bowen was "at once satisfied of the presence of the enemy."[62] As the ranking officer on board, he ordered the *Annie Jacobs* to speed up and push for the north shore, out of artillery range. Despite its evasive maneuvers, the steamer received a number of hits from solid shot and shell, causing panic among the passengers and a great deal of opportunistic looting as well. The boat made it to the north shore, but Private Vincent B. Osborn of the Second Kansas Cavalry had his thigh shattered by flying shell fragments. His leg was amputated in a failed effort to save his life. In contrast to Ryan, who commended only his officers, Colonel Bowen gave Osborn, along with several civilians who tended fires and rallied troops, special mention in his official report. Bowen praised his officers, too, saying, a "less tenacious determination would have surely resulted in the loss of the boats."[63] Private Gaston of the Thirty-third Iowa Infantry, aboard the next steamer, the *Lotus,* left his own account of the affray: "[A]t 3½ P.M. we come up with the Chippawa and her Burning & the Anna Jacobs we got about 2 hundred yds of the Jacobs the rebels opened on us with one piece of Artillery & about 400 or 500 small arms."[64]

A shell passed directly through the *Lotus*'s pilothouse, killing several and causing others to jump into the chilly river. While an undetermined number of passengers were killed, some drowning in the swollen river, the vessel managed to escape irreparable damage. The *Admiral Hines,* not having received a message from Bowen ordering it to remain upriver out of the fray, continued downstream. Luckily for the steamer, an axle broke on the Confederate cannon, rendering it useless. In addition, a nearby Union forage train heard the cannonading and headed toward the river. The Confederates, aware of the wagon train but mistaking it for an artillery unit, decided to retreat into the hills south of the Arkansas River. They released the captured civilians but retained the soldiers.[65]

While the Federal steamers were under assault upriver, Ryan was still in Dardanelle, ardently preparing for what he thought was an imminent attack. On January 18 burned wreckage from the *Chippewa* floated downriver into Dardanelle. This, combined with the testimony of a woman traveler who reported the burning of a Union boat, should have sent Ryan scurrying to reinforce Colonel Bowen and the steamers; however, he irresolutely waited almost thirty-six hours before ordering Captain Hamilton with a detachment of sixty men from the Third Arkansas Cavalry to ride to Bowen's aid.[66] Ryan's hesitation resulted from his myopic concern about a Confederate assault on Dardanelle. He protected the town but failed in his mission to safeguard Union shipping. When confirmation of the attack on the steamers finally came, Ryan belatedly realized that the threat to Dardanelle had passed. After communicating with General Reynolds in Little Rock, Ryan decided a return to Lewisburg was in order.[67]

From a Confederate perspective, the attack on the riverboats had been a definite success. News of the assault reached Lewisburg on the twenty-second, leading Gillet to write tersely, "Rebs burnt one of our Boats." The word upriver was that the troops were marching on the Rebels, but the Butternuts were no longer in the area, save Colonel Newton's Fifth Arkansas Cavalry.[68]

Ryan was still in Dardanelle on January 24 when scouts reported that Newton's troops were twelve miles away at Bogg's Mill. Intelligence reports said that the Confederates planned to grind flour at the mill and be gone before sunrise. Ryan, anxious for some success in this whole Dardanelle affair, sent a detachment of the Third Arkansas Cavalry and 150 men of the Eleventh U.S. Colored Infantry in hopes that they could trap Newton's men. The reports given to Ryan were accurate, and the Federals surprised Newton's command. The Union troops captured twelve hundred bushels of wheat, eighteen horses, twenty stands of arms, and Newton's personal papers, thus giving Ryan some degree of fulfillment in his efforts against the Confederates. He wrote with great satisfaction that "what was left of Newton's regiment was going for Caddo Gap as fast as horseflesh could carry them."[69]

At the last report, Brooks's brigade had been spotted near Caddo Gap, probably waiting for Newton's regiment to bring supplies. Brooks's command later moved south to the Red River for winter quarters, thus bringing an end to the struggle for control of the Arkansas River. Satisfied that nothing else could be done, Ryan's troops began to move out of Dardanelle, with the last returning to Lewisburg on January 27.[70]

The Confederate maneuvering around the Arkansas River in the winter of 1864–1865 proved to be the last major raid into the Federally controlled Arkansas River valley. General Robert E. Lee's surrender came before another advance could be organized, and Arkansas Confederates promptly realized that the cause was lost. While Federal control over Fort Smith had been maintained, it did not stem the flow of refugees into the Union camps as the regimental commanders had hoped. The extreme conditions made nomads of large numbers of civilians. As spring approached, Confederate soldiers recruited in the river valley began to wander toward home. A Confederate lieutenant in Newton's regiment, W. M. Wallis, recalled that most in his outfit were furloughed to go home and cut wheat. Others left to plant corn "before the season was too far gone." Gillet recorded the influx of rebels into Lewisburg: "May 29, 300 Rebs came in with a flag of truce and gave up looked very raged [*sic*] and dirty."[71]

Upon returning home, the soldiers of both the blue and the gray found their "country naked, except a spot here and there, where neighborhoods had been of one mind and had been faithful to each other." A microcosm of the post-surrender difficulties found in the Arkansas River valley was Yell County. Several years after the war, one soldier reflected on his apprehension about returning home: "Dardanelle . . . had been very much divided during the last two years of the war between southern sympathizers, who remained at home, and the families of union sympathizers, who had also remained at home, the people of both parties had been most mercilessly robbed and maltreated by confederate bush-whackers on the one hand, and federal maintained-boomers on the other . . . the feelings of hate and reverage ran high."[72]

The soldier returned safely, but he was careful to travel only after sundown. His prudence was wise because a letter written from Dardanelle in

March 1866 also mentioned that "the people here were divided during the war" and a "good many of the Boomers ha[d] been killed since the war."[73] Likewise, two neighboring counties had their share of Arkansan-on-Arkansan violence. In February 1865 Confederate guerrillas from Conway County murdered a Federal scout for the Third Arkansas Cavalry, Captain Thomas Jefferson Williams, in full view of his family. Williams's son spent months exacting bloody revenge against his neighbors. In the fall of 1865, a former Third Arkansas captain and Pope County sheriff, Archibald Dodson Napier, was killed by local disgruntled Rebels. Old times there were not forgotten either.[74]

The winter skirmishes along the Arkansas River were important for several reasons. It is important to remember that the Federal troops who took part in this struggle of brother against brother were not "damned Yankees," but Arkansans. The recent scholarship of historian Richard N. Current contends that even though homegrown regiments such as the Third Arkansas Cavalry were less than first rate, they did occupy posts, skirmish with the enemy, forage for food, and provide protection and order in the towns along the river. By fulfilling these tasks, they freed other soldiers to engage the Confederates elsewhere and denied the Confederacy the sustaining lifeblood of manpower. Many of those who were not native Arkansans adopted the state as home and prospered. A prime example is Thomas M. Bowen, the officer from the Kansas regiment who saved the Federal boats during the Confederate attack near Roseville. Remaining in Arkansas after the war, Bowen became president of the 1868 constitutional convention and an associate justice of the state supreme court.[75]

The war had been brutal to all, Confederate and Federal soldiers and civilians alike. John Patterson was touched by the suffering of women and children who had nothing to eat but boiled corn, "and not a nuf of thet." To abandon Fort Smith, however meager its effectiveness, would have further jeopardized the lives of the Unionist Arkansans who sought its shelter. To have lost Dardanelle as well would have given the Arkansas River valley and probably northwest Arkansas back to the Confederates. If this had taken place, Unionist morale undoubtedly would have plummeted. Wartime success often involves breaking the will to resist. These Union losses would have strengthened Confederate resolve.

The loss of Arkansas, even at this late stage of the conflict, would have had important ramifications for the Union. A Confederate reoccupation of Fort Smith would have certainly endangered Federal control of the Indian

Territory. The Cherokee Confederate brigadier general Stand Watie did not surrender in April 1865 when Lee did. Neither did he lay down his arms when President Jefferson Davis was captured early in May nor when Confederate general Edmund Kirby Smith surrendered the remains of the Trans-Mississippi to Major General Edward R. S. Canby on May 26. General Watie waited until almost the end of June 1865 before surrendering, becoming the last Confederate general to admit defeat. His will to resist had finally been broken. But if Arkansas had returned to Confederate control in the winter of 1864–1865, and the Indian Territory with it, Fort Gibson would have provided Watie and his pro-Confederate Indians with a new base of operations for raiding into Kansas and Missouri—and a new fighting spirit. The Civil War in the Trans-Mississippi theater would have been prolonged for a people weary of death and destruction. John Patterson, who penned his observations from Lewisburg in May 1865, most certainly represented what many believed in their hearts: "I never want to se another war in my time while I am in life. O but it has bean a crule war."[76]

Chapter 11

"We Cannot Treat Negroes . . . as Prisoners of War": Racial Atrocities and Reprisals in Civil War Arkansas

GREGORY J. W. URWIN

The battle of Poison Spring, April 18, 1864, was one of the most complete victories ever won by Confederate forces in Arkansas. Fewer than four thousand cavalrymen sprang a cleverly laid ambush within the hearing of thirteen thousand Union soldiers in nearby Camden, capturing a large wagon train carrying food for their foes. As the exulting Rebels scattered the train's escort, they refused to take prisoners from its largest unit, the First Kansas Colored Volunteer Infantry Regiment. Thus a glorious Confederate triumph was transformed into Arkansas's most notorious war crime.[1] The atrocities at Poison Spring, along with the retaliatory measures adopted by other African American troops serving in Arkansas, reveal the essence of a savage conflict whose central issue was race.

Though more than 130 years have passed since that terrible day, the memory of Poison Spring still troubles many of those who prefer to view the Civil War in romantic terms. The Arkansas Department of Parks and Tourism, which maintains a historic park at Poison Spring, has tended to ignore the dark deeds that stained that particular patch of hallowed ground. Despite such indifference, the murder of captured black soldiers at Poison Spring deserves a prominent place in any history of the Civil War west of the Mississippi River.[2]

The clash at Poison Spring marked the beginning of the end for the Camden expedition, the last major Federal offensive in Arkansas. In late March 1864, Major General Frederick Steele, the commander of the Union Department of Arkansas and Seventh Army Corps, marched south with roughly fourteen thousand troops drawn from his garrisons at Little Rock and Fort Smith. The five thousand soldiers from the latter post belonged to Brigadier General John M. Thayer's Frontier Division and were veterans of successful operations in Indian Territory. Among Thayer's regiments were the First and Second Kansas Colored Infantry, composed of runaway slaves from Missouri and Arkansas and led by white officers. Steele's column penetrated further into southern Arkansas than the Federals had ever gone before. The expedition also represented the first time that black units in the state were employed as anything more than garrison or labor battalions. Both of these facts struck terror into the hearts of the region's white inhabitants.[3]

Steele carried orders to rendezvous at Shreveport, Louisiana, with a larger Union army and a gunboat flotilla under Major General Nathaniel P. Banks. Once Steele joined him, Banks planned to invade Texas, seizing vast supplies of cotton in the process to enrich Northern speculators. But the two armies were destined never to meet.[4]

Hampered by muddy roads and constantly harassed by more than six thousand Confederate cavalry, Steele pushed southward by starts and stops. A feint toward Washington, the capital of Confederate Arkansas since Little Rock's capture the previous year, threw the Rebels so off balance that Steele was able to march into the fortified town of Camden without a fight on April 15.[5]

The country through which Steele's army passed had been picked over by Confederate foragers since the autumn of 1863. By the time the Federals reached Camden, they had been on half rations for three weeks, and their rations were soon halved again. But relief lay close at hand. Captain Charles A. Henry, Steele's chief quartermaster, learned of the existence of five thousand bushels of corn stored at a point sixteen miles west of Camden. Henry assembled a forage train of 198 wagons to secure the corn.[6]

Steele turned to the Frontier Division for an escort to guard the train, and General Thayer detailed a total of 1,170 troops for that purpose. There were 438 officers and men from the First Kansas Colored Infantry, 383 from the Eighteenth Iowa Infantry, 291 troopers from the Second, Sixth, and Fourteenth Kansas Cavalry, and 58 artillerymen manning four guns. Command of the escort went to James M. Williams, the First Kansas's colonel and an officer known for his zeal, competence, and courage. A lawyer in civilian life, Williams had distinguished himself at several battles in Indian Territory in 1863 and would end the war as a brevet brigadier general of volunteers.[7]

The Confederates destroyed twenty-five hundred bushels of corn before Williams could reach the scene on April 17, but the Federals saved the remainder and loaded it aboard their wagons by midnight. At sunrise the next day, Williams started his column back toward Camden, detaching small parties to gather additional corn from the farms lying near his route. After marching some four miles, Williams encountered Confederate brigadier general John S. Marmaduke with twelve cannon and over 3,600 cavalry deployed for battle at Poison Spring.[8]

Marmaduke's hastily assembled force represented a cross section of Confederate mounted strength in the Trans-Mississippi theater: a brigade and an independent battalion containing 786 of Marmaduke's fellow Missourians; 1,500 Arkansans in brigades led by Brigadier General William L. Cabell and Colonel William A. Crawford; and 655 Texans and 680 Choctaw Indians in a division brought from Indian Territory by Brigadier General Samuel B. Maxey. Most of these horsemen carried infantry rifles, weapons with greater range and stopping power than the Rebel cavalry's traditional carbines and shotguns.[9]

Colonel Williams deployed the First Kansas in an L-shaped line to shield the head and southern side of the forage train from the enemy's main thrust. The black soldiers had only gotten fifteen hours of rest during the past seventy-eight and were now caught in a three-way artillery crossfire. Nevertheless, they held their ground in the face of superior numbers, repulsing two Confederate attacks with rapidly delivered volleys. Many Rebels present, impressed by such tenacity but unwilling to concede that former slaves could match them as soldiers, later stated that the Federals had 1,500 black troops at Poison Spring instead of 438.[10]

By the time Marmaduke was ready to mount a third attack, the First Kansas's ranks had been badly thinned by death and wounds, and ammunition was running low. Advancing with cheers and war whoops, the Rebels turned the battered regiment's flanks and drove the crumbling blue line back through the parked wagons. Colonel Williams rallied as many men as he could and conducted a fighting withdrawal to the comparative safety of a swamp north of the battlefield. From there, he guided what was left of his escort on a circuitous retreat to Camden. The first of these weary fugitives began entering Steele's lines around 8:00 P.M.[11]

A gloating Camden resident watched as Colonel Williams's men "held groups of soldiers in the streets in solemn silence, to hear the story of the fight at Poison Spa [Spring]." The tales spread by the battle's survivors contained elements more horrifying than the experience of military defeat. Williams himself reported, "Many wounded men of the First Kansas Colored Volunteers fell into the hands of the enemy, and I have the most positive assurances from eye-witnesses that they were murdered on the spot." The First Kansas's major and adjutant confirmed the colonel's accusations, as did other members of the escort.[12]

Williams's casualty figures told Steele's veterans at Camden that they could not dismiss these atrocity stories. Of the 301 men listed as killed, wounded, or missing from Williams's escort, 182 belonged to the First Kansas. That by itself proved nothing, as the blacks had borne the brunt of the battle. What aroused suspicion was the disclosure that the First Kansas had suffered 117 slain, but only 65 wounded. "It will be seen," reasoned a trooper in Steele's Third Missouri Cavalry, "that the number of our killed exceeds the number of our wounded in this engagement, an unusual occurrence in warfare of the present day, as it is generally found from the reports of the many battles being daily fought in our land, to be just the contrary. This can be accounted for when it is known as we were informed by one of the 2d Kansas Cavalry who made his escape a few minutes prior to the completion of the struggle, that the inhuman and blood thirsty enemy . . . was engaged in killing the wounded wherever found."[13]

In letters, diaries, reminiscences, and oral testimony handed down from generation to generation, the victors at Poison Spring described the fate that befell those black soldiers who failed to escape. Lieutenant William M. Stafford, a Texas artilleryman in Maxey's Division, confided to his journal, "The surprise of the enemy was complete—at least 400 darkies were killed. [N]o black prisoners were captured." Three different Arkansas cavalrymen expressed pride in the fact that the Union dead were "mostly Negroes." A trooper in the First Arkansas Cavalry boasted, "[W]e almost exterminated the troops that had the train in their charge." "If the negro was wounded," another Arkansas cavalryman wrote to a loved one in Arkadelphia, "our men would shoot him dead as they passed and what negroes that were captured . . . have since been shot." Ordered to remove the captured wagons to a place of greater safety, Cabell's Arkansans drove over the dead and dying blacks, competing to see who could crush the most "nigger heads." When General Edmund Kirby Smith, the commander of the Confederacy's Trans-Mississippi Department, reached the Camden vicinity two days later, his jubilant subordinates informed him that they had left six hundred Federal dead rotting at Poison Spring, "primarily Negroes who neither gave or rec'[eived] quarter." Local civilians were soon referring to the fight as the "Poison Spring Massacre."[14]

Of all those who succumbed to the homicidal frenzy at Poison Spring, none surpassed Colonel Tandy Walker's Choctaws for sheer ferocity. As Lieutenant Stafford scribbled in his journal, "The havoc among the negroes had been tremendous—over a small portion of the field we saw at least 40 dead bodies lying in all conceivable attitudes, some scalped & nearly all stripped by the bloodthirsty Choctaws." "You ought to see Indians fight Negroes—kill and scalp them," marveled Private Charles T. Anderson of the Second Arkansas Cavalry. "Let me tell you, I never expected to see as many dead Negroes again. They were so thick you could walk on them." The Choctaws' behavior was still a topic of conversation when Brigadier General Thomas J. Churchill's Arkansas infantry division arrived in the Camden area a few days after Poison Spring. "The Chocktaw was at Camden when we came up," James McCall Dawson of the Thirty-fourth Arkansas Infantry wrote to his family. "They caught out one Regt of Steels negros and killed all of them They take no prisoners They would shoot a negro as long as he could breathe." Mrs. Elizabeth Godbold Watts, whose home was close enough to Poison Spring to be pressed into service as a field hospital, complained that her slave, Henry, did nothing to protect her hogs from Choctaw foragers "for fear that someone [would] kill him since the negroes were killed so in that fight."[15]

The Choctaws harbored so much animosity for their black victims that killing them was not enough. In addition to scalping and stripping, the Indians devised other ways to desecrate the First Kansas Colored's dead. The *Washington Telegraph* treated its readers to this example of "Choctaw Humor": "After the battle of Poison Springs, the Choctaws buried a Yankee in an ordinary grave. For a headstone they put up a stiff negro buried to the waist. For a footstone another negro reversed, out from the waist to the heels." Three days after the battle, a Union burial detail discovered that three dead white officers from the First Kansas had been scalped, stripped, and turned on their faces as a sign of dishonor, while the corpses of their black soldiers were laid in a circle around them.[16]

News of these atrocities traveled quickly throughout southern Arkansas.[17] For years afterward, Mrs. Martha Holcomb thrilled her children and grandchilden in the little village of Moscow with this version of the battle:

> By noon Marmaduke's men had routed the Federals who had put into the front line of the battle the untrained negro slaves. It was easy enough for these Southern planters when faced to

> face with their own slaves, to attack with a rage which put to flight the unskilled . . . negroes. They fled in terror to hiding places and were pursued by their masters like infuriated demons.
>
> A few miles below the battle field was an old mill with its beautiful pond fed by an abundant spring; here was refuge for the fleeing negroes. These Southern soldiers' revenge was not appeased by flight. The negroes were hunted and either shot or bayonetted in their hiding places.[18]

General Marmaduke and his senior officers never openly admitted that their men had butchered black prisoners, but they strongly hinted that such had been the case in their official reports. "The number of killed of the enemy was very great, especially among the negroes," noted General Cabell. "You could track our troops by the dead bodies lying on the ground." Colonel Walker asserted that during the engagement, his "hungry, half-clothed Choctaws" had been animated solely by the desire to shed "the blood of their despised enemy." Colonel Charles DeMorse, who led the Texas brigade in Maxey's Division, offered this sinister revelation: "But few prisoners were brought in by my command."[19]

While acknowledging no complicity in any war crimes, some of Marmaduke's officers felt the need to justify the carnage committed by their troops. Colonel DeMorse implied that his Texans were outraged to find the Federal forage train "laden with corn, bacon, stolen bed quilts, women's clothing, hogs, geese, and all the *et ceteras* of unscrupulous plunder." Lieutenant Colonel John M. Harrell of Cabell's Brigade recalled that "little children's and women's clothing" were "piled upon the wagons," including "little baby frocks, shoes, stockings, women's bonnets, shawls and cloaks."[20]

It was only natural for Confederates to be infuriated by such discoveries. Brutalized by hunger and the frustrations of campaigning in rough and hostile territory, Steele's bluecoats blazed a path of destruction across southern Arkansas. But that does not explain why the winning side at Poison Spring made the First Kansas Colored the sole object of its vengeance. After all, the First Kansas composed less than half of Colonel Williams's escort, and the African Americans were so drained by a lack of food and rest that they were in poor shape to go ranging about the countryside collecting forage and plunder. By sunup on April 18, 100 black infantrymen were so worn out that Williams classified them as "unfit for duty."[21]

The escort's 291 white Kansas cavalrymen were far better equipped to loot the farms along their route, and they apparently made the most of their opportunities. "Many of the cavalry, in violation of orders, straggled from their commands," Williams fumed. Shortly before the battle broke out, some of these wayward troopers showed up at the home of Mrs. Sarah Elizabeth Gillespie, about three miles from Poison Spring. "The soldiers," wrote Gillespie's great granddaughter, "took what meal, hams and sides of meat, dried beans, peas and fruit that Sarah had not sent deep into the woods and buried."[22] According to the same source, the Kansans were even more ruthless in ransacking the farm next door: "A neighbor of Sarahs climbed up into her meal barrel when the soldiers started to take it, but the man just picked her up and set her out on the floor and took the barrel of meal away. They also took all of her silver. . . . She had one fork left that they did not find. The Federals took feather pillows and mattresses, ripped them open and emptied the feathers out, then used them as sacks to carry their 'loot' in. They could sling them across the backs of their horses if there was no room in the wagons."[23]

From the existing testimony of Confederate civilians who lived in and around Camden during Steele's occupation, it is incontestable that the Union troops to be most feared were white Kansans—especially cavalrymen.[24] "The real yankee's I was not afraid of," insisted Mrs. Clara Dunlap, "they treated me gentlemanly enough, but the Kansas jay hawkers, that were most always sent with the wagon trains I was afraid off, they looked mean enough for any thing, & the officers, as bad as the men!" Dunlap testified, "[The Kansans] took all of our mules, *corn, sugar, molasses, flour, every thing* in the world we had to eat . . . , they even took all my *soap, candles, coffee* & every *hen, chicken,* turkey, eggs &c on the place except two or three setting hens, that ran off in the woods; all my *cooking vessels,* pans, *blankets* &c & then searched the house over, broke the lock on every trunk (but one) & took a good many little things all my good *shoes, stockings, soda,* spirits, even . . . took my *wedding slippers.*" The invaders ravaged the nearby farms of Dunlap's relatives with the same merciless thoroughness. Many of these Jayhawkers bore grudges against Southerners that dated back nearly a decade to "Bleeding Kansas" days, and they rarely missed a chance to settle old scores.[25]

In contrast to their white comrades, Steele's black troops were reasonably well behaved, and the guilt for relatively few depredations can be laid at their door. On the night of April 6–7, 1864, some of the Second Kansas Colored may have burned a cotton barn south of Hot Springs after word got out that the white menfolk from that plantation "were all in the Southern army." A week later, two black soldiers forced their way into a house at Moscow, but all they demanded was food.[26]

For the most part, however, enlisted personnel from the First and Second Kansas Colored gave Confederate civilians few legitimate grounds for complaint. "I did not find the negro soldiers impudent to a firm white man," an anonymous Camden resident informed the *Washington Telegraph.* During the Federal evacuation of the town on April 26, this same observer spotted a black regiment protecting a doctor's home from marauding white stragglers.[27]

Where Steele's black troops deliberately disregarded Southern white sensibilities was in their enforcement of the Emancipation Proclamation. Once at Camden, they wasted no time in notifying local slaves that they were now free to leave their masters and mistresses. Black soldiers also encouraged male slaves to enlist in the Union army, sometimes resorting to press-gang tactics to snare recruits. Yet in all these activities, the men of the First and Second Kansas avoided direct confrontations with whites, and alert slave owners managed to hold onto most slaves who were too timid to go willingly with the Federals. When an armed black squad tried to spirit off the household servants of businessman Henry Merrell, he succeeded in talking the soldiers out of it: "I interposed a long-winded argument to the colored patriots & they listened respectfully enough, until suddenly the drums beat for 'Roll Call,' & my audience vanished in obedience to discipline." Merrell also obtained a speedy release for his body servant, Munroe, who was bullied into enlisting after other black soldiers threatened him with hanging.[28]

If Federal looting really was the primary cause of the Poison Spring Massacre, then the Confederates had as much reason to murder the 120 white prisoners who fell into their hands—and not just the African Americans. The fact that the victims of this massacre belonged exclusively to the First Kansas leads to the conclusion that the perpetrators' motives were racial. The *Washington Telegraph,* the voice of Confederate Arkansas, admitted as much seven weeks after the battle.[29]

With the onset of civil war, John R. Eakin, the *Telegraph*'s editor, dedicated his newspaper to ensuring unwavering public support for the Confederacy across southern Arkansas. His importance as an opinion maker received an enormous boost after Washington became the state's Confederate capital.[30] In a June 8, 1864, editorial titled "The Slave Soldiers," Eakin turned his persuasive talents to justifying Confederate excesses at Poison Spring:

> How shall we treat our slaves arrayed under the banners of the invader, and marching to desolate our homes and firesides? . . . It is a case in which it well becomes our rulers to pray most earnestly for Divine guidance. May they have it soon! Meanwhile the problem has met our soldiers in the heat of battle, where there has been no time for discussion. They have cut the Gordian knot with the sword. They did right. It was not theirs to untangle its knotty folds. It is far better for the deluded victims, as for us, that the fate which may perhaps be considered inevitable, should come upon them in hot blood, and the excitement of the battle field.[31]

African Americans are such a conspicuous and valued part of today's American military that it is difficult to appreciate the revolutionary nature of Abraham Lincoln's decision to let slaves become soldiers. Yet when John Eakin proclaimed, "[T]he crime of Lincoln in seducing our slaves into the ranks of his army [should be ranked] amongst those stupendous wrongs against humanity, shocking to the moral sense of the world, like Herod's massacre of the Innocents, or the eve of St. Bartholomew," multitudes of Confederates on both sides of the Mississippi would have agreed. "All minor and local massacres," Eakin added defensively, "pale before it."[32]

To Eakin and other guardians of Southern slavery, the African American was two persons rolled into one. On the one hand, he was a simple and childlike soul, needing white care and guidance to lead a happy and productive life. On the other hand, he remained a savage at heart, purportedly like his ancestors in Africa, and had to be restrained by slavery. If ever those bonds should slip, he would revert to his animal nature and attempt to kill every white person he came across.[33]

White Arkansans schooled in such prejudices viewed any Northern action against slavery as more than just a threat to their economic and social status, but a deliberate attempt to stir up servile insurrections. If slavery was abolished, whites would either have to exterminate blacks or suffer extermination themselves. The question was literally a matter of life and death, or so whites believed.[34]

When the Lincoln administration followed the Emancipation Proclamation with authorization to accept blacks into the Union army,

Confederates in Arkansas fretted that the South's worst nightmare was about to come true. Little Rock's *True Democrat* accused the Federals of escalating the conflict into "a war for extermination, not only of men, but of women and children." The competing *Arkansas Gazette* anticipated this shift in enemy policy months before it took place, and its reaction was similar to the *Democrat*'s: "Our course is plain. A savage war has been forced upon us. We will have to meet, and deal with it as we find it." In particular, the *Gazette* urged the Confederate government to adopt the following course of action: "Arming negroes, as soldiers or otherwise, or doing any thing to incite them to insurrection is a worse crime than the murder of any one individual: Therefore, all officers and soldiers . . . guilty of such practices . . . should be punished as murderers."[35]

Arkansas journalists charged the North with violating the rules of civilized warfare by fielding black regiments. Only the most drastic action could save the Confederacy and what it represented. "It follows irresistably that we *cannot* treat negroes taken in arms as prisoners of war," proclaimed John Eakin, "without a destruction of the social system for which we contend. In this we must be firm, uncompromising, and unfaltering. We *must* claim the full control of all negroes who may fall into our hands, to punish with death, or any other penalty, or remand to their owners. If the enemy retaliate, we must do likewise; and if the *black flag* follows, the blood be upon their heads."[36]

Eakin's readers shared his indignation, especially after the First and Second Kansas Colored appeared in their midst. Reflecting in 1911 on the depredations committed by white Federals during Steele's stay in Camden, Virginia Stinson revealed, "Only one thing stirred my Southern blood to heat, was when a negro regiment passed my home going to fight our own dear men at Poison Springs. How fierce they did look, it was then that I gave vent to my feelings." When three wounded white prisoners from Poison Spring were delivered to the house of Elizabeth Watts, she taunted them by asking "if they felt as though they were fighting with their equals."[37]

These feelings prevailed at the highest command levels in the Trans-Mississippi Department. Ten months prior to Poison Spring, General Kirby Smith chided one of his senior officers in Louisiana: "I have been unofficially informed that some of your troops have captured negroes in arms. I hope this may not be so, and that your subordinates who may have been in command of capturing parties may have recognized the propriety of giving no quarter to armed negroes and their officers." Fear of Federal retaliation prevented the Confederate government from openly endorsing this draconian policy, but Kirby Smith's subordinates needed little prodding from above to put it into practice. In raids on Pine Bluff and Clarksville, Arkansas, between the fall of 1863 and the spring of 1864, Rebel irregulars shot or hanged captured black soldiers. Confederate guerrillas in Missouri habitually executed any male slaves caught trying to sneak off to Union recruiting stations. In a skirmish south of Lake Providence, Louisiana, on June 29, 1863, a Texas colonel directed his cavalry brigade to charge a fort held by two companies of black infantrymen and to "take none with uniforms on."[38]

As the first black combat unit in the Union army, the First Kansas was the paramount symbol of Yankee malice to every Confederate soldier and guerrilla in "Kirby Smithdom." In a clash that presaged Poison Spring, more than 150 Confederate bushwhackers surprised a foraging party of 25 men from the First Kansas at Sherwood, Missouri, on May 18, 1863. The black soldiers had stacked their rifles to load some corn into wagons, and most could not recover their arms before the Rebels were upon them. The guerrillas showed the defenseless Federals no mercy—shooting, stabbing, or beating thirteen of them to death. The others saved themselves by fleeing into the brush.[39]

Despite this setback, the First Kansas Colored developed into a first-rate regiment, which maddened its enemies all the more. At the battle of Honey Springs in Indian Territory, July 17, 1863, the First Kansas squared off in a head-to-head musketry duel with the dismounted Twenty-ninth Texas Cavalry. The blacks outshot the Twenty-ninth Texas, downing its colors twice and finally putting it to rout. The Texans never got over the humiliation of being bested by former slaves. When the First Kansas and Twenty-ninth Texas next met at Poison Spring, the Texans recognized their opponents and shouted with vindictive glee, "You First Kansas Niggers now buck to the Twenty-ninth Texas!" After the fight, a black soldier feigning death heard the Texans chanting a macabre litany as they searched the battlefield for wounded men to kill. "Where is the First Kansas Nigger now?" one would crow. "All cut to pieces and gone to hell by bad management," another would answer.[40]

An African American did not have to bear arms for the Union to become the object of Confederate wrath. Simply running away to the Federals was considered enough of a threat to Southern society to warrant the severest penalty, as was seen at the battle of Marks' Mills, Arkansas, April 25, 1864.

Like Poison Spring, the clash at Marks' Mills was a consequence of General Steele's logistical problems at Camden. On April 23, he dispatched 240 wagons to Pine Bluff to pick up a load of supplies. Mindful now of the sting of the Confederate cavalry, Steele detailed an entire infantry brigade of three regiments (1,200 men), 240 cavalry, and two artillery sections under Lieutenant Colonel Francis M. Drake as the train's escort. Drake noted that his column was accompanied by "a large number of cotton speculators, Arkansas refugees, sutlers, and other army followers, and 300 negroes." Two days out from Camden, Drake linked up with a relief party of 150 Union cavalry from Pine Bluff.[41]

That same day, 4,000 Confederate horsemen directed by Brigadier Generals James F. Fagan and Joseph O. Shelby converged on Drake's force at Marks' Mills. Hitting the Federals from two directions at once, the Rebels annihilated the escort in short order, taking 1,300 prisoners and the entire supply train. But according to General Fagan, only 150 of the 300 runaway slaves with Drake were taken into custody by the victors. What happened to the others?[42]

The diary of Lieutenant Benjamin Pearson of the Thirty-sixth Iowa Infantry, captured with most of his regiment at Marks' Mills, provides a partial answer: "There was not an armed negro with us & they shot down our Colored servents & teamsters & others what ware following to get from bondage as they would shoot sheep dogs." A wounded Colonel Drake fell into enemy hands midway through the engagement, and he subsequently learned that "a large number [of] negroes . . . were inhumanly butchered by the enemy, and among them [his] own negro servant." A graphic account of this massacre comes from Confederate Major John N. Edwards, the adjutant of Shelby's Brigade. "The battle-field was sickening to behold," Edwards wrote in 1867. "No orders, threats, or commands could restrain the men from vengeance on the negroes, and they were piled in great heaps about the wagons, in the tangled brushwood, and upon the muddy and trampled road." An Arkansas soldier saw General Shelby himself bring a clubbed rifle crashing down on the head of a frightened slave. Then Shelby drew his revolver and casually shot the prostrate black man to death.[43]

The exact number of fugitive slaves killed at Marks' Mills will probably never be known, but it undoubtedly topped 100. The day after the fight, Lieutenant Pearson's captors allowed him to walk the battlefield to search for his son, who was listed as missing. "The number of Negroes I could not get," Pearson complained. "I saw perhaps near 30, & the Rebs pointed out to me a point of woods where they told me they had killed eighty odd negroes men women & children this is their report to me & . . . I fully believe they are hartless enough to do any act that wicked men or devils could conceive." Those few runaways who survived the carnage were apparently hunted down by local whites and carried off to Texas for resale into slavery—much to the chagrin of their original owners.[44]

The war crimes at Poison Spring and Marks' Mills were not isolated outbursts of senseless racial violence, but part of an ongoing program of racial intimidation that took its cues from the basic values of antebellum Southern society. As far as the men who did the killing were concerned, they had simply made examples of some disloyal slaves to deter other blacks from betraying their masters or giving further aid and comfort to the enemy. Fresh from the carnage at Poison Spring, one Arkansas trooper explained the purpose of his comrades' merciless conduct: "Our men are determined not to take negro prisoners and if all the negroes could have seen what occurred today, they would stay at home."[45]

Despite the additional peril, there was no restraining the emancipation movement. When Steele's desperate Federals finally evacuated Camden on the evening of April 26, hundreds of slaves followed in their wake. Likewise, most black men already wearing Union uniforms were not demoralized by the Confederates' no-prisoners policy. A few weeks after Lieutenant William Blain of the Fortieth Iowa Infantry returned from Camden, he encountered a former servant named Alfred who had joined a black regiment at Little Rock. "I asked him," Blain wrote the next day, "if he intended to give the 'rebs' any quarter when he fought with them?" "No Sah," Alfred replied, "dey don't gib us any, and we don't intend to gib dem any. Why sah, dey just kill us like brutes and we's gwine to use dem de same way."[46]

Those were not empty words. Black troops had redeemed Alfred's harsh pledge a full month before Lieutenant Blain first heard it. Within a day of the bloodbath at Poison Spring, Colonel Samuel J. Crawford called the officers of the Second Kansas Colored Infantry into council at Camden to discuss the enemy's treatment of their sister regiment. Before they adjourned, Crawford and his officers solemnly swore this: "That in future the regiment would take no prisoners so long as the Rebels continued to murder our men."[47]

The Second Kansas fulfilled that dreadful oath on April 30, 1864, when Kirby Smith and three Confederate infantry divisions overtook Steele's retreating army amid the flooded bottoms on the south side of the Saline

River at Jenkins' Ferry. At one point in the battle, the Rebels unlimbered two cannon opposite Crawford and his black troops. Crawford accepted the challenge and ordered a charge, which was closely supported by the white Twenty-ninth Iowa Infantry. With one volley, the blacks immobilized the enemy artillery by killing most of its horses, and with a second volley they dispersed a supporting line of infantry. Then the Second Kansas dashed forward with leveled bayonets, the men shouting "Poison Springs" and "Here comes your 'Iron Clads.'" The blacks easily overran the battery position, impaling every Confederate within reach, including three gunners who raised their hands in surrender. Only the timely arrival and forceful intervention of the Twenty-ninth Iowa saved the lives of Lieutenant John O. Lockhart, the commander of the captured cannon, and his five remaining men.[48]

In his 1911 memoirs, Colonel Crawford admitted that the Second Kansas used Jenkins' Ferry to repay the enemy for Poison Spring, but he insisted that his troops behaved in a humane fashion. "After the Poison Springs massacre," Crawford recalled, "we were resolved to take no prisoners. And yet, there lay scores of Rebel wounded all around us; but we left them as they were, to be cared for by their comrades." But Private Milton P. Chambers of the Twenty-ninth Iowa told a very different tale in a letter home seven days after the fight. "The negroes want to kill every wounded reb they come to," he wrote, "and will do it if we did not watch them."[49]

In the fury of their charge, Crawford's vengeful blacks drew no distinction between able-bodied or wounded foes. As Private Chambers related, "One of our boys seen a little negro pounding a wounded reb in the head with the but of his gun and asked him what he was doing. the negro replied he is not dead yet! I tel you they won't give them up as long as they can kick if they can just have their way about it."[50]

Yet even after the heat of combat cooled, the Second Kansas continued to exact revenge for Poison Spring. Having fought Kirby Smith to a standstill, Steele's white regiments started to disengage and slip across the Saline River, leaving behind the Second Kansas for approximately two hours to cover their retreat. Crawford claimed that he utilized that interval to send "men all along where our lines had stood to pick up such of our wounded as might have been overlooked." His soldiers, however, combined this mission of mercy with acts of merciless cruelty.[51]

Earlier in the day, Private John H. Lewis of the Eighteenth Texas Infantry took a bullet in the leg and crawled behind a tree stump for shelter.

"After awhile," Lewis explained, "the firing ceased and our army was gone. Soon I looked around and saw some black negroes cutting our wounded boys' throats, and I thought my time would come next." Forcing himself to walk on his wounded leg, Lewis hobbled away to a place of safety.[52]

Other Confederates, following the Federals at a prudent distance, eventually stumbled across the horrors described by Private Lewis. Surgeon Edward W. Cade of Colonel Horace Randal's Texas Brigade revealed, "Our command fell back, and when they again advanced they found several of our wounded who had their throats cut from ear to ear by the Negroes." James Dawson of the Thirty-fourth Arkansas Infantry wrote to his family that "the negros killed some of [our] Wounded." Assistant Surgeon Junius N. Bragg of the Thirty-third Arkansas Infantry informed his wife that A. J. Williams, the regiment's acting sergeant major, "had his throat cut by a negro" and lived long enough to tell about it.[53] David S. Williams, the Thirty-third's senior surgeon and A. J. Williams's brother, added more details in his own harrowing revelations: "We found that many of our wounded had been mutilated in many ways. Some with ears cut off, throats cut, knife stabs, etc. My brother . . . was shot through the body, had his throat cut through the windpipe and lived several days. I saw several who were treated in the same way. One officer . . . wrote on a bit of paper that his lower jaw and tongue were shot off after the battle was over or during the falling back as referred to above."[54]

News of these reprisals quickly became common knowledge throughout Steele's army, but no one censured the Second Kansas Colored. "It looks hard," Private Chambers conceded, "but the rebs cannot blame the negroes when they are guilty of the same trick."[55] Lieutenant Blain resigned himself to the increasing dehumanization of the conflict as symbolized by Poison Spring and Jenkins' Ferry:

> The "rebs" appear to be determined to show no quarter to Black troops or officers commanding them.
>
> It would not surprise me in the least if this war would ultimately be one of extermination. Its tendencies are in that direction now.[56]

Colonel Crawford liked to pretend that the retaliatory measures he sanctioned at Jenkins' Ferry taught the Rebels to stop killing black prisoners. He was mistaken. Of the 150 badly wounded men that the retreating Federals abandoned at a field hospital on that battlefield, nine belonged to

Crawford's Second Kansas. Before sunset, some Confederate cavalry rode up to the hospital and began robbing the patients. "One," reported an indignant Surgeon William L. Nicholson of the Twenty-ninth Iowa, "dressed like an officer, drew his revolver and shot three wounded 'niggers' who lay in the yard." Two weeks later, the Confederates moved Nicholson and the six surviving Second Kansas men to more permanent accommodations at Princeton, Arkansas. The blacks were lodged in a small storehouse. Shortly after their arrival, Nicholson heard gunshots and someone shouting, "The niggers are catching it." Next he saw a Rebel gripping a revolver in each hand emerge from the storehouse. "I went over at once," Nicholson related, "and found all the poor negroes shot through the head."[57]

The unfortunate First Kansas Colored had several more of its members murdered at a hay-cutting camp fifteen miles from Fort Gibson, Indian Territory, before 1864 came to a close. On September 16, Brigadier General Richard Gano and a brigade of twelve hundred Texas cavalrymen fell on Company H of the First Kansas at Flat Rock. The company's thirty-seven men took shelter in a ravine and kept the Rebels at bay for two hours until their ammunition ran out. At that, the blacks' white lieutenant told them to save themselves, but only four succeeded in getting away. Those few escapees relayed what happened next to Captain John R. Graton, their acting regimental commander: "The men were all killed except a few who concealed themselves in a ravine until dark and then crawled away."[58]

Graton's words jibed well with Confederate accounts. "The negroes were nearly all killed in a little creek into which they had jumped," remembered Private Jefferson P. Boze of the Thirtieth Texas Cavalry. "The water was red with blood of the dead negroes." Private W. T. Sheppard of the Fifth Texas Partisan Rangers rejoiced, "The Federals were short a company of negro troops and after the battle they were all 'good' negroes." To their credit, some of Gano's Texans abstained from the general bloodletting and spared six blacks as prisoners, but up to twenty-seven other Company H men were massacre victims.[59]

The racially motivated killings at Poison Spring, Marks' Mills, Jenkins' Ferry, Princeton, and Flat Rock sprang from deep-seated fears that had permeated white Southern society during two centuries of slavery. Such atrocities were not peculiar to the Trans-Mississippi, even though that theater had earned a reputation for brutality well before black troops entered the Union army. In 1864, incidents like the Poison Spring Massacre occurred from one end of Dixie to the other. To cite only the more conspicuous examples, Confederate soldiers refused to take black prisoners at Fort Pillow in Tennessee and in battles around Petersburg, Virginia.[60]

Confederates regarded the employment of African American soldiers as such a crime against humanity that they felt absolved from any obligation to treat black troops and their white officers as honorable opponents. Rebellious slaves and white abolitionist agitators had to be exterminated to keep other blacks in their place and save a social system based on racial subordination. These convictions added a unique element of savagery to the Civil War, and they persisted for a century after Appomattox. During Reconstruction, many Confederate veterans joined terrorist organizations that frequently assassinated assertive blacks who dared to press for political equality. As heirs to this heritage of racial oppression, the descendants of those veterans would preserve much of the old Southern order down to the 1960s. Thanks to the civil rights movement and the aggressive actions of the national government, expression of much of America's ingrained racial hatred has been driven underground, but students of the dark side of the Civil War should not be surprised to see it still surface from time to time.[61]

Notes

Introduction: The History and Historians of Arkansas's Civil War

The authors wish to thank Willard B. Gatewood, Carl H. Moneyhon, and Patrick G. Williams for their comments on an earlier version of this essay.

1. John M. Harrell, *Arkansas,* vol. 10 in *Confederate Military History,* ed. Clement A. Evans, 12 vols. (Atlanta: Confederate Publishing Company, 1899); Jonathan P. Morrow, Jr., "Confederate Generals from Arkansas," *Arkansas Historical Quarterly* 21 (autumn 1962): 233. *(Arkansas Historical Quarterly* hereafter referred to as *AHQ.)* Although sometimes referred to as "general," Harrell's title came from his postwar militia service. The *Century Magazine* series, which first appeared between November 1884 and November 1887, was published with additional material as Robert Underwood Johnson and Clarene Clough Buel, eds., *Battles and Leaders of the Civil War,* 4 vols. (New York: Century, 1887). U.S. War Department, *The War of the Rebellion: A Compilation of the Official Records of the Union and Confederate Armies,* 128 vols. (Washington, D.C.: GPO, 1880–1901). Wiley Britton, a contemporary of Harrell, published a two-volume history of the war in Missouri, Kansas, and Arkansas during the 1890s, but his principal focus was Missouri. See Britton, *The Civil War on the Border,* 2 vols. (New York: G. P. Putnam's Sons, 1890–99).

2. Thomas S. Staples, *Reconstruction in Arkansas, 1862–1874* (New York: Columbia University Press, 1923).

3. David Y. Thomas, *Arkansas in War and Reconstruction, 1861–1874* (Little Rock: Central Printing Company, 1926), preface; Mary Elizabeth Massey, "David Yancey Thomas: Historian," *AHQ* 7 (autumn 1948): 221–26; Thomas Rothrock, "Dr. David Yancey Thomas," *AHQ* 27 (autumn 1968): 246–57; Fred Arthur Bailey, "Free Speech and the 'Lost Cause' in Arkansas," *AHQ* 55 (summer 1996): 156–63.

4. See also David Y. Thomas, "Calling the Secession Convention in Arkansas," *Southwestern Political and Social Science Quarterly* 5 (December 1924): 246–54.

5. Thomas, *Arkansas in War and Reconstruction,* preface.

6. Myra McAlmont Vaughan, "The First Historical Society of Arkansas," *Publications of the Arkansas Historical Association* (Fayetteville: Arkansas Historical Association, 1906–17), 2:346–53; [David Y. Thomas], "Salutatory," *AHQ* 1 (March 1942): 1–2.

7. [Thomas], "Salutatory," 2–7; Wendy Richter, "Celebrating Fifty Years of the Arkansas Historical Association," *AHQ* 55 (summer 1996): 167–68; J. H. Atkinson, "The Arkansas Historical Association," *AHQ* 20 (summer 1961): 115–17.

8. Fred Harvey Harrington, "Arkansas History: Accomplishments and Opportunities," *AHQ* 11 (spring 1952): 64–65.

9. Fred Harvey Harrington, "Arkansas Defends the Mississippi," *AHQ* 4

(summer 1945): 109–17; Irene Abercrombie, "The Battle of Prairie Grove," *AHQ* 2 (December 1943): 309–15; Harold H. McDonald, "The Battle of Jenkins' Ferry," *AHQ* 7 (spring 1948): 57–67; Jodie Arnold Smith, "Battle Grounds and Soldiers of Arkansas, 1861–1865," *AHQ* 6 (summer 1947): 180–85; Ethel Linder, "Patrick Cleburne, Hero from Helena," *AHQ* 4 (winter 1945): 307–14; Clara B. Eno, "Activities of the Women of Arkansas during the War between the States," *AHQ* 3 (spring 1944): 5–27; Maude Carmichael, "Federal Experiments with Negro Labor on Abandoned Plantations in Arkansas: 1862–1865," *AHQ* 1 (June 1942): 101–16; and Edward E. Dale, "Arkansas and the Cherokees," *AHQ* 8 (summer 1949): 95–114.

10. Elsie Mae Lewis's dissertation, "From Nationalism to Disunion: A Study of the Secession Movement in Arkansas, 1849–1861" (Ph.D. diss., University of Chicago, 1947), would be cited frequently in the coming years, although her own research interests gradually shifted toward African American history and the civil rights movement. Her article was "Economic Conditions in Ante-Bellum Arkansas: 1850–1861," *AHQ* 6 (autumn 1947): 256–74.

11. Jack B. Scroggs, "Arkansas in the Secession Crisis," *AHQ* 12 (autumn 1953): 179–224; Ralph Wooster, "The Arkansas Secession Convention," *AHQ* 13 (summer 1954): 172–95; Elsie Mae Lewis, "Robert Ward Johnson: Militant Spokesman of the Old-South-West," *AHQ* 13 (spring 1954): 16–30; Robert F. Smith, "John R. Eakin: Confederate Propagandist," *AHQ* 12 (winter 1953): 316–26, and "The Confederate Attempt to Counteract Reunion Propaganda in Arkansas: 1863–1865," *AHQ* 16 (spring 1957): 54–62; William Frank Zornow, "State Aid for Indigent Soldiers and Their Families in Arkansas, 1861–1865," *AHQ* 14 (summer 1955): 97–102; Ted R. Worley, "The Arkansas Peace Society of 1861: A Study in Mountain Unionism," *Journal of Southern History* 24 (November 1958): 445–56; and Hugh Park, "Ted R. Worley," *AHQ* 28 (spring 1969): 86–92. Scroggs had written his master's thesis, on secession, under Roman J. Zorn at the University of Arkansas before moving on to doctoral studies at the University of Texas. Smith went to the University of Wisconsin to complete his doctorate in 1958, but his research interests drifted toward diplomatic and general military history. Worley also became a prolific editor of Civil War–era documents, including "Documents Relating to the Arkansas Peace Society of 1861," *AHQ* 17 (spring 1958): 82–111.

12. Richard W. Griffin, "Pro-Industrial Sentiment and Cotton Factories in Arkansas, 1820–1863," *AHQ* 15 (summer 1956): 125–39; Mary Elizabeth Massey, "The Effect of Shortages on the Confederate Homefront," *AHQ* 9 (autumn 1950): 172–93. Barbara L. Bellows wrote an insightful biographical sketch of Massey to introduce a reprint edition of *Ersatz in the Confederacy: Shortages and Substitutes on the Southern Homefront* (Columbia: University of South Carolina Press, 1993), ix–xxi.

13. Daniel O'Flaherty, *General Jo Shelby: Undefeated Rebel* (Chapel Hill: University of North Carolina Press, 1954); Joseph H. Parks, *General Edmund Kirby Smith, C.S.A.* (Baton Rouge: Louisiana State University Press, 1954); Robert H. Hartje, "A Confederate Dilemma across the Mississippi," *AHQ* 17 (summer 1958): 119–31, and *Van Dorn: The Life and Times of a Confederate General* (Nashville: Vanderbilt University Press, 1967); Ralph R. Rea, *Sterling Price: The Lee of the West*

(Little Rock: Pioneer Press, 1959); Robert L. Duncan, *Reluctant General: The Life and Times of Albert Pike* (New York: E. P. Dutton, 1961); Hal Bridges, "A Confederate Hero: General William Y. Slack." *AHQ* 10 (autumn 1951): 233–37; and Harry N. Scheiber, "The Pay of Troops and Confederate Morale in the Trans-Mississippi West," *AHQ* 18 (winter 1959): 350–65. Neal T. Bullock, wrote a masters thesis at the University of Arkansas in 1957 entitled "The Confederate Services of General Ben Mculloch."

14. Ira Don Richards, "The Battle of Poison Spring," *AHQ* 18 (winter 1959): 338–49; James H. Atkinson, *Forty Days of Disaster: The Story of General Frederick Steele's Expedition into Southern Arkansas, March 23 to May 3, 1864* (Little Rock: Pulaski County Historical Society, 1955), and "The Action at Prairie De Ann," *AHQ* 19 (spring 1960): 40–50; Jack B. Scroggs and Donald E. Reynolds, "Arkansas and the Vicksburg Campaign," *Civil War History* 5 (December 1959): 390–401.

15. Jay Monaghan, *Civil War on the Western Border, 1854–1865* (Boston: Little, Brown, 1955); and Ludwell H. Johnson, *Red River Campaign: Politics and Cotton in the Civil War* (Baltimore: Johns Hopkins University, 1958). James J. Hudson, who taught Civil War and military history at the University of Arkansas for many years, criticized Johnson's book in a published review for not devoting more space to Arkansas, but he also acknowledged that Johnson had helped "fill the gap in the comparatively neglected field of Trans-Mississippi West history." *AHQ* 19 (spring 1960): 82–84. Also in 1958, Thomas A. Belser, Jr., produced a doctoral dissertation at Vanderbilt University, drawn largely upon the *Official Records,* entitled, "Military Operations in Missouri and Arkansas, 1861–1865."

16. Walter Lee Brown, "Pea Ridge: Gettysburg of the West," *AHQ* 15 (spring 1956): 15–16. Earlier work on Pea Ridge had included William Baxter's classic *Pea Ridge and Prairie Grove; or, Scenes and Incidents of the War in Arkansas* (Cincinnati: Poe & Hitchcock, 1864); Harvey S. Ford, "Van Dorn and the Pea Ridge Campaign," *Journal of the American Military Institute* 3 (winter 1939): 222–36; Clare N. Moody, *Battle of Pea Ridge; or Elkhorn Tavern* (Little Rock: Arkansas Valley Print Company, 1956); and Faye L. Stewart, "Battle of Pea Ridge," *Missouri Historical Review* 22 (January 1928): 187–92.

17. James J. Hudson, review of *Decisive Battles of the Civil War,* by Joseph B. Mitchell, *AHQ* 15 (autumn 1956): 277.

18. D. Alexander Brown, "The Battle of Pea Ridge: Gettysburg of the West," *Civil War Times Illustrated* 6 (October 1967): 4–11, 46–48; William C. Davis, "The Battle of Prairie Grove," *Civil War Times Illustrated* 7 (July 1968): 12–19; Albert G. Castel, "Fiasco at Helena," *Civil War Times Illustrated* 7 (August 1968): 12–17; Robert S. Huffstot, "Post of Arkansas," *Civil War Times Illustrated* 7 (January 1969): 10–19. For a convenient list of Bearss work in the 1950s and 1960s, see Michael B. Dougan, Tom W. Dillard, and Timothy G. Nutt, comps., *Arkansas History: An Annotated Bibliography* (Westport, Conn.: Greenwood Press, 1995), 46–47; although missing from that list is a series of articles, "The Battle of Pea Ridge," published in *Annals of Iowa,* 3rd series, 36 (spring 1963): 569–89; 37 (summer 1963): 9–41; (autumn 1963): 121–55; (winter 1964): 207–39; and (spring 1964): 304–17.

19. John L. Ferguson, ed., *Arkansas and the Civil War* (Little Rock: Pioneer Press, 1965), v.

20. Leo E. Huff, "Confederate Arkansas, A History of Arkansas during the Civil War" (M.A. thesis, University of Arkansas, 1964); "The Union Expedition against Little Rock, August–September 1863," *AHQ* 22 (autumn 1963): 224–37; "The Last Duel in Arkansas: The Marmaduke-Walker Duel," *AHQ* 23 (spring 1964): 36–49; "The Memphis and Little Rock Railroad during the Civil War," *AHQ* 23 (autumn 1964): 260–70; "The Military Board in Confederate Arkansas," *AHQ* 26 (spring 1967): 75–95; and "Guerrillas, Jayhawkers, and Bushwhackers in Northern Arkansas during the Civil War," *AHQ* 24 (summer 1965): 127–48. Earlier writings about guerrillas in Arkansas included Neva Ingram Hunsicker, "Rayburn the Raider," *AHQ* 7 (spring 1948): 87–91; William E. Sawyer, "The Martin Hart Conspiracy," *AHQ* 23 (summer 1964): 154–65; Barry Roland Weaver, "Jesse James in Arkansas: The War Days," *AHQ* 23 (winter 1964): 359–64; and Boyd W. Johnson, "Cullen Montgomery Baker, The Arkansas-Texas Desperado," *AHQ* 25 (autumn 1966): 229–39. Richard S. Brownlee's book bore the rather misleading title of *Gray Ghosts of the Confederacy: Guerrilla Warfare in the West, 1861–1865* (Baton Rouge: Louisiana State University Press, 1958).

21. Ira Don Richards, "The Engagement at Marks' Mills," *AHQ* 19 (spring 1960): 51–60, and "The Battle of Jenkins' Ferry," *AHQ* 20 (spring 1961): 3–16; Stephen B. Oates, "The Prairie Grove Campaign, 1862," *AHQ* 19 (summer 1960): 119–41, "Cavalry Fight at Cane Hill," *AHQ* 20 (spring 1961): 65–73, and *Confederate Cavalry in the West* (Austin: University of Texas Press, 1961); Alwyn Barr, "Confederate Artillery in Arkansas," *AHQ* 22 (autumn 1963): 238–72; Albert Castel, *General Sterling Price and the Civil War in the West* (Baton Rouge: Louisiana State University Press, 1968). See also Albert Castel, "A New View of the Battle of Pea Ridge," *Missouri Historical Review* 62 (January 1968): 136–51.

22. Calvin A. Collier, *First In—Last Out, the Capitol Guards, Arkansas Brigade* (Little Rock: Pioneer Press, 1961), *"They'll do to tie to!": The Story of the Third Regiment, Arkansas Infantry, C.S.A.* (Little Rock: Pioneer Press, 1959), and *The War Child's Children: The Story of the Third Regiment, Arkansas Cavalry, Confederate States Army* (Little Rock: Pioneer Press, 1965); Wesley T. Leeper, *Rebels Valiant: Second Arkansas Mounted Rifles, Dismounted* (Little Rock: Pioneer Press, 1964); Benjamin Franklin Cooling III, "Gee's Fifteenth Arkansas Infantry in the Forts Henry and Donelson Campaign," *AHQ* 23 (winter 1964): 329–42; and Burton J. Williams, "Missouri State Depredations in Arkansas: A Case of Restitution," *AHQ* 23 (winter 1964): 343–52.

23. Donald Richardson, "A Study of the History of Batesville, Arkansas, 1860–1865" (M.A. thesis, Arkansas State Teachers College, 1963); Martha T. Bridges, "A Study of the Social, Economic, and Personal Problems Experienced by Families Living in Little Rock during the Civil War" (M.A. thesis, Arkansas State Teachers College, 1965); Boyd W. Johnson, *The Civil War in Ouchita County* (Camden, Ark.: Johnson's Book Store, 1968); Ted R. Worley, "The Civil War Comes to Van Buren," *AHQ* 25 (summer 1966): 145–50; Nola A. James, "The Civil War Years in

Independence County," *AHQ* 28 (autumn 1969): 234–74; and Walter Brown, review of *Fight and Survive! A History of Jackson County in the Civil War*, by Lady Elizabeth Watson, *AHQ* 34 (autumn 1975): 286.

24. Edwin C. Bearss, "Federal Generals Squabble over Fort Smith, 1863–64," *AHQ* 29 (summer 1970): 119–51, and "Confederate Action against Fort Smith Post: Early 1864," *AHQ* 29 (autumn 1970): 226–51; Leo E. Huff, "The Martial Law Controversy in Arkansas, 1861–65: A Case History of Internal Confederate Conflict," *AHQ* 37 (summer 1978): 147–67; Donald E. Reynolds, "Union Strategy in Arkansas during the Vicksburg Campaign," *AHQ* 29 (spring 1970): 20–38; and Walter L. Brown, "Albert Pike and the Pea Ridge Atrocities," *AHQ* 38 (winter 1979): 345–59.

25. Michael B. Dougan, "The Little Rock Press Goes to War, 1861–1863," *AHQ* 28 (spring 1969): 14–27, "A Look at the 'Family' in Arkansas Politics, 1858–1865," *AHQ* 29 (summer 1970): 99–111, "Life in Confederate Arkansas," *AHQ* 31 (spring 1972): 15–35, and *Confederate Arkansas: The People and Policies of a Frontier State in Wartime* (University, Ala.: University of Alabama Press, 1976). See also James L. Cox, "Confederate Arkansas: A Study in State Politics" (M.A. thesis, North Texas State University, 1971).

26. Robert L. Kerby, *Kirby Smith's Confederacy: The Trans-Mississippi South, 1863–1865* (New York: Columbia University Press, 1972); Robert E. Shalhope, *Sterling Price: Portrait of a Southerner* (Columbia: University of Missouri Press, 1971); Howell Purdue and Elizabeth Purdue, *Pat Cleburne, Confederate General: A Definitive Biography* (Hillsboro, Tex.: Hill Junior College Press, 1973); Albert Castel, "Theophilus Holmes—Pallbearer of the Confederacy," *Civil War Times Illustrated*, 16 (July 1977): 10-17. See Dougan, Dillard, and Nutt, *Arkansas History*, 54–55, for a list of the Geise articles. Also useful from this period is Maurice G. Fortin, Jr., "Confederate Military Operations in Arkansas, 1861–1865" (M.A. thesis, North Texas State University, 1978).

27. David O. Demuth, "Federal Military Activity in Arkansas in the Fall of 1864 and the Skirmish at Hurricane Creek," *AHQ* 38 (summer 1979): 131–45, and "The Burning of Hopefield," *AHQ* 36 (summer 1977): 123–29; William L. Shea, "Battle at Ditch Bayou," *AHQ* 39 (autumn 1980): 195–207, "The Confederate Defeat at Cache River," *AHQ* 52 (summer 1993): 129–55, and "The Camden Fortifications," *AHQ* 41 (winter 1982): 318–26.

28. Tommy R. Thompson, "Letters Home: From Private Thomas Henry Lochridge, 1861–1862," *AHQ* 33 (autumn 1974): 239–51; LeRoy H. Fischer, "David O. Dodd: Folk Hero of Confederate Arkansas," *AHQ* 37 (summer 1978): 130–46; Earl J. Hess, "Confiscation and the Northern War Effort: The Army of the Southwest at Helena," *AHQ* 44 (spring 1985): 56–75. See also Arthur R. and Robert B. Buckalew, "Hillsboro's Soldier-Citizen: Horatio Gates Perry Williams," *AHQ* 31 (spring 1972): 36–56.

29. James Willis, *Arkansas Confederates in the Western Theater* (Dayton, Ohio: Morningside, 1998); Kim Allen Scott, "The Civil War in a Bottle: Battle of Fayetteville, Arkansas," *AHQ* 54 (autumn 1995): 239–68, "Pursuing an Elusive Quarry: The Battle of Cane Hill, Arkansas" (with Stephen Burgess), *AHQ* 56 (spring

1997): 26–55, and "The Fighting Printers of Company E, Eleventh Kansas Volunteer Infantry," *AHQ* 46 (autumn 1987): 261–81; Anne J. Bailey, *Between the Enemy and Texas: Parsons's Texas Cavalry in the Civil War* (Fort Worth: Texas Christian University Press, 1989), and "The Mississippi Marine Brigade: Fighting Rebel Guerrillas on Western Waters," *Military History of the Southwest* 22 (spring 1992): 31–42; Arthur G. Sharp, "War on the River: The Mississippi Marine Brigade at the Battle of Lake Chicot," *Civil War Times Illustrated* 21 (October 1982): 18–23; Jesse L. Chapman, "The Ellet Family and Riverine Warfare in the West, 1861–1865" (M.A. thesis, Old Dominion University, 1985); and Charles G. Williams, "The Confederate Home Guard in Southwest Arkansas," *AHQ* 49 (summer 1990): 168–72. Examples of recent Arkansas unit histories include Terry Gregory, "4th Arkansas Mounted Infantry, Company C—A Case Study," *Independence County Chronicle* 27 (April–July 1986): 48–69; Floyd R. Barnhill and Calvin L. Collier, *The Fighting Fifth: Pat Cleburne's Cutting Edge, The Fifth Arkansas Infantry Regiment* (Jonesboro, Ark.: privately printed, 1990); James L. Morgan, "The Richland Rangers: Company D, 13th Arkansas Infantry Regiment," *Rivers and Roads and Points in Between* 11 (summer 1983): 14–19; Bryan K. Thomasson, "'We Have Drunk from the Same Canteen': Company H, Sixth Arkansas Regiment, The Camden City Guards" (M.A. thesis, University of Arkansas, 1994); Paul A. Leuschen, "34th Arkansas Infantry, CSA: A Unit History" (M.A. thesis, University of Arkansas, 1996); Anthony C. Rushing, *Ranks of Honor: A Regimental History of the Eleventh Arkansas Infantry Regiment and Poe's Cavalry Battalion* (Little Rock: Eagle Press, 1990), and "Rackensacker Raiders: Crawford's First Arkansas Cavalry," *Civil War Regiments* 1 (1991): 44–69; Joe Fears, "Standing in the Furnace of the Rebellion: The Story of the First Arkansas [Cavalry]" (M.A. thesis, University of Arkansas, 1986); and Wendall P. Beall, "Wildwood Skirmishers: The First Federal Arkansas Cavalry" (M.A. thesis, University of Arkansas, 1988). See also John F. Walter, *Capsule Histories of Arkansas Military Units in the Civil War* (Middle Village, N.Y.: J. F Walter, 1977).

30. James M. Woods, "Devotees and Dissenters: Arkansans in the Confederate Congress, 1861–1865," *AHQ* 38 (autumn 1979): 227–47, and *Rebellion and Realignment: Arkansas's Road to Secession* (Fayetteville: University of Arkansas Press, 1987), 1–4, 170. Lenette Sengel Taylor, "Polemics and Partisanship: The Arkansas Press in the 1860 Election," *AHQ* 44 (winter 1985): 314–35, is also useful.

31. Nate Coulter, "The Impact of the Civil War upon Pulaski County, Arkansas," *AHQ* 41 (spring 1982): 67–82; Carl Moneyhon, "The Civil War and Social-Economic Change in Jackson County, Arkansas," *Stream of History* 18 (November 1979–July 1981): 21–26, "The Civil War in Phillips County, Arkansas," *Phillips County Historical Quarterly* 19 (June–September 1981): 18–36, and "The Impact of the Civil War in Arkansas: Mississippi River Plantation Counties," *AHQ* 51 (summer 1992): 105–18; Wendy Richter, "The Impact of the Civil War on Hot Springs, Arkansas," *AHQ* 43 (summer 1984): 125–42; Carolyn Pollan, "Fort Smith under Union Military Rule, September 1, 1863–Fall 1865," *Fort Smith Historical Journal* 4 (September 1980): 2–11; Gary M. Pecquet, "The Change Shortage and the Private and Public Provisions of Small Currency Denominations in the

Trans-Mississippi States, 1861–1865," *Southern Studies* 25 (spring 1986): 102–10, and "State Finance in Arkansas, 1860–1865," *AHQ* 48 (spring 1989): 65–72; and Diane Neal and Thomas W. Kremm, "An Experiment in Collective Security: The Union Army's Use of Armed Colonies in Arkansas," *Military History of the Southwest* 20 (autumn 1990): 169–81.

32. Michael A. Hughes, "Pea Ridge, or Elkhorn Tavern, Arkansas—March 7–8, 1862: The Campaign, the Battle, and the Men Who Fought for the Fate of Missouri," *Blue and Gray Magazine* 5 (January 1988): 8–36; Alvin M. Josephy, Jr., *The Civil War in the American West* (New York: Alfred A. Knopf, 1991); Stephen D. Engle, "Franz Sigel at Pea Ridge," *AHQ* 50 (autumn 1991): 249–70; David Bosse, "'The Enemy Were Falling Like Autumn Leaves': Fraudulent Newspaper Reports of the Battle of Pea Ridge," *AHQ* 54 (autumn 1992): 359–75; and William L. Shea and Earl J. Hess, *Pea Ridge: Civil War Campaign in the West* (Chapel Hill: University of North Carolina Press, 1992). For an examination of the role of the press similar to that of Bosse, see Brian Dirck, "'We Have Whipped Them Beautifully': The Arkansas Press and Wilson's Creek," *Missouri Historical Review* 84 (April 1990): 270–92. Other useful works include Roy D. Burrow, *The Battle of Pea Ridge* (Charleston, Ill.: Prairie Press, 1970); Dale Edwards, "Arkansas: Pea Ridge and State Division," *Journal of the West* 14 (spring 1975): 167–84; Maynard J. Hanson, "The Battle of Pea Ridge, Arkansas, March 6–8, 1862," *Journal of the West* 19 (October 1980): 39–50.

33. Bobby L. Roberts, "Thomas C. Hindman, Jr.: Secessionist and Confederate General" (M.A. thesis, University of Arkansas, 1972), and "General T. C. Hindman and the Trans-Mississippi District," *AHQ* 32 (winter 1973): 297–311; Carl H. Moneyhon and Bobby L. Roberts, *Portraits of Conflict: A Photographic History of Arkansas in the Civil War* (Fayetteville: University of Arkansas, 1987). The book forms part of a series of the same main title edited by Moneyhon and Roberts for every state of the Confederacy.

34. Carl H. Moneyhon, *The Impact of the Civil War and Reconstruction on Arkansas: Persistence in the Midst of Ruin* (Baton Rouge: Louisiana State University Press, 1994). Also stressing the broad impact of the war was Christina Catalfano-Serio, *The Effect of the Civil War on Ozark Culture* (Little Rock: Arkansas Endowment for the Humanities, 1979).

35. Joseph R. Bellas, "The Forgotten Loyalists: Unionism in Arkansas, 1861–1865" (M.A. thesis, Ohio State University, 1991); Diane Neal, "Treason or Patriotism? Union Peace Societies in Arkansas during the Civil War," *Journal of Confederate History* 1 (autumn 1988): 339–49; Luther E. Warren, *Yellar Rag Boys: The Arkansas Peace Society of 1861 and Other Events in Northern Arkansas, 1861–1865* (Marshall, Ark.: S. L. Weaver, 1992); Robert R. Mackey, "A Self-Inflicted Wound: The Confederacy's Guerrilla Campaign in Arkansas, 1862–1865" (M.A. thesis, Texas A&M University, 1997), and "Bushwhackers, Provosts, and Tories: The Guerrilla War in Arkansas," in *Guerrillas, Unionists, and Violence on the Confederate Home Front,* ed. Daniel E. Sutherland (Fayetteville: University of Arkansas Press, 1999); Jay A. Prier, "Under the Black Flag: The Real War in Washington County, Arkansas, 1861–1865" (M.A. thesis, University of Arkansas, 1998); Russell Baker, "Yellow Doc, The

Ranger—An Arkansas Legend: A Daring Adventure—In Skirts," *Rivers and Roads and Points in Between* 14 (spring 1986): 10–12; Barry A. Crouch and Donaly E. Brice, *Cullen Montgomery Baker: Reconstruction Desperado* (Baton Rouge: Louisiana State University Press, 1997); James B. Martin, "The Third War: Irregular Warfare on the Westen Border, 1861–1865" (Ph.D. diss., University of Texas, 1997); John F. Bradbury, "'Buckwheat Cake Philanthropy': Refugees and the Union Army in the Ozarks," *AHQ* 57 (autumn 1998): 233–54; and Clea Lutz Bunch, "Confederate Women of Arkansas Face 'the Fiends in Human Shape,'" *Military History of the West* 27 (autumn 1997): 173–87.

36. Orville W. Taylor, *Negro Slavery in Arkansas* (Durham, N.C.: Duke University Press, 1958). Also useful is a recent issue of *AHQ* devoted to slavery in the state. *AHQ* 58 (spring 1999).

37. Larry Wesley Pearce, "The American Missionary Association and the Freedmen in Arkansas, 1863–1878," *AHQ* 30 (summer 1971): 123–44; Thomas C. Kennedy, "Southland College: The Society of Friends and Black Education in Arkansas," *AHQ* 42 (autumn 1983): 207–38; Randy Finley, *From Slavery to Uncertain Freedom: The Freedmen's Bureau in Arkansas, 1865–1869* (Fayetteville: University of Arkansas Press, 1996), and "In War's Wake: Health Care and Arkansas Freedmen, 1863–1868," *AHQ* 51 (summer 1992): 135–63; Howard C. Westwood, "The Reverend Fountain Brown: Alleged Violator of the Emancipation Proclamation," *AHQ* 49 (summer 1990): 107–23; Bobby L. Lovett, "African Americans, Civil War, and Aftermath in Arkansas," *AHQ* 54 (autumn 1995): 304–58; Paul D. Lack, "An Urban Slave Community: Little Rock, 1831–1862," *AHQ* 41 (autumn 1982): 258–87; and A. F. Kaufman, "The Fifty-Fourth U.S. Colored Infantry: The Forgotten Regiment," *Ozark Historical Review* 16 (spring 1987): 1–8.

38. Brown, "Albert Pike and the Pea Ridge Atrocities"; Roy A. Clifford, "The Indian Regiments in the Battle of Pea Ridge," *Chronicles of Oklahoma* 25 (winter 1947–48): 314–22; Shea and Hess, *Pea Ridge;* Annie Heloise Abel, *The American Indian as Participant in the Civil War* (Cleveland: Arthur H. Clark, 1919); Wiley Britton, *The Union Indian Brigade in the Civil War* (Kansas City: F. Hudson, 1922); Edward Everett Dale, "The Cherokees in the Confederacy," *Journal of Southern History* 13 (May 1947): 160–85; Edwin C. Bearss, "General Cooper's CSA Indians Threaten Fort Smith," *AHQ* 26 (autumn 1967): 257–84; Leroy H. Fischer and Jerry Gill, "Confederate Indian Forces Outside of Indian Territory," *Chronicles of Oklahoma* 46 (autumn 1968): 249–84; William H. Graves, "Indian Soldiers for the Gray Army: Confederate Recruitment in Indian Territory," *Chronicles of Oklahoma* 69 (summer 1991): 134–45; Frank Cunningham, *General Stand Watie's Confederate Indians* (San Antonio: Naylor, 1959); Kenny A. Franks, *Stand Watie and the Agony of the Cherokee Nation* (Memphis: Memphis State University Press, 1979); Gary E. Moulton, *John Ross, Cherokee Chief* (Athens: University of Georgia Press, 1978); and W. Craig Gaines, *The Confederate Cherokees: John Drew's Regiment of Mounted Rifles* (Baton Rouge: Louisiana State University Press, 1989).

39. William B. Hesseltine and Larry Gara, "Arkansas' Confederate Leaders after the War," *AHQ* 9 (winter 1950): 259–69; Ruth Caroline Cowen, "Reorganization

of Federal Arkansas, 1862–1865," *AHQ* 18 (summer 1959): 132–57; Martha A. Ellenburg, "Reconstruction in Arkansas" (Ph.D. diss., University of Missouri, 1967); George H. Thompson, *Arkansas and Reconstruction: The Influence of Geography, Economics, and Personality* (Port Washington, N.Y.: Kennikat Press, 1976); Diane Neal and Thomas W. Kremm, "Loyal Government on Trial: The Union versus Arkansas," *Southern Studies* 25 (summer 1986): 148–62; Conrid C. Berry, "Arkansas and Abraham Lincoln: Wartime Reconstruction and the President's Plan for the State" (Ph.D. diss., University of Mississippi, 1992); and Benjamin Boulden, "'So Long as Strangers Are the Rulers': Gen. Frederick Steele and the Politics of Wartime Reconstruction in Arkansas" (M.A. thesis, University of Arkansas, 1992). Most recently, William C. Harris, *With Charity for All: Lincoln and the Restoration of the Union* (Lexington: University Press of Kentucky, 1997), has placed Arkansas in the broader context of wartime Reconstruction.

40. Mark K. Christ, ed., *Rugged and Sublime: The Civil War in Arkansas* (Fayetteville: University of Arkansas Press, 1994); Mike Fisher, "Remember Poison Spring," *Missouri Historical Review* 74 (autumn 1980): 323–42; Samuel T. Gill, "The Pain of Pyrrhic Victory: Battle at Jenkins' Ferry," *Civil War Times Illustrated* 23 (May 1984): 8–15; Ival L. Gregory, "The Battle of Prairie Grove, December 7, 1862," *Journal of the West* 19 (October 1980): 63–75; Michael Banasik, *Embattled Arkansas: The Prairie Grove Campaign of 1862* (Wilmington, N.C.: Broadfoot, 1996); Henry F. Hartsell, "The Battle of Cane Hill, Arkansas, November 28, 1862," *Journal of the West* 19 (October 1980): 51–62; Glenn T. Nelson and John D. Squier, "The Confederate Defense of Northeast Arkansas and the Battle of Cotton Plant, Arkansas, July 7, 1862," *Rivers and Roads and Points in Between* 14 (1989): 5–27; Scott H. Akridge and Emmett E. Powers, *A Severe and Bloody Fight: The Battle of Whitney's Lane and Military Occupation of White County, Arkansas, May and June 1862* (Searcy, Ark.: White County Historical Museum, 1996); Richard L. Kiper, "John Alexander McClernand and the Arkansas Post Campaign," *AHQ* 56 (spring 1997): 56–79; Anne J. Bailey, "The Texas Cavalry's Race to Reinforce Arkansas Post, January 1863," *East Texas Historical Journal* 28 (winter 1990): 45–56, and "The Abandoned Western Theater: Confederate National Policy toward the Trans-Mississippi Region," *Journal of Confederate History* 5 (autumn 1990): 35–54; Barry R. Sude, "Federal Military Policy and Strategy in Missouri and Arkansas, 1861–1863: A Study of Command Level Conflict" (Ph.D. diss., Temple University, 1987); Tom Franzmann, "The Final Campaign: The Confederate Offensive of 1864," *Chronicles of Oklahoma* 63 (autumn 1985): 266–79; Robert T. Maberry, "Texans and the Defense of the Confederate Northwest, April 1861–April 1862: A Social and Military History" (Ph.D. diss., Texas Christian University, 1992); Gregory J. W. Urwin, "'The Lord Has Not Forsaken Me and I Won't Forsake Him': Religion in Frederick Steele's Union Army, 1863–1864," *AHQ* 52 (autumn 1993): 318–40; and Anne J. Bailey, "Was There a Massacre at Poison Spring?" *Military History of the Southwest* 20 (autumn 1990): 157–68.

41. Craig L. Symonds, *Stonewall of the West: Patrick Cleburne and the Civil War* (Lawrence: University Press of Kansas, 1997); Mauriel Phillips Joslyn, ed., *A Meteor Shining Brightly: Essays on Maj. Gen. Patrick R. Cleburne* (Milledgeville, Ga.: Terrell

House, 1997); Barbara C. Ruby, "General Patrick Cleburne's Proposal to Arm Southern Slaves," *AHQ* 30 (autumn 1971): 193–212; Paul R. Fessler, "The Case of the Missing Promotion: Historians and the Military Career of Major General Patrick Ronayne Cleburne, C.S.A.," *AHQ* 53 (summer 1994): 211–31; Wiley Sword, "The Other Stonewall," *Civil War Times Illustrated* 36 (February 1998): 36–44; Sam Connor, "Cleburne and the Unthinkable," *Civil War Times Illustrated* 36 (February 1998): 45–47; Diane Neal and Thomas W. Kremm, "'The King of the Revolution Is the Bayonet': General Thomas C. Hindman's Proposal to Arm the Slaves," *Journal of Confederate History* 7 (1991): 81–96, and *The Lion of the South: General Thomas C. Hindman* (Macon, Ga.: Mercer University Press, 1993); Walter Lee Brown, *A Life of Albert Pike* (Fayetteville: University of Arkansas Press, 1997); Thomas W. Cutrer, *Ben McCulloch and the Frontier Military Tradition* (Chapel Hill: Univesity of North Carolina Press, 1993); and Daniel E. Sutherland, "No Better Officer in the Confederacy: The Wartime Career of Daniel C. Govan," *AHQ* 54 (autumn 1995): 269–303.

42. Moneyhon, *Impact of the Civil War and Reconstruction on Arkansas,* 9; Bailey, "Free Speech and the 'Lost Cause' in Arkansas."

Chapter 1: Henry McCulloch's Texans and the Defense of Arkansas in 1862

1. W. H. Parsons to W. H. Getzendaner, June 24, 1878, in *A Brief and Condensed History of Parsons' Texas Cavalry Br*igade . . . (Waxahachie, Tex.: J. M. Flemister, Printer, 1892), 21, 23. Parsons, who had been a firebrand newspaper editor in Waco, Texas, before the war, served under Henry McCulloch in 1862 and 1863. Although never promoted, he was highly popular with his men and commanded a brigade. Following the war he was an outspoken critic of those who criticized the men serving in the Trans-Mississippi Department. For more on the general situation in Arkansas, see Michael B. Dougan, *Confederate Arkansas: The People and Policies of a Frontier State in Wartime* (University, Ala.: University of Alabama Press, 1976.)

2. For military events in Arkansas in 1862, see William L. Shea, "1862: A Continual Thunder," in *Rugged and Sublime: The Civil War in Arkansas,* ed. Mark K. Christ (Fayetteville: University of Arkansas Press, 1992.) Additional information on Ben McCulloch's death is found in Thomas W. Cutrer, *Ben McCulloch and the Frontier Military Tradition* (Chapel Hill: University of North Carolina Press, 1993); and William L. Shea and Earl J. Hess, *Pea Ridge: Civil War Campaign in the West* (Chapel Hill: University of North Carolina Press, 1992). For more on Van Dorn in Arkansas, see Arthur B. Carter, *The Tarnished Cavalier: Major General Earl Van Dorn* (Knoxville: University of Tennessee Press, 1999); Robert G. Hartje, *Van Dorn: The Life and Times of a Confederate General* (Nashville: Vanderbilt University Press, 1967); and Emily Van Dorn Miller, ed., *A Soldier's Honor, With Reminiscences of Major-General Earl Van Dorn* (New York: Abbey Press, 1902.)

3. Additional information on Samuel Curtis is found in Ruth C. Gallaher, "Samuel Ryan Curtis," *Iowa Journal of History and Politics* 25 (1927): 331–58.

4. Ibid.; John M. Harrell, "Arkansas," in *Confederate Military History,* ed.

Clement A. Evans, vol. 10, *Louisiana and Arkansas* (Atlanta: Confederate Publishing Co., 1899), 99; *Little Rock True Democrat,* May 22, 1862. See also Edwin C. Bearss, "The White River Expedition, June 10–July 15, 1862," *Arkansas Historical Quarterly* 21 (winter 1962): 305–62.

5. J. P. Benjamin to P. O. Hébert, February 24, 1862, U.S. War Department, *The War of the Rebellion: A Compilation of the Official Records of the Union and Confederate Armies,* 128 vols. (Washington, D.C.: GPO, 1880–1901), ser. 1, vol. 9, 700 (hereafter cited as *OR;* unless otherwise indicated, all references are to series 1); P. O. Hébert to George W. Randolph, April 19, 1861, ibid., 707.

6. Henry McCulloch to Samuel Cooper, May 26, 1862, Compiled Military Service Record of Henry E. McCulloch, Compiled Confederate Military Service Records, RG 109, National Archives; General Orders No. 5, *OR,* vol. 9, 718. McCulloch, born in Tennessee in 1816, moved to Texas in 1837. He had a colorful career as an Indian fighter, sheriff, member of the Texas house and senate, captain of a company of Texas Rangers in the Mexican War, and, when the Civil War began, he was serving as United States marshal for the Eastern District of Texas. McCulloch was commissioned a brigadier general on March 14, 1862. He died March 12, 1895.

7. E. S. C. Robertson to Mary Robertson, June 24, 1862, Robertson Colony Collection, Special Collections, University of Texas at Arlington. Born in Tennessee, Robertson came to Texas in 1832 at the age of twelve. His father was one of the founders of the Nashville Colony, which owned much of the land in central Texas. Appointed aide-de-camp to Henry McCulloch, he served with him until both men returned to Texas. See also Organization of the Trans-Mississippi Department, December 12, 1862, *OR,* vol. 22, pt. 1, 903–4; Consolidated Report of the Army of the Confederate States of America, January 1863, *OR,* ser. 4, pt. 2, 380.

8. See also Diane Neal and Thomas Kremm, *The Lion of the South: General Thomas C. Hindman* (Macon, Ga.: Mercer University Press, 1993); and Bobby L. Roberts, "General T. C. Hindman and the Trans-Mississippi District," *Arkansas Historical Quarterly* 32 (winter 1973): 297–311.

9. E. S. C. Robertson to Mary Robertson, September 22, 1862, Robertson Colony Collection; Report of T. C. Hindman, June 19, 1863, *OR,* vol. 13, 28–44.

10. George W. Ingram to Martha Ingram, June 11, 1862, in *Civil War Letters of George W. And Martha F. Ingram 1861–1865,* comp. Henry L. Ingram (College Station: Texas A&M University Press, 1973), 23. Ingram, a native of North Carolina, was first lieutenant and later captain of Co. A, Twelfth Texas Cavalry Regiment. Roger Q. Mills to wife, September 5, 1862, Mrs. Charles Mills Papers, Dallas County Historical Society Archives, Dallas, Texas. Mills became colonel of the Tenth Texas Regiment when Allison Nelson was promoted to brigadier general. The regiment was captured at Arkansas Post in January 1863.

11. Report of Charles E. Hovey, July 7, 1862, *OR,* vol. 13, 143–45; Bryan Marsh to Araminta Marsh, July 29, 1862, in "The Confederate Letters of Bryan Marsh," *Chronicles of Smith County* 14 (1975): 14–15. Marsh, a native of Alabama, came to Texas in 1854. Elected captain of Co. C, Seventeenth Texas Cavalry (dismounted), his regiment was among those captured at Arkansas Post and, following exchange, was

assigned to the Army of Tennessee. See also William L. Shea, "The Confederate Defeat at Cache River," *Arkansas Historical Quarterly* 52 (summer 1993): 129–55.

12. Report of T. C. Hindman, dated June 19, 1863 (the date is located on page 43 in a footnoted correction of the date Hindman gave in the report), *OR*, vol. 13, 28–44; T. H. Holmes to George W. Randolph, September 8, 1862, ibid., 877–78.

13. E. S. C. Robertson to Mary Robertson, July 10, August 4, 30, and September 12, 1862, Robertson Colony Collection.

14. Special Orders No. 39, September 28, 1862, and Special Orders No. 42, September 30, 1862, *OR*, vol. 13, 883–85, 978. See also Albert Castel, "Theophilus Holmes—Pallbearer of the Confederacy," *Civil War Times Illustrated* 16 (July 1977): 11–17.

15. E. S. C. Robertson to Mary Robertson, September 30, October 3, 8, 9, 11, 1862, Robertson Colony Collection.

16. J. P. Blessington, *The Campaigns of Walker's Texas Division by a Private Soldier* (New York: Lang, Little & Co., 1875), 42. Blessington, an Irishman, arrived in Texas on the eve of the war. He joined Co. H, Sixteenth Texas Infantry, and by 1864 had risen to corporal on the personal staff of his brigade commander, William R. Scurry. His excellent narrative is a standard reference for the division's history. Z. H. Crow to Martha Crow, October 17, 1862, in "Letters of Z. H. Crow," ed. F. Lee Lawrence and Robert W. Glover, *Chronicles of Smith County* 4 (1965): 13–14. Born in South Carolina, Crow served in Co. C, Seventeenth Texas Cavalry (dismounted), but there is no record that he was captured with the regiment at Arkansas Post. E. S. C. Robertson to Mary Robertson, October 28, 1862, Robertson Colony Collection.

17. Bryan Marsh to Araminta Marsh, August 29, 1862; E. S. C. Robertson to Mary Robertson, November 14, 1862, Robertson Colony Collection.

18. Samuel Cooper to T. H. Holmes, October 15, 1862, *OR*, vol. 13, 888; T. H. Holmes to Samuel Cooper, October 19 and 26, 1862, ibid., 889, 898–99.

19. Samuel Cooper to T. H. Hindman, November 19, 1862, ibid., 921.

20. T. H. Holmes to Samuel Cooper, December 5, 1862, *OR*, vol. 17, pt. 2, 783–84.

21. Samuel Cooper to T. H. Holmes, December 6, 1862, ibid., 786; T. H. Holmes to Samuel Cooper, December 8, 1862, ibid,, 787–88.

22. John Simmons to Nancy Simmons, December 29, 1862, in "Civil War Letters of John Simmons," ed. Jon Harrison, *Chronicles of Smith County* 14 (1975): 29–30. Born in Georgia, John Simmons came to Texas about 1850. The unit he joined became Co. I, Twenty-second Texas Infantry. Blessington, *Walker's Texas Division,* 63.

23. For the response of some of the Texans, see M. Jane Johansson, *Peculiar Honor: A History of the Twenty-Eighth Texas Cavalry, 1862–1865* (Fayetteville: University of Arkansas Press, 1998), 39.

24. Blessington, *Walker's Texas Division,* 67.

25. Elijah P. Petty to Margaret Petty, January 10, 1863, in *Journey to Pleasant Hill: The Civil War Letters of Captain Elijah P. Petty, Walker's Texas Division CSA,* ed. Norman D. Brown (San Antonio: Institute of Texas Cultures, 1982), 127. Petty, a native of Tennessee, was the commander of Co. F, Seventeenth Texas Infantry. He died at the battle of Pleasant Hill in April 1864.

26. Henry G. Orr to James D. Orr, January 21, 1863, in *Campaigning with Parsons' Texas Cavalry Brigade, CSA,* ed. John Q. Anderson (Hillsboro, Tex.: Hill Junior College Press, 1967), 90. Four brothers served in the Confederate army. Two were with Parsons' cavalry brigade, and the other two were in regiments captured at Arkansas Post, thus his grief was understandable. After exchange, the two who were taken prisoner became soldiers in the Army of Tennessee.

27. Blessington, *Walker's Texas Division,* 70; John Simmons to Nancy Simmons, February 5, 1863, Harrison, ed., "Civil War Letters of John Simmons."

28. Blessington, *Walker's Texas Division,* 70; John Simmons to Nancy Simmons, February 5, 1863, Harrison, ed., "Civil War Letters of John Simmons."; Smith Diary, January 21, 1863, Thomas B. Smith Diaries, Layland Museum, Cleburne, Texas. Smith served as captain of Co. I, Eleventh Texas Infantry Regiment. He died at Princeton, Arkansas, of pneumonia on May 9, 1864.

29. McCulloch fought at Milliken's Bend, Louisiana, in June 1863, but his performance in combat was so poor that he was replaced and transferred back to Texas. In September 1863, he took command of the Northern Subdistrict of Texas, where he remained until the war's end. For more on his later career, see David Paul Smith, *Frontier Defense in the Civil War: Texas' Rangers and Rebels* (College Station: Texas A&M University Press, 1992.)

Chapter 2: Wartime Gristmill Destruction in Northwest Arkansas and Military Farm Colonies

1. Ninety-eight of the 771 actions, or 12.7 percent. Frederick H. Dyer, *Compendium of the War of the Rebellion* (Des Moines: Dyer Publishing, 1908), 582.

2. There were approximately 3,045 Union casualties. Compiled from Dyer, *Compendium of the War,* 385–98.

3. Bureau of the Census, *Agriculture of the United States in 1860, Compiled from the Original Returns of the Eighth Census* (Washington, D.C., 1867), 6–9; Bureau of the Census, *Manufactures of the United States in 1860, Compiled from the Original Returns of the Eighth Census* (Washington, D.C., 1867), 15–19.

4. Northwest Arkansas includes the counties of Benton, Carroll, Crawford, Madison, Johnson, and Washington. Bureau of the Census, "Arkansas, Products of Industry, 1860," manuscript, Special Collections, Mullins Library, University of Arkansas, Fayetteville.

5. There were 1,493 slaves and 14,673 residents. Bureau of the Census, *Eighth Census of the United States, 1860: Population of the United States in 1860* (Washington, D.C.: GPO, 1864), 12–22.

6. Lyman G. Bennett and Wm. M. Haigh, *History of the Thirty-Sixth Regiment, Illinois Volunteers* (Aurora, Ill.: Knickerbocker & Hodder, 1876), 120–21.

7. U.S. War Department, *The War of the Rebellion: A Compilation of the Official Records of the Union and Confederate Armies,* 128 vols. (Washington, D.C.: GPO, 1880–1901), ser. 1, vol. 13, 577 (hereafter cited as *OR;* unless otherwise indicated, all references are to series 1).

8. Ibid., 506.

9. Ibid., vol. 3, 728.

10. Philip H. Sheridan, *Personal Memoirs of P. H. Sheridan* (New York: C. L. Webster, 1888), 129–31.

11. *OR,* ser. 2, vol. 2, 801.

12. Ibid., ser. 1, vol. 3, 738.

13. William Baxter, *Pea Ridge and Prairie Grove* (Cincinnati: Poe & Hitchcock, 1864), 53.

14. Marian Tebbetts Bane, "The Tebbetts Family History," *Flashback* (Washington County Historical Society, March 1971): 11.

15. *OR,* vol. 13, 574.

16. Ibid., 583.

17. "Arkansas, Products of Industry, 1860."

18. *OR,* vol. 13, 582, 584.

19. William H. Tunnard, A *Southern Record: The History of the Third Louisiana Infantry* (Baton Rouge: Louisiana State University Press, 1866), 126.

20. *OR,* vol. 3, 737, and vol. 8, 589.

21. Ibid., vol. 8, 497.

22. Tunnard, *A Southern Record,* 111; *OR,* vol. 8, 68–69, 208–9.

23. *OR,* vol. 8, 598–99, 759.

24. Ibid., 768.

25. Ibid., 765.

26. Ibid., 49.

27. "An Interesting Civil War Record," *Flashback* (Washington County Historical Society, March 1958):13; "W. H. Rhea . . . Totals His Losses," ibid. (May 1956): 17–18.

28. "W. H. Rhea . . . Totals His Losses," 17–18.

29. Clarence Evans, ed., "Memoirs, Letters, and Diary Entries of German Settlers in Northwest Arkansas, 1853–1863," *Arkansas Historical Quarterly* 6 (autumn 1947): 243.

30. *OR,* vol. 34, pt. 2, 605.

31. W. J. Lemke, ed., *The Mecklin Letters,* Washington County Historical Society Bulletin, 1955, 43.

32. *OR,* vol. 41, pt. 1, 267–68.

33. Ibid., 266–70.

34. "Arkansas, Products of Industry, 1860."

35. Ibid.

36. Untitled article, *Flashback* (Washington County Historical Society, September 1958): 13.

37. Bureau of the Census, "Arkansas, Products of Industry, 1870," manuscript, Special Collections, Mullins Library, University of Arkansas, Fayetteville.

38. *OR,* vol. 34, pt. 3, 8.

39. Ibid., vol. 48, pt. 1, 741.

40. Ibid., 1120–21.

41. Ibid., pt. 2, 295.

42. *OR,* vol. 34, pt. 2, 605–6.

43. Ibid., pt. 3, 640.

44. Ibid., 595 596, 640.

45. *OR,* vol. 48, pt. 1, 931–32.

46. Ibid., pt. 2, 295.

47. Ibid., pt. 1, 1210.

48. *OR,* vol. 34, pt. 4, 84; ibid., vol. 48, pt. 1, 1121.

49. U.S. Congress, *Report of the Adjutant General of Arkansas,* by Albert W. Bishop, 39th Cong., 2nd sess., 1867, S. Doc. 53, 265.

50. *OR,* vol. 48, pt. 2, 135.

51. Ibid., vol. 34, pt. 3, 8.

52. Ibid., vol. 48, pt. 2, 1210.

53. "Destitute" roll of Union Valley Colony, undated, signed by Captain J. R. Rutherford, Rutherford Collection, Special Collections, Mullins Library, University of Arkansas, Fayetteville.

54. *OR,* vol. 48, pt. 1, 1169; ibid., pt. 2, 369.

55. Ibid., vol. 34, pt. 3, 642.

56. Ibid., vol. 41, pt. 4, 917.

57. Ibid., vol. 48, pt. 1, 743, 848.

58. U.S. Congress, *Report of the Adjutant General of Arkansas,* 267; *OR,* vol. 48, pt. 1, 1293–94.

59. U.S. Congress, *Report of the Adjutant General of Arkansas,* 274.

60. Ibid.

61. Carol N. Wenzel, "Freedmen's Farm Letters of Samuel and Louisa Mallory . . . ," *Journal of the Illinois State Historical Society* 73 (autumn 1980): 165–66, 168. See also Diane Neal and Thomas W. Kremm, "An Experiment in Collective Security: The Union Army's Use of Armed Colonies in Arkansas," *Military History of the Southwest* 20 (autumn 1990): 169–81.

62. *OR,* vol. 48, pt. 1, 791.

63. U.S. Congress, *Report of the Adjutant General of Arkansas,* 267; *OR,* vol. 48, pt. 1, 1294.

64. Grant's General Order No. 3, *OR,* vol. 34, pt. 3, 9; *OR,* vol. 41, pt. 2, 499.

65. *OR,* vol. 48, pt. 2, 135.

66. Letter of Lafayette Gregg to Joseph R. Rutherford, July 22, 1865, Rutherford Collection.

67. *OR,* vol. 48, pt. 1, 1210.

68. U.S. Congress, *Report of the Adjutant General of Arkansas,* 274.

69. *OR,* vol. 48, pt. 1, 1168.

70. Ibid., 1178.

71. Ibid., 1293–94.

72. Thomas S. Staples, *Reconstruction in Arkansas, 1862–1874* (New York: Columbia University Press, 1923), 186.

73. Ibid., 190–91.

74. Ibid., 190; James W. Leslie, "Family's Letters Reflect P[ine] B[luff] during Reconstruction," *Pine Bluff (Arkansas) Commercial,* September 2, 1981, 17; Wenzel, "Freedmen's Farm," 168, 171–73.

75. Staples, *Reconstruction,* 187–88; *OR,* vol. 34, pt. 3, 482.

76. *OR,* vol. 34, pt. 3, 642; ibid., vol. 48, pt. 1, 1178–79.

77. *OR,* vol. 48, pt. 1, 1294.

78. "Destitute" roll, Rutherford Collection.

79. *OR,* vol. 48, pt 1, 1177; ibid., pt 2, 529.

80. *OR,* vol. 48, pt. 2, 529.

81. Ibid., pt. 1, 1120.

82. Ibid., 847–48.

83. Ibid., 1120–21, 1151.

84. Ibid., 1168–69.

85. Ibid., 1179.

86. Ibid., pt. 2, 369.

87. Ibid., pt. 1, 1302.

88. Ibid., pt. 1, 178, and pt. 2, 369.

89. *OR,* vol. 48, pt. 1, 1302.

90. Ibid., pt. 3, 305.

91. Ibid., pt. 2, 305, 369.

92. Ibid., pt. 1, 1294.

93. Ibid., pt. 2, 369.

94. Ibid., pt. 1, 1120–21.

95. Special Order No. 6, Headquarters Post, Fayetteville, Arkansas, March 14, 1865, manuscript, Rutherford Collection.

96. Letter from George A. Purdy to Capt. J. R. Rutherford, April 14, 1865, Rutherford Collection.

Chapter 3: Bullets for Johnny Reb: Confederate Nitre and Mining Bureau in Arkansas

1. P. Gary Eller, "Saltpeter Production from Cave Sediments—An Important and Early American Chemical Industry," *Cave Research Foundation 1976 Annual Report* (1976): 48; Josiah Gorgas, *The Ordnance Manual for the Use of the Officers of the Confederate States Army* (1863; reprint, Dayton, Ohio: Morningside, 1976), 224 (hereafter cited as *Ordnance Manual*). "The origin of nitrate deposits is still an open problem. Fixation of nitrogen by lightning, leaching of guano deposits, leaching of nitrates produced by nitrifying bacteria, a volcanic origin, and other suggestions have been made." W. A. Tarr, *Introductory Economic Geology* (New York: McGraw-Hill, 1930), 565. "Free nitric acid, formed in moist air by the discharge of atmospheric electricity (lightning), is found to a very slight extent in rain water and is also formed in the soil by the oxidation of nitrogenous organic matter. It is neutralized by the basic substances in the soil to form nitrates, principally saltpetre, KNO_3, and Chile saltpetre, $NaNO_3$, the latter being found in greater abundance and concentrations." "Nitric

Acid and Nitrates," *Encyclopaedia Britannica* (Chicago: Encyclopedia Britannica, 1956), 16:324. "*Nitre,* also spelled Niter, or called Saltpetre, also Saltpeter, naturally occurring potassium nitrate KNO_3; soda nitre, also known as cubic nitre or Chile saltpetre, is sodium nitrate, $NaNO_3$. Nitre was employed in the 13th century in the preparation of nitric acid and the manufacture of gunpowder and fireworks. It occurs as crusts on the surface of the Earth, on walls and rocks, and in caves. It forms in certain soils in Spain, Italy, Egypt, Iran, India and occurs with soda nitre in Chile and in caves in the Mississippi Valley." *The New Encyclopaedia Britannica* (Chicago: Encyclopedia Britannica, 1984), 7:358. The Ozark mountaineers referred to saltpeter, not niter. W. B. Flippin, "Early History—Marion County as She Was When Settled in 1836," *Yellville (Arkansas) Mountain Echo,* June 23, 1899, c. 1, p. 3.

2. Major George W. Rains, *Notes on Making Saltpetre from the Earth of Caves* (Augusta, Ga., 1861; reprint, n.p.: National Speleological Society, 1973).

3. "Gunpowder for the Confederate Army," *Confederate Veteran* 14 (1906): 119. See also footnote 1 for guano as saltpeter source, and below; "*guano*, accumulated excrement and remains of birds, bats and seals, valued as fertilizer. Bat guano comes mainly from islands off the coasts of Peru, Baja California, and Africa heavily populated by cormorants, pelicans, and gannets. Bat guano is found in caves throughout the world. Seal guano has accumulated to great depths on the Islas Lobos de Tierra, and the Islas Lobos de Afuera, off northwestern Peru. Bat and seal guano are lower in fertilizer value than bird guano, which contains about 11 to 16 percent nitrogen, 8 to 12 percent phosphoric acid, and 2 to 3 percent potash." *The New Encyclopaedia Britannica,* 4:769. "The guano deposits of insectivorous bats are used for agricultural fertilizer in many countries and in the past were used as a source of nitrogen and phosphorous for munitions," *The New Encyclopaedia Britannica,* 4:430.

4. "Cave in the Ozarks Furnished Powder for the Southern Army," *McCrory Arkansas Central Leader,* May 15, 1930, p. 2; George W. Foster, Co. A, Twenty-seventh Arkansas Infantry, Compiled Service Records, RG 109, National Archives (hereafter cited as NA).

5. Rains, *Notes on Making Saltpetre.*

6. *Ordnance Manual,* 224–25.

7. J. W. Mallet, "Work of the Ordnance Bureau," *Southern Historical Society Papers* 37 (1909): 10.

8. Bobbie Jones McLane and Capitola Hensley Glazner, *1850 Mortality Schedules of Arkansas* (Hot Springs , Ark. privately printed, 1968), 64; David Dale Owen, *First Report of a Geological Reconnaissance of the Northern Counties of Arkansas, Made during the years 1857 and 1858* (Little Rock, 1858), 53–55, 224–26.

9. Josiah Gorgas, "Contributions to the History of the Confederate Ordnance Department," *Southern Historical Society Papers* 12 (1884): 70.

10. Ibid.

11. Ibid., 68–76; "To Manufacture Saltpetre," *Little Rock True Democrat,* June 19, 1862, c. 2, p. 1.

12. John M. Harrell, *Arkansas,* vol. 10 in *Confederate Military History,* ed.

Clement A. Evans, 12 vols. (Atlanta: Confederate Publishing Company, 1899), 16; Mallet, "Work of the Ordnance Bureau," 3.

13. "Army and Munitions for War," *Little Rock Arkansas Gazette,* May 18, 1861; "Manufactures in Arkansas," *True Democrat,* January 1, 1862, c. 2, p. 2.

14. U.S. War Department, *The War of the Rebellion: A Compilation of the Official Records of the Union and Confederate Armies,* 128 vols. (Washington, D.C.: GPO, 1880–1901), ser. 4, vol. 1, 355 (hereafter cited as *OR*); "Transfer of Arms," *Arkansas State Gazette,* July 20, 1861.

15. Letter from P. S. McNamara in Captain Patrick S. McNamara, Nitre and Mining Bureau, Compiled Confederate Military Service Records, RG 109, (hereafter cited as CSA N&M Bureau), NA; Bureau of the Census,*1860 Population Census, Johnson County, Tennessee,* National Archives microflm, M653, reel 1259; 1862 Newton County Tax Records, Arkansas History Commission, Little Rock; "Cave in the Ozarks Furnished Powder for the Southern Army," *McCrory Arkansas Central Leader,* May 15, 1930, c. 1, p. 2; travel voucher dated February 7, 1863, in Major Isaac Read, CSA N&M Bureau, NA.

16. "Saltpeter in Arkansas," *Des Arc Weekly Citizen,* October 16, 1861, 2:2; Mrs. Elmer Kirk, "The Saltpeter Mine of 1862," *Batesville (Ark.) Independence County Chronicle,* April 1962.

17. *OR,* ser. 4, vol. 1, 535.

18. Rains, *Notes on Making Saltpetre.*

19. Ibid.

20. "Army and Munitions for War," *Arkansas Gazette,* May 18, 1861; "Col. Borland's Orders," ibid., December 14, 1861.

21. "Improvements at the Arsenal," *Arkansas Gazette,* December 14, 1861, c. 2, p. 2; "Manufactures in Arkansas," *True Democrat,* January 1, 1862; Gorgas, "Contributions," 74; Mallet, "Work of the Ordnance Bureau," 5–6. In Camden, Arrington V. Dedman had an iron forge, valued at $20,000, which processed eighty tons of pig iron valued at $2,800 annually. He employed ten men at $65 per month and used an eight-horse steam engine to produce plows, hollow ware, and engine machinery worth $42,000 per annum. At Little Rock, Robert Brodie had a foundry, valued at $25,000, which used $2,000 worth of iron and coal annually. He employed seven men at $100 per month and used steam power to produce 60,000 pounds of machinery castings at $42,000 per annum. Also at Little Rock, Drake and Byrd had a $5,000 foundry, steam powered, to produce mostly machinery valued at $10,000 per annum. Annually they used the following raw materials: 50 tons of pig iron at $20,000, 20,000 pounds of bar iron at $1,200, coal and coke at $60, and firewood at $250. Bureau of the Census, Eighth Census of the United States 1860, "Arkansas, Products of Industry, 1860," manuscript, Special Collections, Mullins Library, University of Arkansas, Fayetteville. Drake and Byrd advertised in the *Arkansas Gazette* that they had acquired an iron lathe and planer. They would make castings and advertised that they had efficient workmen in molding, blacksmithing, pattern making, and finishing. Drake and Byrd could make gin gears, dog irons, plow points, gudgeons, and boxes. "New Foundry," *Arkansas Gazette,* May 11, c. 5, p. 4.

22. Gorgas, "Contributions," 70–72, 84; "Cave in the Ozarks Furnished Powder for Southern Army," *McCrory Arkansas Central Leader,* May 15, 1930, p. 2; "The Saltpeter Cave Rivals Mammoth," *Texarkana (Arkansas) Daily Texarkanian,* January 4, 1909, p. 9; "Manufactures in Arkansas," *True Democrat,* January 1, 1862.

23. Kenneth L. Smith, "The Seven Kettles," *Arkansas Gazette,* November 29, 1959, p. E-2; Charles H. Lothrop, *A History of the First Regiment Iowa Cavalry Veteran Volunteers, From Its Organization in 1861 to Its Muster out of the United States Service in 1866* (Lyons, Iowa, 1890), 98–99. Note that Lothrop locates the niter mines at Kingston, Madison County, but the official report (*OR,* ser. 1, vol. 22, pt. 1, 213–14) places it fourteen miles beyond Kingston on the Buffalo River. See Viola Dickey Gibson, "This Old Kettle," *Boone County Historian* 13 (1989): 174.

24. *OR,* ser. 1, vol. 8, 636–37; Earl Berry, *History of Marion County* (Little Rock, Ark.: International Graphics, 1977), 76–77.

25. *OR,* ser. 1, vol. 8, 59–60.

26. Ibid., 371; George Haddock, *Report of a Geological Reconnaissance of a Part of the State of Arkansas, Made during the Years 1871–72* (Little Rock, Ark., 1873), 57; Owen, *First Report,* 38; Kirk, *ibid.*; Captain Patrick S. McNamara, CSA N&M Bureau, NA. McNamara settled Cubbins's account with the Little Rock arsenal on August 8, 1862. Cubbins received $1,000 for 2,000 pounds of saltpeter.

27. *OR,* ser. 4, vol. 1, 1054–55, 1115–16, 1139; Gorgas, "Contributions," 76.

28. *OR,* ser. 4, vol. 2, 26–30.

29. Ibid.; Lothrop, *A History of the First Regiment Iowa Cavalry,* 98–99.

30. Gorgas, "Contributions," 76.

31. Ibid., 77.

32. *OR,* ser. 4, vol. 8, 29.

33. Ibid., ser. 1, vol. 8, 28–44, 832–33.

34. McNamara, Dunnington, and Frederick P. Leavenworth, CSA N&M Bureau, NA; "Statement of Receipts and Expenditures, September 1862," Little Rock Arsenal Record, 1862–1863, Civil War: Miscellaneous Records, RG 109, (hereafter cited as LR Arsenal), NA.

35. H. B. McKenzie, "Confederate Manufactures in Southwest Arkansas," *Arkansas Historical Association Publications* (Fayetteville, Ark.) 2 (1908): 207. The Bellah and Davis mines are both located in northwestern Sevier County (see appendix 2 at end of chap. 3). The Davis mine was opened in 1843 for lead ore and was operated intermittently until 1916. The Bellah mine produced lead ore, iron pyrites, and copper ores. When David D. Owen visited the mine in 1859 he saw a ditch six to ten feet deep and nearly one hundred yards long, and some six other shafts where efforts had been made to explore the copper and iron pyrites vein. He comments that the debris around the diggings prove the vein was rich. Since no one was around the mine, Owen wrote to Richard W. Bellah, one of the owners, in Texas, who replied that there were three principal shafts sunk, two were thirty feet deep and the other was seventeen feet, as well as several smaller shafts six to twelve feet deep, which produced five tons or more of ore. Bellah had the ore assayed in Liverpool, England, and the assayers reported that the ore yielded 73 percent lead and 148 ounces of silver per ton. Raymond B. Stroud,

Robert H. Arndt, Frank B. Fulkerson, and W. G. Diamond, *Mineral Resources and Industries of Arkansas,* Bureau of Mines Bulletin 645 (Washington, D.C.: GPO, 1969), 373; David Dale Owen, *Second Report of a Geological Reconnaissance of the Southern Counties of Arkansas, Made during the years 1859 and 1860* (Philadelphia, 1860), 110–11; "To Manufacture Saltpetre," *True Democrat,* June 19, 1862, c. 2, p. 1; "How Women Make Powder," *True Democrat,* June 19, 1862, c. 3, p. 3.

36. "Encouraging Home Manufactures," *Arkansas Gazette,* June 14, 1862, c. 4, p. 1.

37. "Estimate of Funds required in the Ordnance Department for the month of August 1862" and "Estimate of Funds required by Ordnance Department for 3rd Quarter 1862," in Colonel John W. Dunnington, CSA N&M Bureau, NA; Return of Hired Men Employed at Little Rock Arsenal for Month of August 1862, LR Arsenal, NA.

38. *OR,* ser. 1, vol. 8, 34.

39. Colonel John W. Dunnington, CSA N&M Bureau, NA; Lieutenant R. LaMar Sprigg and Major Isaac Read, ibid.

40. Major Isaac Read, CSA N&M Bureau, NA; Owen, *Second Report,* 106.

41. *OR,* ser. 1, vol. 22, pt. I, 159–61, 794.

42. Travel voucher dated February 7, 1863, Major Isaac Read, CSA N&M Bureau, NA; Confederate States, Account Current, LR Arsenal, NA.

43. *OR,* ser. 1, vol. 22, pt. I, 213–14; ibid., ser. 1, vol. 34, pt. 1, 93.

44. Lieutenant R. LaMar Sprigg, CSA N&M Bureau, NA; *OR,* ser. 1, vol. 34, pt. 1, 64–66; John Campbell, C. S. Nitre and Mining Service voucher, Union Provost Marshal's File of Papers Relating to Individual Civilians, RG 109, NA; *A Reminiscent History of the Ozark Region* (Chicago: Goodspeed, 1894), 639–40.

45. Interview with Leland Henley, St. Joe, Ark., December 23, 1977 (notes in author's collection); interview with Bee Still, Morning Star, Ark., December 23, 1977 (notes in author's collection); "Helped Make Powder in Civil War," *Marshall (Arkansas) Republican,* newspaper clipping ca. 1915 (photocopy in author's collection). Point Peter Mountain at the mouth of Richland Creek, the Diggins about two miles up Richland Creek, and Peter Cave on the south side of Buffalo River, about seven miles below Richland Creek mouth, are other locations, in western Searcy County, which are identified with early niter production, but not with Confederate niter mining. Orville J. McInturff, "War Kettles and Powder," *Marshall (Arkansas) Mountain Wave,* March 8, 1979, p. 9.

46. Newton County 1862 Tax Record, Arkansas History Commission, Little Rock; Bureau of the Census, *Searcy County 1860 Census, Slave Schedule,* National Archives Microfilm, M653, reel 54; Lieutenant R. LaMar Sprigg, CSA N&M Bureau, NA; Thomas Jerome Estes, *Early Days and War Times in Northern Arkansas* (Lubbock, Tex., n. d.), 11; Bureau of the Census, *Agriculture of the United States in 1860, Compiled from the Original Returns of the Eighth Census, Under the Direction of the Secretary of the Interior* (Washington, D.C., 1864), 224, quoted in Dwight T. Pitcaithley, *Let the River Be: A History of the Ozark's Buffalo River* (Santa Fe, N. M.: n.d.), 42.

47. S. C. Turnbo, unpublished manuscript, quoted in Berry, *History of Marion County,* 78–79.

48. Muster Roll, Co. F, Thirty-second Arkansas Infantry, February 29, 1864, RG 109, NA; Muster Roll, Co. D, Twenty-seventh Arkansas Infantry, February 29, 1864, RG 109, NA; *OR*, ser. 1, vol. 22, pt. 2, 871–73.

49. James Bratton, Sr., "Used Turtle Shell for a Cradle," *Marshall Mountain Wave,* August 25, 1919.

50. Albert W. Bishop, *Report of the Adjutant General of Arkansas, 1861–1866* (Washington, D.C.: GPO, 1867), 131–33, 121–24; Muster Rolls, Co. D, Twenty-seventh Arkansas Infantry, and Co. F, Thirty-second Arkansas Infantry, RG 109, NA. The Rose family which lived near the Big Creek saltpeter cave recalls an incident which was probably Napier's recruiting expedition, and which helps to explain the lack of employable men in north Arkansas: "Grandfather Isaac Rose did not wish to be drafted into the army as he wished to obey the Commandment "Thou Shalt Not Kill" so he fled southward [from Missouri] to Spring Creek near Big Flat, Arkansas . . . Near the log cabin on Spring Creek, Grandma was shearing her sheep one day while Grandpa kept watch on a high ridge above the Salt Peter Cave where some men made ammunition. A kindly old neighbor man decided it would be safe to help shear the sheep. This he did, for a while. Grandma begged him to go and hide as soldiers had gathered some recruits lately. Before the old fellow could escape some soldiers caught him and hanged him on a tree that stood between two pine trees. Poor Grandmother had to witness the awful cruel deed." May Adams, "Civil War Happenings Concerning People in Searcy County," *Marshall Mountain Wave,* n.d. (clipping in author's collection).

51. "Resources of the Confederacy in February 1865," *Southern Historical Society Papers* 2 (1874): 58–63.

52. Mallet, "Work of the Ordnance Bureau," 3; *OR*, ser. 4, vol. 2, 222–23; Gorgas, "Contributions," 74.

53. *OR*, ser. 1, vol. 22, pt. 2, 871–73.

54. Ibid., ser. 1, vol. 22, pt. 2, 909–11, and pt. 1, 521,604–8.

55. Ibid., pt. 1, 684–85, and pt. 2, 1141–42.

56. Ibid., pt. 2, 953, 1139–40.

57. Ibid., pt. 1, 65–66, 640; Muster Roll, Co. C, Seventh Arkansas Cavalry, December 31, 1863, RG 109, NA.

58. George T. Maddox, *Hard Trials and Tribulations of an Old Confederate Soldier* (Van Buren, Ark., 1897), 16–17; Estes, *Early Days and Wartimes in Northern Arkansas,* 11.

Chapter 4: A Semi-Savage State: The Image of Arkansas in the Civil War

1. Foy Lisenby, "A Survey of Arkansas' Image Problems," *Arkansas Historical Quarterly* 30 (1971): 60–71; C. Fred Williams, "The Bear State Image: Arkansas in the Nineteenth Century," ibid., 39 (1980): 99–111; Elmo Howell, "Mark Twain's Arkansas," ibid., 29 (1970): 195–208; Lee A. Dew, "'On a Slow Train through Arkansas'—The Negative Image of Arkansas in the Early Twentieth Century," ibid., 29

(1980): 125–35; E. J. Friedlander, "'The Miasmatic Jungles': Reactions to H. L. Mencken's 1921 Attack on Arkansas," ibid., 38 (1979): 63–71; David M. Tucker, *Arkansas: A People and Their Reputation* (Memphis: Memphis State University Press, 1985).

2. Addison A. Stuart, *Iowa Colonels and Regiments: Being a History of Iowa Regiments in the War of the Rebellion* (Des Moines, 1865), 44.

3. Othmar A. Abbott, *Recollections of a Pioneer Lawyer* (Lincoln: Nebraska State Historical Society, 1929), 36. The Army of the Southwest was composed primarily of men from Illinois, Iowa, Indiana, and Missouri, with smaller contingents from Wisconsin, Ohio, and Kansas. U.S. War Department, *The War of the Rebellion: A Compilation of the Official Records of the Union and Confederate Armies,* 128 vols (Washington, D.C.: GPO, 1880–1901), ser. 1, vol. 8, 204–06; Samuel P. Curtis, "The Army of the South-West, and the First Campaign in Arkansas," *Annals of Iowa* 7 (1869): 11–12.

4. George W. Herr, *Episodes of the Civil War: Nine Campaigns in Nine States* (San Francisco, 1890), 90; Henry Cummings to his wife, April 30, 1862, H. B. J. Cummings Papers, State Historical Society of Iowa, Des Moines (hereafter cited as SHSI); April 10, 1862, entry in Lines L. Parker Diary, Illinois State Historical Library, Springfield (hereafter cited as ISHL); Byron Carr to his father, April 24, 1862, Byron O. Carr Letters, U.S. Army Military History Institute, Carlisle, Penn. (hereafter cited as USAMHI).

5. M. M. Hughes letter in *Muncie (Indiana) Delaware County Free Press,* January 8, 1862; Robert Gooding to his brother, April 13, 1862, Robert Gooding Letters, Western Historical Manuscript Collection and State Historical Society of Missouri Manuscripts, University of Missouri-Columbia (hereafter cited as WHMC-Columbia, also there are manuscripts at WHMC-Rolla); William N. Tyler, *The Dispatch Carrier* (Port Byron, Ill., 1892), 20; Silas Miller letter in *Aurora (Illinois) Beacon,* May 22, 1862; Thomas Priestly to his sister, July 28, 1862, Thomas Priestly Papers, State Historical Society of Wisconsin, Madison (hereafter cited as SHSW).

6. David P. Bond to Rowland S. Mantor, May 18, 1862, Rowland S. Mantor Letters, WHMC-Columbia; William P. Black to his mother, March 5, 1862, John C. Black Family Papers, ISHL; Charles Calkins to his mother, April 12, 1862, Charles Calkins Papers, ISHL.

7. David Lathrop, *The History of the Fifty-Ninth Regiment Illinois Volunteers* (Indianapolis, 1865); April 10, 1862, entry in Frederick N. Boyer Diary, Minnesota Historical Society, Minneapolis.

8. Lyman G. Bennett, "A Cartographer Speaks," *White River Valley Historical Quarterly* 2 (1966): 7; "Correspondent" letter in *Chicago Tribune,* May 2, 1862; March 18 and 23, 1862, entries in Henry J. Seaman Diary, USAMHI.

9. C. D. letter in *Indianapolis Daily Journal,* February 20, 1862; Silas Miller letter in *Aurora (Illinois) Beacon,* May 22, 1862; William Black to his mother, March 5, 1862, Black Family Papers, ISHL; June 24, 1862, entry in M. W. Wood Journal, E. B. Quiner Papers, SHSW.

10. Lyman G. Bennett and William M. Haigh, *History of the Thirty-Sixth Regiment Illinois Volunteers, During the War of the Rebellion* (Aurora, Ill., 1876),

187–88; Herr, *Episodes of the Civil War,* 90; Wallace P. Benson, *A Soldier's Diary* ([Algonquin, Ill.], 1919), 15; "P" letter in *Aurora (Illinois) Beacon*, June 5, 1862.

11. William Black to his mother, March 5, 1862, Black Family Papers, ISHL; S. S. Marrett to his wife, April 13, 1862, S. S. Marrett Papers, Duke University; Samuel P. Curtis, "Army of the South-West," *Annals of Iowa* 6 (1868): 266; Sam Black, *A Soldier's Recollection of the Civil War* (Minco, Okla.,: Minco Minstrel, 1912), 11; July 7, 1862, entry in Joseph L. Trego Diary, Kansas State Historical Society, Topeka (hereafter cited as KSHS); Henry Cummings to his wife, May 7, 1862, Cummings Papers, SHSI.

12. William Black to his mother, May 12, 1862, Black Family Papers, ISHL; John Higgins to his wife, June 5, 1862, John Higgins Papers, ISHL; "Special Correspondent" letter in *New York Tribune,* March 20, 1862; E. D. Harris letter in *Monmouth (Illinois) Atlas,* April 11, 1862; Alonzo Abernethy, "Incidents of an Iowa Soldier's Life, or Four Years in Dixie," *Annals of Iowa* 12 (1920): 410.

13. Albert O. Marshall, *Army Life; From a Soldier's Journal* (Joliet, Ill., 1884), 93; March 11, 1862, entry in Lyman G. Bennett diary, Lyman G. Bennett Papers, WHMC-Rolla; David Bond to Rowland Mantor, May 18, 1862, Mantor Letters, WHMC-Columbia; G. B. Kirkpatrick to Cynthia, June 20, 1862, private collection of Bruce Roberts, Knoxville. The intensely negative view of Arkansans noted in the text was not unanimous. According to one Federal soldier, "the people of Arkansas seem to be more intelligent and have a better idea of the state of affairs than did the Missourians." George P. Ela to his wife, May 7, 1862, George P. Ela Papers, Illinois State University. Almost identical comments were made by S. S. Marrett to his wife, May 5, 1862, Marrett Papers, Duke University; and by Myron G. Love to his sister, April 23, 1862, Myron G. Love Papers, University of Georgia. In the category of damning with faint praise was this observation by an Illinois officer: "My impressions of Arkansas and its people have been much changed. *They* are no wild and savage race. *It* is no desert but compares favorably with Missouri. The people seem a primitive simple class who live at ease, in plenty, undisturbed and undisturbing." John C. Black to his mother, February 25, 1862, Black Family Papers, ISHL.

14. Daniel Prosser to Miss Ingram, June 19, 1862, O. V. Brown Papers, Indiana State Library; William M. Fogo to [?], July 20, 1862, Quiner Papers, SHSW; "Junius" letter in *Cincinnati Daily Gazette,* March 18, 1862.

15. "Leon" letter in *St. Louis Missouri Republican,* May 13, 1862; Norman E. Clarke, ed., *Warfare along the Mississippi: The Letters of Lieutenant Colonel George E. Currie* (Mount Pleasant, Mich.: Central Michigan University Press, 1961), 36. The Ozark Plateau was and is not representative of the entire state, but the Federals had no way of knowing that. They assumed that what they saw was typical. Such an assumption was quite natural from a Midwestern perspective. One region of mid-nineteenth-century Iowa or Illinois was very much like another in terms of geography and culture.

16. David Bond to Rowland Mantor, May 18, 1862, Mantor Letters, WHMC-Columbia; Henry T. Noble et al, *Military History and Reminiscences of the Thirteenth Regiment of Illinois Volunteer Infantry in the Civil War in the United States, 1861–1865* (Chicago, 1892), 170; April 3, 1862, entry in Bennett diary, Bennett Papers, WHMC-Rolla.

17. John Black to his sister, February 24, 1862, Black Family Papers, ISHL; February 25, 1862, entry in Henry Kircher diary, Engelmann-Kircher Collection, ISHL; March 18, 1862, entry in James Boyle Journal, SHSI; "Special Correspondent" letter in *New York Tribune,* March 10, 1862; June 21, 1862, entry in Wood journal, Quiner Papers, SHSW; "Junius" letter in *Cincinnati Daily Gazette,* March 18, 1862.

18. *Pocahontas (Arkansas) Division Register,* May 1, 1862 (reprinted in *Memphis Daily Appeal,* July 10, 1862).

19. William Fogo to [?], July 20, 1862, Quiner Papers, SHSW; March 22, 1862, entry in Seaman Diary, USAMHI; George Ela to his wife, May 1, 1862, Ela Papers, Illinois State University; Henry Curtis, Jr., to his wife, May 15, 1862, Henry Curtis, Jr., Papers, USAMHI; editorial in *Peoria (Illinois) Daily Transcript,* July 17, 1862; John W. Moulton to his parents, June 15, 1862, William P. Palmer Collection, Western Reserve Historical Society, Cleveland; William H. Kinsman to Grenville M. Dodge, April 17, 1862, Grenville M. Dodge Papers, SHSI; Silas Miller letter in *Aurora (Illinois) Beacon,* May 22, 1862; John [?] to Rachel Love, Love Papers, University of Georgia.

20. Noble et al., *Military History and Reminiscences,* 192; T. I. McKinney letter in *Keokuk (Iowa) Daily Gate City,* June 18, 1862; Myron Love to his sister, May 27, 1862, Love Papers, University of Georgia; J. W. letter in *Greenville (Illinois) Advocate,* May 29, 1862; Henry Cummings to his wife, May 7, 1862, Cummings Papers, SHSI; G. B. Kirkpatrick to Cynthia, June 20, 1862, private collection of Bruce Roberts, Knoxville.

21. Bennett and Haigh, *History of the Thirty-Sixth Regiment,* 193; May 5, 1862, entry in George A. Cummins Diary, ISHL; Curtis, "Army of the South-West," *Annals of Iowa* 7 (1869): 6; Day Elmore to his parents, May 4, 1862, Day Elmore Papers, Chicago Historical Society; George Ela to his wife, May 22, 1862, Ela Papers, Illinois State University; Jonathan Kershner letter in *Greenville (Illinois) Advocate,* May 29, 1862.

22. Marshall, *Army Life,* 97; Henry Cummings to his wife, July 1, 1862, Cummings Papers, SHSI; Curtis, "Army of the South-West," *Annals of Iowa* 7 (1869): 127; Samuel T. Bryant letter in *Greenville (Illinois) Advocate,* August 14, 1862; July 5, 1862, entry in Lot Abraham diary, Lot Abraham Papers, University of Iowa; Myron Love to his sister, May 6, 1862, Love Papers, University of Georgia; George Ela to his wife, May 12, 1862, Ela Papers, Illinois State University.

23. Albert G. Brackett, "A Memorable March," *United Service* 4 (1890): 336; S. S. Marrett to his wife, June 15, 1862, Marrett Papers, Duke University; Abbott, *Recollections,* 40; Black, *Soldier's Recollection,* 16; James M. Miller et al., *History of the Sixteenth Battery of Ohio Volunteer Light Artillery, U.S.A.* (n.p., 1906), 19.

24. William F. Scott, *The Story of a Cavalry Regiment: The Career of the Fourth Iowa Veteran Volunteers from Kansas to Georgia, 1861–1865* (New York, 1893), 39; Samuel T. Bryant letter in *Greenville (Illinois) Advocate,* August 14, 1862; Abbott, *Recollections,* 41; May 5, 1862, entry in Abraham diary, Abraham Papers, University of Iowa.

25. June 10 and 27, 1862 entries in Abraham diary, Abraham Papers, University of Iowa; May 12, 1862, entry in Cummins Diary, ISHL; April 23, 1862, entry in Chesley A. Mosman diary in Herr, *Episodes of the Civil War,* 373.

26. Abbott, *Recollections,* 40; T. I. McKinney letter in *Keokuk (Iowa) Daily Gate City,* July 28, 1862; "P" letter in *Aurora (Illinois) Beacon,* July 24, 1862.

27. Edward Ingraham to his wife, May 12, 1862, Edward Ingraham Papers, ISHL; July 15 and 16, 1862 entries in Wood journal, Quiner Papers, SHSW.

28. A. J. Huntoon to his wife, July 22, 1862, A. J. Huntoon Collection, KSHS; Brackett, "Memorable March," 339. The Second Confiscation Act of July 1862 authorized Federal commanders to confiscate and free the slaves of Confederate supporters, but it became law after the close of the Pea Ridge campaign. Curtis struck at slavery in Arkansas on his own authority or, more accurately, without any legal authority at all.

29. W. H. H. Barker Memoir, 42, USAMHI; S. S. Marrett to his wife, June 9, 1862, Marrett Papers, Duke University; William Marsh to his father, August 14, 1862, William Marsh Papers, ISHL; William S. Burns, *Recollections of the Fourth Missouri Cavalry* (Dayton, Ohio: Morningside, 1988), 42; Henry Cummings to his wife, July 15, 1862, Cummings Papers, SHSI; Fred T. Ledergerber to his uncle, September 2, 1862, Engelmann-Kircher Collection, ISHL. For purposes of comparison see the comments of Federal soldiers presented in Bell I. Wiley, *The Life of Billy Yank: The Common Soldier of the Union* (Indianapolis: Bobbs-Merrill, 1952), 40–44, 109–23; and Joseph T. Glatthaar, *The March to the Sea and Beyond: Sherman's Troops in the Savannah and Carolina Campaigns* (New York: New York University Press, 1985), 52–65.

30. William Fayel report in *St. Louis Daily Missouri Democrat,* July 17, 1862; Thomas Priestly to his sister, July 18, 1862, Priestly Papers, SHSW; C. P. M. and T. I. McKinney letters in *Keokuk (Iowa) Daily Gate City,* July 28, 1862; Samuel T. Bryant letter in *Greenville (Illinois) Advocate,* August 14, 1862; Stuart, *Iowa Colonels and Regiments,* 44–45; September 1, 1862, entry in Achilles H. Fretageot journal, Fretageot Family Papers, Indiana Historical Society, Indianapolis. At least one Federal soldier insisted that Helena " is one of the most pleasant places I have yet seen in the South. The buildings are fine, the streets are clean and nice, and everything has the appearance of wealth and elegance." William Fogo to [?], July 20, 1862, Quiner Papers, SHSW.

31. F. O. W. letter in *Aurora (Illinois) Beacon,* June 12, 1862; July 8 and 9, 1862, entries in Abraham diary, Abraham Papers, University of Iowa; John M. Bowling to his brother (printed in the *Little Rock Arkansas Democrat,* July 10, 1862, after a Federal mail pouch was captured by the Confederates); Lathrop, *History of the Fifty-Ninth Regiment,* 105. See also the comments in the French Brownlee letter in the *Monmouth (Illinois) Atlas,* May 16, 1862.

32. A fine analysis of Federal attitudes toward the Ozark region in general is John F. Bradbury, Jr., "'Good Water & Wood but the Country is a Miserable Botch': Flatland Soldiers Confront the Ozarks," *Missouri Historical Review* 90 (1996): 166–86. A more traditional account of the impact of wartime passions is Wiley, *Life of Billy Yank,* 96–108. The hardening effect of two additional years of war on Federal soldiers, including many veterans of the Pea Ridge campaign, is described in Glatthaar, *March to the Sea,* 66–80.

33. George W. Guess to his wife, July 29, 1862, George W. Guess Letters, Louisiana State University, Baton Rouge. Another Texan was more succinct: "I am very tired of Arkansas and want to get out of it very much for it is no place for Texans." Charleen P. Pollard, ed., "Civil War Letters of George W. Allen," *Southwestern Historical Quarterly* 83 (1979): 49.

Chapter 5: The Preacher, the Lawyer, and the Spoils of War

1. William F. Cloud to Thomas Ewing, Jr., December 13, 1862. Thomas Ewing, Jr., Papers, Manuscripts Division, Library of Congress (hereafter cited as Ewing Papers).

2. "Civil War and Other Records of a Washington County Merchant," *Flashback* 10 (July 1960): 22. This transcription of receipts from the G. W. McClure store at Evansville shows that on September 15, 1962, Edmiston sold two mules to Captain J. B. Mayes of the First Cherokee Batalion, C.S.A., for $400; but in the Washington County Tax Records for 1861, Edmiston listed the value of the mules to be only $150.

3. "Washington County, Arkansas, Sheriff's Census, 1865," p. 111, in Special Collections, Mullins Library, University of Arkansas, Fayetteville.

4. William F. Cloud to Thomas Ewing, Jr., December 13, 1862, Ewing Papers; Robert M. Owings et al., statement, Cane Hill, Arkansas, December 13, 1862, Ewing Papers.

5. William E. Treadway, "The Gilded Age in Kansas," *Kansas Historical Quarterly* 40 (spring 1974): 14–15.

6. Ibid., 15.

7. Ibid.

8. Thomas Ewing, Jr., to Thomas Ewing, Sr., August 23, 1862, Ewing Papers.

9. Edgar Landsdorf, ed., "The Letters of Joseph H. Trego, 1857–1864, Linn County Pioneer," *Kansas Historical Quarterly* 19 (winter 1951): 391 n.

10. [Kansas Adjutant General], *Official Military History of Kansas Regiments during the War for the Suppression of the Great Rebellion* (Leavenworth: W. S. Burke, 1870), 16–22; *History of Jasper County, Missouri* (Des Moines: Mills and Company, 1883), 330–31.

11. U.S. War Department, *The War of the Rebellion: A Compilation of the Official Records of the Union and Confederate Armies,* 128 vols. (Washington, D.C.: GPO, 1880–1901), ser. 1, vol. 3, 160 (hereafter cited as *OR*).

12. Louise Barry, "Legal Hangings in Kansas," *Kansas Historical Quarterly* 18 (autumn 1950): 281; Kansas Adjutant General, *Official Military History of Kansas Regiments,* 32.

13. Wiley Britton, "A Day with Colonel W. F. Cloud," *Chronicles of Oklahoma* 5 (September 1927): 311.

14. Ibid., 317.

15. Thomas Ewing, Jr., to Ellen Ewing, November 25, 1862, Ewing Papers.

16. Ibid.

17. A search through series 1, volumes 13, 22, and 34, of the *The War of the Rebellion (OR)* has failed to produce a complete copy of this order. These volumes record the actions of the Army of the Frontier.

18. Minos Miller to Martha Hormandy, August 12, 1862, Minos Miller Letters, Special Collections, Mullins Library, University of Arkansas, Fayetteville.

19. John Howard Kitts, "The Civil War Diary of John Howard Kitts," in *Kansas Historical Collections, 1915–1918*, vol. 14 (Topeka: State Printing Office, 1918): 325.

20. William F. Cloud to Thomas Ewing, Jr., December 23, 1862, Ewing Papers; Walter J. Lemke, *The Hermanns of Old Hermannsburg* (Fayetteville: Washington County Historical Society, 1965), 50.

21. *Cane Hill (Arkansas) Buck and Ball*, December 6–15, 1862, p. 4.

22. Thomas Ewing, Jr., to Ellen Ewing, December 2, 1862, Ewing Papers.

23. *OR*, ser. 1, vol. 22, pt. 1, 41–52, passim.

24. Thomas Ewing, Jr., to Ellen Ewing, December 2, 1862, Ewing Papers.

25. William Frederick Cloud, "General Order No. 15," December 4, 1862, Ewing Papers.

26. William F. Cloud to Thomas Ewing, Jr., December 13, 1862, Ewing Papers; William V. Phillips to Thomas Ewing, Jr., December 13, 1862, Ewing Papers.

27. William F. Cloud to Thomas Ewing, Jr., December 13, 1862, Ewing Papers; William V. Phillips to Thomas Ewing, Jr., December 13, 1862, Ewing Papers; unsigned statement, Cane Hill, Arkansas, dated December 21, 1862, Ewing Papers.

28. William F. Cloud to Thomas Ewing, Jr., December 13, 1862, Ewing Papers.

29. Memorandum, William F. Cloud to Thomas Ewing, Jr., December 13, 1862, Ewing Papers.

30. William V. Phillips to Thomas Ewing, Jr., December 13, 1862, Ewing Papers.

31. Robert M. Owings et. al., signed statement, Cane Hill, Arkansas, December 13, 1862 (addendum signed by Harvey Henderson Edmiston), Ewing Papers.

32. Ibid., addendum signed by Thomas Ewing, Jr.

33. William F. Cloud to Thomas Ewing, Jr., December 15, 1862, Ewing Papers.

34. Thomas Ewing, Jr., to James H. Lane, December 14, 1862, Ewing Papers.

35. Amanda Braly to Carrick Braly, November 15, 1862, Amanda Malvina Fitzallen McClellan Braly Family Papers, Special Collections, Mullins Library, University of Arkansas, Fayetteville.

36. Lemke, *Hermanns of Old Hermannsburg*, 50.

37. Albert O. McCollum to Robert McCollum, February 1, 1863, Robert McCollum Family Papers, Special Collections, Mullins Library, University of Arkansas, Fayetteville.

38. Thomas Ewing, Jr., to James H. Lane, December 14, 1862, Ewing Papers.

39. Thomas Ewing, Jr., to William F. Cloud, December 20, 1862 (addendum signed by William F. Cloud), Ewing Papers.

40. Memorandum, J. D. Adams to Thomas Ewing, Jr., December 21, 1862 (addendum signed by Thomas Ewing, Jr., and William F. Cloud), Ewing Papers.

41. *OR*, ser. 1, vol. 22, pt. 1, 90.

42. Thomas Ewing, Jr., to Ellen Ewing, December 18, 1862, Ewing Papers.

43. *OR,* ser. 1, vol. 22, pt. 1, 93.

44. Thomas Ewing, Jr., to Ellen Ewing, December 18, 1862, Ewing Papers; *OR,* ser. 1, vol. 22, pt. 1, 889.

45. *OR,* ser. 1, vol. 22, pt. 1, 889.

46. "Veteran of Two Wars," *Kansas City (Kansas) Sun,* March 5, 1905.

47. Ibid.; W. F. Cloud, *Church and State, or, Mexican Politics from Cortez to Diaz under X-Rays.*(Kansas City: Peck and Clark, 1896).

48. "Famous Personages of the Civil War in Missouri," *Missouri Historical Review* 56 (April 1962): back cover; Mark Mayo Boatner III, *The Civil War Dictionary* (New York: David McKay Company, 1959), 270.

49. Patricia L. Faust, ed., *Historical Times Illustrated Encyclopedia of the Civil War* (New York: Harper & Row, 1986), 302–3.

50. "Famous Personages," back cover; Boatner, *Civil War Dictionary,* 270.

51. Fayetteville Chamber of Commerce, *Pioneer Farm Family Award,* September 4, 1987. Award presented to the Harvey Henderson Edmiston Family in cooperation with the Washington County Farm Bureau.

52. Roster, June 30, 1964, "Muster Roll of Captain George Gibson's Company B of the Brooks Regiment of Arkansas Infantry, Army of the Confederate States of America," Fontaine Richard Earle, Military and Other Records, Special Collections, Mullins Library, University of Arkansas, Fayetteville.

53. Walter J. Lemke, "Claims for Forage and Other Supplies Taken by U.S. Army," *Flashback* 8 (September 1958): 8. The original manuscript volume of George W. M. Reed cited by Lemke in his article is at the Fayetteville Public Library. Edmiston's claim is recorded on page 38 with a notation by Reed that the case would be forwarded to September 29, 1873. There is no record of the ultimate disposition of this claim in Reed's book.

Chapter 6: Disloyalty and Class Consciousness in Southwestern Arkansas

1. For discussion of the varieties of centripetal forces at work in the Confederacy see E. Merton Coulter, *The Confederate States of America, 1861–1865* (Baton Rouge: Louisiana State University Press, 1950), 374–404; Clement Eaton, *A History of the Southern Confederacy* (New York: McMillan Company, 1954); David Donald, "Died of Democracy," and David M. Potter, "Jefferson Davis and the Political Factors in Confederate Defeat," in *Why the North Won the Civil War,* ed. David Donald (Baton Rouge: Louisiana State University Press, 1960), 79–90; Richard E. Beringer et al. *Why the South Lost the Civil War* (Athens: University of Georgia Press, 1986). Carl Degler, *The Other South: Southern Dissenters in the Nineteenth Century* (New York: Harper & Row, 1974), offers an overview of sources of internal opposition to the Confederate government. Ideas concerning class conflict are presented in Emory Thomas, *The Confederate Nation, 1861–1865* (New York: Harper & Row, 1979), especially see 233–36.

2. Albert B. Moore, *Conscription and Conflict in the Confederacy* (New York: McMillan Co., 1924), 17; Ella Lonn, *Desertion during the Civil War* (New York: McMillan Co., 1928), 3–20.

3. Some early studies emphasizing class conflict in the urban setting include Stephen E. Ambrose, "Yeoman Discontent in the Confederacy," *Civil War History* 8 (December 1962): 259–68; and Paul D. Escott, "Southern Yeomen and the Confederacy," *South Atlantic Quarterly* 77 (spring 1978): 146–58. See also Wayne K. Durrill, *War of Another Kind: A Southern Community in the Great Rebellion* (New York: Oxford University Press, 1990).

4. Thomas, *The Confederate Nation,* 234.

5. T. Holmes to J. Davis, December 29, 1862, Correspondence of General T. H. Holmes, Records of the War Department, Collection of Confederate Records, RG 109, National Archives (hereafter cited as Holmes Correspondence, NA).

6. Bureau of the Census, *Population of the United States in 1860: Compiled from the Original Returns of the Eighth Census* (Washington, D.C., 1864), 7.

7. Evidence of the nature of antebellum society in this area is limited. Samuel H. Chester, a member of Union County's elite provides some insight into the ideology of equality within the community, at least as perceived by the elites, in his *Pioneer Days in Arkansas* (Richmond, Va.: Presbyterian Committee of Publication, 1927). My own studies of mobility in antebellum Union County show that there was a degree of upward mobility among the propertyless in that county, with some 15 percent of that class in 1850 persisting in the county until 1860 and some 89 percent of these acquiring property. Carl H. Moneyhon, *The Impact of the Civil War and Reconstruction on Arkansas: Persistence in the Midst of Ruin* (Bation Rouge: Louisiana State University Press, 1994), 55.

8. John Brown Diary, November 6, 1860, February 2, 1861, Arkansas History Commission, Little Rock, Arkansas (hereafter cited as Brown Diary).

9. Ibid., May 30, 1861; *Biographical and Historical Memoirs of Southern Arkansas* (Chicago: Goodspeed Publishing Company, 1890), 649–50, 818.

10. T. H. Holmes to Jefferson Davis, December 29, 1862, Holmes Correspondence, NA; Jefferson Davis to T. H. Holmes, October 21, 1862, in *Jefferson Davis, Constitutionalist: His Letters, Papers, and Speeches,* ed. Dunbar Rowland (Jackson: Mississippi Department of Archives and History, 1923), 5:357; U.S. War Department, *The War of the Rebellion: A Compilation of the Official Records of the Union and Confederate Armies,* 128 vols. (Washington, D.C.: GPO, 1880–1901), ser. 1, vol. 11, 160 (hereafter cited as *OR*).

11. T. J. Boldger and others to Harris Flanagin, January 17, 1863, and L. C. Ross to Harris Flanagin, January 1863 in Kie Oldham Collection, Arkansas History Commission (hereafter cited as Kie Oldham Collection).

12. T. Holmes to Jefferson Davis, March 25, 1865, Holmes Correspondence, NA; Brown Diary, February 26, 1863; Newell P. Brooks Case File (Ouachita County), and Deposition of John H. Haslow, James Byrne Case File (Calhoun County), Southern Claims Commission case files, RG 217, NA; William H. Pierre to Samuel R. Curtis, January 13, 1863, *OR,* ser. 1, vol. 22, pt. 2, 36–37. Newell P. Brooks

identifies as active Unionists in Ouachita County the following men in addition to himself: Joseph Bean, William Bigger, Patrick Brison, Elliott [*sic*], John Gibson, William Ivy, William Jones, George Mapkin, Jacob Lavender, Doc. Parsell, Hannibal Parsell, John Parsell, William Riggs, Lewis Taylor, Jink Wheat, John Wheat, and Marion Wheat. James Byrne identifies as Unionists in Calhoun County the following: Dick Gammell, Elijah Harkan, John H. Haslam, Benjamin Nutt, Cabet Sillimore, and William Whyat (other sources spell this name William Wyatt).

13. Brown Diary, March 19, 1863; *Little Rock True Democrat,* February 4 and 11, 1863; M. La Rue Harrison to Samuel R. Curtis, March 9, 1863, *OR,* ser. 1, vol. 22, pt. 1, 229; Report of Henry C. Caldwell, *OR,* ser. 1, vol. 22, pt. 1, 753.

14. *True Democrat,* February 4 and 11, 1863; *Washington Telegraph,* January 28, 1863; James L. Skinner III, ed., *The Autobiography of Henry Merrell, Industrial Missionary to the South* (Athens: University of Georgia Press, 1991), 319.

15. Brown Diary, March 19, 1863.

16. Brown Diary, February 26, 1863, March 19, 1863; S. M. Scott to Harris Flanagin, April 27, 1863, Kie Oldham Collection.

17. Names came from the Southern Claims Commission Papers, RG 217, NA, and these were compared against census and tax returns for the counties. Ten of sixteen were found in Ouachita County. Seven of eight were found in Calhoun County. The average age of participants in the two counties was 38.9 and 41.7 years of age, respectively. The average personal property reported in the 1860 census was $660 and $887, respectively. The average real property value at the same time was $545 and $453, respectively. All reported their occupations as being either farmers or laborers. All were native-born Southerners.

18. *Washington Telegraph,* December 17, 1862.

19. Ibid.

20. Ibid., February 4, 1863.

21. Ibid., March 25, 1863.

22. T. Holmes to Jefferson Davis, December 29, 1863; Holmes to S. J. Hinsdale, R. C. Holmes or H. S. Holmes, March 25, 1863; Holmes to R. W. Johnson, February 16, 1863; Holmes to J. Walker, February 8, 1863, all in Holmes Correspondence, NA; *Washington Telegraph,* February 18, 1863.

23. T. Holmes to R. W. Johnson, February 16, 1863, and Holmes to Jefferson Davis, March 6, 1863, Holmes Correspondence, NA; *Washington Telegraph,* February 18, 1863. Apparently most of the companies used in the suppression of the internal opposition and in enforcing conscription were state units raised locally under the authority of the provost marshal or Benjamin F. Danley, commandant of conscripts. I was unable to find any letters, diaries, or memoirs of a participant in Holmes's crackdown on dissidents among the numerous published or unpublished materials on Arkansas and Texas troops who served in the area during the war.

24. Elliott's biography was written by his son in a letter to the Arkansas History Commission in 1906. Despite his wartime role, Elliott was elected a Republican congressman from the Third District in 1868 and to the state senate in 1870. See James T. Elliott, Individual File, Arkansas History Commission.

25. T. Holmes to S. J. Hinsdale, R. C. Holmes, or H. S. Holmes, March 25, 1863, and Holmes to Jefferson Davis, February 16, March 6, 1863, Holmes Correspondence, NA; Brown Diary, February 26, 1863.

26. Skinner, *Autobiography of Henry Merrell,* 320; *Little Rock True Democrat,* February 4, 1863; *Washington Telegraph,* January 28, 1863.

27. *Little Rock Arkansas Gazette,* June 27, 1863; Henry G. Orr to "Dear Sister," April 30, 1863, and Henry G. Orr to "Friends at Home," May 22, 1863, in *Campaigning with Parsons' Texas Cavalry Brigade, C.S.A.,* ed. John Q. Anderson (Hillsboro, Tex.: Hill Junior College Press, 1967), 96, 100; Calhoun County Circuit Court Records, Book B, case 812, pp. 272, 194, Arkansas History Commission.

28. M. La Rue Harrison to Samuel R. Curtis, March 9, 1863, *OR,* ser. 1, vol. 22, pt. 1, 2290; *Arkansas Conference Journal,* quoted in *Little Rock Arkansas Patriot,* March 5, 1863.

29. *True Democrat,* April 8, 1863; Brown Diary, March 19, 1863.

30. *Little Rock Constitutional Union,* June 15, 1865.

31. B. F. Danley to Harris Flanagin, April 4, 1863; J. T. Elliott to H. Flanagin, April 6, 1863; and L. B. Green to H. Flanagin, no date, all in Kie Oldham Collection; *Washington Telegraph,* July 1, 1863.

32. *True Democrat,* February 25, 1863; T. H. Holmes to S. J. Hisdale, R. C. Holmes, or H. S. Holmes, March 25, 1863, and T. H. Holmes to Jefferson Davis, April 7, 1863 (quotes), Holmes Correspondence, NA; T. H. Holmes to Jefferson Davis, March 6, 1863, *OR,* ser. 1, vol. 22, pt. 2, 297.

33. S. M. Scott to Flanagin, April 27, 1863, Kie Oldham Collection.

34. *Washington Telegraph,* September 2, 1863; S. M. Scott to Harris Flanagin, April 27, 1863, Kie Oldham Collection.

35. Brown Diary, July 27, 1863; Skinner, *Autobiography of Henry Merrell,* 320.

36. B. F. Danley to Harris Flanagin, September 30, 1863, and B. J. Brown to H. Flanagin, October 6, 1863, Kie Oldham Collection.

37. Report of Henry C. Caldwell, *OR,* ser. 1, vol. 22, pt. 1, 764.

38. Brown Diary, August 15, October 13, 1863; B. J. Brown to Harris Flanagin, October 6, 1863, Kie Oldham Collection; W. H. Ferrell to S. D. Jackman, May 21, 1863, *OR,* ser. 1, vol. 34, pt. 3, 835 (quote).

39. Brown Diary, May 23, 24, and 28, 1865.

40. M. La Rue Harrison to Samuel R. Curtis, March 9, 1863, *OR,* ser. 1, vol. 22, pt. 1, 229; H. C. Caldwell to A. S. Montgomery, November 18, 1863, *OR,* ser. 1, vol. 22, pt. 1, 752–54.

41. Brown Diary, March 21, 1864, May 28, June 12, 1865.

42. *Little Rock Republican,* February 2, 1868.

Chapter 7: Guerrillas: The Real War in Arkansas

1. U.S. War Department, *The War of the Rebellion: A Compilation of the Official Records of the Union and Confederate Armies,* 128 vols. (Washington, D.C.:

GPO, 1880–1901), ser. 1, vol. 13, 396 (hereafter cited as *OR*, and all references are to series 1).

2. Among the most widely cited general works are Irwin R. Blacker, ed., *Irregulars, Partisans, Guerrillas: Great Stories from Roger's Rangers to the Haganah* (New York: Simon and Schuster, 1954); Charles W. Thayer, *Guerrilla* (New York: Harper & Row, 1963); N. I. Klonis, *Guerrilla Warfare: Analysis and Projections* (New York: Robert Speller and Sons, 1972); Robert B. Asprey, *War in the Shadows: The Guerrilla in History*, 2 vols. (Garden City, N.Y.: Doubleday, 1975); John Ellis, *From the Barrel of a Gun: A History of Guerrilla, Revolutionary, and Counter-Insurgency Warfare, from the Romans to the Present* (London: Greenhill, 1995); Walter Laqueur, *Guerrilla: A Historical and Critical Study* (Boston: Little, Brown, 1976); Anthony James Joes, *Guerrilla Conflict before the Cold War* (Westport, Conn.: Praeger, 1996).

3. Virgil Carrington Jones, *Gray Ghosts and Rebel Raiders* (New York: Henry Holt, 1956); Richard S. Brownlee, *Gray Ghosts of the Confederacy: Guerrilla Warfare in the West, 1861–1865* (Baton Rouge: Louisiana State University Press, 1958). A still useful article published at this same time is Carl E. Grant's "Partisan Warfare, Model 1861–1865," *Military Review* 8 (November 1958): 42–56. See also Ethelbert C. Barksdale, "Semi-Regular and Irregular Warfare in the Civil War" (Ph.D. diss., University of Texas, 1941); and a series of articles written in 1960 and 1961 by Barnes F. Lathrop on partisan activities in Louisiana, most notably "The Lafourche District in 1862: Militia and Partisan Rangers," *Louisiana History* 1 (summer 1960): 230–44.

4. Albert Castel, "The Guerrilla War, 1861–1865," *Civil War Times Illustrated*, Special Issue (October 1974): 4–50; and Don R. Bowen, "Guerrilla War in Western Missouri, 1862–1865: Historical Extensions of the Relative Deprivation Hypothesis," *Comparative Studies in Society and History* 19 (January 1977): 30–51, "Quantrill, James, Younger, et al.: Leadership in a Guerrilla Movement, Missouri, 1861–1865," *Military Affairs* 41 (February 1977): 42–48, and "Counterrevolutionary Guerrilla War: Missouri, 1861–1865," *Conflict* 8 (1988): 69–78.

5. Philip S. Paludan, *Victims: A True Story of the Civil War* (Knoxville: University of Tennessee Press, 1981); Michael Fellman, *Inside War: The Guerrilla Conflict in Missouri during the American Civil War* (New York: Oxford University Press, 1989); Thomas Goodrich, *Bloody Dawn: The Story of the Lawrence Massacre* (Kent, Ohio: Kent State University Press, 1991), and *Black Flag: Guerrilla Warfare on the Western Border, 1861–1865* (Bloomington: Indiana University Press, 1995); Stephen V. Ash, *When the Yankees Came: Conflict and Chaos in the Occupied South, 1861–1865* (Chapel Hill: University of North Carolina, 1995); Samuel C. Hyde, Jr., "Bushwhacking and Barn Burning: Civil War Operations and the Florida Parishes' Tradition of Violence," *Louisiana History* 36 (spring 1995): 171–86; Edward E. Leslie, *The Devil Knows How to Ride: The True Story of William Clarke Quantrill and His Confederate Raiders* (New York: Random House, 1996); Benjamin Franklin Cooling, *Fort Donelson's Legacy: War and Society in Kentucky and Tennessee, 1862–1863* (Knoxville: University of Tennessee Press, 1997); Noel C. Fisher, *War at Every Door: Partisan Politics and Guerrilla Violence in East Tennessee, 1860–1869* (Chapel Hill: University of North Carolina Press, 1997); Kenneth W. Noe and Shannon H. Wilson,

eds., *The Civil War in Appalachia: Collected Essays* (Knoxville: University of Tennessee Press, 1997); Stephen S. Michot, "'War Is Still Raging in This Part of the Country': Oath-Taking, Conscription, and Guerrilla War in Louisiana's Lafourche Region," *Louisiana History* 38 (spring 1997): 157–84; Thomas Goodrich and Albert Castel, *Bloody Bill Anderson: The Short, Savage Life of a Civil War Guerrilla* (Harrisburg, Pa.: Stackpole, 1998); Daniel E. Sutherland, "Without Mercy, and without the Blessing of God," *North and South* 1 (August 1998): 12–21; Daniel E. Sutherland, ed., *Guerrillas, Unionists, and Violence on the Confederate Home Front* (Fayetteville: University of Arkansas Press, 1999).

6. Leo E. Huff, "Guerrillas, Jayhawkers, and Bushwhackers in Northern Arkansas during the Civil War," *Arkansas Historical Quarterly* 24 (summer 1965): 127–48; Wendell P. Beall, "Wildwood Skirmishers: The First Federal Arkansas Cavalry" (M.A. thesis, University of Arkansas, Fayetteville, 1988); Joseph R. Bellas, "The Forgotten Loyalists: Unionism in Arkansas, 1861–1865" (M.A. thesis, Ohio State University, 1991); Thomas A. Belser, Jr., "Military Operations in Missouri and Arkansas, 1861–1865" (Ph.D. diss., Vanderbilt University, 1958); Benjamin Boulden, "So Long as Strangers Are the Rulers: General Frederick Steele and the Politics of Wartime Reconstruction in Arkansas" (M.A. thesis, University of Arkansas, Fayetteville, 1992); Maurice G. Fortin, Jr., "Confederate Military Operations in Arkansas, 1861–1865" (M.A. thesis, North Texas State University, 1978); Barry R. Sude, "Federal Military Policy and Strategy in Missouri and Arkansas, 1861–1863: A Study of Command Level Conflict" (Ph.D. diss., Temple University., 1987); Jayme Lynne Stone, "Brother against Brother: The Winter Skirmishes along the Arkansas River, 1864–1865," *Military History of the West* 25 (spring 1995): 24–49; Robert R. Mackey, "A Self-Inflicted Wound: The Confederacy's Guerrilla Campaign in Arkansas, 1862–1865" (M.A. thesis, Texas A&M University, 1997), and "Bushwhackers, Provosts, and Tories: The Guerrilla War in Arkansas," in Sutherland, ed., *Guerrillas, Unionists, and Violence;* Jay A. Prier, "Under the Black Flag: The Real War in Washington County, Arkansas, 1861–1864" (M.A. thesis, University of Arkansas, Fayetteville, 1998). The guerrilla war is mentioned in the two most important recent works on Civil War Arkansas: Carl H. Moneyhon, *The Impact of the Civil War and Reconstruction in Arkansas* (Baton Rouge: Louisiana State University Press, 1994); and Mark K. Christ, ed., *Rugged and Sublime: The Civil War in Arkansas* (Fayetteville: University of Arkansas Press, 1994), but without the amount of attention it deserves.

7. Virgil C. Jones, "The Problem of Writing about the Guerrillas," *Military Affairs* 21 (summer 1958): 21–25, discusses the problems of sources. For the significance of the oral tradition see James J. Johnston, "Jayhawker Stories: Historical Lore in the Arkansas Ozarks," *Mid-South Folklore* 4 (spring 1976): 3–10; Desmond Walls Allen, ed., *Turnbo's Tales of the Ozarks: War and Guerrilla Stories*, rev. ed. (Conway, Ark.: n.p., 1989); Luther E. Warren, *Yellar Rag Boys: The Arkansas Peace Society of 1861 and Other Events in Northern Arkansas, 1861–1865* (Marshall, Ark.: S. L. Weaver, 1992), 1. Another problem is that of definition. The term *partisan* generally applied to irregulars sanctioned and controlled by the Confederate government; *guerrillas, bushwhackers, jayhawkers,* and similar designations generally referred to freebooters

and renegades who, feeling little loyalty to either North or South, used the war for private gain. The distinction has merit and should not be discounted. Yet so confused did the use of these terms become in practice, especially in Arkansas, where there seem to have been very few official "partisan" units, that, except in a few instances, they will be used interchangeably in this essay.

8. Elmo Ingenthron, *Borderland Rebellion: A History of the Civil War on the Missouri-Arkansas Border* (Branson, Mo.: Ozarks Mountaineer, 1980), 298–99; Drury Connally to Ann Kilgore Connally, May 5, 1862, War Letters of Drury Connally, Trans-Mississippi Research Group Collection, Special Collections, Mullins Library, University of Arkansas, Fayetteville (hereafter cited as TMRGC).

9. Sude, "Federal Military Policy and Strategy," 73; Bellas, "The Forgotten Loyalists," 20–21; Bobby L. Roberts, "General T. C. Hindman and the Trans-Mississippi District," *Arkansas Historical Quarterly* 32 (winter 1973): 302–4; Diane Neal and Thomas W. Kremm, *Lion of the South: General Thomas C. Hindman* (Macon, Ga.: Mercer University Press, 1993), 127–28; Robert L. Kerby, *Kirby Smith's Confederacy: The Trans-Mississippi South, 1863–1865* (Tuscaloosa: University of Alabama Press, 1972), 31–32; Fellman, *Inside War,* 97–98; *OR,* vol. 13, 835. See also an advertisement in *Little Rock True Democrat,* July 18, 1861, p. 2, for "persons that feel inclined to go into guerrilla or independent service."

10. Kerby, *Kirby Smith's Confederacy,* 46; George T. Maddox, *Hard Trials and Tribulations of an Old Confederate Soldier* (Van Buren, Ark.: Argus, 1897), 11–12; Joseph M. Bailey, "Memoirs of Captain J. M. Bailey," 46–47, typescript in Special Collections, Mullins Library, University of Arkansas, Fayetteville; Drury Connally to Ann Kilgore Connally, June 28, 1862, War Letters of Drury Connally, TMRGC. Many of these reactions would fall into the category of "blood sport," as described by Fellman, *Inside War,* 176–84.

11. *OR,* vol. 13, 10–11; Joe M. Scott, *Four Years' Service in the Southern Army* (1897; reprint, Fayetteville, Ark.: Washington County Historical Society, 1958), 31–32; T. D. Hill to Harris Flanagin, June 1, 1863, Kie Oldham Collection, Arkansas History Commission, Little Rock. This desire to protect their families supports the "relative deprivation" theory of Bowen, "Guerrilla War in Western Missouri,"42–48, although Bowen's emphasis on prosperous, slaveholding families probably does not fit the situation in Arkansas. Stephen V. Ash, *Middle Tennesee Transformed, 1860–1870: War and Peace in the Upper South* (Baton Rouge: Lousiana State University Press, 1988), 148–51, and *When the Yankees Came,* 64–67, also stresses the ties between guerrillas and their communities.

12. Details of Love's career from correspondence of J. C. Love of Leachville, Arkansas, and James J. Johnston of Fayetteville, Arkansas, courtesy of Mr. Johnston; *OR,* vol. 13, 835; Nola A. James, "The Civil War Years in Independence County," *Arkansas Historical Quarterly* 28 (autumn 1969): 247.

13. *OR,* vol. 13, 769–70.

14. Fellman, *Inside War,* 52–54, 62–65, 138–39, 184–92; David Y. Thomas, *Arkansas in War and Reconstruction, 1861–1874* (Little Rock: Central Printing Company, 1926), 198–99; Allen, *Turnbo's Tales of the Ozarks,* 30–31, 61–62, 103–104; J. Bailey, "Memoirs," 47, 70. The ultimate act of revenge associated with guerrilla war-

fare is Quantrill's sacking of Lawrence, Kansas. For revenge as a motive among Civil War soldiers generally, see James M. McPherson, *For Cause and Comrades: Why Men Fought in the Civil War* (New York: Oxford University Press, 1997), 148–62.

15. "Discussion of Jayhawkers," n.d., in Dandridge McRae Papers, Arkansas History Commission, Little Rock; J. Bailey, "Memoirs," 75; Maddox, *Hard Trails and Tribulations,* 81–82.

16. Carl von Clausewitz, *On War,* ed. and trans. by Michael Howard and Peter Paret (Princeton, N.J.: Princeton University Press, 1976), 380–82; *OR,* vol. 22, pt. 2, 518; Drury Connally to Ann Kilgore Connally, June 28, 1862, War Letters of Drury Connally, TMRGC. Anne J. Bailey, "The Mississippi Marine Brigade: Fighting Rebel Guerrillas on Western Waters," *Military History of the Southwest* 22 (spring 1992): 31–32, 41–42; and Richard Beringer et al., *Why the South Lost the Civil War* (Athens: University of Georgia Press, 1986), 171–73, also draw on Clausewitz, although the latter work fails to comment on the situation in Arkansas.

17. *OR,* vol. 13, 33, 35. For a good description of a guerrilla band stalking a Federal supply train—and the fear it instilled in the Yankees—see A. M. Rich, "Remarkable Scouting in Arkansas," *Confederate Veteran* 14 (April 1906): 183–83.

18. Boulden, "So Long as Strangers Are the Rulers," 62; *OR,* vol. 22, pt. 2, 308–9, vol. 34, pt. 1, 858–59, pt. 3, 30, 89, vol. 41, pt. 2, 219, 635, pt. 3, 320. See also Ingenthron, *Borderland Rebellion,* 209–10; and "Proceedings of Military Commission at St. Louis, Headquarters, Department of Missouri, November 7, 1864," in Sarah Jane Smith Records, Special Collections, Mullins Library, University of Arkansas, Fayetteville, for women as "irregulars."

19. *OR,* vol. 22, pt. 2, 15, 309, vol. 34, pt. 1, 689, 930, vol. 41, pt. 2, 42; B. F. Riggs, "Capture of the *J. H. Miller,*" *Confederate Veteran* 15 (February 1907): 73–77; Harry Forrest Lupold, ed., "An Ohio Doctor Views Campaigning on the White River, 1864," *Arkansas Historical Quarterly* 34 (winter 1975): 336, 346; Jonathan MacLean to Daniel H. Reynolds, March 10, 1864, Daniel Harris Reynolds Papers, Special Collections, Mullins Library, University of Arkansas, Fayetteville (hereafter cited as UAF). While apparently never engaged on Arkansas waters, the Mississippi Marine Brigade, commissioned by Abraham Lincoln in November 1862 to interdict partisan pirates, was active along the Mississippi shore. See A. Bailey, "Mississippi Marine Brigade," 34–41. For an action by the brigade ashore in Arkansas, see Norman E. Clarke, ed., *Warfare along the Mississippi: The Letters of Lieutenant Colonel George E. Currie* (Mt. Pleasant: Central Michigan University, 1960), 101–11.

20. Fellman, *Inside War,* 23; Minos Miller to Mother, May 20, 1864, Minos Miller Papers, Special Collections, Mullins Library, University of Arkansas, Fayetteville; *OR,* vol. 22, pt. 2, 186, 756.

21. *OR,* vol. 34, pt. 2, 631.

22. Boulden, "So Long as Strangers Are the Rulers," 59–63; *OR,* vol. 41, pt. 2, 234, 502; H. H. to Daniel H. Reynolds, July 24, 1864, Reynolds Papers, UAF. While not referring directly to the election of 1864, Fellman, *Inside War,* 109–10, describes Sterling Price's Missouri raid of September–October 1864 as a "revitalization movement" for the Confederacy.

23. Daniel E. Sutherland, "Mansfield Lovell's Quest for Justice: Another Look at the Fall of New Orleans," *Louisiana History* 24 (summer 1983): 233–59; Michael B. Dougan, *Confederate Arkansas: The People and Policies of a Frontier State in Wartime* (Tuscaloosa: University of Alabama Press, 1976), 87–88.

24. *OR,* vol. 13, 33, 36, 43, 827–28; Ingenthron, *Borderland Rebellion,* 255. For a firsthand account of partisans at Lone Jack, see Richard L. Norton, ed., *Behind Enemy Lines: The Memoirs and Writings of Brigadier General Sidney Drake Jackman* (Springfield, Mo.: Oak Hills, 1997).

25. Robert W. Williams, Jr., and Ralph A. Wooster, eds., "With Wharton's Cavalry: The Civil War Letters of Private Isaac Dunbar Affleck," *Arkansas Historical Quarterly* 21 (autumn 1962): 260; *OR,* vol. 41, pt. 2, 330; Neva Ingram Hunsicker, "Rayburn the Raider," *Arkansas Historical Quarterly* 7 (September 1948): 87–91; Russell Baker, "Yellow Doc, The Ranger—An Arkansas Legend: A Daring Adventure—In Skirts," *Rivers and Roads and Points in Between* 14 (spring 1986): 10–12.

26. Quoted in Anne J. Bailey, *Between the Enemy and Texas: Parsons's Texas Cavalry in the Civil War* (Fort Worth: Texas Christian University Press, 1989), 80, 93; Drury Connally to Ann Kilgore Connally, June 6, 1862, War Letters of Drury Connally, TMRGC; John Q. Anderson, ed., *Campaigning with Parsons' Texas Cavalry Brigade, C.S.A.: The War Journals and Letters of the Four Orr Brothers, 12th Texas Cavalry Regiment* (Hillsboro, Tex.: Hill Junior College Press, 1967), 49.

27. Edward E. Leslie, *The Devil Knows How to Ride: The True Story of William Clarke Quantrill and His Confederate Raiders* (New York: Random House, 1996), 157, 159–64; *OR,* vol. 22, pt. 1, 307, vol. 34, pt. 1, 86.

28. *OR,* vol. 34, pt. 1, 925, 928, pt. 3, 829, pt. 4, 143, 633, 652–53. Price also made skillful use of guerrillas based in Missouri. See Albert Castel, *General Sterling Price and the Civil War in the West* (Baton Rouge: Louisiana State University Press, 1968), 199; Kerby, *Kirby Smith's Confederacy,* 339–41.

29. *OR,* vol. 34, pt. 4, 652–53.

30. *OR,* vol. 22, pt. 2, 845, 851, vol. 34, pt. 1, 925, 928, pt. 3, 829, pt. 4, 633, 652–53. Theophilus Holmes had made similar use of partisan bands, going so far as to assign them duty as provost guards. See Holmes to Samuel Cooper, October 8, 1862, Correspondence of General T. H. Holmes, Records of War Department, Collection of Confederate Records, chap. 2, vol. 358, RG 109, NA.

31. Mackey, "A Self-Inflicted Wound," 36–44; Prier, "Under the Black Flag," 19; *OR,* vol. 22, pt. 2, 845, vol. 34, pt. 4, 670, vol. 41, pt. 2, 1073–74.

32. Prier, "Under the Black Flag," 22; *OR,* vol. 22, pt. 1, 165. For the plight of the refugee, see Mrs. J. N. Bromley, *Biography of John W. Morris* (Marshall, Ark.: privately printed, 1916), 70–73; Walter F. Lackey, *History of Newton County, Arkansas* (Independence, Mo.: Zion's Print and Publishing Company, 1950), 357–59; Martha M. Mills Brown, "Reminiscences of the Life of Martha M. Brown nee Mills," typescript courtesy of James J. Johnston, Fayetteville.

33. Examples of genuine outlaws, like William Darke of Searcy County, are found in John Hallum, *Reminiscences of the Civil War,* 2 vols. (Little Rock: Tunnah

and Pittard, 1903), 1:95–104. For the partisan captain, see John Connally to Harris Flanagin, February 29, 1864, July 17, 1864, Kie Oldham Collection. See also Thomas, *Arkansas in War and Reconstruction,* 195; *OR,* vol. 22, pt. 1, 30–31.

34. Maddox, *Hard Trials and Tribulations,* 80–81; James H. Campbell, "Reminiscence Experiences during the Civil War," typescript in possession of Eli Taylor Campbell, St. Joseph, Missouri.

35. Jonathan MacLean to Daniel H. Reynolds, October 16, 1864, and H. H. to Daniel H. Reynolds, July 24, 1864, Reynolds Papers, UAF.

36. *OR,* vol. 22, pt. 2, 1058–60; Boulden, "So Long as Strangers Are the Rulers," 7–11; *OR,* vol. 22, pt. 2, 860–61, vol. 34, pt. 4, 690–91.

37. Drury Connally to Ann Kilgore Connally, July 14, December 16, 1862, War Letters of Drury Connally, TMRGC; *OR,* vol. 34, pt. 3, 829, pt. 4, 633.

38. Mackey, "A Self-Inflicted Wound," ii, believes, with some justification, that the Confederates failed to make effective use of guerrillas in Arkansas. He points to the inability of the Confederacy to develop a strategic plan that could effectively control them, the success of Union counterguerrilla measures, and the growing antiguerrilla sentiments of the civilian population.

39. *OR,* vol. 13, 622, 647–48.

40. *OR,* vol. 13, 682–83. As in so much else, Ulysses S. Grant and Sherman agreed on this point. See A. Bailey, "Mississippi Marine Brigade," 32. When Union generals like Grant and Sherman embraced a strategy of exhaustion against the Rebels later in the war, they pursued policies identical to the ones they had earlier used against guerrillas. See James M. McPherson, *Drawn with the Sword: Reflections on the American Civil War* (New York: Oxford University Press, 1996), 66–86; Mark Grimsley, *The Hard Hand of War: Union Military Policy toward Southern Civilians, 1861–1865* (Cambridge: Cambridge University Press, 1995), 111–19; Daniel E. Sutherland, "Abraham Lincoln, John Pope, and the Origins of Total War," *Journal of Military History* 56 (October 1992): 578–79.

41. *OR,* vol. 13, 726–27. In time, many partisan units wore captured Federal uniforms, both as a means of deceiving the Yanks and because Federal uniforms were better made than their own. Such deception also required a system of signals among blue-clad Confederates to avoid firing on each other. See Scott, *Four Years' Service in the Southern Army,* 30; Maddox, *Hard Trials and Tribulations,* 32–34.

42. *OR,* vol. 22, pt. 2, 237–39; Sutherland, "Lincoln, Pope, and Total War," 584–85.

43. *OR,* vol. 13, 106–7, 108–9.

44. *OR.* vol. 22, pt. 2, 164, 701; Sutherland, "Lincoln, Pope, and Total War," 580–85; Goodrich, *Bloody Dawn,* 21–24, 152–53. The fullest reviews of Federal methods of retaliation are Mackey, "A Self-Inflicted Wound," 75–119; and Mackey, "Bushwhackers, Provosts, and Tories."

45. *OR,* vol. 34, pt 2, 23–24, 64–66; Editors of Life-Time Books, *Spies, Scouts, and Raiders: Irregular Operations* (New York: Time-Life Books, 1985), 155. Kerby, *Kirby Smith's Confederacy,* 44–50, asserts that Missouri guerrillas had a similar impact.

46. Quoted in Belser, "Military Operations in Missouri and Arkansas," 606;

OR, vol. 34, pt. 2, 51–52, pt. 3, 621, 676, 706; Scott, *Four Years' Service in the Southern Army,* 36.

47. *OR,* vol. 22, pt. 2, 197–98. See also Charles G. Williams, ed., "A Saline Guard: The Civil War Letters of Col. William Ayers Crawford, C.S.A., 1861–1865," pt. 2, *Arkansas Historical Quarterly* 32 (spring 1973): 78; David O. Demuth, " The Burning of Hopefield," *Arkansas Historical Quarterly* 36 (summer 1977): 123–29.

48. *OR,* vol. 22, pt. 2, 186–87, 189–90, 480–81, 617–18. For recruitment of Arkansas Unionists generally, see Richard N. Current, *Lincoln's Loyalists: Union Soldiers from the Confederacy* (Boston: Northeastern University Press, 1992), 73–87.

49. Mackey, "A Self-Inflicted Wound," 100–4; *OR,* vol. 22, pt. 2, 772–75, 778, 784–85, 828–29, vol. 34, pt. 1, 924; William E. Sawyer, "The Martin Hart Conspiracy," *Arkansas Historical Quarterly* 23 (summer 1964): 154–65.

50. Edwin C. Bearss, "General William Steele Fights to Hold onto Northwest Arkansas," *Arkansas Historical Quarterly* 25 (spring 1966): 40–44; A. B. Lewis, "Chasing Guerrillas in Arkansas," *Confederate Veteran* 29 (June 1921): 220–22; Barry Popchock, ed., *Soldier Boy: The Civil War Letters of Charles O. Musser, 29th Iowa* (Iowa City: University of Iowa Press, 1995), 85.

51. *OR,* vol. 22, pt. 2, 824–25; Prier, "Under the Black Flag," 121–50.

52. *OR,* vol. 34, pt. 1, 924–25, 926–27, vol. 41, pt. 1, 14, 643, vol. 22, pt. 1, 310, pt. 2, 103, vol. 34, pt. 3, 182–83, 706; quote in Michael A. Hughes, "Wartime Gristmill Destruction in Northwest Arkansas and Military-Farm Colonies," *Arkansas Historical Quarterly* 46 (summer 1987): 177–78. The Federal antiguerrilla marine brigade disbanded largely because it too frequently imitated the worst excesses of its prey. See A. Bailey, "Mississippi Marine Brigade," 39–41. Consider, too, that both sides used outrages perpetrated by the other as propoganda. See Robert F. Smith, "Confederate Attempts to Influence Public Opinion in Arkansas, 1861–1865" (M.A. thesis, University of Arkansas, Fayetteville, 1952), 42–43; Bellas, "The Forgotten Loyalists," 78–79.

53. Clarke, *Warfare along the Mississippi,* 101; Edwin C. Bearss, ed., *The Civil War Letters of Major William G. Thompson of the 20th Iowa Infantry Regiment* (Fayetteville, Ark.: Washington County Historical Society, 1966), 42–43.

54. Sude, "Federal Military Policy and Strategy," 73–75, 98; Belser, "Military Operations in Missouri and Arkansas," 398. Many of these same partisans, with the addition of Buck Brown, continued to harass Federals in northwest Arkansas through most of the war. See, for example, Edwin C. Bearss, "The Confederate Attempt to Regain Fort Smith," *Arkansas Historical Quarterly* 28 (winter 1969): 342–80.

55. *OR,* vol. 22, pt. 1, 165, 781, 526, 534, 579, 674.

56. *OR,* vol. 22, pt. 2, 689; Fortin, "Confederate Military Operations in Arkansas," 88–89.

57. Hughes, "Wartime Gristmill Destruction," 175–76. Federal troops proved less successful in destroying niter mills on which guerrillas depended. See James J. Johnston, "Bullets for Johnny Reb: Confederate Nitre and Mining Bureau in Arkansas," *Arkansas Historical Quarterly* 49 (summer 1990): 141, 158–62.

58. Hughes, "Wartime Gristmill Destruction," 179–86; Bellas, "The Forgotten Loyalists," 107–14; Diane Neal and Thomas W. Kremm, "An Experiment in

Collective Security: The Union Army's Use of Armed Colonies in Arkansas," *Military History of the Southwest* 20 (autumn 1990): 169–81.

59. *OR,* vol. 41, pt. 1, 69–70, pt. 4, 877, 943, vol. 34, pt. 4, 231–32. See also Alice E. Andrews, ed., *Christopher C. Andrews: Recollections, 1829–1922* (Cleveland: Arthur H. Clark, 1928), 179–80.

Chapter 8: The Williams Clan: Mountain Farmers and Union Fighters in North Central Arkansas

1. Albert Webb Bishop, *Loyalty on the Frontier, or Sketches of Union Men of the Southwest* (St. Louis: R. P. Studley, 1863); James W. Demby, *Mysteries and Miseries of Arkansas, or a Defence of the Loyalty of the State* (St. Louis: n.p., 1863).

2. Note the two earliest surveys of the war in Arkansas: John Harrell, *Arkansas,* vol. 10 of *Confederate Military History,* 12 vols. (Atlanta: Confederate Publishing Company, 1899); and David Y. Thomas, *Arkansas in War and Reconstruction* (Little Rock: Central Printing Company, 1926).

3. See the excellent discussions of Unionist views in James M. Woods, *Rebellion and Realignment: Arkansas's Road to Secession* (Fayetteville: University of Arkansas Press, 1987); John L. Ferguson, ed., *Arkansas and the Civil War* (Little Rock: Pioneer Press, 1965); Michael B. Dougan, *Confederate Arkansas: The People and Policies of a Frontier State in Wartime* (University, Ala.:University of Alabama Press, 1976).

4. Exceptions here are the story of an Arkansas Unionist from Searcy County written by his daughter, Mrs. J. N. Bromley, *Biography of John W. Morris* (Marshall, Ark.: privately printed, 1916); Ted Worley's work on the Arkansas Peace Society, "The Arkansas Peace Society of 1861: A Study in Mountain Unionism," *Journal of Southern History* 24 (November 1958): 445–56, and "Documents Relating to the Arkansas Peace Society of 1861," *Arkansas Historical Quarterly* 17 (spring 1958): 82–111; and Joseph R. Bellas, "The Forgotten Loyalists: Unionism in Arkansas, 1861–1865" (M.A. thesis, Ohio State University, 1991). See also the section on Arkansas in Richard Nelson Current's *Lincoln's Loyalists: Union Soldiers from the Confederacy* (Boston: Northeastern University Press, 1991).

5. See the examination of regional variation in demography and economics in pre–Civil War Arkansas in Woods, *Rebellion and Realignment,* 35–67. The Williams men seem typical of Southern Unionists in general; see Richard Nelson Current's chapter, "What Manner of Men," in his *Lincoln's Loyalists,* 133–57.

6. Military Department of Tennessee, Office of the Adjutant General, "Cherokee War," 114, Tennessee State Library, Nashville. See Thurman Wilkin's account of the journey in his *Cherokee Tragedy: The Story of the Ridge Family and the Decimation of a People* (New York: Macmillan, 1970), 304–5.

7. Bureau of the Census, *Seventh Census of the United States, 1850, Population Schedule, Conway County, Arkansas,* and *Eighth Census of the United States, 1860, Population Schedule, Conway, Arkansas*, National Archives, Microfilm, M432, reel 25, and M653, reel 39. The other slaveowner, Henson Scroggins, in Lick Mountain township owned a female slave and her two children. Two sons of Henson Scroggins married daughters of Jeff Williams. The Scroggins family also supported the Union in

wartime. Bureau of the Census, *Eighth Census of the United States, 1860, Population Schedule, Conway, Arkansas*, National Archives, Microfilm, M653, reel 53.

8. *Little Rock Arkansas Gazette*, January 19, 1861.

9. *Arkansas Gazette*, January 12, 1861, and February 2, 1861.

10. *Historical Reminiscences and Biographical Memoirs of Conway County, Arkansas* (Little Rock: Arkansas Publishing Company, 1890), 16–17; Harrell, *Arkansas*, 306.

11. For information on the Peace Society see Worley, "The Arkansas Peace Society of 1861;" Worley, "Documents Relating to the Arkansas Peace Society of 1861;" Diane Neal, "Treason or Patrioism? Union Peace Societies in Arkansas during the Civil War," *Journal of Confederate History* 1 (fall 1988): 339–49.

12. Bishop, *Loyalty on the Frontier*, 133; and Bromley, *Biography of John Morris*, both suggest that chapters of the Peace Society existed in Conway County. When arrested, Ananias Stobaugh had in his possession one of the surviving oaths of the Peace Society. See Kie Oldham Collection, box 2, item 110d, Arkansas History Commission, Little Rock. See also*Conway County: Our Land, Our Home, Our People* (Little Rock: Historical Publications of Arkansas, 1989), 460; John L. Williams, deposition of February 2, 1891, Ananias Stobaugh Pension File, RG 15, National Archives (hereafter cited as NA).

13. See Carl Degler's, *The Other South: Southern Dissenters in the Nineteenth Century* (New York: Harper & Row, 1974); Current, *Lincoln's Loyalists*, 146.

14. U.S. War Department, *The War of Rebellion: A Compilation of the Official Records of the Union and Confederate Armies*, 128 vols. (Washington, D.C.: GPO, 1880–1901), ser. 1, vol. 13, 66 (hereafter cited as *OR*); see Confederate general Thomas Hindman's report of conditions in Arkansas when he assumed command there in May 1862. In *OR*, ser. 1, vol. 13, 30.

15. Harrell, *Arkansas*, 100–101; *OR*, ser. 1, vol. 13, 30, 66.

16. *Historical Reminiscences of Conway County*, 15–16; *OR*, ser. 1. vol. 13, 418, 436; Bishop, *Loyalty on the Frontier*, 11; Leroy Williams Pension File, RG 15, NA.

17. Leroy Williams Pension File, RG 15, NA; Senate, *Report of the Adjutant General of State of Arkansas*, by Albert Webb Bishop, 39th Cong., 2nd sess., 1866, Senate Misc. Doc. 53, 245.

18. William H. D. Wilson to Arabella Wilson, August 5, 1862, Arabella Lanktree Wilson Papers, Special Collections, Mullins Library, University of Arkansas, Fayetteville.

19. *OR*, ser. 1, vol. 13, 66, 434, 447.

20. Demby, *Mysteries and Miseries of Arkansas*, 11–12, 44; Senate, *Report of the Adjutant General*, 245.

21. *OR*, ser. 1, vol. 13, 144–45; Leroy Williams Pension File, 12–13, RG 15, NA. Quote from William L. Shea, "A Semi-Savage State: The Image of Arkansas in the Civil War," *Arkansas Historical Quarterly* 48 (winter 1989): 321; see also Thomas Arvin Belser, Jr., "Military Operations in Missouri and Arkansas, 1861–1865," (Ph.D. diss., Vanderbilt University, 1958), 390–98.

22. The entire muster roll of the First Battalion is in Senate, *Report of the Adjutant General*, 236–45; Demby, *Mysteries and Miseries of Arkansas*, 37, 39.

23. Quotes from Shea, "Image of Arkansas in the Civil War," 323–25; U.S. Congress, *Report of the Adjutant General,* 245; Demby, *Mysteries and Miseries of Arkansas,* 22.

24. Demby, *Mysteries and Miseries of Arkansas,* 37; U.S. Congress, *Report of the Adjutant General,* 245; and James W. Demby, ed., *The Home Aegis and Monthly Review* 1, no. 3 (July 1864): 97. For conditions in Helena, see *OR,* ser. 1, vol. 13, 684, 752.

25. Leroy Williams Pension File, RG 15, NA; *OR,* ser. 1, vol. 13, 738, 752; Demby, *Mysteries and Miseries of Arkansas,* 45; Union Service Documents, Arkansas, First Battalion, Infantry, microfilm at the Arkansas History Commission, Little Rock; U.S. Congress, *Report of the Adjutant General,* 245; Morton W. Williams Pension File, RG 15, NA.

26. Demby, *Mysteries and Miseries of Arkansas,* 43–44.

27. U.S. Congress, *Report of the Adjutant General,* 245; Union Service Documents, Arkansas, First Battalion, Infantry, microfilm at the Arkansas History Commission, Little Rock.

28. Demby, *Mysteries and Miseries of Arkansas,* 39.

29. Depositions by Daniel Webster Williams and Henry Clay Williams, September 1899, Morton W. Williams Pension File, RG 15, NA. Conway County indeed became a dangerous place for civilians in the early months of 1863. In March one woman wrote to her cousin from Cadron, "Everybody here is alarmed about the jayhawkers. One man has gone to the army from this settlement to keep them from getting hold and there is two here now waiting for a steamboat to go to Little Rock. One of them has his family along with him and the other one is leaving his family. Mr. Benedict (the one with the family) his house was burned by jayhawkers last Sunday night and they have threatened to burn two or three more families in a few miles of here." Fannie Harrison to R. P. Harrison, March 8, 1863, Jim and R. P. Morrison Papers, microfilm, Special Collections, Mullins Library, University of Arkansas, Fayetteville.

30. Harrell, *Arkansas,* 167; Leroy Williams Pension File, RG 15, NA.

31. George T. Bird Pension File, RG 15, NA; *Historical Reminiscences of Conway County,* 101, 120; Leroy Williams Pension File, RG 15, NA; *OR,* ser. 1, vol. 22, pt. 2, 525; Herbert Jones's memoirs, quoted in *Conway County: Our Land, Our Home, Our People,* 12.

32. *OR,* ser. 1, vol. 22, pt. 2, 533; Union Service Documents, Arkansas, First Battalion, Infantry, microfilm, Arkansas History Commission, Little Rock; Daniel Webster Williams and Thomas Wells depositions, Morton W. Williams Pension File, RG 15, NA; Alexander McCuin Pension File, RG 15, NA. McCuin applied for a pension in 1890 for his service in Jeff Williams's independent company. The War Department rejected his claim because he did not serve in a regular Union unit.

33. *Conway County: Our Land, Our Home, Our People,* 12; *OR,* ser. 1, vol. 22, pt. 2, 699, 709–12, 741.

34. Thomas, *Arkansas in War and Reconstruction,* 249; *OR,* ser. 1, vol. 22, pt. 2, 699, 756. For the most insightful study of guerrilla war in neighboring Missouri, see Michael Fellman, *Inside War: The Guerrilla Conflict in Missouri during the American Civil War* (New York: Oxford University Press, 1989).

35. U.S. Congress, *Report of the Adjutant General,* 134; Leroy Williams Pension File, RG 15, NA; Thomas Jefferson Williams Pension File, RG 15, NA; Henry Clay Williams deposition, Morton W. Williams Pension File, RG 15, NA.

36. *OR,* ser. 1, vol. 24, pt. 3, 703; ser. 1, vol. 26, pt. 2, 3–5; ser. 1, vol. 27, pt 2, 786; ser. 1, vol. 34, pt. 1, 91–92–96; ser. 2, vol. 5, 732; *Confederate Veteran* 6 (November 1898): 529; *Historical Reminiscences of Conway County,* 15.

37. Witt's men did maintain some contact with the Confederate command in southwest Arkansas. In November 1863 Col. Witt's men carried a letter from one soldier in the Rebel camp just north of Washington to his wife in Quitman. W. W. Garner to Henrietta Garner, November 23, 1863, May Hope Moose Papers, Special Collections, Mullins Library, University of Arkansas, Fayetteville.

38. *OR,* ser. 1, vol. 48, pt. 1, 885, 920; pt. 2, 844; Confederate Service Records, Tenth Arkansas, RG 109, NA; W. W. Garner to Henrietta Garner, November 21, 1863, May Hope Moose Papers, Special Collections, Mullins Library, University of Arkansas, Fayetteville. For a discussion of the terms, guerrilla, Jayhawker, and bushwhacker, see Leo E. Huff, "Guerrillas, Jayhawkers, and Bushwhackers in Northern Arkansas during the Civil War," *Arkansas Historical Quarterly* 24 (summer 1965): 127–48.

39. *OR,* ser. 1, vol. 34, pt. 3, 717; pt. 4, 31–32; ser. 1, vol. 41, pt. 3, 69; Leroy Williams Pension File.

40. See the entries for Newton Franklin Chandler and John H. Rhoades in *Arkansas 1911 Census of Confederate Veterans,* ed. Bobbie J. McLane and Capitola Glazner, 3 vols. (Hot Springs, Ark.: n.p., 1981); Leroy Williams Pension File, RG 15, NA.

41. *OR,* ser. 1, vol. 34, pt. 1, 924–28; pt. 3, 635, 670–71, 930–32.

42. *OR,* ser. 1, vol. 34, pt. 3, 717; pt. 1, 930–32.

43. Johnny Mason, interview with Polly Church, April 29, 1978. Mr. Mason was a remarkable oral source, a "griot" for the history of Conway County and the Williams clan. Born in 1899 and orphaned as a boy, he was adopted by Frank Williams's son and was told these stories about the Williams family by Frank and Leroy Williams. He later earned a masters degree in history and was a history teacher and school principal. Besides his clear memory of stories he heard in childhood, he was also conscious of the need to preserve them in written and audiotape form. In this instance he recalled that the person shot was "a McGinty boy." Mrs. Ruth Cupit of Overcup, Arkansas, identifies the man as John McGinty, her great-grandfather. She says he died three years later of this gunshot wound which never healed. Ruth Cupit interview, February 15, 1992, with Kenneth C. Barnes. One piece of written evidence that corroborates Mason's account is an intestate record filed by William Day Williams's heirs after the war which stated that he died in June 1864. Intestate Record Book, 1859–1885, p. 102, Conway County Courthouse, Morrilton.

44. Regimental Order Number 31, July 18, 1864, Regimental Letters and Orders, Third Arkansas Cavalry, RG 94, NA; *OR,* ser. 1, vol. 34, pt. 3, 258; *OR,* ser. 1, vol. 41, pt. 2, 665. See Edwards' account of Shelby's activities in John N. Edwards, *Shelby and His Men: or, The War in the West* (Cincinnati: Miami Printing and

Publishing Company, 1867), 298–360; Edwards' account must be taken with a degree of skepticism. See also Albert Castel, *Sterling Price and the Civil War in the West* (Baton Rouge: Louisiana State University Press, 1968), 197, 203.

45. John C. Darr, "Price's Raid into Missouri," *Confederate Veteran* 11 (1903): 359–62; Castel, *Sterling Price,* 203–4; *OR,* ser. 1, vol. 41, pt. 3, 104; Leroy Williams Pension File, RG 15, NA.

46. Darr, "Price's Raid into Missouri," 359; *OR,* ser. 1, vol. 41, pt. 3, 116–17, 139, 223; pt. 4, 643.

47. This story was recounted by Joe Stobaugh, interview of February 2, 1992; Arlie Williams, interview of February 7, 1992; and Thelma Hensley, interview of February 8, 1992, with Kenneth C. Barnes. Small details in each of their tellings differ, e.g., one version has seven bullet holes, another thirteen; Stobaugh has Williams sleeping on the front porch of the Williams's log house, and Hensley has him in a bedroom inside.

48. *OR,* ser. 1, vol. 48, pt. 1, 111; Lonnie Maxwell, interview with Polly Church, summer 1963; Ruth Cupit interview; Arlie Williams interview. Information in Jeff Williams's Widows Pension application, made in 1891, corroborates the descendants' oral history of the event, Thomas Jefferson Williams Pension File, RG 15, NA.

49. Lonnie Maxwell interview; Arlie Williams interview; Thelma Hensley interview; and Martha Nell Smith, interview of February 1992 with Kenneth C. Barnes. These Williams descendants all recounted this story although their tellings differed slightly on details.

50. Arlie Williams, interview; and Ruth Cupit, interview. For a comparison of these oral history accounts to other Civil War folklore, see James L. Johnston, "Jawhawker Stories: Historical Lore in the Arkansas Ozarks," *Midsouth Folklore* (spring 1976): 3–9.

51. *OR,* ser. 1, vol. 48, pt. 1, 111, 885; Ted Worley, ed., "Diary of Lieutenant Orville Gillet, U.S.A., 1864–1865," *Arkansas Historical Quarterly* 17 (summer 1958): 189. Gillet was a member of Ryan's detachment, which chased Witt's men after the killing of Jeff Williams. His account and the *War of the Rebellion (OR)* confirm the outline, if not the details, of family oral history of these events.

52. Arlie Williams, interview; and Ruth Cupit, interview. Descendants of Clinton Confederates tell the same story; see Emma Sue Beavers, interview of May 8, 1992; and Maxine Kelly, interview of April 12, 1992, with Kenneth C. Barnes. Emma Sue Beavers is the descendant of Ant Bradley, the man who, according to Williams tradition, pulled the trigger on Jeff Williams. John Mason also recounts this story and cites the Pate family as his source, John Mason to Ernie Dean, February 26, 1980, Individual File, John Madison [*sic*] Clayton, Arkansas History Commission, Little Rock.

53. James Demby, "Death of T. J. Williams, and Son, of Conway County," *Home Aegis and Monthly Review* 9 (February 1865): 209; U. S. Senate, *Report of the Adjutant General,* 272.

54. *OR,* ser. 1, vol. 48, pt. 2, 494–95, 844–45.

55. Henry Clay Williams deposition, Morton W. Williams Pension File, RG 15,

NA; Maxine Kelly interview; Mary Holmes, interview with Polly Church, November 1977; Leroy Williams Pension File, RG 15, NA; Lonnie Maxwell interview.

56. A listing of the members of the militia can be found in the Conway County Court Record Book, July 1868–May 1871, Conway County Courthouse, Morrilton, Arkansas. Leroy Williams, four other Williams men, and several additional veterans of the old company served in the militia. With Republicans now controlling county offices, they each were paid $2.86 for their militia service from the country coffers. In his pension application years later, Leroy Williams recalled that Governor Powell Clayton asked him to form a company to go to Bradley County, in his words, "to keep the Night Riders from killing niggers." Leroy got the men together, but they never made it all the way to south Arkansas.

57. John Mortimer Harrell, *The Brooks and Baxter War: A History of the Reconstruction Period in Arkansas* (St. Louis, 1893), 72. See accounts of the race war in the *Arkansas Gazette*, August 28–September 15, 1868; and Powell Clayton, *The Aftermath of the Civil War in Arkansas* (New York: Neale Publishing, 1915), 144–51.

58. Clayton, *The Aftermath of the Civil War in Arkansas*, 151–63; *Arkansas Gazette*, December 10, 1868–January 5, 1869. See also Otis Singletary, "Militia Disturbances in Arkansas during Reconstruction," *Arkansas Historical Quarterly* 15 (summer 1956): 140–50.

59. *Historical Reminiscences of Conway County*, 19; see Witt's obituary in *Arkansas Baptist*, May 6, 1903, 12; Current, *Lincoln's Loyalists*, 199–205.

60. See House, "John M. Clayton vs. C. R. Breckinridge," in *Digest of Contested Elections*, 51st Cong., 2nd sess., 1891, House Misc. Doc. 137.

61. *Historical Reminiscences of Conway County*, 19; *Morrilton (Arkansas) Pilot*, September 16, 1892; *Arkansas Gazette*, August 30, 1890, September 2, 1890, September 13, 1890.

62. *Arkansas Gazette*, October 9, 11, 12, 1890, and November 9, 1990; *Morrilton Pilot*, November 21, 1890. Frank Williams was convicted by a jury of assault and fined ten dollars. Galloway Williams was found not guilty. Conway County Circuit Court, Criminal Record Book, March 1889–October 1899, pp. 138–39, Conway County Courthouse, Morrilton, Arkansas.

63. Curtis Barnes, interview of February 1992 with Kenneth C. Barnes, remembers James Stobaugh, one of the veterans of Company B, leading the celebration by "shooting the anvil." This involved digging a pit into which one placed gunpowder underneath an anvil. A gunpowder trail went out of the hole through a narrow trench to a safe distance where it was ignited. A terrific noise rang out as the anvil bounced up from the force of the explosion.

64. Mrs. Grant Reddig, interview of October 23, 1992; Marvin Barnes, interview of October 17, 1992; Beva Winningham, interview of October 23; Robert Morrow, interview of October 22, 1992, with Kennth C. Barnes.

Chapter 9: From Slave to Free Labor: The Federal Plantation Experiment in Arkansas

1. For examples of work done on specific areas or general issues see Willie Lee Rose, *Rehearsal for Reconstruction: The Port Royal Experiment* (New York: Vintage Books, 1967); Lawrence N. Powell, *New Masters: Northern Planters during Civil War and Reconstruction* (New Haven: Yale University Press, 1980); Louis S. Gerteis, *From Contraband to Freedman: Federal Policy towards Southern Blacks, 1861–1865* (Westport, Conn.: Greenwood, 1973); and Ira Berlin, ed., *Freedom: A Documentary History of Emancipation*, vol. 3, *The Wartime Genesis of Free Labor: The Lower South* (Cambridge: Cambridge University Press, 1991), see particularly 80, 83. The one study of the experiment in Arkansas is Dale Kirkman, "The Leased Plantations," *Phillips County Historical Quarterly* 4 (September 1966): 14; in addition the published primary sources concerning the experiment have been dealt with in Maude Carmichael, "The Plantation System in Arkansas, 1850–1860" (Ph.D. diss., Radcliffe College, 1935). Much of Carmichael's work has appeared in John William Graves's *Town and Country: Race Relations in an Urban-Rural Context, Arkansas, 1865–1905* (Fayetteville: University of Arkansas Press, 1990), 72–74.

2. George P. Rawick, comp., *The American Slave: A Composite Biography*, vol. 8, *Arkansas Narratives* (Westport, Conn.: Greenwood, 1972), pt. 1, 169.

3. B. M. Prentiss to Commanding Office, Cairo, Ill., March 11, 1863, Letters Sent, District of Eastern Arkansas, Department of Arkansas, RG 393, National Archives (hereafter cited as NA); N. B. Buford to H. Binmore, October 20, 1863, Letters Received, ser. 391, 16th Army Corps, RG 393, NA; A. McFarland to Wm. P. Mellen, March 11, 1864 (quote), Reports of A. McFarland, Skipwith's District, 2nd Agency, RG 366, NA. In this and subsequent footnotes, record group numbers correspond with the following collections: RG 56, General Records of the Department of the Treasury; RG 94, Records of the Adjutant Generals Office; RG 105, Records of the Bureau of Refugees, Freedmen, and Abandoned Lands; RG 366, Records of the Civil War Special Agencies of the Treasury Department; and RG 393, Records of the United States Army Continental Commands.

4. Edwin M. Stanton to Lorenzo Thomas, March 25, 1863; Circular, October 27, 1863, in U.S. War Department, *The War of the Rebellion: A Compilation of the Official Records of the Union and Confederate Armies*, 128 vols. (Washington, D.C.: GPO, 1880–1901), ser. 3, vol. 3, 100 (first quote), 939 (second quote), (hereafter cited as *OR*); Lorenzo Thomas to E. M. Stanton, April 12, 1863, in Powell, *New Masters*, 3, offers Thomas's earliest idea about the new system. See also John Eaton, *Grant, Lincoln, and the Freedmen: Reminiscences of the Civil War with Special Reference to the Work for the Contrabands and Freedmen of the Mississippi Valley* (London: Longmans, Green, and Company, 1907), 59–60, for a discussion of the initial lease system.

5. Special Orders No. 12, April 18, 1863, Lorenzo Thomas Letters & Orders, Generals' Papers & Books, RG 94, NA; Major W. G. Sargent to Col. John Eaton, Jr., March 1, 1864, in letter of Sargent to A. A. General C. H. Dyer, May 17, 1864,

Miscellaneous Letters & Reports Sent & Reports Received, District of Little Rock, Army of Arkansas, RG 393, NA.

6. *OR,* ser. 3, vol. 3, 872; William B. Mellen, *Report Relative to Leasing Abandoned Plantations,* (Washington, D.C.: McGill & Witherow, 1864), 3–5, 8; James E. Yeatman, *Report to the Western Sanitary Commission in Regard to Leasing Abandoned Plantations, with Rules and Regulations Governing the Same* (St. Louis: Western Sanitary Commission, 1864), 3–4.

7. Special Orders No. 94, November 5, 1863, in John Eaton,*Report of the General Superintendent of Freedmen, Department of the Tennessee and the State of Arkansas for 1864* (Memphis, 1865).

8. A. McFarland to Wm. P. Mellen, March 11, 1864, Reports of A. McFarland, Skipwith's District, 2nd Special Agency; M. D. Landon to Wm. P. Mellon, May 12, 1864, General Letters Received, Records of the General Agent; A. M. McFarland to Wm. P. Mellen, October 10, 1864, Loyal Case to Mellen, January 1, 1864, Loyal Case to Mellen, February 10, 1864, Letters Received: Special Agents, Records of the General Agent, all in RG 366, NA; Eaton, *Report of the General Superintendent . . . for 1864,* 36.

9. Report of T. C. Callicot, March 1, 1864, Papers of T. C. Callicot, Helena District, 2nd Special Agency, RG 366, NA; M. D. Landon to Wm. P. Mellen, May 12, 1864, General Letters Received, Records of the General Agent, RG 366, NA; Eaton, *Report of the General Superintendent . . . for 1864,* 36; Mellen, *Report Relative to Leasing Abandoned Plantations,* 13.

10. Thomas Heaton to Wm. P. Mellen, September 24, 1864, A. M. McFarland to Mellen, October 10, 1864, Letters Received: Special Agents, Records of the General Agent, RG 366, NA; Report of T. C. Callicot, March 1, 1864, Papers of T. C. Callicot, Helena District, 2nd Special Agency, RG 366, NA; M. D. Landon to Wm. P. Mellen, May 12, 1864, General Letters Received, Records of the General Agent, RG 366, NA; Mellen, *Report Relative to Leasing Abandoned Plantations,* 14 (for regulations concerning the size of leases), 36 (for total plantations supervised).

11. L. Thomas to Edwin M. Stanton, February 20, 1864, *OR,* ser. 3, vol. 4, 124; A. Lincoln to L. Thomas, February 28, 1864, ibid., 143; L. Thomas, Orders No. 9, March 11, 1864, ibid., 170, see also 138; for Thomas's concession see Wm. P. Mellen to S. P. Chase, March 29, 1864, Letters Received by the Division, Division of Captured Property, Claim, & Land, RG 56, NA; Eaton, *Report of the General Superintendent . . . for 1864,* 6.

12. Loyal Case to W. P. Mellen, February 16, 1864, Letters Received: Special Agents, Records of the General Agent, RG 366, NA; Mellen, *Report Relative to Leasing Abandoned Plantations,* 14–16; W. G. Sargent to John Eaton, Jr., July 1, 1864, Letters Received, Department of Arkansas, 7th Army Corps and 4th Military District, RG 393, NA.

13. Loyal Case to W. P. Mellen, February 17, 1864, Jno. Wilmer Seidelman to P. H. Campbell, May 17, 1864, Letters Received: Special Agents, Records of the General Agent, RG 366, NA; Order No. 9, March 11, 1864, *OR,* ser. 3, vol. 4, 166–70.

14. Mellen, *Report Relative to Leasing Abandoned Plantations,* 13, 15.

15. Order No. 9, March 11, 1864, *OR*, ser. 3, vol. 4, 166–70.

16. Contract of January 26, 1864, Letters Sent, Reports Affidavits, & Court Papers, Jacksonport, Arkansas Field Office Papers, RG 105, NA; Agreement between William P. Mellen and Thomas W. Jordan, March 5, 1865, Letters Received: General Records of the General Agent, RG 366, NA. Treasury guidelines allowed contracts for an interest in the share of profits in lieu of regular wages and did not specify what it considered an equitable share, Mellen, *Report Relative to Leasing Abandoned Plantations*, 15.

17. Permits to Lease Plantations, 1864, Helena District, 2nd Agency, RG 366, NA; A. McFarland to Wm. P. Mellen, March 11, 1864, Reports of A. McFarland, Skipwith's District, 2nd Agency, RG 366, NA; Lists of Freedmen and Their Employers, Department of Arkansas and the 7th Army Corps and 4th Military District, RG 393, NA.

18. Report of July 1, 1864, Office of Superintendent of Freedmen, State of Arkansas, Department of Arkansas, RG 393, NA; Eaton,*Report of the General Superintendent . . . for 1864*, 53.

19. Orders No. 9, March 11, 1864, *OR*, ser. 3, vol. 4, 166–69.

20. Tho. Heaton to Wm. P. Mellen, September 24, 16, 1864, Letters Received; Special Agent, Records of the General Agent, RG 366, NA; see E. T. Diamond to Col. McDowell, October 4, 1864, G. Hammond to Jno. A. McDowell, October 4, 1864, and George P. Peters to Jno. A. McDowell, October 4, 1864, Letters Received: General Records of the General Agent, RG 366, NA; Eaton, *Report of the General Superintendent . . . for 1864*, 34; Mellen, *Report Relative to Leasing Abandoned Plantations*, 7 (quote); William W. Orme to Frederick Steele, November 23, 1864, Letters Received, Department of Arkansas, 7th Army Corps and 4th Military District, RG 393, NA.

21. Eaton, *Report of the General Superintendent . . . for 1864*, 37 (first quote), 73 (second quote); Thomas Heaton to Wm. P. Mellen, September 24, 1864, Letters Received: Special Agents, Records of the General Agent, RG 366, NA; Report of T. C. Callicot, March 1, 1864, Papers of T. C. Callicot, 2nd Special Agency, Helena District, RG 366, NA; Report of J. N. Locke, Superintendent of Freedmen, Helena, July 1864, Helena Officer, Arkansas Field Office Records, RG 105, NA.

22. Jno. Adair McDowell to Wm. P. Mellen, October 8, 1864, Warren Rabb to Col. Heaton, August 24, 1864, Letters Received: General Records of the General Agent, RG 366, NA; Report of J. N. Locke, Superintendent of Freedmen, Helena, Helena Office, Arkansas Field Office Records, RG 105, NA.

23. M. D. Landon to Wm. P. Mellen, May 12, 1864, and E. L. Floyd, W. Warwick, and J. B. Tobing to Supervising Special Agent Treasury Department, February 1, 1864, Letters Received: General, Records of the General Agent, RG 366, NA.

24. Thos. Heaton to D. G. Barritz, August 4 (quote), 8, 1864, and Thos. Heaton to Wm. P. Mellen, September 24, 1864, Letters Received: Special Agents, Records of the General Agent, RG 366, NA.

25. Eaton, *Report of the General Superintendent . . . for 1864*, 36; B. F. Tuttle to

W. P. Mellen, October 27, 1864, and A. M. McFarland to Wm. P. Mellen, October 10, 1864, Letters Received, Special Agents, Records of the General Agent, RG 366, NA.

26. Eaton, *Report of the General Superintendent . . . for 1864,* 48.

27. Ibid., 29–30.

28. Ibid., 29, 30, 33–34, 45 (first quote, fourth quote), 30, 58 (second quote); Order No. 9, March 11, 1864, *OR,* ser. 3, vol. 4, 166–70; M. D. Landon to Wm. P. Mellen, May 12, 1864, September 5, 1864 (third quote), Letters Received: General, Records of the General Agent, RG 366, NA.

29. M. D. Landon to Wm. P. Mellen, May 12, 1864, September 5, 1864 (quote), Letters Received: General, Records of the General Agent, RG 366, NA.

30. Eaton, *Report of the General Superintendent . . . 1864,* 29, 36, 67 (quote).

31. Ibid., 35, 67.

32. Ibid., 45–46.

33. Ibid., 36 (quote), 34, 45, 67.

34. Ibid., 32, 60–61, 73.

35. J. H. Rains to W. G. Sargent, March 31, 1865, Quarterly Report, March 31, 1865, Retained Copies of Reports, Reports Received, and Misc. Papers, 1864–1865, Little Rock Office, Arkansas, Field Office Records, RG 105, NA.

36. Ibid.

37. Eaton, *Report of the General Superintendent . . . for 1864,* 52 quote), 61.

38. J. I. Herrick to Wm. P. Mellen, October 12, 1864, Letters Received, General, Records of the General Agent, RG 366, NA; J. I. Herrick to Gen. Buford, November 30, 1864, in N. B. Buford to W. W. Orme, December 27, 1864, Case Files of Claims for Cotton & Captured & Abandoned Property, Miscellaneous Division, RG 56, NA; N. P. Buford to W. P. Mellen, November 29, 1864, Letters Received: General, Records of the General Agent, RG 366, NA.

39. Statement Showing the Leasing of Plantations in the Little Rock District, Ark., for the year 1865 to 9th May, Special Agent at Little Rock, Register of Plantations Made by Owner, 1865, Helena District, 2nd Special Agency, RG 366, NA; B. F. Tuttle to W. W. Orme, January 28, March 9, 1865, and Enoch Howard to W. W. Orme, November 25, 1864, Second Special Agency, General Records, Letters Received by the Supervising Special Agent of the Second Special District, RG 366, NA; C. W. Montross to W. P. Mellen, March 23, 1865, Letters Received: Assistant Special Agents, Correspondence of the General Agent, RG 366, NA.

40. Register of Plantations Made by Owner, 1865, Helena District, 2nd Special Agency, RG 366, NA.

41. William Sanderson to Wm. P. Mellen, November 29, 1864, Letters Received: General, Records of the General Agent, RG 366, NA.

42. E. T. Diamond to Col. Jno. Adair McDowell, October 4, 1864, and George B. Peters to McDowel and G. Hammond to McDowell, October 4, 1864, Letters Received: General, Records of the General Agent, RG 366, NA; Register of Plantations Made by Owner, 8165, Helena District, Statement Showing the Registering of Plantations in the Little Rock District, Ark., for the Year 1865 to 9th May, Special Agent at Little Rock, 2nd Special Agency, RG 366, NA.

43. Wm. Sanderson to Wm. P. Mellen, November 29, 1864, Letters Received: General, Records of the General Agent, RG 366, NA; Quarterly Report, March 31, 1865, District of Arkansas, J. H. Rains to W. G. Sargent, March 31, 1865, Retained Copies of Reports, Reports Received and Miscellaneous Papers Arkansas, RG 105, NA.

44. Quarterly Report, March 31, 1865, District of Arkansas, J. H. Rains to W. G. Sargent, March 31, 1865, Retained Copies of Reports, Reports Received and Miscellaneous Papers, Major Sargent's Papers, Little Rock Office, Arkansas Field Office Papers, RG 105, NA; H. Sweeney to Sargent, April 5, 1865, Little Rock, Letters and Orders Received, Arkansas Field Office Records, RG 105, NA; Quarterly Report of Refugees and Freedmen for the Eastern District of Arkansas, June 30, 1865, Letters Received, Department of Arkansas, 7th Army Corps and the 4th Military District, RG 393, NA.

45. A. McD. McCook to J. H. Nixon, March 26, 1865, Helena Reports, Arkansas Field Office Records, Report of James H. Rains, August 30, 1865, Arkansas, RG 105, NA.

46. Quarterly Report of Refugees and Freedmen for the Eastern District of Arkansas, June 30, 1865, Letters Received, Department of Arkansas, 7th Army Corps and the 4th Military District.

47. Eaton, *Report of the General Superintendent . . . for 1864*, 67 (first quote); Quarterly Report of Refugees and Freedmen for Eastern District of Arkansas, June 30, 1865 (second quote), Letters Received, Department of Arkansas, 7th Army Corps and 4th Military District, RG 393, NA.

Chapter 10: Brother against Brother: The Winter Skirmishes along the Arkansas River, 1864—1865

The author wishes to thank Susan R. Spellins and Meei-tyng Loh for their assistance in preparing this essay for publication.

1. Michael Fellman, *Inside War: The Guerrilla Conflict in Missouri during the American Civil War* (New York: Oxford University Press, 1989), v.

2. Edwin C. Bearss, "The Federal Struggle to Hold on to Fort Smith," *Arkansas Historical Quarterly* 24 (summer 1965): 149–79; Harry S. Ashmore, *Arkansas: A History* (New York: W. W. Norton & Co., 1978), 79.

3. John L. Ferguson, *Arkansas and the Civil War* (Little Rock: Pioneer, 1961), 261–62; Ashmore, *Arkansas*, 82; Carl H. Moneyhon, *The Impact of the Civil War and Reconstruction on Arkansas: Persistence in the Midst of Ruin* (Baton Rouge: Louisiana State University Press, 1994), 128.

4. Albert W. Bishop, *Loyalty on the Frontier, or Sketches of Union Men of the South-West; with Incidents and Adventures in Rebellion on the Border* (St. Louis, Mo.: R. P. Studley and Co., 1863), 13, 20–28. For the most exhaustive study of Pea Ridge, see William L. Shea and Earl J. Hess, *Pea Ridge: Civil War Campaign in the West* (Chapel Hill: University of North Carolina Press, 1992).

5. Bishop, *Loyalty on the Frontier*, 11; [James W. Demby], *Mysteries and Miseries of Arkansas: or, a Defense of the Loyalty of the State, By a Refugee* (St. Louis, Mo.: printed by author, 1863), 7–8.

6. Adjutant General (Arkansas), *The Report of the Adjutant General of the State of Arkansas for the Period of the Late Rebellion and to November 1, 1866,* prepared by Albert W. Bishop (Washington, D.C.: GPO, 1867), 134; Desmond Walls Allen, *The Third Arkansas Union Cavalry* (Conway, Ark.: D. W. Allen, 1987), 8; General Danridge McRae, undated letter, Danridge McRae Papers, box 1, Arkansas History Commission, Little Rock; Moneyhon, *Impact of the Civil War,* 130–33; Daniel E. Sutherland, "Guerrillas: The Real War in Arkansas," *Arkansas Historical Quarterly* 52 (autumn 1994): 258–85.

7. Bishop, *Loyalty on the Frontier;* 134.

8. *Little Rock National Democrat,* February 20, 1864.

9. Ibid.; Descriptive Book, Third Arkansas Cavalry, Regimental Books, Records of the Adjutant General's Office, 1780s–1917, RG 94, National Archives (hereafter cited as NA); Desmond Walls Allen, *Arkansas' Damned Yankees: An Index to Union Soldiers in Arkansas Regiments* (Conway, Ark.: D. W. Allen, 1987), 5; W. K. Patterson to Governor Flanagin, November 20, 1863, quoted in *Confederate Arkansas: The People and Politics of a Frontier State in Wartime,* by Michael B. Dougan (Tuscaloosa: University of Alabama Press, 1976), 119.

10. Gretchen C. Greeson, "Sentiment or Survival? Company G, 3rd Arkansas Cavalry, USV," *Faulkner Facts and Fiddlings* 22 (1980): 7–8.

11. For an outstanding study of Federal troops from Southern states, see Richard Nelson Current's *Lincoln's Loyalists: Union Soldiers from the Confederacy* (Boston: Northeastern University Press, 1992), 73–85, 133–57. Also see Kenneth C. Barnes, "The Williams Clan: Mountain Farmers and Union Fighters in North Central Arkansas," *Arkansas Historical Quarterly* 52 (autumn 1993): 286–317; Gregory J. W. Urwin, "An Arkansas Unionist," *Civil War Times Illustrated* 31 (March–April 1992): 27.

12. U.S. War Department, *The War of the Rebellion: A Compilation of the Official Records of the Union and Confederate Armies,* 128 vols. (Washington, D.C.: GPO, 1880–1901), ser. 1, vol. 34, pt. 1, 33 (hereafter cited as *OR*).

13. J. T. Knight to Susan F. Knight, February 18, 1865, quoted in Dougan, *Confederate Arkansas,* 3.

14. *OR,* ser. 1, vol. 48, pt. 1, 516; Bearss, "Federal Struggle," 166.

15. Dougan, *Confederate Arkansas,* 106; Wiley Britton, *The Civil War on the Border: A Narrative of Military Operations in Missouri, Kansas, Arkansas, and the Indian Territory, During the Years 1863–1865,* 2 vols. (New York: G. P. Putnam's Sons, 1899), 343–45.

16. *OR,* ser. 1, vol. 48, pt. 1, 515; Allen, *Third Arkansas,* 8.

17. Isaac Murphy was a representative from Huntsville in the Arkansas secession convention. When the final vote was counted, Murphy was the only delegate who voted against the split with the Union. This loyalty paid off when the state returned to Federal control and he was appointed military governor. Bishop, *Loyalty on the Frontier,* 259–61.

18. *OR,* ser. 1, vol. 41, pt. 4, 711, 836; Bearss, "Federal Struggle," 150; Sutherland, "Guerrillas," 285.

19. Bishop, *Loyalty on the Frontier,* 261; Alvin M. Josephy, Jr., *The Civil War in*

the American West (New York: Alfred A. Knopf, 1991), 320–52; Robert E. Waterman and Thomas Rothrock, eds., "The Earle-Buchanan Letters of 1861–1876," *Arkansas Historical Quarterly* 33 (summer 1974): 148.

20. *OR,* ser. 1, vol. 48, pt. 1, 1135–36; Bishop, *Loyalty on the Frontier,* 261–63.

21. Carolyn Pollan, "Fort Smith under Union Military Rule, September 1, 1863, through Fall 1865," *Fort Smith Historical Society Journal* 6 (April 1982): 25; *OR,* ser. 1, vol. 48, pt. 1403, 473; ibid., vol. 41, pt. 4, 962; Bearss, "Federal Struggle," 163–64: Bishop, *Loyalty on the Frontier,* 264–69.

22. *OR,* ser. 1, vol. 48, pt. 1, 466–67.

23. Ted R. Worley, ed., "Diary of Lieutenant Orville Gillet, U.S.A., 1864–1865," *Arkansas Historical Quarterly* 17 (summer 1958): 184. The manuscript is in the General Miscellaneous File, Arkansas History Commission.

24. *OR,* ser. 1, vol. 48, pt. 1, 393; Bearss, "Federal Struggle," 158–59; Joseph O. Shelby was, indeed, a legend in his own time. As leader of the Fourth Missouri Cavalry Brigade, called the Iron Brigade, Shelby was known for his use of subterfuge. Often dressing in Union uniforms, with nothing but a sprig of red sumac to identify them, the men of the Iron Brigade launched daring raids throughout Arkansas and Missouri.

25. Thirty-fourth Arkansas Mounted Infantry, microfilm 317, rolls 215–19, Confederate Service Records, Arkansas History Commission; Arkansas Cavalry Battalion, microfilm 317, rolls 13–14, Confederate Service Records, Arkansas History Commission; Erasmus Stirman to Rebecca, April 3 and 27, 1862, *In Fine Spirits: The Civil War Letters of Ras Stirman with Historical Comments by Pat Carr,* by Erasums Stirman (Fayetteville, Ark.: Washington County Historical Society, 1986), 34–36, 70–71.

26. *Little Rock Arkansas Gazette,* June 3, 1887; Robert C. Newton, Muster Roll, Company C, Arkansas Mounted Volunteers, State Troops (Newton's Tenth Arkansas Cavalry), Small Manuscript Collection, box 49, no. 37, Arkansas History Commission. The recollections of W. M. Wallis, third lieutenant in Company C, were recorded at Hope, Arkansas, in October 1912 and are included in this collection. This, and a few scattered service cards, are the only solid evidence of Newton's regiment—which apparently was renamed the Tenth Arkansas Cavalry when it changed from state to Confederate service in October 1864.

27. *OR,* ser. 1, vol. 48, pt. 1, 1330; Bearss, "Federal Struggle," 159; *Washington County Flashback* 4 (1954): 20; Fontaine Richard Earle to Arnanda Buchanan, August 18, 1864, in "Earle-Buchanan Letters," Waterman and Rothrock, 155.

28. *OR,* ser. 1, vol. 41, pt. 3, 1137; ibid., vol. 48, pt. 1, 16, 395–96, 1330; Bearss, "Federal Struggle," 159–60; David Y. Thomas, *Arkansas in War and Reconstruction, 1861–1874* (Little Rock: Central Printing Company, 1926), 302.

29. Worley, "Diary of Lieutenant Orville Gillet," 184–85; John Patterson to Sarah Patterson, December 9, 1864, Small Manuscript Collection, box 5, no. 17, Arkansas History Commission.

30. *OR,* ser. 1, vol. 48, pt. 1, 404, 412, 430; Bearss, "Federal Struggle," 160–62. Dardanelle is one of the oldest settlements in Arkansas. It had close access to a military road and was considered the best landing on the river—well above flood stage.

31. *OR,* ser. 1, vol. 48, pt. 1, 420, 430, 446–47; Bearss, "Federal Struggle," 161–62.

32. *OR*, ser. 1, vol. 48, pt. 1, 430; Worley, "Diary of Lieutenant Orville Gillet," 185–86.

33. *OR*, ser. 1, vol. 48, pt. 1, 12, 509; Bearss, "Federal Struggle," 167; Cyrus Gaston Diary, January 14, 1865, State Historical Society of Iowa, Des Moines, Iowa. All the official accounts refer to the *Ad. Hines* in its abbreviated form.

34. Worley, "Diary of Lieutenant Orville Gillet," 186; *OR*, ser. 1, vol. 48, pt. 1, 12; Bearss, "Federal Struggle," 166–68.

35. *OR*, ser. 1, vol. 48, pt. 1, 497.

36. Gaston Diary, January 14, 1865.

37. *OR*, ser. 1, vol. 48, pt. 1, 12, 531–32; Bearss, "Federal Struggle," 168.

38. Worley, "Diary of Lieutenant Orville Gillet," 186; *OR*, ser. 1, vol. 48, pt. 1, 12.

39. U.S. Congress, *Medal of Honor Recipients, 1863–1978*, 96th Cong., 1st sess., 1979, Committee Print 3, 81; *OR*, ser. 1, vol. 48, pt. 1, 12, 14; Worley, "Diary of Lieutenant Orville Gillet," 186; *The Goodspeed Biographical and Historical Memoirs of Western Arkansas* (Chicago: Southern Publishing Co., 1891), 16, 69; Wayne Banks, *The History of Yell County* (Van Buren, Ark.: Press Argus, 1959), 136; Wayne Banks, *The History of Yell County, Arkansas*, vol. 2 (Dardanelle, Ark.: Dardanelle Printers, 1992), 122. As late as 1959, when Banks wrote his *History of Yell County*, attitudes toward the Federal occupation of Dardanelle were decidedly mixed. Banks claimed that the deed Sergeant Ellis performed to receive the Congressional Medal of Honor was unknown, but theorized that Ellis earned his medal for helping destroy the town's Baptist and Presbyterian churches. Banks's bias is indicative of the deep feelings that thrived in Arkansas society almost a century after the war. Banks recently updated his work and, to his credit, did correct the misinformation concerning the citation. However, he created another misimpression by saying that since Ellis was born in England, his real purpose in Arkansas must have been to sell English munitions. Banks, *History of Yell County*, 136.

40. Mary Lee Chapter #87, United Daughters of the Confederacy, Small Manuscript Collection, p. 131, Arkansas History Commission; *OR*, ser. 1, vol. 48, pt. 1, 12; Banks, *History of Yell County*, 140–42.

41. William Deloss Love, *Wisconsin in the War of the Rebellion: A History of All Regiments and Battteries* (Chicago: Church and Goodman, 1866), 1127; Bearss, "Federal Struggle," 168–69; Pollan, "Fort Smith," 26.

42. *OR*, ser. 1, vol. 48, pt. 1, 12, 16, 531–32, 541; Worley, "Diary of Lieutenant Orville Gillet," 86; Bearss, "Federal Struggle," 168–69.

43. *OR*, ser. 1, vol. 48, pt. 1, 16; Banks, *History of Yell County*, 140–42.

44. *OR*, ser. 1, vol. 48, pt. 1, 16, 541; Bearss, "Federal Struggle," 158–59; Banks, *History of Yell County*, 142.

45. *OR*, ser. 1, vol. 48, pt. 1, 532, 541; Bearss, "Federal Struggle," 169.

46. Worley, "Diary of Lieutenant Orville Gillet," 186; *OR*, ser. 1, vol. 48, pt. 1, 532, 563; Bearss, "Federal Struggle," 169–70; Pollan, "Fort Smith," 26.

47. *OR*, ser. 1, vol. 48, pt. 1, 403, 428, 466, 473, 516, 532; ibid., vol. 41, pt. 4, 768– 769; Bearss, "Federal Struggle," 165, 188; Pollan, "Fort Smith," 25–26.

48. *OR*, ser. 1, vol. 48, pt. 1, 532.

49. Ibid., 12–13.

50. Ibid., vol. 34, pt. 1, 927; Barnes, "Williams Clan," 27; Bobby Roberts and Carl Moneyhon, *Portraits of Conflict: A Photographic History of Arkansas in the Civil War* (Fayetteville: University of Arkansas Press, 1987), 175–76. Military regulations required vaccinations against smallpox, but the high incidence of the disease in Arkansas during the second half of the Civil War indicates carelessness on the part of both the military and civilian populations. For more information, see Paul E. Steiner, *Disease in the Civil War: Natural Biological Warfare in 1861–1865* (Springfield, Ill.: Charles C. Thomas, 1968), 222.

51. *OR,* ser. 1, vol. 34, pt. 3, 717, and pt. 1, 930–32; Barnes, "Williams Clan," 28; Greeson, "Sentiment or Survival?" 9; Paul P. Steed, Jr., *Arkansas Fed: James Scott Nunnally Jr. and the Third Arkansas Cavalry (USA),* Pamphlet 3451, Arkansas History Commission.

52. Bearss, "Federal Struggle," 170.

53. *Dardanelle Post Dispatch,* February 14, 1895, quoted in "Early Twin Cities of Arkansas: Dardanelle and Norristown," by Ernestine Gravley, *Arkansas Historical Quarterly 10* (summer 1951): 180. Barry's account refers to Colonel A. H. Ryan as Colonel A. J. Bryan; however, it is quite obvious that the difference is just a slip in memory of a man referring to events occurring thirty years before. Medal of Honor recipient Sergeant William Ellis, of course, had been wounded in the skirmish two days earlier and did not take part in the destruction, despite the supposition of Wayne Banks in his *History of Yell County,* 136.

54. Trustees of the Baptist Church of Dardanelle, Arkansas, Pamphlet 2831, 1908, Arkansas History Commission.

55. *OR,* ser. 1, vol .48, pt. 1, 13, 532, 541; Bearss, "Federal Struggle," 170–71.

56. *OR,* ser. 1, vol. 48, pt. 1, 576.

57. Worley, "Diary of Lieutenant Orville Gillet," 186.

58. Bearss, "Federal Struggle," 171; Anne J. Bailey, *Between the Enemy and Texas: Parsons's Texas Cavalry in the Civil War* (Fort Worth: Texas Christian University Press, 1989), 198–205.

59. John Patterson to Sarah Patterson, December 9, 1864, box 5, number 17, Small Manuscript Collection, Arkansas History Commission. In this letter, dated as being written in early December in Waldron but actually sent at the end of the month from Fort Smith, Patterson gives a detailed description of the suffering he experienced. Also see *Fort Smith New Era,* January 21, 1865.

60. *OR,* ser. 1, vol. 48, pt. 1, 13–14; Bearss, "Federal Struggle," 173–74, 178.

61. *OR,* ser. 1, vol. 48, pt. 1, 13, 16–17; *Fort Smith New Era,* January 21, 1865; Bearss, "Federal Struggle," 173; Banks, *History of Yell County,* 142; Banks, *History of Yell County*, vol. 2, 119; Pollan, "Fort Smith," 26; Thomas, *Arkansas in War and Reconstruction,* 302. The *Chippewa* is referred in some accounts as the *New Chippewa* or the *Chipaway.*

62. *OR,* ser. 1, vol. 48, pt. 1, 14.

63. Ibid., 14–16, 613; Bearss, "Federal Struggle," 174–76; Pollan, "Fort Smith," 26.

64. Gaston Diary, January 17, 1865.

65. *OR,* ser. 1, vol. 48, pt. 1, 14–17; *Fort Smith New Era,* January 28, 1865; Gaston Diary, January 17, 1865; Bearss, "Federal Struggle," 176–77; Banks, *History of Yell County,* 143; Pollan, "Fort Smith," 26.

66. *OR,* ser. 1, vol. 48, pt. 1, 576; Bearss, "Federal Struggle," 171, 178.

67. *OR,* ser. 1, vol. 48, pt. 1, 583, 613, 619; Bearss, "Federal Struggle," 178.

68. Worley, "Diary of Lieutenant Orville Gillet," 187.

69. *OR,* ser. 1, vol. 48, pt. 1, 13, 630, 664; Bearss, "Federal Struggle," 178–79; Thomas, *Arkansas in War and Reconstruction,* 302; Banks, *History of Yell County,* 143.

70. *OR,* ser. 1, vol. 48, pt. 1, 655; Banks, *History of Yell County,* 143; Bearss, "Federal Struggle," 179.

71. Worley, "Diary of Lieutenant Orville Gillet," 197; Newton Collection, Small Manuscript Collection, box 49, no. 37, Arkansas History Commission; Nettie Frances Blevins, *Scrapbook 1* (Dardanelle Ark.: privately printed, 1979).

72. Blevins, *Scrapbook 1*; James Reed Elson, ed., "A Letter from Dardanelle to Jonesville, South Carolina," *Arkansas Historical Quarterly* 28 (spring 1969): 74.

73. Blevins, *Scrapbook 1*; James Reed Eison, ed., "A Letter from Dardanelle to Jonesville, South Carolina," *Arkansas Historical Quarterly* 28 (spring 1969): 74.

74. Worley, "Diary of Lieutenant Orville Gillet," 189; Barnes, "Williams Clan," 286–317; Moneyhon, *Impact of the Civil War,* 191–92.

75. Current, *Lincoln's Loyalists,* 195. Current's statistics are quite telling. Arkansas had roughly 60,000 men join the Confederate cause while another 9,000 to 10,000 whites and 5,000 African Americans were organized in Union regiments. Not factoring in the black troops, since there was little chance of their being used by the Confederacy as soldiers, the numbers translate into a 14.3 percent loss of potential troops for the South. And not only can those Arkansans be subtracted from Rebel strength in Arkansas, but they can be added to the Union's effectiveness. Tally in the 5,000 African Amencans, and 20 percent of the fighting men in this Confederate state joined forces with the Union. *Goodspeed Biographical and Historical Memoirs,* 30, 39, 69; Milton C. Tucker, comp., "A New York Newspaper Reporter Provides Extensive, on-the-site Coverage of the Pope County, Arkansas, Revolt against Reconstruction," 18, Arkansas Tech University Locked File, Russellville, Arkansas.

76. "Civil War Letters of John Patterson," *Pulaski County Historical Society Review* 6 (June 1958): 33–34. These and other letters can be found in the Small Manuscript Collection, box 5, no. 17, Arkansas History Commission. Although Stand Watie did finally surrender, another famous figure of the Trans-Mississippi theater, Jo Shelby, did not. He and his Iron Brigade fled to Mexico instead, eventually returning to Missouri years later.

Chapter 11: "We Cannot Treat Negroes . . . as Prisoners of War": Racial Atrocities and Reprisals in Civil War Arkansas

1. Henry Merrell, "'Receipts' Book (Diary)," April 18, 27, 1864, Henry Merrell Papers, Southwest Arkansas Regional Archives, Washington, Arkansas; *Fort Smith New Era,* May 7, 21, 1864; For a recent overview of military operations in Arkansas, one that places the Poison Spring affair in context, see Mark K. Christ, ed., *Rugged and Sublime: The Civil War in Arkansas* (Fayetteville: University of Arkansas Press, 1994).

2. Jay S. Miller and Elwin Goolsby, *The Red River Campaign in Arkansas* (Little Rock: Arkansas State Parks, 1989), 1–4; *Little Rock Arkansas Democrat Gazette,* September 11, 1994.

3. Wiley Britton to his wife, "The Camden Expedition," June 1, 1864, 1, 10, Wiley Britton Letters, J. N. Heiskell Historical Collection, H-4, 13, UALR Archives and Special Collections, UALR Library, University of Arkansas at Little Rock, Little Rock, Arkansas (hereafter cited as UALR Archives); Wiley Britton, *The Union Indian Brigade in the Civil War* (Kansas City, Mo.: Franklin Hudson Publishing Co., 1922), 346–47, 355–56; Dudley Taylor Cornish, "Kansas Negro Regiments in the Civil War," *Kansas Historical Quarterly* 21 (May 1953): 420–27; *Lafayette County (Arkansas) Democrat,* July 8, 1971; John M. Harrell, "Arkansas," in *Confederate Military History,* vol. 10, ed. Clement A. Evans (Seacaucus, N.J.: Blue & Grey Press, 1975), 239; "An Abstract of Facts in Case of John Taylor, Co. C. 79th U.S.C. Troops," ca. 1891, Military File of John Taylor, Military Service Branch, RG 94, NA.

4. Ludwell H. Johnson, *Red River Campaign: Politics and Cotton in the Civil War* (Baltimore: Johns Hopkins University Press, 1958; reprint, Kent, Ohio: Kent State University Press, 1993), 46–48, 81, 85 (page citations are to the reprint edition).

5. James A. Campbell, "Diary," March 25, 1864, J. N. Heiskell Historical Collection, H-16, box 1, file 4, UALR Archives; U.S. War Department, *The War of the Rebellion: A Compilation of the Official Records of the Union and Confederate Armies,* 128 vols. (Washington, D.C.: GPO, 1880–1901), ser. 1, vol. 34, pt. 1, 660–63 (hereafter cited as *OR,* with all references to ser. 1, vol. 34, pt. 1, unless otherwise noted); Roman J. Zorn, ed., "Campaigning in Southern Arkansas: A Memoir by C. T. Anderson," *Arkansas Historical Quarterly* 8 (autumn 1949): 241–42; John N. Edwards, *Shelby and His Men: or, The War in the West* (Cincinnati: Miami Printing and Publishing Company, 1867), 263; Harrell, "Arkansas," 238–39.

6. Carl H. Moneyhon, *The Impact of the Civil War and Reconstruction on Arkansas: Persistence in the Midst of Ruin* (Baton Rouge: Louisiana State University Press, 1994), 116, 129; Lenore Routon, "The Carrigans: Family History," 1945, 129, MsF# 326, Southwest Arkansas Regional Archives, Washington, Arkansas; George Boddie to Mary E. Boddie, February 2, 1864, and George Boddie to Mary E. Boddie, February 12, 1864, in *Sisters, Seeds, and Cedars: Rediscovering Nineteenth-Century Life through Correspondence from Rural Arkansas and Alabama,* ed. Sarah M. Fountain (Conway: University of Central Arkansas Press, 1995), 174–75; John W. Brown, "Diary," April 20, 1864, Arkansas History Commission, Little Rock, Arkansas; *OR,*

661, 679–80; Campbell, "Diary," April 15, 1864; A. W. M. Petty, *A History of the Third Missouri Cavalry from Its Organization at Palmyra, Missouri, 1861, up to November Sixth, 1864: With an Appendix and Recapitulation* (Little Rock: J. William Denby Publisher, 1865), 67–68; Merrell, "Diary," April 23, 1864; Britton, *Union Indian Brigade,* 360–61.

7. *OR,* 743–44, 746; Britton, *Union Indian Brigade,* 362–63; Glenn L. Carle, "The First Kansas Colored," *American Heritage,* 42 (February/March 1992): 79–80, 82–90.

8. *OR,* 680, 743–44, 819, 828, 848, 849.

9. *OR,* 819, 828, 848, 849; James L. Skinner III, ed., *The Autobiography of Henry Merrell: Industrial Missionary to the South* (Athens: University of Georgia Press, 1991), 352; Harrell, "Arkansas," 238–39.

10. *OR,* 745, 751–54, 792, 818–19, 842; *Fort Smith New Era,* May 21, 1864; Britton, *Union Indian Brigade,* 369; William M. Stafford, "Battery Journal," April 18, 1864, M. D. Hutcheson Papers, Camden, Arkansas.

11. *OR,* 745–46, 752–53, 755–56, 829; Britton, *Union Indian Brigade,* 370–72.

12. *Washington (Arkansas) Telegraph,* May 25, 1864; Campbell, "Diary," April 18, 1864; Merrell, "Diary," April 18, 1864; *OR,* 746, 748, 754, 756; *New Era,* May 7, 21, 1864; Britton, *Union Indian Brigade,* 372–73.

13. *OR,* 746, 753; *Fort Smith New Era,* May 7, 28, 1864; Petty, *Third Missouri Cavalry,* 76.

14. Stafford, "Battery Journal," April 18, 1864; John C. Wright, *Memoirs of Colonel John C. Wright* (Pine Bluff, Ark.: Rare Book Publishers, 1982), 142; J. T. Kidd, "The History of J. T. Kidd from March 18th, 1862, until May 28th, 1865," n.d., 12, SF# 101, Southwest Arkansas Regional Archives; "A Confederate Veteran's Story," in *The Old Town Speaks: Washington, Hempstead County, Arkansas,* ed. Charlean Moss Williams (Houston, Tex.: Anson Jones Press, 1951), 91; *Lafayette County Democrat,* July 15, 1971; Anonymous to "Dear Sally," n.d., transcribed copy on loan to the Old State House Museum, Little Rock, Arkansas; Ralph R. Rea, *Sterling Price: The Lee of the West* (Little Rock: Pioneer Press, 1959), 106; *Washington Telegraph,* May 11, 1864; Edmund Kirby Smith to his wife, April 20, 1864, Edmund Kirby Smith Papers, Southern Historical Collection, Manuscripts Department, Wilson Library, University of North Carolina, Chapel Hill, North Carolina; Skinner, *Autobiography of Henry Merrell,* 367–68.

15. Stafford, "Battery Journal," April 18, 1864; Zorn, "Campaigning in Southern Arkansas," 242–43; James McCall Dawson to "Dear Father Sister and Brothers," May 5, 1864, in "'Stand We in Jeopardy Every Hour': A Confederate Letter, 1864," ed. James Reed Eison, *Pulaski County Historical Review* 31 (autumn 1993): 52. For another account of the massacre by a different member of Dawson's regiment, see W. C. Braly to "My Dear Ma," May 7, 1864, Amanda Malvina Fitzallen McClellan Braly Papers, Special Collections Division, Mullins Library, University of Arkansas, Fayetteville, Arkansas; Elizabeth Godbold Watts to John Comer Watts, May 9, 1864, in "Poison Springs Battle Recalled by 1864 Letter," *Ouachita County Historical Quarterly* 19 (September 1987): 14; *Fort Smith New Era,* May 21, 1864.

16. *Washington Telegraph,* May 11, 1864; Charles H. Lothrop, *A History of the*

First Regiment Iowa Cavalry Veteran Volunteers, from Its Organization in 1861 to Its Muster Out of the United States Service in 1866 (Lyons, Iowa: Beers & Eaton, Printers, 1890), 182; For more on the Choctaws' implacable hatred for black Union troops, see Henry Cathey, ed., "Extracts from the Memoirs of William Franklin Avera," *Arkansas Historical Quarterly* 22 (summer 1963): 103, 107; Wright, *Memoirs,* 146; John Hallum, *Reminiscences of the Civil War* (Little Rock: Yunnah & Pittard Printers, 1903), 1:115–16, 315–16; *New Era,* May 28, 1864; *Washington Telegraph,* August 3, 1864; Skinner, *Autobiography of Henry Merrell,* 367–68; *OR,* 843, 849; Tom L. Franzmann, "'Peculiarly Situated between Rebellion and Loyalty': Civilized Tribes, Savagery, and the American Civil War," *Chronicles of Oklahoma* 76 (summer 1978): 140–59.

17. Hellice Gillespie Burton, *Arkansas' Role in the War between the States, 1861–1865* (Houston, Tex.: privately printed, 1986), 12; Cathey, "Avera Memoirs," 107; Mary Elizabeth Moore Carrigan, "Diary," May 2, 3, 1864, SMF# 479, Southwest Arkansas Regional Archives; Merrell, "Diary," April 18, 1864.

18. Artie Whiteside Vardy, "The Battle of Moscow: As It Was Told to Me by My Grandmother, Martha Holcomb," n.d., 2, SMF# 191, Southwest Arkansas Regional Archives.

19. *OR,* 781, 791–92, 820, 842–43, 847–49. For additional consideration of this point, see Ira Don Richards, "The Battle of Poison Spring," *Arkansas Historical Quarterly* 18 (winter 1959): 349; Anne J. Bailey, "Was There a Massacre at Poison Spring?" *Military History of the Southwest* 20 (autumn 1990): 161.

20. *OR,* 847; Harrell, "Arkansas," 250; *Lafayette County Democrat,* July 15, 1971.

21. Aside from officers of the First Kansas, the Confederates may have murdered at least one white Federal soldier at Poison Spring. But the motive was racial even in this case, as the Unionist *New Era* reported: "An officer . . . saw a man who was wounded taken out of the ambulance by the rebels and asked what command he belonged to, he told them the 18th Iowa, they called him a *damned liar,* and said he belonged to the 12th Kansas, brigaded with the negroes and knocked his brain out with the butt of a gun." *OR,* 743–44; *New Era,* May 7, 1864.

22. *OR,* 744, 748; Britton, *Union Indian Brigade,* 365; Burton, *Arkansas' Role,* 11.

23. Burton, *Arkansas' Role,* 12.

24. Brown, "Diary," April 17, 24, 1864; *Washington Telegraph,* May 25, 1864; United Confederate Veterans, Arkansas Division, *Confederate Women of Arkansas in the Civil War, 1861–'65: Memorial Reminiscences* (Little Rock: H. G. Pugh Printing Co., 1907), 41, 49–52. See also "The Federal Occupation of Camden as Set Forth in the Diary of a Union Officer," *Arkansas Historical Quarterly* 9 (autumn 1950): 216–17.

25. Clara Dunlap to "Dear Dear Sister," July 24, 1864, Fred J. Herring Collection, Small Manuscripts Collection, Arkansas History Commission. For more on the depredations committed by Kansas cavalrymen in the Trans-Mississippi, see Stephen Z. Starr, *Jennison's Jayhawkers: A Civil War Cavalry Regiment and Its Commander* (Baton Rouge: Louisiana State University Press, 1973); Arabella Lanktree Wilson to William H. D. Wilson, November 2, 1863, in "Arabella Lanktree Wilson's Civil War Letter," ed. James W. Leslie, *Arkansas Historical Quarterly* 47 (autumn 1988): 257–72.

26. Lonnie J. White, ed., "A Bluecoat's Account of the Camden Expedition," *Arkansas Historical Quarterly* 24 (spring 1965): 84; Vardy, "Battle of Moscow," 2.

27. *Washington Telegraph,* May 25, 1864.

28. Vardy, "Battle of Moscow," 2; Merrell, "Diary," April 18, 1864; Skinner, *Autobiography of Henry Merrell,* 372–73; Brown, "Diary," April 15, 17, 26, 1864; Virginia Mc'Collum Stinson, "Memories," in *The Garden of Memory: Stories of the Civil War as Told by Veterans and Daughters of the Confederacy,* comp. Mrs. M. A. Elliott (Camden, Ark.: Brown Printing Co., 1911), 33–34.

29. *OR,* 820, 826.

30. Robert Freeman Smith, "John R. Eakin: Confederate Propagandist," *Arkansas Historical Quarterly* 12 (winter 1953): 316–26.

31. *Washington Telegraph,* May 25, 1864.

32. Ibid. For more on the Confederate reaction to blacks in the Union army, see Joseph T. Glatthaar, *Forged in Battle: The Civil War Alliance of Black Soldiers and White Officers* (New York: Free Press, 1990), 155–59; Dudley Taylor Cornish, *The Sable Arm: Black Troops in the Union Army, 1861–1865* (New York: Longmans Green & Co., 1956; reprint, Lawrence: University Press of Kansas, 1987), 157–80 (page citations are to reprint edition); Michael Fellman, *Inside War: The Guerrilla Conflict in Missouri during the American Civil War* (New York: Oxford University Press, 1989), 69–70; Michael E. Stevens, ed., *As If It Were Glory: Robert Beecham's Civil War from the Iron Brigade to the Black Regiments* (Madison, Wis.: Madison House, 1998), 181–89, 192–93; James G. Hollandsworth, Jr., *The Louisiana Native Guards: The Black Military Experience during the Civil War* (Baton Rouge: Louisiana State University Press, 1995), 65, 70–71.

33. Skinner, *Autobiography of Henry Merrell,* 24, 38–39, 44, 260; Wright, *Memoirs,* 266–67; Clara Dunlap to Clarissa Dickson, October 7, 1863, in *Sisters, Seeds, and Cedars,* Fountain, 152; *Washington Telegraph,* July 27, 1864, January 13, 1865; *Little Rock Arkansas Gazette,* November 4, 1853, April 6, June 15, 1855.

34. *Washington Telegraph,* October 15, 1862, June 8, 1864; *Helena (Arkansas) Southern Shield,* December 20, 1862; *Arkansas Gazette,* October 11, 1862; Moneyhon, *The Impact of the Civil War,* 62, 81, 93–94.

35. *Little Rock True Democrat,* April 22, 1863; *Arkansas Gazette,* October 11, 1862; *Washington Telegraph,* October 15, 1862.

36. *Washington Telegraph,* June 8, 1864.

37. Stinson, "Memories," 31; Elizabeth Godbold Watts to John Comer Watts, May 9, 1864, in "Poison Spring Letter," 14.

38. *OR,* ser. 2, vol. 6, 21–22; James G. Hollandsworth, Jr., "The Execution of White Officers from Black Units by Confederate Forces during the Civil War," *Louisiana History* 35 (autumn 1994): 475–89; Mrs. J. S. Adamson, "Personal Reminiscences of the Civil War," *Pulaski County Historical Society Review* 7 (March 1959): 2–3; *New Era,* April 9, 1864; Glatthaar, *Forged in Battle,* 69–70; Richard B. Sheridan, "From Slavery in Missouri to Freedom in Kansas: The Influx of Black Fugitives and Contrabands into Kansas, 1854–1865," *Kansas History* 12 (spring 1989): 36; Michael Fellman, "Emancipation in Missouri," *Missouri Historical Review* 83

(October 1988): 50; Excerpt from Testimony of R. A. Watt, November 30, 1863, in *Freedom: A Documentary History of Emancipation, 1861–1867,* Series 2, *The Black Military Experience,* ed. Ira Berlin, Joseph P. Reidy, and Leslie S. Rowland (Cambridge: Cambridge University Press, 1982), 235–36; Henry Orr to "Dear Sister," July 2, 1863, in *Campaigning with Parsons' Texas Cavalry Brigade, C.S.A.: The War Journals and Letters of the Four Orr Brothers, 12th Texas Cavalry,* ed. John Q. Anderson (Hillsboro, Tex.: Hill Junior College Press, 1967), 111–12; Junius N. Bragg to "My Dear Wife," July 1, 1863, in *Letters of a Confederate Surgeon, 1861–1865,* ed. Mrs. T. J. Gaughan (Camden, Ark.: privately printed, 1960), 142–44; *OR,* ser. 1, vol. 24, pt. 2, 450–66; Anne J. Bailey, "A Texas Cavalry Raid: Reaction to Black Soldiers and Contrabands," *Civil War History* 35 (June 1989): 138–52.

39. Britton, *Union Indian Brigade,* 176–77, 242; John R. Graton to "My Dear Wife," May 22, 1863, John R. Graton Papers, 1838–1910, Kansas State Historical Society, Topeka, Kansas; Joseph T. Wilson, *The Black Phalanx* (Hartford, Conn.: American Publishing Company, 1890), 231–32; Cornish, "Kansas Negro Regiments," 425.

40. Charles DeMorse was the colonel of the 29th Texas at Honey Springs, and he took a bullet in the right arm in the first volley fired by the 1st Kansas Colored. Recovered from his wound, DeMorse commanded a brigade at Poison Spring (consisting of the 29th, 30th, and 31st Texas Cavalry), which, as he put it, took "but few prisoners." *OR,* ser. 1, vol. 22, pt. 1, 447–52; Britton, *Union Indian Brigade,* 242, 277, 279–84, 367, 372–73; Cornish, "Kansas Negro Regiments," 425; *OR,* 848; Rea, *Sterling Price,* 105.

41. *OR,* 712–13; F. M. Drake, "Campaign of General Steele," in *War Sketches and Incidents as Related by Companions of the Iowa Commandery of the Loyal Legion of the United States* (Des Moines: Press of P. C. Kenyon, 1893), 1:65–66, 68–69; Charles H. Lothrop, "The Fight at Marks' Mills," n.d., 1, Civil War Manuscripts, State Historical Society of Iowa, Des Moines, Iowa; Ira Don Richards, "The Engagement at Marks' Mills," *Arkansas Historical Quarterly* 19 (spring 1960): 54–55.

42. *OR,* 713–15, 788–99; Harrell, "Arkansas," 255, 259; Richards, "Marks' Mills," 55–60; Elizabeth Titsworth, ed., "The Civil War Diary of a Logan County Soldier," *Wagon Wheels* 1 (winter 1981): 19. For more on the fight at Marks' Mills, see Orr Kelly and Mary Davis Kelly, *Dream's End: Two Iowa Brothers in the Civil War* (New York: Kodansha International, 1998), 158–74.

43. R. P. Marshall of Shelby's Brigade defended the excesses committed by his comrades at Marks' Mills and other locations with these words: "People called us rough and Savages we had to be we had to lay aside the Golden Rule with the Federals and treat them just like they treat us. [A]nd as old David Haram said do it First." "Benjamin Pearson's War Diary," part 5, *Annals of Iowa* 15 (October 1926): 441; *OR,* 714–15; Edwards, *Shelby and His Men,* 279; Rea, *Sterling Price,* 110; Lurton Dunham Ingersoll, *Iowa and the Rebellion: A History of the Troops Furnished by the State of Iowa to the Volunteer Armies of the Union, which Conquered the Great Southern Rebellion of 1861–5* (Philadelphia: J. B. Lippincott & Co., 1866), 658; Carhey, "Avera Memoirs," 107; R. P. Marshall to W. L. Skaggs, February 20, 1912, W. L. Skaggs Collection, Arkansas History Commission.

44. "Pearson's War Diary," 441; George Boddie to Mary E. Boddie, June 11, 1864, in Fountain, *Sisters, Seeds, and Cedars,* 179. For more on the problem of stolen Arkansas slaves being sold illegally to new owners in Texas, see John Hudson to Harris Flanagin, May 30, 1864, Kie Oldham Papers, Arkansas History Commission; John Hugh Reynolds, ed., "Official Orders of Governor Harris Flanagin, Commander in Chief of the Militia of Arkansas," in *Publications of the Arkansas Historical Association,* ed. John Hugh Reynolds (Fayetteville: Arkansas Historical Association, 1908), 2:400–401.

45. *Washington Telegraph,* June 1, August 3, 1864; Elizabeth Godbold Watts to John Comer Watts, May 9, 1864, in "Poison Spring Letter," 14; Vardy, "Battle of Moscow," 2; Anonymous to "Dear Sally," n.d.

46. A. F. Sperry, *History of the 33d Iowa Infantry Volunteer Regiment, 1863–6* (Des Moines: Mills & Company, 1866), 94; Stinson, "Memories," 33–4; Brown, "Diary," April 26, 1864; Clara Dunlap to "Dear Dear Sister," July 24, 1864, Herring Collection; William Blain to "Dear Wife," June 1, 1864, in *Rouse Stevens Ancestry and Allied Families,* comp. Dolly Bottens (Carthage, Mo.: privately printed, 1970), 110A.

47. Samuel J. Crawford, *Kansas in the Sixties* (Chicago: A. C. McClurg & Co., 1911), 117; *Washington Telegraph,* May 25, 1864.

48. The Second Kansas Colored was nicknamed the "Iron Clads" soon after its formation in 1863. *OR,* 697–98, 781, 813; *Little Rock Unconditional Union,* May 13, 20, 1864; George Carr to "Dear Father," May 2, 1864, Eugene A. Carr Papers, Archives Branch, U.S. Army Military History Institute, Carlisle Barracks, Pennsylvania; John W. Long to "Sir," May 17, 1864, in "A Union Soldier's Personal Account of the Red River Expedition and the Battle of Jenkins Ferry," *Grassroots* 8 (July 1988): 3; Crawford, *Kansas in the Sixties,* 124, 128; White, "Camden Expedition," 87–88; William E. McLean, *Forty-Third Regiment of Indiana Volunteers: An Historic Sketch of Its Career and Services* (Terre Haute: C. W. Brown, Printer and Binder, 1903), 26; Samuel J. Crawford to James T. Wilson, December 31, 1885, in *Black Phalanx,* Wilson, 242; *Fort Scott (Kansas) Union Monitor,* October 22, 1863; Skinner, *Autobiography of Henry Merrell,* 368.

49. Crawford, *Kansas in the Sixties,* 124; Milton P. Chambers to "Dear Brother," May 7, 1864, Milton P. Chambers Papers, Special Collections Division, Mullins Library, University of Arkansas, Fayetteville, Arkansas.

50. Milton P. Chambers to "Dear Brother," May 7, 1864.

51. Crawford, *Kansas in the Sixties,* 131-32; *OR,* 759; Samuel J. Crawford to James T. Wilson, December 31, 1885, in *Black Phalanx,* Wilson, 245; William L. Nicholson, "The Engagement at Jenkins' Ferry," *Annals of Iowa* 11 (October 1914): 511.

52. Mamie Yeary, comp., *Reminiscences of the Boys in Gray, 1861–1865* (Dallas, Tex.: Smith & Lamar, 1912), 437.

53. Edward W. Cade to "My dear Wife," May 6, 1864, Edward W. and Allie Cade Correspondence, John Q. Anderson Collection, Texas State Archives, Austin, Texas; James McCall Dawson to "Dear Father Sisters and Brothers," May 5, 1864, in "'Stand We in Jeopardy,'" Eison, 52; Junius N. Bragg to Anna Josephine Goddard Bragg, May 5, 1864, in *Letters,* Gaughan, 230; *OR,* 817; Yeary, *Reminiscences of the Boys in Gray,* 390.

54. Yeary, *Reminiscences of the Boys in Gray,* 799.

55. Milton P. Chambers to "Dear Brother," May 7, 1864; *OR,* 671, 698; White, "Camden Expedition," 87.

56. William Blain to "Dear Wife," May 17, 1864, in *Rouse Stevens Ancestry,* Bottens, 108B.

57. Nicholson's story was corroborated by two other captured Union officers, Lieutenant John Hayes of the 2nd Kansas Colored and Surgeon C. R. Stuckslager of the 12th Kansas Infantry, who were interviewed for the *New Era* following their release from prison camp. Nicholson, "Jenkins' Ferry," 509, 511-15, 519; *New Era,* June 16, August 6, 1864.

58. In another irony, Gano's Brigade included three regiments that participated in the Poison Spring Massacre—the 29th, 30th, and 31st Texas Cavalry. Marvin J. Hancock, "The Second Battle of Cabin Creek," *Chronicles of Oklahoma* 39 (winter 1961-62): 416-18; Larry C. Rampp, "Negro Troop Activity in Indian Territory," *Chronicles of Oklahoma* 47 (spring 1969): 550-53; Britton, *Union Indian Brigade,* 437, 439-40; John R. Graton to "Dear Wife," September 29, 1864, Graton Papers.

59. Yeary, *Reminiscences of the Boys in Gray,* 46, 352-53, 684, 812, 831; John R. Graton to "My Dear Wife," March 12, 1865, Graton Papers.

60. For balanced accounts of these and other anti-black atrocities committed in 1864, see Brian Steel Wills, *A Battle from the Start: The Life of Nathan Bedford Forrest* (New York: HarperCollins Publishers, 1992); Richard L. Fuchs, *An Unerring Fire: The Massacre at Fort Pillow* (Rutherford, Madison, and Teaneck, N.J.: Fairleigh Dickinson University Press, 1994); Michael A. Cavanaugh and William Marvel, *The Battle of the Crater: "The 'Horrid Pit,'" June 25-August 6, 1864* (Lynchburg, Va.: H. E. Howard, Inc., 1989); Richard J. Sommers, *Richmond Redeemed: The Siege at Petersburg* (Garden City, N.Y.: Doubleday & Company, 1981); Edward A. Miller, Jr., *The Black Civil War Soldiers of Illinois: The Story of the Twenty-ninth U.S. Colored Infantry* (Columbia: University of South Carolina Press, 1998).

61. For more on the role of racial violence in Reconstruction and the Jim Crow South, see George C. Rable, *But There Was No Peace: The Role of Violence in the Politics of Reconstruction* (Athens: University of Georgia Press, 1984); Eric Foner, *Reconstruction: America's Unfinished Revolution, 1863-1877* (New York: Harper & Row, Publishers, 1988); Nell Irvin Painter, *Exodusters: Black Migration to Kansas after Reconstruction* (New York: Alfred A. Knopf, 1977; reprint, Lawrence: University Press of Kansas, 1986); Kenneth C. Barnes, *Who Killed John Clayton: Political Violence and the Emergence of the New South, 1861-1893* (Durham, N.C.: Duke University Press, 1998).

Index